POLICYMAKING IN
CONTEMPORARY JAPAN

POLICYMAKING IN CONTEMPORARY JAPAN

edited by T. J. PEMPEL

CORNELL UNIVERSITY PRESS
ITHACA AND LONDON

First published 1977 by Cornell University Press.
Published in the United Kingdom by Cornell University Press Ltd.,
2–4 Brook Street, London W1Y 1AA.

International Standard Book Number 0-8014-1048-7
Library of Congress Catalog Card Number 77-4514
Printed in the United States of America by Vail-Ballou Press, Inc.
Librarians: Library of Congress cataloging information appears on the last page of the book.

Contents

Acknowledgments 7

Abbreviations and a Note on Japanese Names 8

Contributors 9

1. Introduction *T. J. Pempel* 13

2. Studies in Policymaking: A Review of the Literature *Haruhiro Fukui* 22

3. Tanaka Goes to Peking: A Case Study in Foreign Policymaking *Haruhiro Fukui* 60

4. Compensation for Repatriates: A Case Study of Interest-Group Politics and Party-Government Negotiations in Japan *John Creighton Campbell* 103

5. Setting the Price of Rice: A Study in Political Decisionmaking *Michael W. Donnelly* 143

6. Pollution and Policymaking *Margaret A. McKean* 201

7. Policymaking in Japan: An Organizing Perspective *Bradley M. Richardson* 239

8. Patterns of Policymaking: Higher Education *T. J. Pempel* 269

9. Conclusion *T. J. Pempel* 308

Annotated Bibliography 325

Index 337

84575

Tables

5–1. Rice-price offers compared to final decisions   175

7–1. Basic rationales and roles in Japanese policymaking
processes   249

7–2. Participation and role taking in seven Japanese
policy processes, 1968   262–263

8–1. Patterns of Japanese policymaking   278

Acknowledgments

Because of my longstanding interest in Japanese political problems, I organized in April 1974 a panel meeting for the Annual Convention of the Association for Asian Studies. As a result of my participation I was encouraged to consider the possibilities for publication of a book on policymaking in contemporary Japan. Amended versions of several papers presented at the convention appear in this book, as well as other contributions of particular interest prepared especially for this volume.

I would like to thank David A. Titus for initially encouraging the panel, and Frank Langdon and William E. Steslicke for their thoughtful participation and fruitful comments. In addition, Peter Katzenstein and Robert Weissberg provided particularly useful suggestions on my own contributions. Laurie Ann Schlansky and Yvonne Yung provided research help, and Gertrude Fitzpatrick and Charlotte Shull and their respective staffs at Cornell's Government Department and China-Japan Program were generous and patient with their help in preparing the manuscript for publication. The staff of Cornell University Press was consistently helpful in bringing this project to completion. Finally, I would like to thank my fellow contributors for their stimulating and generous suggestions, but more especially for their unflagging good nature in the face of my constant cajolery, criticism, and deadlines.

T. J. PEMPEL

Ithaca, New York

Abbreviations and a Note on Japanese Names

The following abbreviations appear frequently in the text:

CGP   Clean Government Party (also known as Kōmeitō)
DSP   Democratic Socialist Party
EPA   Economic Planning Agency
FEO   Federation of Economic Organizations
JCED Japan Committee for Economic Development
JCP   Japan Communist Party
JFEA Japan Federation of Employers' Associations
JSP   Japan Socialist Party
LDP   Liberal Democratic Party
MAF   Ministry of Agriculture and Forestry
MHW   Ministry of Health and Welfare
MITI Ministry of International Trade and Industry
MOF   Ministry of Finance
PMO   Prime Minister's Office

Japanese names are given in their Japanese order, family name first, except in citations for English-language works by Japanese or Japanese-American authors, where the name is given in Western fashion.

Contributors

John Creighton Campbell is Assistant Professor of Political Science at the University of Michigan. He served as a staff member of the Social Science Research Council and is the author of *Contemporary Japanese Budget Politics*. He is currently engaged in research on Japanese governmental policy toward the aged.

Michael W. Donnelly is Visiting Instructor at the University of Toronto. He was a Visiting Research Fellow at the Institute of Developing Economies, Tokyo, from 1970 to 1973. He also served as a staff member of the Social Science Research Council and has just completed his dissertation on "The Political Management of Japan's Rice Economy."

Haruhiro Fukui is Associate Professor of Political Science at the University of California, Santa Barbara. He has been a research associate at the Brookings Institution and is the author of several books, including *Party in Power*, and numerous articles. His most recent book is *Managing an Alliance: The Politics of U.S.–Japanese Relations*.

Margaret A. McKean is Assistant Professor of Political Science at Duke University. She has written numerous articles on problems of pollution in Japan and is finishing a book on this subject.

T. J. Pempel is Associate Professor of Government at Cornell University. He is the author of the forthcoming *Patterns of Japanese Policymaking* as well as several articles on Japanese politics. He is currently engaged in a comparative study of the political role of the Japanese bureaucracy.

Bradley M. Richardson is Professor of Political Science at Ohio State University. He is the author of *The Political Culture of Japan*. His articles have appeared in *Asian Survey*, the *American Political Science Review*, *Comparative Political Studies*, *Journal of Asian Studies*, and elsewhere.

POLICYMAKING IN
CONTEMPORARY JAPAN

1. Introduction
T. J. Pempel

The earliest Western writings on Japan, largely those of missionaries, overseas traders, journalists, government officials, and miscellaneous part-time or permanent expatriates, are conspicuously marked by sweeping attempts to portray for a bemused and captivated West the idiosyncracies of an overwhelmingly alien culture. With the Pacific War, awe gave way to scorn and scepticism in the face of brutish expansionism and internal repression. Though the generalizations were different they were at least as rampant. After the war, an increasing number of scholars, many themselves directly involved in the war and the subsequent military Occupation of Japan, looked backward to the war seeking its causes, or forward to the probabilities for the success or failure of the Occupation-induced reforms, particularly as these could affect future amity between Japan and the West. Though increasingly more focused, the topics of investigation, nevertheless, remained characterized by efforts to understand and explain the totality or broad sectors of Japan. Culturally deterministic interpretations were dominant; Japanese uniqueness for better or worse was largely taken for granted; understanding was presumed to be primarily a function of extremely long exposure and isolated examination.

As more and more knowledge has emerged about Japan, and as social scientists studying the country have become somewhat more sensitive to broader disciplinary questions transcending national boundaries, gaps and inconsistencies demanding further investigation have become apparent. Moreover, as World War II and the Korean War have become rather dim memories and as Cold War rigidities soften, previous concerns with Japan's role in the "high politics" of confrontation, war, and interstate activities have given way to a realization of the relevance of "normal" politics and an increased sensitivity to some of the many new issues that have begun to attract the attention of the Japanese political community.

One of the foremost areas where these trends have now begun to intersect is at the point of public policymaking. Policymaking studies of the United States and Western Europe for many years involved either very general attempts to delineate universally applicable rules of policymaking or else intensive investigations of single cases of policy formation. Though each approach has inherent merits and strong supporters, as with comparative politics generally, it has now become virtually a truism that greater attention must be devoted to "middle-level theory," to the generating of studies which are empirically based but which involve more than a single case; studies which seek to develop or test hypotheses without becoming so abstract as to render the evolving propositions meaningless for those concerned with the explanation or prediction of day-to-day activity.

While a great deal of theoretical and empirical work has been done on the problems of public policymaking in the United States and Western Europe, the paucity of studies on contemporary Japanese policymaking has mooted, to some extent, the issue of theory versus empiricism. Many political scientists, both generalists and Japan specialists, would welcome increased study of Japanese policymaking at *any* level. One must immediately recognize the simple need for more facts and information about Japanese policymaking. At the same time, "facts and information" can take many forms, not all of which are of equal utility and insight. It is within this context that the present volume takes on its significance. The authors have tried to meet the need for more "facts" about public policymaking and public policy in a host of different areas, largely by providing insightful case studies. As in all case studies the advantage of tremendous detail in information is counterbalanced by the disadvantage of having to decide the relevance of the particular case within some broader context: Of what is it a case? The authors generally seek to provide theoretical insights and present findings from a wide array of empirical situations so as to give the volume some relevance for those concerned with broader aspects of Japanese politics, those whose interests are in subfields such as foreign policy, education, or pollution and those interested in policymaking within industrial societies generally. In short, the essays are middle-level studies of policymaking within diverse but representative political contexts in contemporary Japan.

At base, each author seeks to address a broadly comparable set of questions concerning the nature of political power in Japan as it relates to the operative constraints on public policymaking and public policy. As a result, all address the dynamic interaction between state and society in Japan: Which is the more powerful? In which instances? Through what institutional linkages do the two interact? With what consequences? Though such questions undergird most of the analyses, each author is interested in getting into the "black box" of policymaking through whichever door seems easiest to jar open and most likely to provide a useful field of vision for the specific cases involved. Such latitude has allowed each author to seek an appropriate level of subtlety and richness without the constraints of an overarching model or framework of analysis. Nevertheless, the findings of the individual chapters do triangulate around certain common themes which will be examined in the last chapter. Before this is done, however, it would be well to highlight several aspects of each of the chapters.

In his opening essay, Haruhiro Fukui provides a broad overview of the existing literature on Japanese policymaking, covering both English- and Japanese-language studies. He argues first that there is no clear consensus on the basic nature of Japanese policymaking and that a fundamental dichotomy exists in assessments of the nature of the process. Many scholars have interpreted Japanese policymaking to be highly elitist— dominated by a ruling triumvirate of the Liberal Democratic Party (LDP), senior bureaucrats, and the peak associations of big business. Others suggest far more openness and pluralism than notions of such a ruling triumvirate can accommodate.

Within this broad debate, Fukui takes up a number of other conclusions that emerge from the literature, many of which he finds mutually contradictory. He concludes by discussing the need for more paradigmatic analysis and suggesting some of the more fruitful lines along which it could develop.

Fukui follows this with a second chapter of much more particularistic concern: the Japanese government's decision that Prime Minister Tanaka should visit Peking, a trip which resulted in a major reversal of Japanese foreign policy and the extention of diplomatic recognition to the People's Republic of China. Based on extensive interviews with most of the major participants in the decision, the chapter not only provides a detailed analysis of the complexities of reaching any single decision, but also a number of broader insights. While overall Fukui concludes that the process was dominated by a very small number of people, drawn primarily from the ranks of senior bureaucrats in the Foreign Ministry and top officials in the LDP, he finds that businessmen were largely absent from the process while some of the truly important individuals were from opposition parties, a finding which forces some rethinking about the alleged impotence and irrelevance of the opposition parties as well as about the closed nature and presumed significance of the alleged ruling triumvirate.

John Creighton Campbell follows with an essay dealing with a classical example of pressure-group, or interest-group, politics. All Japanese citizens throughout Japan's Asian empire were forced at the end of World War II to return to the four main islands which constitute present-day Japan. In the process many of them left behind businesses, homes, and other assets. Campbell analyzes the way in which these repatriates organized to seek remuneration from the Japanese government for their lost property. Using a strategy which took advantage of Japan's unusual electoral system, the repatriates were able to convince LDP politicians of their potential significance with the result that the party eventually entered into negotiations with the Finance Ministry and both agreed on a policy of remuneration. The bulk of the policymaking involved a series of public rallies and electoral threats by the pressure group, allegedly technical and apolitical investigations of the problem by government advisory groups, support and miscellaneous involvement by a host of other actors, and, finally, a tough all-night bargaining session between a narrow group composed of some key members of the LDP and top Finance Ministry officials. Campbell analyzes both the decision to pay and the decision regarding the precise amount awarded, noting ironically in conclusion that the presumed electoral significance of the repatriates was probably vastly overrated by the LDP, a fact which in no way prevented them from achieving a visible measure of success.

A second case of pressure-group politics aimed at financial remuneration is taken up by Michael Donnelly in Chapter 5, which analyzes the long-term efforts made by Japan's rice farmers to insure two things: first that the government continue its long-standing policy of official purchase and sale of almost all the nation's rice crop and, more importantly, that it pay the highest prices possible for the rice produced. In contrast to the single payment sought by the wartime repatriates, the farmers' battle recurs annually in what Donnelly calls the "rice-price cycle." The recurring necessity for the government to decide what price it will officially pay for rice provides Donnelly with an opportunity to study a particular instance of policymaking over a long period of time, one in which social, economic, and political changes provide an ever shifting policymaking context. The rice-price problem takes on particular significance because of Japan's rapid transition from a society in which at the end of the war approximately one-half of the population was engaged in agriculture to one which is now highly industrialized and in which farmers make up fewer than 15 per cent of the work force. At the same time, however, the ruling LDP remains electorally dependent on a strong rural vote, giving the farmers a useful lever in exerting political influence.

Coping with a diminishing agricultural sector is but one problem associated with Japan's rapid industrial development. In addition the country faces a problem now common to virtually all industrial societies, namely, high levels of industrial pollution. The rapidity of Japan's growth and the limited geographical area within which industrial development has been concentrated, however, have made the Japanese problem even more acute than that in other countries, resulting in hundreds of hideous pollution-related deaths and illnesses. How the government did and did not respond to this problem is analyzed by Margaret McKean in Chapter 6.

She shows that at the national governmental level, major divisions on the pollution question existed for over ten years. The Ministry of Health and Welfare sought to legislate tighter pollution controls, while the "economic ministries" such as Finance and International Trade and Industry were far more receptive to the claims of business federations that pollution was less serious a problem than was contended and that pollution controls should not be forced on industry in ways detrimental to economic growth. McKean traces the arguments and political maneuvering at this level, showing how eventually in the face of overwhelming evidence and mass political pressure a number of legislative measures were enacted to try to bring pollution under control during the "Pollution Diet" of 1970. Above and beyond such central governmental action however, numerous citizens' groups were formed to take countermeasures against individual industries polluting their local areas. In many instances these groups forced city and prefectural governmental action; in others they brought successful court suits which resulted in extensive damages being paid to pollution victims by the polluting firms. As a result, argues McKean, local governments proved themselves far more significant innovators of policy than has usually been believed, while the courts have been catapulted into a significant policymaking role they heretofore did not exert.

In Chapter 7, Bradley Richardson analyzes a number of different patterns of policymaking over the course of a single year. In what is probably the first attempt to use quantified newspaper coverage to examine policymaking in Japan, he isolates some of the principle ways in which policy was formulated in seven specific instances, chosen for variation in political cleavage. He finds that different actors, working from dramatically different motivations, play in their time, as Shakespeare suggested, many different parts. Thus, he concludes, there is wide variation in the processes of policymaking and the positions of policymakers even within so narrow a time frame as a single year. All the same, his concern for patterns is clear; he makes no argument that each and every case of policymaking is unique, in contrast to the implicit assumption behind many existing case studies.

In my own essay on policymaking within the area of higher education, I argue essentially that different higher educational issues have been resolved through dramatically different policymaking procedures. Three ideal types of processes are analyzed: policymaking through camp conflict, pressure-group policymaking, and incremental policymaking. These ideal types suggest important patterns that approximate policymaking realities, even though significant variations are found within each pattern. The first type is associated with the highly ideological and conflict-ridden process surrounding efforts to increase government control over the administration of Japanese universities, where the political left generally combined with the university community against government efforts. The second type, pressure-group policymaking, is analyzed in two situations. In the first the business community was largely successful in efforts to have the national government adopt policies which would make the universities far more responsive to the technological and scientific demands of the industrial community; in the second the private universities were eventually successful in their efforts to win financial support from the government. Finally I examine the incremental policies which led to the expansion of enrollment in Japanese universities. Japan is now second in the world in the percentage of the 18-to-22-year-old age cohort attending higher educational institutions. This, I argue, is a result of a series of rather discrete and evolutionary steps that provided the basis for the policy. The central argument throughout is that variations in the nature of an issue, combined with variations in the nature of political structure, result in different policymaking processes.

The concluding essay is one to which some readers may wish to turn immediately since it attempts to highlight certain themes arising from the various essays. It may therefore provide useful guidelines to the more empirical and data-rich es-

says. Others will prefer to read the essays first, and then evaluate my conclusions in the light of their own. For the latter,
however, it may be useful to highlight here the key aspects that
I see emerging from the volume as a whole. Although the
essays suggest a wide variety of policymaking situations and
solutions, there are certain similarities and commonalities
among them. To make sense out of the competing strands of
diversity and similarity, it is important to keep in mind that
while each author is basically concerned with explaining policymaking process as a dependent variable, there are three sets of
independent variables which are used in the endeavor, usually
with no author relying on more than one or two. To some, the
nature of the issue at stake is a prominent cause of policymaking variation; to others, political structures are vital; finally, still
others lay stress on the importance of the role perceptions of
the individual and group actors involved. Further, some
chapters work at an intrastate level of analysis; others examine
societal and state interactions. Which factors or combinations of
factors are stressed obviously influences the perceptions one
gets of the policymaking processes, but I argue that the three
viewpoints and two levels of analysis are far more complementary than competitive, with all leading to compatible conclusions.

The final point that the reader may wish to keep in mind is
that policymaking studies should have some broader import. It
is easy to become seduced by facts and to loose sight of their
collective significance. What do the studies suggest about the
nature of Japanese politics? How open and how closed do the
political processes appear to be? Which groups and which institutions dominate; which are dominated? Just how democratic is
Japan? Answers to these questions do not jump unambiguously
from the essays; reality is far more complex. Yet a sensitivity to
such questions allows the reader to confront his or her own values and standards and to measure Japan in terms perhaps a bit
less simplistic than has all too often been the case in the past.

It is these issues that the conclusion attempts to examine and
which provide, I feel, the overarching structure to the book. At
the same time, they should not be artificially imposed on the individual chapters which were written from perspectives slightly

or dramatically different. If the essays must be seen in their own light, as well as the editor's, the reader should surely feel free to apply still a third lamp to them. Surely in this way the cumulative illumination will be even greater.

2. Studies in Policymaking: A Review of the Literature
Haruhiro Fukui

This chapter is divided into two sections. The first discusses the substantive findings, generalizations, and propositions about the nature of policymaking in contemporary Japan found in the current scholarly literature. Using the elitist-pluralist debate as the main organizing principle, I examine the major points of agreement and disagreement among the various authors reviewed. The second section attempts to bring the discussion into a broader theoretical and methodological perspective by exploring the state-to-be of the art and suggesting some alternative conceptions of policy processes and research strategies.

This review seeks to assess the state of the field prior to the publication of this volume. Therefore, my comments are made without reference to the new evidence presented and new ideas advanced in the studies that follow. Where the reader finds my comments or judgments to be inconsistent with them, this circumstance should be kept in mind.

Competing Models and Perspectives
The Elitist Perspective

The elite model, probably the single most popular and influential model of policymaking in contemporary Japan identifiable in the existing literature, is based on the concept of a tripartite power elite composed of leaders of the ruling Liberal Democratic Party (LDP), senior bureaucrats, and big businessmen. There are some important variations, depending on which of the three groups is regarded as the most or more powerful, but that the three major groups comprise a regular and effective alliance and control decisionmaking on major policy issues is an article of faith among most specialists and members of the attentive public in Japan. Whether explicitly or implicitly, many American specialists also subscribe to this view. A parallel view of American politics and policymaking made famous by C. Wright Mills some twenty years ago still enjoys a relatively small but devoted following among contemporary American political scientists and sociologists.[1] Among students of Japanese politics, by way of contrast, the power-elite model is the orthodoxy and its critics are the heretics.

The basic line of argument underlying the ruling-triumvirate model is familiar. It may be summarized roughly as follows. In postwar Japan elected members of the Diet nominally monopolize legislative power and control the executive and administrative branches of government. However, the virtually permanent and frozen divisions of opinion along party lines, aggravated by the scarcity of time and skills at the disposal of Diet members, make it impossible for the Diet to function as an effective decisionmaking body. Its main role has thus become one of ratifying decisions and actions made by the LDP, instead of generating its own policies based on a genuine give-and-take between the ruling and opposition parties.

The LDP is, however, not a self-sufficient policymaking group, so the argument goes. For its electoral success it depends on those who can supply it with votes or funds or both. The party also needs expert advice and assistance in formulating its policies. Furthermore, individual LDP members are incapable of meeting by themselves the multifarious demands placed on them by their constituents. For votes the LDP depends mainly on local supporters of its individual members, the so-called kōenkai (support associations). For campaign funds it turns to businessmen and their organizations, both officially as a party and through the intraparty factions and individual members. For expertise in policymaking and policy implemen-

1. See C. Wright Mills, *The Power Elite* (New York: Oxford University Press, 1956). For contemporary application of the theory to an analysis of American politics, see Thomas R. Dye and L. Harmon Zeigler, *The Irony of Democracy* (Belmont, Cal.: Wadsworth, 1970).

tation it relies on the government bureaucracy. All of these groups are essential to the survival and success of the LDP, but since support associations are too dispersed and fragmented to constitute an effectively united political force only the businessmen and bureaucrats are sufficiently united to function as cohesive groups cooperating with the LDP.

The argument runs further. Businessmen and bureaucrats in turn both need and depend on each other and the LDP. Businessmen collectively wish to see the capitalist free-enterprise system continued and consequently work to keep the conservatives in power. Individual businessmen and various business sectors are also interested in having particular legislative bills promoted or blocked in the Diet in accord with their best interests. Bureaucrats, meanwhile, look to LDP politicians for actions favorable to them in budget appropriations and jurisdictional aggrandizement. Furthermore, many senior bureaucrats hope to enter politics after early retirement, and the friendship of influential politicians is especially helpful to them. Other retiring officials seek to find new jobs in private firms and for this reason they cultivate the friendship of their clients while still in office by manipulating their regulatory and licensing authority. The three groups thus are seen to complement each other, forming a natural and happy alliance.

This elite model of Japanese politics was certainly familiar to students of Japanese politics in the 1950's. A series of articles published in the 1960's by some of the most prominent Japanese political scientists, however, elevated it to its present respectability and authority. Probably the most important in this respect were two articles published in the 1960 issue of the official annals of the Japanese Political Science Association. Under the general title "Japanese Pressure Groups," Nagai Yōnosuke, then a Hokkaidō University political scientist, and Ishida Takeshi, a political scientist at Tokyo University, argued that, in the final analysis, government and governmental decisionmaking in Japan were dominated and manipulated by an alliance of the LDP, the bureaucracy, and influential pressure groups. Nagai explained that, smug in the position of "overwhelming" strength that was assured by their command of skills essential to effective administration and legislation, upper- and middle-level bureaucrats constantly expanded their influence over the LDP by manipulating various interest groups.[2] In the process a tripartite alliance of the three emerged and became firmly entrenched as an elite in control of the Diet and its committees. Among the pressure groups thus participating in the power-elite alliance the most powerful and effective were those representing the nation's "monopoly capitalists," whose interests were "basically identical" with those of official policymakers.[3] Ishida supported this view, pointing out that the three groups mentioned were often so closely interconnected that it was impossible to separate them.[4] Both also argued that while relatively small and weak pressure groups were dependent on bureaucrats for their access to government funds and various other favors, the larger and more powerful employer groups manipulated and used almost at will, and could if necessary negotiate directly with, the leadership of the ruling class.[5]

The arguments and conclusions of Nagai and Ishida were subsequently embraced and expanded by many others. In an introductory political science textbook published in 1965 another Tokyo University political scientist, Shinohara Hajime, joined Nagai in expounding the same view.[6] Two years later the annals of the Japanese Political Science Association, under the general title "Political Parties and Bureaucracy in Modern Japan," carried an oft-quoted article by a Saitama University political scientist, Misawa Shigeo, which argued the same general point.[7]

2. Nagai Yōnosuke, "Atsuryoku Seiji no Nihonteki Kōzō" [The Japanese patterns of pressure-group politics], in Nihon Seiji Gakkai (ed.), *Nihon no Atsuryoku Dantai* [Pressure groups in Japan] (Tokyo: Iwanami Shoten, 1960), 18–19.

3. *Ibid.*, 12.

4. Ishida Takeshi, "Waga Kuni ni okeru Atsuryoku Dantai Hassei no Rekishiteki Jōken to sono Tokushitsu" [The historical conditions and characteristics of the origins of pressure groups in Japan], in *Nihon no Atsuryoku Dantai*, 33.

5. *Ibid.*, 38.

6. Shinohara Hajime and Nagai Yōnosuke (eds.), *Gendai Seijigaku Nyūmon* [An introduction to contemporary political science] (Tokyo: Yūhikaku, 1965).

7. Misawa Shigeo, "Seisaku Kettei Katei no Gaikan" [An outline of the policymaking process in Japan], in Nihon Seiji Gakkai (ed.), *Gendai Nihon no Seitō to Kanryō: Hoshu Gōdō Igo* [Parties and the bureaucracy in contemporary

About the same time, a public law professor at Rikkyō University, Ikeda Masaaki, made essentially the same point in his discussion of legislative process and decisionmaking in postwar Japan.[8] Echoing Nagai's argument of seven years earlier, he saw the Diet standing committees as the main conduits and arenas of collaboration and collusion among representatives of the allied elite groups. More recently, a 1969 discussion of the "economic bureaucrats" by a *Nihon Keizai Shimbun* editorial staffer, Suzuki Yukio, spoke knowingly of the alliance among Finance Ministry bureaucrats, LDP leaders, and big businessmen.[9]

A book titled *Sōridaijin* [The prime minister], based on serialized articles originally published in the *Yomiuri Shimbun* in 1970, also contains explicit and wholehearted endorsement of the elite model by several prominent people.[10] In one discussion, Tokyo University political scientist Tsuji Kiyoaki, Iwai Akira of the pro-left General Council of Japanese Trade Unions (Sōhyō), and a director of the influential pro-LDP Federation of Economic Organizations (Keidanren), Shinojima Hideo, all refer matter-of-factly to this tripartite ruling elite.[11] Two other academic participants in the discussion, Nagai Yōnosuke and Watanuki Jōji, emphasize the influence of bureaucrats on the LDP, while Meiji University professor Taguchi Fukuji and Tokyo University professor Kobayashi Naoki refer especially to the power of big-business leaders.[12]

One could list many more examples. Anyone familiar with Japanese intellectual and semi-intellectual magazines, such as *Sekai, Chūō Kōron, Ekonomisuto, Asahi Jānaru,* and others, will

Japan: since the conservative merger], (Tokyo: Iwanami Shoten, 1967), 5–33. For the English translation of the article, see "An Outline of the Policy-Making Process in Japan," in Hiroshi Itoh (ed.), *Japanese Politics: An Inside View* (Ithaca, N.Y.: Cornell University Press, 1973), 12–48.

  8. Ikeda Masaaki, "Rippō Katei no Mondaiten" [Problems in the legislative process], in Ashibe Nobuyoshi (ed.), *Gendai no Rippō* [Modern legislation] (Tokyo: Iwanami Shoten, 1967), 244–45.

  9. Suzuki Yukio, *Keizai Kanryō: Shin Sangyō Kokka no Purojūsā* [The economic bureaucrats: producers of a new industrial state] (Tokyo: Nihon Keizai Shimbunsha, 1969), 173–74.

  10. Yomiuri Shimbun Seijibu (ed.), *Sōridaijin* [The prime minister] (Tokyo: Yomiuri Shimbunsha, 1971).

  11. *Ibid.,* 238, 256, 299.   12. *Ibid.,* 254, 295–98.

readily agree that this view of policymaking power in postwar Japan indeed represents an orthodoxy among Japanese social scientists in general and political scientists in particular. Japanese scholars and journalists are not alone, however, in espousing the elite model outlined above. In one of the most popular English-language textbooks on postwar Japanese politics, Robert A. Scalapino and Tokyo Metropolitan University political scientist Junnosuke Masumi argue that "conservative dominance in Japan is the product of a triple alliance between the bureaucracy, key national interest groups, and the Liberal Democratic Party." [13] Two books on the LDP, one by Nathaniel Thayer and the other by myself, basically subscribe to the same view.[14] In making his point Thayer quotes Kōno Kenzō, then vice-president of the House of Councillors: "The businessmen have influence over the politicians, the politicians control the bureaucracy, and the bureaucrats keep the businessmen in line. It's a natural system of checks and balances." [15] My own acceptance of the same view is more explicit in a 1972 article on economic planning in postwar Japan.[16]

Those who support, explicitly or implicitly, the power-elite model of Japanese policymaking all seem to agree that the three groups identified are the principal actors. There is less agreement on which is the more powerful. Many see the bureaucracy as pivotal. In the works already cited, Ishida, Misawa, and Ikeda, for example, emphasize the saliency and importance of the LDP-bureaucracy linkage in the alliance.[17] In his contribution to a recently published symposium on the Japa-

13. Robert A. Scalapino and Junnosuke Masumi, *Parties and Politics in Contemporary Japan* (Berkeley: University of California Press, 1962), 93.

14. Nathaniel B. Thayer, *How the Conservatives Rule Japan* (Princeton, N.J.: Princeton University Press, 1969); Haruhiro Fukui, *Party in Power: The Japanese Liberal-Democrats and Policy-making* (Berkeley and Los Angeles: University of California Press, 1970).

15. Thayer, *How the Conservatives Rule Japan,* 70; See also chapters 3 and 8.

16. Haruhiro Fukui, "Economic Planning in Postwar Japan: A Case Study in Policy Making," *Asian Survey* 12 (April 1972), 327–48.

17. Ishida, "Waga Kuni ni okeru Atsuryoku Dantai," 37–38; Misawa, "Seisaku Kettei Katei," 14–15; Ikeda, "Rippō Katei no Mondaiten," 271, 275; see also Masumi Junnosuke, "Jiyūminshutō no Soshiki to Kinō" [The organization and functions of the Liberal-Democratic Party], *Gendai Nihon no Seitō to Kanryō,* 65–66; and Soma Masao, "Chihō Seitō no Kōzō to Kinō" [The structure and functions of local political parties], *ibid.,* 132.

nese bureaucracy a Seikei University political scientist, Kawanaka Nikō, argues:

In Japan administrators are deeply involved in the political activities of
the government; "professional" administrators recommend policies,
see to it that they are adopted, integrate them, and move them forward. . . . Major obstacles to their policymaking activities lie within
the administrative branch itself; they face obstacles raised by various
bureaus and departments within ministries, the Budget Bureau, and
the [Cabinet] Legislation Bureau. Once these internal obstacles are
overcome, they may still face some resistance from other interested
groups [outside the bureaucracy] but this can be crushed, by cavalier
means if necessary. . . . The role [of bureaucrats] replaces the political role of those political leaders who are accountable to the people.
Thus [policies] are manipulated behind the doors of ministry offices.
. . . It is hard to call rational a system which permits the limbs to
displace the head. . . . We need to analyze this displacement of politics by administration which characterizes policymaking in Japan.[18]

Several American writers also see the role of bureaucrats as
particularly conspicuous and important.[19] Ehud Harari main-
tains: "with the entrenchment of the conservative parties in
power, the conservative character of bureaucracy was strongly
reinforced, and a close alliance developed between the bureaucracy and the conservative parties." [20] Citing the works by
Thayer, Misawa, and myself, T. J. Pempel suggests one explanation for the linkage: "the LDP exercises strong personnel
controls over promotions within the bureaucracy, making it effectively impossible for any bureaucrat unacceptable to the
party to rise above the level of bureau chief. With the passage
of time, such control over bureaucratic mobility increasingly in-
sures the institutionalization of organizational ties between the

18. Kawanaka Nikō, "Nihon ni okeru Seisaku Kettei no Seiji Katei" [The
political process of policymaking in Japan], in Taniuchi Ken et al. (eds.), Gendai
Gyōsei to Kanryōsei [Contemporary administration and bureaucracy] (Tokyo:
Tōkyō Daigaku Shuppankai, 1974), II, 7; see also 17–18.
19. See, for example, Nobutaka Ike, Japanese Politics: Patron-Client Democracy
(New York: Alfred A. Knopf, 1972), 117–19, 126–127; Hans Baerwald, Japan's
Parliament: An Introduction (London and New York: Cambridge University
Press, 1974), 102, 123, 137.
20. Ehud Harari, The Politics of Labor Legislation in Japan: National-Interna-
tional Interaction (Berkeley and Los Angeles: University of California Press,
1973), 91.

LDP and the bureaucracy. In turn this means that the LDP and
the Cabinet it controls have come increasingly to depend on the
bureaucracy for the formulation of both laws and party policy." [21]
   On the other hand, the role of big business has been emphasized with equal or even greater vehemence by some writers.
Predictably, Marxist and quasi-Marxist scholars advocate the
extreme view that big business, usually referred to as monopoly
capital, controls and directs the Japanese government and all of
its functions. Classic examples are found in a 1960 book on
postwar Japanese political power, in which Ōe Shinobu, of
Tokyo University of Education, typically argues that "none
other than Japan's own monopoly capitalists have been ruling
Japan since the peace treaty." In his view the successive conservative cabinets have been no more than agents for the omnipotent monopoly capital; through them the ruling capitalists have
controlled the nation's education, strengthened the oppressive
functions of the police, and brought about the revision of the
U.S.-Japan Mutual Security Treaty in 1960.[22] In his study of
Japan's urban problems, an Osaka City University professor,
Miyamoto Ken'ichi, defines Japan as a "business enterprise
state" (*kigyō kokka*), contending that the Japanese state is "subject to the will of monopolistic big businesses." [23] In another
book on the same subject members of the Urban Problems
Study Society see the government and the LDP as spokesmen
for American and Japanese monopoly capital.[24] A recent book
by Jon Halliday and Gavan McCormack takes a similar approach in analyzing and interpreting "Japanese imperialism
today." [25]

   21. T. J. Pempel, "The Bureaucratization of Policymaking in Postwar
Japan," *American Journal of Political Science* 18 (November 1974), 653.
   22. Gendaishi Kenkyūkai (ed.), *Sengo Nihon no Kokka Kenryoku* [State power
in postwar Japan] (Tokyo: San'ichi Shobō, 1960), 240, 240–43, 263–76.
   23. Miyamoto Ken'ichi, *Nihon no Toshi Mondai: Sono Seiji Keizaiteki Kōsatsu*
[Urban problems in Japan: a political and economic analysis] (Tokyo: Chikuma
Shobō, 1969), 64, 106.
   24. Jichitai Mondai Kenkyūkai and Toshi Mondai Kenkyūkai (eds.),
Toshi Mondai no Shiten [A standpoint on urban problems] (Tokyo: Jichitai Kenkyūkai, 1969), 222.
   25. Jon Halliday and Gavan McCormack, *Japanese Imperialism Today* (New
York: Monthly Review Press, 1973).

Among non-Marxist scholars Chitoshi Yanaga emphasizes
the dominant role of big business, the *zaikai,* more sweepingly
than most others:

Zaikai's interest in national affairs is not in any way limited, except in
the degree to which it participates. It has a vital interest in the administrative structure and proposes reforms aimed at making government operations more efficient. It participates in the formulation of
the legislative program, the budget, and fiscal and financial policies.
Defense policy and defense production are of direct and immediate
concern to business. Zaikai plays a decisive role in economic planning,
which embraces industrial structure planning, regional planning, and
zoning, as well as trade and tariff policy and tax structure. Economic
cooperation (with technical assistance to developing nations), international cooperation, and foreign trade are activities in which zaikai provides both initiative and leadership. It also concerns itself with education, employment, public health, social security and welfare,
labor-management relations, and public safety.[26]

Even those who reject the view that big business is omnipotent support the notion that it wields considerable influence on
Japanese policymaking, especially in the field of economic policy, usually in close cooperation with the bureaucracy and the
LDP leadership. In an early examination of the subject, Frank
C. Langdon identifies two kinds of organization through which
business channeled its political influence, namely, the specialized trade associations and the umbrella national federations,
typically the Federation of Economic Organizations (Keidanren). He goes on to argue: "Both levels of associations then
urge their policy upon the party and the government, making
use of the top-level leadership where needed. Such advocacy is
not easily set aside. Because of the technical importance of the
recommendations or the part to be played in a policy by the
businesses concerned, the lowest components of big business
(the big member companies) thus have a share in policy-
forming and political power." [27] In his later works Langdon
continues to maintain essentially the same view.[28]

26. Chitoshi Yanaga, *Big Business in Japanese Politics* (New Haven: Yale University Press, 1968), 63–64.
27. Frank C. Langdon, "Organized Interests in Japan and Their Influence
on Political Parties," *Pacific Affairs* 34 (Fall 1961), 274.
28. See Arnold J. Heidenheimer and Frank C. Langdon, *Business Associations
and the Financing of Political Parties: A Comparative Study of the Evolution of Prac-*

James R. Soukup's 1965 discussion is quite similar. He argues that "the business elite certainly have excellent 'access' to political decision makers. By virtue of their financial resources and networks of personal ties with the government and party elite, they are assured ample opportunities to explain their views." He carefully cautions, however, that "the Marxist image of business domination is an exaggeration. Such thinking ignores the fact that bureaucrats and especially bureaucrat-politicians can and sometimes do resist business pressures."[29] More recently, discussing Japanese policy in the field of research and development, John K. Emmerson emphasizes the importance of business inputs but makes it clear that in his view the relationship between business and government in Japan is one of coordination rather than any domination of one by the other: "one can see that the financial responsibility of the Government for science and technology is limited and that of the industrialists very great indeed. This does not mean that the government loses control of policy; it means, in fact, that it is the 'government-industrial complex' which bears responsibility for the promotion of science and technology, including the determination of national policy."[30] The essential contributions of government-business cooperation to the making and implementation of economic policy in postwar Japan have also been fully documented and analyzed in detail in several case studies, notably those by William W. Lockwood, Martin Bronfenbrenner, Kozo Yamamura, and Kazushi Ohkawa and Henry Rosovsky.[31]

A supportive, though not necessarily integral, component of

tices in Germany, Norway and Japan (The Hague: Martinus Nijhoff, 1968), 189, 199–201.

29. James R. Soukup, "Business Political Participation in Japan," in Robert K. Sakai (ed.), Studies on Asia, 1965 (Lincoln: University of Nebraska Press, 1965), 171, 172. Soukup then goes on to support Langdon's view.

30. John K. Emmerson, Arms, Yen and Power: The Japanese Dilemma (New York: Dunellen, 1971), 316.

31. William W. Lockwood, "Japan's 'New Capitalism,' " in William W. Lockwood (ed.), The State and Economic Enterprise in Japan (Princeton: Princeton University Press, 1965), 458; Martin Bronfenbrenner, "Income-Doubling Plan," ibid., 540; Kozo Yamamura, Economic Policy in Postwar Japan: Growth versus Economic Democracy (Berkeley and Los Angeles: University of California Press, 1967), passim; Kazushi Ohkawa and Henry Rosovsky, Japanese Economic Growth: Trend Acceleration in the Twentieth Century (Stanford: Stanford University Press, 1973), 222–23.

the power-elite perspective is the widely shared impression that
the Diet, which is constitutionally the most important and authoritative institution of representation and decisionmaking,
does not in practice function as it is supposed to. Not surprisingly, Ōe dismisses it as just another agency of the reigning monopoly capital.[32] Most non-Marxist scholars are more cir-
cumspect, but argue that the Diet's role is generally more
symbolic than real. According to Masumi, the role of the Diet
was still important before the emergence of what he calls "the
1955 system," namely, the appearance of a pseudo-two-party
system following the socialist and conservative party mergers in
that year. It has, however, since become largely nominal as a
decisionmaking body under the permanent domination of the
conservative majority. As Masumi puts it, the Diet's importance
is as the major mechanism of legitimization for the conservative
rule.[33] Pempel echoes Masumi's view and argues:

a parliament can exercise independence in at least two ways. First, individual members and opposition parties can introduce their own
legislative proposals, and second, they can serve as opponents of
government-proposed legislation. Thus not all legislation passed need
be that proposed by the cabinet, and not all legislation need pass
unopposed. The evidence suggests, however, that legislative independence, as measured by both of these, is declining in the face of a
growth in the combined legislative power of the bureaucracy and the
ruling conservative party, particularly since 1955 when the two conservative parties, the Liberals and the Democrats, merged to form the
since-dominant Liberal Democratic Party (LDP).

Pempel then proceeds to support his thesis by pointing to three
explicit criteria by which the independent legislative power of
the Diet can be measured: "success rates of governmental and
individual member bills; the declining rate of amendments
added; and the singular lack of success for opposition-spon-
sored bills." [34] He reaffirms a similar view in "The Dilemma of
Parliamentary Opposition in Japan," which explores the problems faced by the opposition parties.[35]

    32. Gendaishi Kenkyūkai, *Sengo Nihon no Kokka Kenryoku*, 297.
    33. Masumi Junnosuke, *Gendai Nihon no Seiji Taisei* [The political structure
of contemporary Japan] (Tokyo: Iwanami Shoten, 1969), 305–7, 310.
    34. Pempel, "The Bureaucratization of Policymaking," 648.
    35. T. J. Pempel, "The Dilemma of Parliamentary Opposition in Japan," *Pol-
ity* 8 (Fall 1975), 63–79.

As the title of Pempel's paper suggests, the downgrading of
the decisionmaking role of the Diet reflects the prevalent view
that the opposition parties and groups allied with them are
weak and ineffectual and hardly in a position to challenge and
compete with the tripartite elite alliance. The often heard comment that Japan has a "one-and-a-half-party system" reflects
this popular view. In the conclusion to my discussion of decisionmaking in the economic planning of postwar Japan I
wrote: "The study presented above of the politics of postwar
economic planning thus reveals rather conclusively the precari-
ousness and marginality of the role played by the opposition
groups in authoritative policymaking processes in postwar
Japan and, conversely, the predominant, almost exclusive role
of the tripartite coalition." [36] Baerwald makes the same point
less bluntly: "There is within the framework of the system very
little room—if any—for compromise, so that amendments of
any significance that are sponsored by the Opposition to a legislative proposal made by the Cabinet and supported by the majority party have little chance of being adopted." [37]

The vulnerabilities, both organizational and political, of op-
position-led pressure groups, especially labor groups, have
been pointed out and examined by many. Especially pertinent
comments are found in the 1960 issue of the annals of the Japanese Political Science Association. There Nagai and Ishida
both emphasize the weaknesses of Japanese labor unions and
the labor movement resulting from the traditional system of
lifetime employment, corporate familism, and company unions.
According to Ishida, mass actions such as street demonstrations
and strikes to which labor unions frequently resort may have
some limited impact on policymaking but if and only if the
power elite decides to respond to their demands so as to maintain the stability of the existing structure of reward allocation.[38]
The same thesis was further elaborated by a Hōsei University
political scientist, Matsushita Keiichi.[39]

Among American observers Richard J. Willey in 1964

36. Fukui, "Economic Planning," 348.
37. Baerwald, *Japan's Parliament*, 126.
38. Nagai, "Atsuryoku Seiji," 24–36; Ishida, "Waga Kuni ni okeru Atsuryoku
Dantai," 41.
39. Matsushita Keiichi, "Rōdō Kumiai no Seiji Katsudō" [Political activities of labor unions], *Nihon no Atsuryoku Dantai*, especially 91–94, 108.

argued that the General Council of Japanese Trade Unions was
not an effective participant in the nation's policymaking because of factionalism among its own ranks and its "radical"
ideology. He concluded: "Sohyo has not provided an effective
counterforce to the pressure of commercial and industrial interests, its chief economic rivals. It has succeeded in pressing its
demands upon decisionmakers only in a very limited way. Perhaps it has best succeeded in advancing the general interest of
the working class in a rather negative and unintended manner.
As a grim spectre lurking over the horizon, it has cautioned
Japanese conservatives to be not too heedless of the interests of
labor." [40] In their separate studies of the Japan Teachers
Union and its battles with the Education Ministry Donald R.
Thurston and Benjamin C. Duke reach similar conclusions
about the general effectiveness of this particularly militant
labor group.[41]

   In the absence of effective and forceful opposition groups,
the argument goes, the power elite dominates the nation's policymaking with few constraints on its freedom of action. There
are, to be sure, a large number of policy advisory commissions
on which scholars and labor representatives as well as high-
ranking officials and influential businessmen serve to advise
and assist various government ministries and agencies.[42] According to Pempel, these groups are "major organizational
tools in overall policy formulation." But, as he also points out,
they depend for information and advice on the very ministries
and agencies which they are supposed to advise.[43] This view
agrees with the conclusion presented somewhat more tenta-
tively by Ikeda in his 1967 work.[44] Since local government and

   40. Richard J. Willey, "Pressure Group Politics: The Case of Sohyo," *Western
Political Quarterly* 17 (December 1964), 718–19.
   41. Donald R. Thurston, *Teachers and Politics in Japan* (Princeton: Princeton
University Press, 1973), especially 129–55, 196 ff.; Benjamin C. Duke, *Japan's
Militant Teachers* (Honolulu: University of Hawaii Press, 1973), 143, 154–55,
159, 161, 198.
   42. As of January 1975 there were a total of 246 such commissions. See
Gyōsei Kanrichō (ed.), *Shingikai Sōran: Shōwa Gojūnen Ban* [General list of
public advisory commissions 1975 ed.] (Tokyo: Ōkurashō Insatsukyoku,
1975).
   43. Pempel, "The Bureaucratization of Policymaking," 658, 659; see also
661, 663.
   44. Ikeda, "Rippō Katei no Mondaiten," 263–64.

politics, too, are said to be dominated by the central ministries through extensive "policy guidance" and the manipulation of centrally administered grants-in-aid,[45] the influence of the power-elite alliance appears virtually unlimited both functionally and geographically.

In the face of such expert opinions and the evidence marshaled to back them up, one is tempted to say that where there is so much smoke there must be fire. This may be true, but the smoke may exaggerate the real size of the fire. In any event, a considerable amount of evidence in the literature suggests that the power elite-model grossly oversimplifies the reality.

The Pluralistic Perspective

As the foregoing discussion suggests, the power-elite model of Japanese policymaking stands on three basic propositions: first, the major groups comprising the elite triumvirate are united, normally if not always, both in purpose and action; second, they participate in most, if not all, important policy decisions; third, individuals and groups other than those included in the elite categories are regularly excluded from decisionmaking processes involving important policy issues. According to the findings of several case studies, however, none of these propositions is entirely correct.

To begin with the first, frequent and intense conflicts of opinion have been reported by many observers. References to the perpetual factional strife within the LDP are common to virtually all discussions of postwar Japanese politics. In fact, the causes, functions, and consequences of the LDP factions have been discussed in much greater detail than any other single aspect of contemporary Japanese politics.[46] Furthermore, there

45. Kawanaka, "Nihon ni okeru Seisaku Kettei," 11–14; Kawanaka Nikō, "Chiiki Seisaku to Chihō Gyōsei" [Regional policy and local administration], *Gendai Nihon no Seitō to Kanryō,* especially 106–7, 121; Soma, "Chihō Seitō," 134–35.

46. See the following: Thayer, *How the Conservatives Rule Japan,* chapter 2; Fukui, *Party in Power,* chapter 5; Haruhiro Fukui, "Japan: Factionalism in a Dominant Party System," in Frank P. Belloni and Dennis Beller (eds.), *Faction Politics* (Santa Barbara, Cal.: ABC-Cleo, forthcoming); J. A. A. Stockwin, "A Comparison of Political Factionalism in Japan and India," *Australian Journal of Politics and History* 16 (December 1970), 361–74. In another article Stockwin points out the function of LDP factionalism as the "lubricant of the system of

is an unusually high level of consensus about the importance of
these intraparty groups in the understanding of Japanese parliamentary and party politics. Baerwald sums up this consensus
as follows:

> Appearances of unity within each of the parties during formal divi-
> sions in the Diet are deceptive, for they hide the intense bargaining
> that has taken place inside the parliamentary parties at earlier stages
> of the policy-making and legislative processes. Especially in the cases
> of the LDP and JSP, the facade of unity during Diet votes that each
> party seeks to project to the public obscures the considerable amount
> of strife that exists fairly constantly in each. It is the factions (*habatsu*)
> which are the real actors in intra-party politics in Japan. Their impor-
> tance, especially in the LDP, cannot be overemphasized. It is the fac-
> tions which have provided the most crucial leavening element in what
> might otherwise have become an LDP bulldozer and a relatively dull
> scene.[47]

There is not much evidence to show that the LDP factions
themselves act as initiators or promoters of particular policies.
There is, however, a large amount of evidence that they can
crystallize intraparty opposition to particular policies and decisions. Classic examples are reported by Donald C. Hellmann
in his study of the 1956 Soviet-Japanese peace settlement and
by George R. Packard in his study of the 1960 Security Treaty
crisis. According to Hellmann, the LDP factional struggle "became synonymous with the foreign policy-making process,"
completely overshadowing the roles of formal party organs.[48]
Packard tells how LDP factionalism constrained Prime Minister
Kishi Nobusuke's actions during the crisis and eventually drove
him from power: "If Kishi had enjoyed full support from all

---

power elite rule: "From 1955 . . . political power was effectively restricted to
elites within the LDP, the bureaucracy and sections of business. Within and between those groups, factional compromises and accommodations . . . proved
the lubricant of a complex and bewildering system. Between this 'power elite'
on the one hand, and labor and the opposition parties on the other, compromises indeed took place, but on a much lesser scale" ("Is Japan a Post-Marxist
Society?" *Pacific Affairs* 41 [Summer 1968] 197).

47. Baerwald, *Japan's Parliament*, 46–47.

48. Donald C. Hellmann, *Japanese Foreign Policy and Domestic Politics* (Berkeley and Los Angeles: University of California Press, 1969), 56; see also 19, 41,
68, 69.

LDP factions in May–June 1960, he would not have had to resign over the crisis; it was this potential for an anti-mainstream coalition—or even for defection—and this alone that kept the Prime Minister within acceptable bounds of authority." [49] Martin E. Weinstein, too, notes the decisive impact of LDP factional dissension on the Prime Minister's actions during the same crisis and the Police Law revision controversy which immediately preceded it.[50]

The factions thus are seen to represent an important, perhaps the most persistent, form of dissension within the LDP. They are, however, by no means the only or necessarily the most important source of division on policy matters in the ruling party. Nonfactional or cross-factional divisions emerge from time to time on specific policy questions. In his study of the International Labor Organization Convention 87 case Harari presents a detailed analysis of such divisions.[51] William E. Steslicke in his study of the Japan Medical Association and its efforts to influence policymaking in the disputes over medical fee increases also emphasizes differences of opinion among top LDP leaders based mainly on personal convictions and commitments.[52] The LDP is thus divided against itself frequently, if not every time it faces a controversial policy issue.

Nor is the bureaucracy any more effectively united either in purpose or in action. According to Itō Daiichi, Finance and MITI bureaucrats bitterly fought each other over the Income-Doubling Plan during the last years of Kishi's government in the late 1950's and the first years of Ikeda's in the early 1960s. Individuals within the Finance Ministry opposed the plan in order to prevent their rivals in MITI from sharing their "secrets of control" over government fiscal policy, so as to maintain their own monopoly over the formulation of the "master

49. George R. Packard III, *Protest in Tokyo: The Security Treaty Crisis of 1960* (Princeton: Princeton University Press, 1966), 347; see also 72–77, 80–81, 187–191.

50. Martin E. Weinstein, *Japan's Postwar Defense Policy, 1947–1968* (New York: Columbia University Press, 1971), especially 91–94.

51. Harari, *The Politics of Labor Legislation,* especially 176; on the activities of cross-factional intraparty groups, see 141–42.

52. William E. Steslicke, *Doctors in Politics: The Political Life of the Japan Medical Association* (New York: Praeger, 1973), especially 167–68.

plan" for national economic policy.[53] The New Industrial City Program, which grew out of the Income-Doubling Plan in the mid-1960's, also became a major bone of contention among several ministries. As Masumi explains, the ministries of Home Affairs, Agriculture and Forestry, International Trade and Industry, Construction, and Transportation all came forward with their own pet programs and competed for cabinet endorsement and funding.[54] These disagreements among the bureaucrats enormously complicated the legislative process, adding to the confusion created by the competition among prefectural governments and LDP Diet members all speaking, either individually or through temporary coalitions, for separate constituents and clients. In his book on urban problems Miyamoto relates an even more prevalent fragmentation of interest and opinion among the ministries of Finance, Health and Welfare, Agriculture and Forestry, International Trade and Industry, and Transportation, plus the National Tax Administration and the Food Agency. Over such issues as pollution control, industrial relocation, and regional development a bevy of ministries, agencies, and their subdivisions wage relentless struggles against one another for greater shares of control over programs and funds.[55] These examples all point to the prevalence and ferocity of intrabureaucratic conflicts, a situation Kawanaka refers to as "jungle warfare." [56] They certainly give credence to Steslicke's observation: "The fact of great bureaucratic influence and control over governmental functions and the important role of the bureaucracy in modern Japanese history is too well known to require detailed comment here. What must be emphasized, however, is that Japanese bureaucracy is by no means monolithic. Like the political parties, the national administration is also factionalized both by ministry and within ministries." [57]

53. Itō Daiichi, "Keizai Kanryō no Kōdō Yōshiki" [The economic bureaucrats' pattern of behavior], *Gendai Nihon no Seitō to Kanryō*, 92.
54. Miyamoto, *Nihon no Toshi Mondai*, 410–13. See also Kawanaka, "Chiiki Seisaku," 125–26.
55. Miyamoto, *Nihon no Toshi Mondai*, 109, 113, 116, 200.
56. Kawanaka, "Nihon ni okeru Seisaku Kettei," 8.
57. Steslicke, *Doctors in Politics*, 28; see also Ike, *Japanese Politics*, 71–72.

Unsurprisingly, "big business" also turns out to be many things, rather than a simple monolithic group, when dealing with specific policy questions. Soukup and Misawa both point out serious divergences of opinion among individual businessmen and their groups.[58] The point is made very eloquently by Lockwood in "Japan's New Capitalism": "Powerful as Big Business may be, and close as its relations with the Ministries, it is itself divided in its interests and counsels. Only on the broadest issues can it present a united front. In politics, too, it faces a more open and competitive situation in which strong, though often unequal, countervailing forces come into play from other sectors of Japanese society. On this score there are marked changes, even revolutionary changes, from the old order of the twenties and thirties."[59] In a recent study of the political influence of big business in Japan, Gerald L. Curtis emphasizes the importance of changes in the nation's economy and society since 1955 as a factor in the decline of *zaikai* influence. These changes, he argues, have made the business community "increasingly pluralistic," and as a result there are important conflicts of interest within the big-business community "that neither *Keidanren* nor any other organization can effectively mediate."[60]

In addition to all these divisions within the ranks of each group, differences and conflicts among the three groups themselves are said to be serious and prevalent. For example, Steslicke describes the fierce battles on a proposed raise in medical fees which were fought out between Health and Welfare Ministry bureaucrats on the one hand and, on the other, the Japan Medical Association and the LDP Special Committee for Medical Care Policy. To further complicate the situation, the influential and usually pro-LDP Federation of Economic Organizations was allied in this instance with the militantly antibusiness

58. Soukup, "Business Political Participation," 172–73; Misawa, "Seisaku Kettei Katei," 18.
59. Lockwood, "Japan's 'New Capitalism,'" 498; for further elaboration, see 495–97.
60. Gerald L. Curtis, "Big Business and Political Influence," in Ezra F. Vogel (ed.), *Modern Japanese Organization and Decision-making* (Berkeley and Los Angeles: University of California Press, 1975), 60.

and anti-LDP General Council of Japanese Trade Unions against the alliance of the Japan Medical Association and the LDP special committee.[61]

In his discussion of Japanese budget politics Kojima Akira, then of the National Diet Library's Legislative Reference Department, takes issue with the assumption which John C. Campbell allegedly makes in his forthcoming work on the same subject about a stable relationship of mutual role expectations between LDP policy groups and Finance Ministry budget makers. As support, Kojima points to the fact that politicians' aggressive bids for supremacy and ministry officials' strong reactions over allocation decisions involving politically sensitive budget items result in intense conflicts between the two.[62]

The bureaucracy and big business do not always get along very well either. According to Yamamura, the 1963 Temporary Promotion of Specified Industries Bill was vigorously pushed by MITI but was killed by the strong opposition of, among others, the "large corporate sector." In the conclusion to his study of the antimonopoly policy and its demise in postwar Japan Yamamura offers the following thought:

> In postwar Japan, to equate the interests and views of large firms with those of the policy-makers is to make a serious error. These two positions are separate, as has become increasingly clear to all but doctrinaire Marxists. It is perhaps accurate to state that in the early stages of postwar growth the policies appeared to reflect the views of this group as the policies coincided with the oligopolist position. However, . . . when these two views began to diverge, especially after 1958, the oligopolist position on some fundamental issues came into direct conflict with that of the policy-makers.[63]

Lockwood's view in "Japan's New Capitalism" is only marginally less emphatic of the conflictual elements in the bureaucracy-business relationship.[64]

The situation resulting from these conflicts and incompati-

---

61. Steslicke, *Doctors in Politics,* 140 ff., 234.
62. Kojima Akira, "Gendai Yosan Seiji Shiron" [A preliminary discussion of contemporary budget politics], *Gendai Gyōsei to Kanryōsei,* II, 113–14; John Creighton Campbell, *Contemporary Japanese Budget Politics* (Berkeley and Los Angeles: University of California Press, 1977).
63. Yamamura, *Economic Policy,* 83, 179.
64. Lockwood, "Japan's 'New Capitalism,' " especially 503–4.

bilities within and among the elite groups is what Steslicke describes as "a diffusion of power at the upper levels of the policymaking structure in contemporary Japan."[65] In such a situation unified and effective initiatives for specific policy decisions are unlikely to come from the power elite. Several other case studies seem to corroborate this inference either by identifying a few LDP politicians, notably the prime minister and his close associates, as the major initiators and promoters of particular policies or by pointing to significant, if not decisive, inputs of nonelite interest groups.

Weinstein, for example, attributes the initiative for Japanese decisions relating to the 1951 peace treaty and the conclusion of the original U.S.-Japanese Mutual Security Treaty almost exclusively to Prime Minister Yoshida Shigeru and Foreign Minister Ashida Hitoshi.[66] Likewise, according to Masumi, the Income-Doubling Plan of the early 1960's grew out of an improvised campaign slogan used by the prime ministerial hopeful, Ikeda Hayato, in his challenge to the incumbent, Kishi.[67] In its origin, then, it was an ambitious politician's tactical move, rather than a plan carefully developed by either the ruling party or the bureaucracy. The revision of the U.S.-Japan Mutual Security Treaty in 1960 was accomplished under the initiative of Kishi and his foreign minister, Fujiyama Aiichirō, very much against the wishes, not only of the opposition parties, but of certain fellow LDP members as well.[68] My recent article on decisionmaking regarding the Okinawa reversion highlights the central role of Prime Minister Satō Eisaku and his primarily political motivation in pushing the policy.[69]

Sometimes a leading LDP politician other than the prime minister sponsors and promotes a particular policy. Naoki Kobayashi, in his case study of the Small and Medium-Sized En-

65. Steslicke, *Doctors in Politics,* 30.
66. Weinstein, *Japan's Postwar Defense Policy,* 21 ff.
67. Masumi, "Jiyūminshutō no Soshiki to Kinō," 67–68, 72.
68. Packard, *Protest in Tokyo, passim.*
69. Haruhiro Fukui, "Okinawa Henkan Kōshō: Nihon Seifu ni okeru Kettei Katei" [Okinawa reversion: decisionmaking in the Japanese government], in Nihon Kokusai Seijigakkai (ed.), *Okinawa Henkan Kōshō no Seiji Katei* [The political process of Okinawa reversion] (Tokyo: Yūhikaku, 1975), 97–124.

terprises Organization Bill in the mid-1950's, mentions LDP Diet member Nakasone Yasuhiro as the principal promoter of the legislation during its early phase.[70] A major policy commitment by the LDP in 1968 to take action on urban problems resulted largely from the efforts of Tanaka Kakuei, who was then chairman of the LDP Urban Policy Council.[71] Steslicke identifies Health and Welfare Minister Furui Yoshimi as the "central figure" in the 1961 controversy over medical fees.[72]

These examples are by no means exhaustive, but they do represent a major thrust of most case studies in Japanese policymaking. Almost unanimously they point to the critical role played by the political and personal judgments of particular LDP leaders rather than the collective will of an elite alliance as a dominant factor in the critical policy decisions examined. Baerwald expresses the idea nicely when he says: "It is they who make the choices of which bill to push forward and which to be given a lesser priority." [73]

On the basis of such evidence the power-elite model is criticized as defining the scope of the participation in the active initiation and promotion of a policy much too broadly by equating it with the three constituent groups of the elite alliance. Fault is also found with the model for an opposite reason. Several cases show that those groups which the elite model dismisses as powerless and inconsequential do in fact contribute significantly to important policy decisions.

Few dispute the fact that the Diet has not functioned as the nation's supreme institution of representation and decisionmaking. However, some have found its work to be much more than an automatic ratification and legitimization of the policy decisions taken by the majority party. While pointing to the steady decline of the Diet's authority and influence, Misawa suggests that through both deliberations on bills and criticisms

70. Naoki Kobayashi, "The Small and Medium-Sized Enterprises Organization Law," in *Japanese Politics: An Inside View*, 50.
71. Noguchi Yūichirō, "Toshi Seisaku to Keizai Seisaku" [Urban policy and economic policy], in Miyamoto Ken'ichi et al. (eds.), *Gendai Toshi Seisaku* [Contemporary urban policy] (Tokyo: Iwanami Shoten, 1973), 171–74.
72. Steslicke, *Doctors in Politics*, especially 203.
73. Baerwald, *Japan's Parliament*, 125.

of government policies it nevertheless exerts substantive pressure on policy decisions. He also reminds his readers that a majority of bills are debated in a friendly, nonpartisan manner and many are amended by the joint efforts of government and opposition-party members.[74] In the opening chapter of his 1968 book on the JSP, J. A. A. Stockwin points out that even on such a controversial issue as China Policy there has been substantial understanding, and presumably agreement, between the LDP and the JSP.[75] The Diet is also seen to have a limited but meaningful role both as a formal public forum of debate on policy issues and as the "sole lawmaking organ of the state" by authors of several case studies. Thurston, for example, describes how the Japan Teachers Union used the Diet education committees to bring their views to public attention. He adds: "although in most cases the LDP listens to, but does not accept, the views of the JTU and the JSP, a few bills containing the essence of a particular JTU policy or demand have nevertheless been passed by the Diet." [76] In his discussion of the ILO case Harari lists Diet plenary sessions and committee meetings as major forums of formal debate on the issue. He then argues: "The opposition elements and the neutrals were as significant in defining the issue and subissues, and in making detailed proposals for their solutions, as were the LDP members and their traditional allies." [77] Packard goes much further in emphasizing the role of the Diet in his work on the Security Treaty crisis. He says:

demonstrators who marched to the Diet showed with their feet that they knew the locus of state power. Protesting Hungarian students had marched against the State security forces and then against the Soviet troops, with results that were all too tragic. In Japan, the last serious attempt to overthrow the government was in the February 26, 1936 Incident, when Army officers took over government buildings, ignoring the Diet completely. In 1960, the Diet was at the heart of the

74. Misawa, "Seisaku Kettei Katei," 12–13, 25.
75. J. A. A. Stockwin, *The Japanese Socialist Party and Neutralism: A Study of a Political Party and Its Foreign Policy* (Melbourne: Melbourne University Press, 1968), 3.
76. Thurston, *Teachers and Politics,* especially 252–53.
77. Harari, *The Politics of Labor Legislation,* 178.

crisis at all times; the simple fact that it survived offered hope for the future.[78]

Activities in or through the Diet are, however, not the only or necessarily the most effective means by which nonelite groups have their cases heard. Nor are labor unions and radical students who work closely with the opposition parties the only nonelite groups demanding government attention and action. In their battles with big business the small businessmen described in Kobayashi's early case study managed to overwhelm the latter's resistance. Typically, leaders of the group chose to negotiate directly with top LDP leaders to get their way.[79] And as mentioned earlier, the Japan Medical Association took on, at one time or another, both the MHW bureaucracy and big-business insurer groups, managing not only to survive but eventually to prevail over both. Like Kobayashi's small businessmen, Steslicke's doctors negotiated directly with the "Big Three" of the LDP.[80] In one of my own case studies I describe the defiance of the MOF bureaucracy and LDP leadership by former landowners during the latter's campaigns for governmental compensation for property expropriated from them during the postwar land reform.[81]

In order to be effective in putting pressure on and getting attention from the government, groups have to be well organized under good leadership. As Ike puts it:

bureaucrats and party leaders exert a great influence on public policy, but there are instances in which those outside the elite group can be effective. Under certain conditions, the elite can be persuaded or even compelled to adopt policies it may not particularly favor. If a sizable number of individuals have a common grievance, they may be able to organize for the purpose of seeking a political solution to their problem. To be successful, the group will need good leadership, a workable strategy, and—above all—political clout.[82]

78. Packard, *Protest in Tokyo,* 350.
79. Kobayashi, "The Small and Medium-Sized Enterprises Organization Law," 83–84, 73.
80. Steslicke, *Doctors in Politics,* 155, 177–89.
81. Fukui, *Party in Power,* chapter 7.
82. Ike, *Japanese Politics,* 119–20; See also Langdon, "Organized Interests," 276–77.

In this scheme of things, then, there seems to be little room for public opinion as such to become an important factor in policymaking. In his investigation of the policymaking process of the 1956 Soviet-Japanese peace settlement Hellmann concludes that "public opinion and the policy-formulation process seemed to function independently, in parallel planes, with no discernible interconnections." Packard concurs with Hellmann's judgment.[83] However, some evidence is found in the literature which suggests that it would be rash to dismiss public opinion as totally inconsequential.

First of all, some studies point out that Japanese public opinion has been particularly sensitive to and influential on issues of defense and security. Particularly explosive and requiring extreme caution on the part of policymakers have been issues related to nuclear weapons. Weinstein describes how in 1955 the governments in Tokyo and Washington gave up their attempt to bring atomic warheads for the Honest John missiles to Japan, in large part because of public opposition.[84] Similarly, Emmerson cites the bitter debates in the Diet in recent years on such issues as the arrival of B-52 strategic bombers in Okinawa, the calls at Japanese ports of the nuclear-powered aircraft carrier *Enterprise,* the use of Japanese bases by E-112 "spy planes," and so forth. He argues: "While the LDP government with its comfortable majority did not need to bend its policies to meet the verbiage of the opposition, nevertheless, the voice of public opinion being louder in Japan than in most democracies, the Japanese leadership was never insensitive to the effect on the public of its decisions and actions." [85] The critical role of public opinion, whether spontaneous or organized, in the Okinawa reversion issue has also been pointed out by a Tokyo University political scientist, Watanabe Akio, among others.[86]

83. Hellmann, *Japanese Foreign Policy,* 78, 109; Packard, *Protest in Tokyo,* 45, 147–52, 344.

84. Weinstein, *Japan's Postwar Defense Policy,* 82–83.

85. Emmerson, *Arms, Yen and Power,* 114.

86. See Akio Watanabe, *The Okinawa Problem: A Chapter in Japan-U.S. Relations* (Melbourne: Melbourne University Press, 1970), chapter 11; Watanabe Akio, "Okinawa Henkan wo meguru Seiji Katei: Minkan Shūdan no Yakuwari wo Chūshin to shite" [The roles of nongovernmental groups in Okinawa reversion], *Okinawa Henkan Kōshō no Seiji Katei,* 65–97; Higa Mikio, "Okinawa no Fukki Undō" [The reversion movement in Okinawa], *ibid.,* 5–26; Hiyane

In the arena of local politics and on such domestic issues as pollution, public health, regional development, and so forth, the influence of "citizens' movements" also appear increasingly visible and effective.

A Seikei University professor, Kawanaka Nikō, referred in a 1967 article to citizens' movements against industrial pollution in many rapidly growing industrial centers, such as Yokkaichi, Mizushima, Matsuyama, Mishima, and Numazu.[87] Seven years later he argued that a "new procedure" for the initiation and articulation of policies was emerging as a result of the new-style pressure politics developed by various citizen groups. The growth of the citizens' movements constrains the freedom of action on the part of bureaucrats in the central government ministries while broadening the scope of participation by local political leaders and an emergent class of policy planners in private firms.[88] Similarly, in his 1969 book Miyamoto Ken'ichi saw the development of citizens' movements as a proof of growing grass-roots democracy and democratic control over public policymaking at the local level, but he also emphasized their vulnerability to the pressures of big-business groups and the bureaucracy. In a book on urban policy he edited in 1973, however, Miyamoto strikes a much more positive note by pointing to the successes of an increasing number of opposition candidates in gubernatorial and mayoral elections, especially in the nation's largest cities.[89] The significance of the steady increase in the number of "progressive heads of local governments" between 1963 and 1973 and the promotion of citizen participation in local policymaking is the central topic of another article in the same book by the JSP-supported mayor of Yokohama, Asukata Ichio.[90] Two recent Ph.D. dis-

---

Teruo and Gabe Masao, "Tochi Tōsō no Igi" [The significance of the land struggle], *ibid.*, 27–46.

87. Kawanaka, "Chiiki Seisaku," 128–29.

88. Kawanaka, "Nihon ni okeru Seisaku Kettei," 24–27, 36–37.

89. Miyamoto, *Nihon no Toshi Mondai*, 96 ff.; "Toshi Mondai kara Toshi Seisaku e" [From urban problems to urban policy], *Gendai Toshi Seisaku*, 8, 31.

90. Asukata Ichio, "Nihon no Seiji Gyōsei Kōzō no Tenkan" [For a change in the Japanese political and administrative structure], *Gendai Toshi Seisaku*, 40, 55, 57–58. See also Sankei Shimbun Chihōjichi Han, *Kakushin Jichitai* [Progressive local governments] (Tokyo: Sankei Shimbunsha, 1973); Ōshima Tarō, "Kakushin Jichitai to Kanryōsei" [The progressive local governments and the bureaucracy], *Gendai Gyōsei to Kanryōsei*, II, 293–322.

sertations, by Jack G. Lewis and Margaret A. McKean, also focus on the same general theme.[91]

As we have seen above, most case studies and generalizations based on their findings present interpretations and arguments that challenge key aspects of the power-elite model. Collectively, they draw a picture of Japanese policymaking characterized by fluidity, complexity, and variability, rather than by the regularity, stability, and constancy which the power-elite perspective projects. The general picture emerging from these studies is much more pluralistic, as Steslicke points out in the introductory chapter of his book.[92] In his conclusion Curtis is more explicit than most others in his critique of the elite model and his advocacy of a pluralistic perspective. He states:

> The ruling elite model of Japanese politics has had to make a number of false assumptions about the organizational unity of the business community, its unanimity of views on specific issues, and its involvement in a broad range of governmental decisions. There are few case studies of decision-making in contemporary Japan, but it may be hypothesized that such studies would show what they have shown in the United States: that different groups participate in the decision-making process depending on the issue involved.[93]

The findings and conclusions of the case studies, however, do not quite add up to an integrated model or theory of pluralism. They deal with different cases, focus on different aspects or phases of policymaking, and, above all, ask different sets of questions. As a result, they agree with one another in some respects, but they also disagree on other important points. Intuitively one may be tempted to say that the more complex pluralist perspective is more realistic and plausible than the simplistic elite perspective, but given the free-for-all, grab-what-you-want character of much of the current literature, it is really not possible to choose one position against the other with anything like total confidence. Surely those who subscribe to the elite-trium-

91. Jack G. Lewis, "Hokaku Rengo: The Politics of Conservative-Progressive Cooperation in a Japanese City" (Ph.D. dissertation, Stanford University, 1975); Margaret A. McKean, "The Potentials for Grass-Roots Democracy in Postwar Japan: The Anti-Pollution Movement as a Case Study in Political Activism" (Ph.D. dissertation, University of California, Berkeley, 1974). For a relevant comment, see Ike, *Japanese Politics*, 122.
92. Steslicke, *Doctors in Politics*, 3–4.   93. Curtis, "Big Business," 68.

virate model would be quick to argue that the specific findings of the individual case studies are basically insignificant in the face of what they would see as the more generally overwhelming power of the ruling elite.

According to Thomas S. Kuhn, frequent and deep debates over legitimate methods, problems, and standards of solution serve "rather to define schools than to produce agreement" and are characteristic of what he calls the "pre-paradigmatic period" in the history of a science. He says, "in the early stages of the development of any science different men confronting the same range of phenomena, but not usually the same particular phenomena, describe and interpret them in different ways. What is surprising . . . is that such initial divergences should ever largely disappear." [94] Whether the differences of opinion between the two schools of students of Japanese policymaking discussed above will ever disappear, as Kuhn predicts for a true "science," is not so certain at this point. In fact, it is no more certain that the study of politics can ever be what he calls "normal science," with a single dominant paradigm eventually overcoming all its competitors and reigning as the orthodox way of selecting and ordering methods and data. What is necessary, as far as we are concerned, seems to be to recognize these perspectives as competing, not complementary. From there we must move toward a more comprehensive and reliable empirical model of Japanese policymaking, and perhaps eventually to a theory of policymaking in general, which will allow us to evaluate the different perspectives more astutely. But to do this we shall need information that is not only more accurate and detailed but also more suitable to integration and generalization. Apart from its quantitative limitations, which are only too obvious, the existing literature on Japanese policymaking is qualitatively inadequate and deficient. In the following pages I shall consider how we might be able to cope with this problem.

94. Thomas S. Kuhn, *The Structure of Scientific Revolutions* (Chicago: University of Chicago Press, 1962), 47–48, 17.

The State-to-Be of the Art
Need for a Common Typology of Policy Issues

Lest there be any misunderstandings, let us state clearly at the outset that whatever else we may need for a better understanding of Japanese policymaking, we shall need many more good case studies. These are an essential source of knowledge and understanding and the only sound basis on which to build generalizations. Models and theories will be only as good as the case studies from which they are derived.

The question, though, is not whether we need more case studies but rather the kind of case studies we need. This is also to ask: What are good case studies? Are not those reviewed in the preceding section good case studies?

It seems to me that there are two troublesome problems in the current literature, especially among the case studies, which demand our careful attention. The first is the problem of typicality and representativeness, the typological framework of our research and writing. The second relates to the systematic description and analysis of the elements of complexity and dynamism found in each case. This involves the problem of defining, identifying, and classifying a range of relevant variables in each case study. In both areas we can and should improve our scholarly endeavors.

More than ten years ago in his well-known review of the book mentioned in the quotation Theodore J. Lowi observed:

American Business and Public Policy, despite its richness as a case study in the politics of foreign trade, suffers the one debilitating handicap of all case-studies, the problem of uniqueness. . . . How are we to know the extent to which the patterns the authors discover apply to all cases? How are we to know at least toward what *class* of cases we can generalize? . . . If their findings are to be judged for their applicability to all of national policy-making, then we are about where we were before the book was published, except for some healthy negative insights as to prevailing "theories." [95]

Lowi's comment is applicable to most of the current case studies in Japanese policymaking.

95. Theodore J. Lowi, "American Business, Public Policy, Case Studies, and Political Theory," *World Politics* 16 (July 1964), 686–88.

The works reviewed in the preceding section were not consciously and explictly designed to be typical or representative. As a rule, the cases studied were chosen for other reasons. Even though they were not meant to represent the universe of real-world policy issue areas, however defined, visibility and topicality were at least a moderately important factor in the authors' choice of subject matter. Beyond this, we find no evidence to show that some explicit and systematic criteria of representativeness guided and determined their selection. Though substantial agreement exists among the findings of many case studies, this seems to have been more a fortuitous coincidence than proof of systematic coordination in research design and replication. The many points of disagreement suggest, on the other hand, that the cases were also different in certain respects. It is not at all clear in what respects and to what extent the findings of these studies can or cannot be meaningfully compared with one another, much less how and to what extent they can be integrated into meaningful generalizations. The "models" or "theories" we can currently force out of the literature inevitably take on the character which Lowi attributed to their American counterparts ten years ago. As he pointed out, both the pluralist and elitist "models" are inadequate to explain a specific policymaking case and thus are not true "models" but merely "self-validating standpoints." He concluded: "The pluralist approach suggests what to look for and the elitist model suggests perhaps what not to look for. Since neither is a theory, neither has much bearing on specific cases." [96]

Assuming for the moment that the variations in the case-study literature on Japanese policymaking arise mainly from differences in the data, rather than from the authors' handling of the data, it is sensible to suggest that we need a common typology of important policy issues in contemporary Japan. Such a typology would bring some order to our future research endeavors and help us build a firmer basis for more meaningful generalizations.

One common-sense approach to typology building would be to use the functional divisions of the nation's public services.

96. *Ibid.*, 685–86.

The ministries and agencies of the Japanese government and their subdivisions are each responsible for issues in a particular functional area. The organization of the government bureaucracy is thus based on and represents a typology of policy issue areas. Surprisingly, however, none of the case studies in Japanese policymaking uses, or even refers to, these seemingly most obvious divisions as a basis of issue classification.[97]

In discussions by Japanese scholars one finds much simpler schemes. For example, Masumi divides policymaking processes into two types: the ordinary and the extraordinary.[98] The ordinary process is characterized by the prominent roles played by LDP factions, the bureaucracy, pressure groups, and constituents and is typified by the policymaking process of the Income-Doubling Plan. On the other hand, an extraordinary case is characterized by confrontation between the LDP and the opposition parties, mobilization of the masses, revolts by antimainstream LDP factions against the mainstream coalition, and the active intervention of big business. This type is represented by the case of the Mutual Security Treaty crisis. Ikeda suggests a slightly more complex typology. He classifies legislation by their major promoters—the LDP, the bureaucracy, and interest groups—and then adds two other types respectively called the social welfare and the local government types.[99] Neither of these proposals may be very inspiring, but they may at least serve as clues to better typologies.

Compared to the general lack of typological concern among students of Japanese policymaking, those working on policymaking in the United States have shown a much greater interest. Among the several alternative typologies suggested, the simplest and apparently the most popular are the incremental-fundamental dichotomy and its variations, roughly corre-

97. For relevant comments see David H. Davis, *How the Bureaucracy Makes Foreign Policy: An Exchange Analysis* (Lexington, Mass.: D.C. Heath, 1972), 6; A. W. Marshall, *Bureaucratic Behavior and the Strategic Arms Competition* (Santa Monica, Cal.: Southern California Arms Control and Foreign Policy Seminar, 1971), 9.

98. Masumi, *Gendai Nihon no Seiji Taisei*, 414–15; Masumi, "Jiyūminshutō no Soshiki to Kinō," 75.

99. Ikeda, "Rippō Katei no Mondaiten," 269–70.

sponding to Masumi's twofold classification.[100] A more complex scheme is Lowi's, first presented in the 1964 review article quoted earlier. There he identified three policy arenas—distributive, regulatory, and redistributive—and three corresponding patterns of power—coalition, pluralist, and elitist. Subsequently, he rearranged the three arenas into elitist, logrolling, and regulatory, and eventually he arrived at a fourfold typology.[101] In a 1973 article William Zimmerman proposed a substantially revised and expanded version of Lowi's classification for application in studies of foreign policymaking, adding two new dimensions—the symmetrical-asymmetrical nature of the domestic impact of the issue involved and the tangibility-intangibility of the political goods at stake. Emmette E. Redford's threefold scheme classifies issue areas into micropolitical, subsystem, and macropolitical types. In his 1975 textbook James E. Anderson proposes a fourfold classification: broad benefits and broad costs, broad benefits and narrow costs, narrow benefits and broad costs, and narrow benefits and narrow costs—"broad" and "narrow" referring to the size of population affected by the particular policies.[102]

All of these typologies are no doubt useful for the specific purposes for which they were devised. However, all assume, consciously or unconsciously, a high level of factual knowledge and understanding of the world dealt with. The categories used are abstract and analytical, rather than concrete and descriptive. At the present stage of our own scholarship and sophistication, the use of such hyperabstract and often hypersimplified categories may well prove counterproductive. I

100. See, for example, Amitai Etzioni, "Mixed-Scanning: A 'Third' Approach to Decision-Making," *Public Administration Review* 27 (December 1967), especially 389; Davis, *How the Bureaucracy Makes Foreign Policy*, 137–38.

101. Lowi, "American Business," 690–91; "Making Democracy Safe for the World: National Politics and Foreign Policy," in James N. Rosenau (ed.), *Domestic Sources of Foreign Policy* (New York: Free Press, 1967), 324–25; "Four Systems of Policy, Politics and Choice," *Public Administration Review* 32 (July 1972), 298–310.

102. William Zimmerman, "Issue Area and Foreign-Policy Process," *American Political Science Review* 67 (December 1973), 1207–8; Emmette S. Redford, *Democracy in the Administrative State* (New York: Oxford University Press, 1969), 4–5; James E. Anderson, *Public Policy-making* (New York: Praeger, 1975), 155–59.

would therefore suggest that we begin with identifying and classifying concrete policy issues as they occur and exist in contemporary Japanese society. The next logical step would be to ask ourselves questions such as the following: Do issues falling in some concrete categories tend to be more "ordinary" than "extraordinary," more "distributive" than "regulatory" or "redistributive," more "micropolitical" than "subsystem" or "macropolitical"? If so, why? Do some issues within one category tend to be more "ordinary," "distributive," "micropolitical," and so forth than others in the same category? If so, why? Which categories and which issues in those categories need to be selected for further investigation in our future case studies and according to what typological criteria—"ordinary"/"extraordinary"? "distributive"/"regulatory"/"redistributive"? "micropolitical"/"subsystem"/"macropolitical"?

In any event, there is a pressing need to develop a common typology of policy issues if we are meaningfully to compare and evaluate the frequently divergent and conflicting findings and generalizations found in the existing literature on the subject.

Beyond Typologies

A typological perspective, as it is conceived here, is basically static. It orders and clusters policy issues at a given time; it does not focus on the complexity of relationships among the issues or on the dynamism of the developmental process through which each issue moves. Thus a second major problem concerns the way we deal with these elements of complexity and dynamism.

Reading the existing case studies leaves one with the distinct impression of tremendous diversity and fluidity in any actual policymaking process. Each case appears to have been so complex that one is almost tempted to conclude that any attempt to relate one to another and make generalizations about "Japanese policymaking" is foolhardy and futile. Such an impression may be sound and even desirable; indeed, reality may be more complex and confusing than even the existing case studies lead us to believe. As an antidote to what appears to be the unrealistically simplistic view of the elitist model, the impact of the existing case studies may serve a very useful purpose, forcing attention to the complexity of actual policymaking processes. Yet it is still necessary to deal with that complexity more systematically and effectively.

In a real-world situation the elements of complexity may appear to pervade an entire policymaking process. For purposes of description and analysis, however, it is possible to separate and divide cases along several distinct dimensions: (1) actors and their definitions of a policy issue; (2) interissue relationships; and (3) issue evolution and process continuity.

All the case studies reviewed earlier start with the implicit assumption that each policy issue under consideration involved a relatively small and well-defined group of actors who could and should be identified. Few, however, explicitly distinguish between different types of actors. In order to avoid confusion and to reduce the degree of complexity to a manageable level, distinctions need to be made between those whose roles are central and those whose roles are peripheral, between those who participate directly and regularly and those who do so only indirectly and sporadically, between those who have authority and those who lack it, and so forth. Such distinctions will bring at least some order to the confusing array of data on actors encountered in the case-study literature.

More important and potentially more useful will be to distinguish and type actors in terms of their perceptions of the issue or issues involved. According to most case-study descriptions, no issue is so simple as to be seen in exactly the same light by all actors or actor groups. To Prime Minister Kishi and Foreign Minister Fujiyama the issue of the Security Treaty revision in 1960 may have been one of stabilizing the Japanese alliance with the United States by removing aspects of inequality in the existing treaty and making it more palatable to an increasingly independent-minded Japanese public. To his critics in the LDP, however, the issue was whether Kishi and his mainstream coalition should be permitted a diplomatic coup and a consolidation of their power and control of the party leadership and accompanying privileges. To many critics in the opposition parties the real issue was Japan's relationships with the Soviet Union and the People's Republic of China and the future of Japanese alignments. To many university professors and students the issue involved the rules and procedures of democratic government. To still others the central focus was the excitement or inconvenience caused by the massive riots. Similarly, the issue of compensating former landlords as it evolved in the 1950's and early 1960's was to many politicians an issue of whether they should risk offending an important group of voters and endanger their own chances of success in future Diet elections. To MOF bureaucrats the issue was one of accepting an additional burden on the government treasury and potentially setting a precedent for similar demands from other groups, such as the repatriates. To LDP leaders the issue was how to avoid alienating either the bureaucrats or the landlords. To many citizens the issue centered around the legitimacy and desirability of pressure-group politics. As Morton H. Halperin puts it: "Each participant, depending on where he sits, will see a somewhat different face of an issue, because his perception of the issue will be heavily shaded by his particular concerns." [103] Like beauty, the nature of an issue is in the eyes of the beholder. A policymaking process is therefore to an important extent a process of competition among contending definitions of the issue involved. This subjective nature and fragmentation of definitions of a policy issue are an important source of complexity. By explicitly and systematically identifying the range and contents of important definitions of the given issue and their promoters we may come closer to bringing the problem of complexity under control.

The second dimension of the problem of complexity relates to the way two or more policy issues become linked. Since issues involve subjective psychological elements, some actors perceive issues to be interrelated in one way or another. One might say again that interissue linkages develop differently in the eyes of different actors, on the basis of which they make choices and decisions. As I have already suggested, the landlord-compensation issue was linked to the issue of compensation for repatriates in the minds of some bureaucrats and many repatriates. The landlord-compensation problem had in turn been stimulated by its association with the successful demand of

103. Morton H. Halperin, *Bureaucratic Politics and Foreign Policy* (Washington, D.C.: Brookings Institution, 1974), 16.

veterans for bigger pensions.[104] In a 1955 controversy over the
proposed expansion of an American Air Force base in Niigata
Prefecture the local farmers and fishermen opposed to the proposal saw relationships between the base issue on the one hand
and, on the other, the proposed abolition of the rice-price support system by the government and their own demands for
larger national government subsidies for local public works
projects.[105] Harari notes in the conclusion of his study of the
ILO Convention 87 case that "it reflected the strong linkage between labor legislation and several other issue-areas of the Japanese political system—primarily those of education and internal security."[106]

Such interconnections among issues can have important consequences for an actor's decisions and actions. At the minimum, simultaneous preoccupation with multiple issues will severely constrain his freedom of action on any single issue.[107]
The interissue relationships also enormously complicate our
task of describing and analyzing any given policymaking case.
Instead of leaving the problem implicit or completely ignoring
its implications for our conclusions, as has been our usual practice in the past, it will be better to deal with it explicitly and systematically. We should ask how and why certain issues become
linked to one another, how the perceptions of the linkages affect an actor's behavior, how this phenomenon affects policy
outputs, and so forth.

Finally, another important dimension of complexity is found
in the simple fact that policymaking is a historical process and a
policy issue is a variable in that process. Issues change over
time; they develop, evolve, or transform. This is a factor of
fundamental importance in the study of policymaking. In the
conclusion to his recent study of public advisory bodies in Japanese politics, Harari points out: "The same PAB, with practically the same membership, may perform under changing environmental conditions different instrumental as well as

104. Nagai, "Atsuryoku Seiji," 11.
105. Shibuya Takeshi, "Niigata Hikōjō Kakuchō Hantai Kisei Dōmei
[The league against the expansion of the Niigata Air Force base], *Nihon no
Atsuryoku Dantai*, 143.
106. Harari, *The Politics of Labor Legislation*, 176.
107. Halperin, *Bureaucratic Politics*, 120.

systemic functions." [108] Essentially the same thought is expressed by Lowi when he points out that an issue may move from one of his arenas to another, and by Anderson when he says that "the nature of the problem at which policy is directed may change while policy is being developed or applied." [109]

The idea that policymaking is a historical process has another important implication for future research. It is that an issue evolves continuously. As Anderson puts it: "the process of policy-making on most problems—certainly those of any magnitude—is continuous." [110] This continuity makes it difficult to separate and isolate the *making* of policy from its *implementation and evaluation.*[111] There is an inherent difficulty in our practice of talking about and confining our attention to *policymaking.* Furthermore, the practice is based on or justified by the implicit assumption that policies *made* normally are *implemented* without much difficulty. By focusing on the *making* of policies, then, we should be able to know also what policies are actually administered in the society. Despite the strong elements of continuity in any policy process, however, policies that are made may not actually be implemented.

In a recent study of this problem in the case of Economic Development Administration projects in Oakland, California, Jeffrey L. Pressman and Aaron B. Wildavsky present some amazing and disturbing data. For the implementation of an EDA public works program the authors identify thirty "decision points" involving a cumulative total of seventy agreements which are required to move a program to successful completion. They then calculate that, if the probability of agreement by every actor at every decision point was 99 per cent, the program would have been successfully implemented about forty-nine times in a hundred (.489). If, however, that probability was 90 per cent, the likelihood of implementation would drop to slightly over six in ten thousand (.000644); if the probability of agreement among all actors at every point was 80 per cent,

108. Ehud Harari, "Japanese Politics of Advice in Comparative Perspective: A Framework for Analysis and a Case Study," *Public Policy* 22 (Fall 1974), 576.

109. Lowi, "American Business," 699; Anderson, *Public Policy-making,* 153.

110. Anderson, *Public Policy-making,* 161.

111. See also Halperin's comment in *Bureaucratic Politics,* 281, n. 7.

which would be a far more realistic expectation, the chance of the ultimate success of the program fell to one in a million (.000000125). But is this an exceptional case? The authors explain:

We have chosen to analyze the EDA public works program in Oakland precisely because it lacks those elements that permit easy explanations. . . . The EDA's involvement in Oakland lacks both drama and conflict. . . . There were no obvious conflicting interests and contradictory legislative criteria . . . there was no opposition on the local level. In EDA public works, all the major participants throughout the program's history insisted that they believed in the program and that there were no fundamental disagreements among them. The happenings we record are important to us for their everyday prosaic character. These are the kinds of things—changing actors, diverse perspectives, multiple clearances—that are found in any program.[112]

It will be neither necessary nor useful to speculate at this point on the relevance to Japan of the substantive findings and conclusions of the Pressman and Wildavsky study. There are as yet no comparable studies in the literature on Japanese policymaking. But until we study Japanese cases of policy implementation we can neither prove nor disprove the applicability of the experience of a single American case.

The addition of the time dimension to our research design and, especially, the inclusion of policy implementation, and perhaps even policy evaluation, in the scope of our investigation will no doubt considerably complicate our work. Nevertheless, such complexity and dynamism inhere in the reality with which we deal. It is not helpful to ignore or cover up such elements, however intractable they may appear to be. Here again the important thing is to recognize the problem explicitly and try to find ways of dealing with it systematically and meaningfully as another important factor in our analysis.

The two major types of problems on which I have focused in the foregoing discussion concern primarily the study of *Japanese* policymaking in a single-nation perspective. For a fuller

112. Jeffrey L. Pressman and Aaron B. Wildavsky, *Implementation* (Berkeley and Los Angeles: University of California Press, 1973), 92–93, 102–10; see also 123. I am grateful to Biliana Ambrecht for bringing this fascinating little book to my attention.

and more meaningful discussion of the theoretical and methodological issues raised here, however, these problems need to be viewed also in a broader cross-national comparative perspective. Such a perspective is emergent in some recent works, but it too needs to be more explicitly defined and systematically articulated.[113]

The state-to-be of the art which I envisage will thus be characterized by more case studies and generalizations based on them which are informed and guided by greater concern with and sensitivity to the problems of representativeness, complexity, dynamism, and cross-national comparability. I hope that the studies in this volume will mark an important step in that direction.

113. Campbell's *Contemporary Japanese Budget Politics* adopts such a cross-national comparative perspective more systematically than any I have reviewed in this chapter. See also Kojima, "Gendai Yosan Seiji Shiron," 117–25; Curtis, "Big Business," *passim.*

3. Tanaka Goes to Peking: A Case Study in Foreign Policymaking

Haruhiro Fukui

Introduction

In the absence of a comprehensive typology of policy issues and representative patterns of policymaking in contemporary Japan (or anywhere else for that matter) it is not possible to select a particular case for investigation from which a large number of generalizations may be extracted about policymaking in Japan, much less policymaking in general. It is, in fact, like putting the cart before the horse to undertake an investigation of a particular case before determining what class of cases it belongs to and where that class falls in the general spectrum of all cases. On the other hand, it is no more possible to construct a useful typology until we have examined and identified a sufficient number of empirical cases. We thus face a basic dilemma of the chicken-and-egg variety. Even at this pretaxonomic stage of our explorations in policymaking in an advanced industrial society we can and should try to look at cases as systematically as possible. One way of doing so would be to pick and study a case or cases prima facie similar to those which have been previously investigated with a view to confirming or challenging or modifying the findings of those previous studies.

One group of cases appear particularly amenable to this approach and hold special interest to a political scientist because of their unusual visibility and controversiality in the society. These are the cases which may be called, in the absence of a better label, "critical" cases. For example, the 1951 peace settlement at San Francisco, the 1956 peace-making with the Soviet Union, and the 1960 revision of the U.S.-Japan Mutual Security Treaty were all cases of this variety. They were not cases of "crisis" decisionmaking, as the term is used in the specialized literature on international crises.[1] They were in fact all *domestic political disturbances* caused by or related to specific foreign-policy issues. Of the three elements attribued to an international crisis by Charles F. Hermann and others—short decision time, high perceived threat to the decisionmakers' central values or goals, and surprise—these cases shared, more or less, the first and the second but not, or only very weakly, the last. They were nevertheless clearly distinguishable from the routine operations of government. Unlike the latter, which consist mainly of incremental adjustments by and among bureaucrats, they involved a series of distinctive and relatively easily identifiable *decisions* by political leaders. These decisions were regarded both by the decisionmakers and by observers as exceptionally important to Japanese foreign relations and domestic politics in the long run. In other words, they were perceived to be watersheds in the foreign policy of postwar Japan involving "critical" decisions. Largely for this reason several scholars have studied these cases in detail, as my review of the literature in Chapter 2 indicated. Moreover, these case studies have generated a number of important, interesting, and reasonably explicit propositions about the general patterns of Japanese policymaking in critical situations. It will be sensible to build on this existing basis of scholarship by adding a few more studies of similar cases and either verifying or modifying those proposi-

1. The term "critical" is used here to distinguish the type of policymaking situation examined in this chapter from a "crisis" situation defined by Charles F. Hermann and others. A "critical" policymaking case, as the term is provisionally used here, differs from the process of routinized and incremental adjustments and shares some but not all of the properties attributed to a "crisis." Such a definition is obviously much too loose and unsatisfactory for a general organizing concept in our future research and will either be refined or replaced by a better term in my future explorations. For relevant discussions of "crisis" in foreign policy and international relations, see Charles F. Hermann, (ed.), *International Crises* (New York: Free Press, 1972), especially parts 1 and 6. See also Charles F. Hermann, *Crises in Foreign Policy: A Simulation Analysis* (Indianapolis and New York: Bobbs-Merrill, 1969); James A. Robinson, "Crisis Decision-Making: An Inventory and Appraisal of Concepts, Theories, Hypotheses, and Techniques of Analysis," in James A. Robinson (ed.), *Political Science Annual: An International Review* 2 (Indianapolis and New York: Bobbs-Merrill, 1969), 111–48.

tions so as to expand our cumulative knowledge of foreign policymaking in contemporary Japan.

With this in mind I have undertaken a case study of Prime Minister Tanaka's trip to Peking in September 1972. The purpose of the trip was to extend the formal recognition of the Japanese government to the government of the People's Republic of China (PRC) and to establish normal diplomatic relations between the two governments. This was an event of political significance comparable to the critical cases mentioned above. It represented a series of complex and difficult policy decisions in the Japanese government. Why did Tanaka decide to go to Peking at that particular time? Why did he consent to signing the joint communiqué which spelled out the terms of reconciliation? Who advocated and who opposed Tanaka's trip in Japan and why? How was the opposition overcome and at what political costs to whom? More specifically, how did the LDP behave in the situation? What effects, if any, did intraparty factionalism have on the process of decisionmaking? Did ministry bureaucrats lead or follow politicians? How about big businessmen? What was the role of the Diet? How about the opposition parties and their leaders? What about the press and public opinion? Was there an identifiable group of decisionmakers, and if so, who belonged to it? And, finally, what does the experience of this particular case add to our knowledge about foreign policymaking in Japanese government?

Answers to these and related questions will help us clarify some of the questions that have been left by the previous case studies as well as test the general applicability of the specific propositions based on those studies. As I have suggested already, this is one way, though by no means the only or even the best way, to expand the horizon of our knowledge about foreign policymaking in contemporary Japan and, ultimately, policymaking in a complex and rapidly changing industrial society in general.

Background

Until the summer of 1971 the policy of the Japanese government toward the PRC remained generally consistent in its studied passivity and inaction. As I pointed out in my previous study of the subject, the policy amounted to an implicit recognition of two Chinas, a policy that was justified by the so-called principle of the separation of politics and economics.[2] During his seven and a half years as prime minister, Satō Eisaku was preoccupied in the field of foreign policy mainly with the reversion of Okinawa to Japanese administration. His remaining time and energy were expended largely on such other controversial issues as the normalization of relations with South Korea (1965) and the textile dispute with the United States (1969–1971).[3] Under the circumstances Satō had neither the will nor the time to take the initiative in reorienting Japan's posture of political noninvolvement toward the PRC, until he was jolted by the "Nixon shocks" of the summer of 1971 into a reluctant reappraisal of the situation.

This jolt came at a time when the Chinese had been leveling numerous charges against Japan for alleged militarism. Such charges were not new. In fact, the first explicit charge of this kind had been made in the preamble of the 1950 Sino-Soviet Alliance Treaty, and it had been repeated sporadically during the early 1960's.[4] After the Satō-Nixon Joint Communiqué of November 1969, however, references to Japanese militarism began to appear in Chinese official statements and press reports with noticeable frequency. The triggering occasion was no doubt the mention in the Satō-Nixon communiqué of "the

2. Haruhiro Fukui, *Party in Power: The Japanese Liberal-Democrats and Policy-making,* (Berkeley and Los Angeles: University of California Press, 1970), chapter 9. See also the following: Herbert Passin, *China's Cultural Diplomacy,* (New York: Praeger, 1962); A. M. Halpern, "China and Japan" in Tan Tsou (ed.), *China in Crisis* (Chicago: University of Chicago Press, 1968), II, 441–57; Frank C. Langdon, "Japanese Liberal Democratic Factional Discord on China Policy," *Pacific Affairs* 41 (Fall 1968), 403–15; Chae-Jin Lee, "The Politics of Sino-Japanese Trade Relations, 1963–68," *Pacific Affairs* 42 (Summer 1969), 129–44.

3. Details of the Okinawa reversion and textile negotiations will be examined in forthcoming case studies by a group of Brookings Institution scholars, Priscilla Clapp, I. M. Destler, Hideo Sato, and myself. On the Japan–South Korea normalization treaty negotiation, see Hans H. Baerwald, "Nikkan Kokkai: The Japan–Korea Treaty Diet," in Lucian W. Pye (ed.), *Cases in Comparative Politics: Asia* (Boston: Little, Brown, 1970), 19–57.

4. For a chronological list of relevant statements by the PRC government and the Chinese press, see Eiichi Suga *et al., Nitchū Mondai: Gendai Chūgoku to Kōryū no Shikaku* [The Japan-China problem: a standpoint on exchanges with contemporary China] (Tokyo: Sanseidō, 1971), 57–59.

maintenance of peace and security in the Taiwan area" as "a most important factor for the security of Japan." [5] Beginning with the *People's Daily* editorial of November 28 condemning the "criminal conspiracy of the reactionary groups in the United States and Japan," the theme of reviving Japanese militarism and Satō's imperialistic designs appeared with regularity throughout 1970 and 1971. As late as September of 1971 Premier Chou En-lai made it very clear to a visiting Japanese delegation led by an LDP Diet member, Kawasaki Hideji, that he still believed that Japanese militarism was reviving and that he had no intention whatever of negotiating with the Satō government.[6] Nor did a Democratic Socialist Party (DSP) delegation led by Chairman Kasuga Ikkō find the PRC line softening a bit in December of that year.[7] Only after President Nixon's trip to Peking in February 1972 did the PRC cease to hurl charges of militarism against Tokyo, at least officially; after about May more positive indications of a change in Peking's attitude began to attract the attention of the Japanese government and press.

In May 1972 a Clean Government Party (CGP) delegation led by Vice-Chairman Ninomiya Bunzō visited Peking. This was followed by the visit of a single LDP Diet member, Furui Yoshimi. Both received a clear signal from Chou that the PRC government was willing, in fact eager, to discuss normalization of relations with whoever might succeed Satō as prime minister. The only condition was that the new prime minister must accept the so-called "Three Principles"—that the PRC was the sole legitimate government representing China, that Taiwan was part of China, and that the Japan–Republic of China Peace Treaty was null and void.[8] About a week earlier a *Peking Daily* Tokyo correspondent, Wang T'ai-p'ing, explained to me that, whoever it might be, the next prime minister and his cabinet would have to come to terms with the PRC because the "objec-

5. For text, see *New York Times*, November 22, 1969.
6. *Nihon Keizai Shimbun*, September 17, 1971.
7. Interview: Ōuchi Keigo (director, DSP Education and Information Bureau), March 2, 1973.
8. *Mainichi Shimbun*, May 17, 1972; *Nihon Keizai Shimbun*, May 24, 1972; Furui Yoshimi, "Nitchū Kokkō Seijōka no Hiwa" [Secret records of the normalization of Japan-China relations], *Chūō Kōron*, December 1972, 143.

tive circumstances" would give him no other choice.[9] He thought highly of such pro-Peking LDP leaders as Miki Takeo and Fujiyama Aiichirō, but he insisted that the PRC government would not prejudge any candidate and that, from his government's point of view, actual performance after assuming power would be far more important than past words. It should be noted that even at this point the PRC firmly maintained that there could be no reconciliation with the Japanese government so long as Satō remained prime minister.

Satō had survived the barrage of Peking's strong charges for six and a half years until the summer of 1971. The "Nixon shocks," however, made his position clearly untenable and his early resignation unavoidable. The shock waves of Nixon's July 1971 announcement of his forthcoming visit to Peking were felt literally in every corner of the Japanese establishment. Every LDP leader I have since interviewed has related his great consternation at the news.[10] Every senior official of the Foreign Ministry I have met echoed the politicians' amazement.[11] There was a sense of crisis in the ruling party, in the bureaucracy, and even in the mass media.[12] And most people naturally blamed Satō and his inner circle for the loss of face and humiliation suffered by the entire nation. Just as naturally, Satō and his friends tried desperately to extricate themselves from the deepening trouble, but in vain. In fact, two well-publicized events in the fall of 1971 further compounded their mounting difficulties.

The first involved a secret letter addressed to the PRC government written by LDP Secretary-General Hori Shigeru in early October and carried by Tokyo Governor Minobe Ryō-

9. Interview: Wang T'ai-p'ing, May 8, 1972.
10. Interviews: Satō Eisaku (former prime minister), February 26, 1973; Kishi Nobusuke (former prime minister), March 6, 1973; Ōhira Masayoshi (former foreign minister), February 7, 1972; Kosaka Zentarō (former foreign minister), March 8, 1972; Fujiyama Aiichirō (former foreign minister), February 17, 1973; Noda Takeo (chairman, LDP China Committee), February 5, 1972.
11. Interviews: Yoshino Bunroku (director, American Affairs Bureau), October 14, 1971; Hōgen Shinsaku (deputy vice-minister), October 25, 1971; Ushiba Nobuhiko (ambassador, Embassy of Japan, Washington, D.C.), October 25, 1972; Yoshida Kenzō (director, Asian Affairs Bureau), March 6, 1973; Ōgawara Yoshio (director, American Affairs Bureau), March 1, 1973.
12. See various newspapers of July 16–18, 1971.

kichi to Peking during the latter's tour of the PRC and North
Korea shortly afterward. The idea apparently originated in
conversations Hori had had with Tagawa Seiichi, a well-known
friend of Peking in the LDP and former personal secretary to
Matsumura Kenzō,[13] and reached Minobe through the governor's "brain-truster," Komori Takeshi of the Tokyo Municipal Administration Research Association. Ever since the visit of
the American table tennis team to the PRC in the spring and
particularly President Nixon's July announcement, Satō and
his inner circle had been seeking an opening to Peking. They
knew well that pressure for immediate recognition of the PRC
government was growing in Japan and that unless they responded quickly and positively it would soon overwhelm them.
Satō's political life seemed now to hang on his immediate reconciliation with the leadership of the PRC government. Given
the rigid attitude of the latter, this was a virtual impossibility,
but Satō tried. First, he asked the chairman of the newly appointed LDP China Committee, Noda Takeo, to go to Peking
on his behalf. Noda, an ardent advocate of early reconciliation
with the PRC, agreed to run the errand for Satō, but the
plan aborted owing to the lack of response from the Chinese
side.[14] Noda nevertheless drafted in June a three-part proposal
for normalization, which explicitly recognized the PRC as the
legitimate government of China and Taiwan as part of Chinese
territory but which did not deny the validity of the 1952 peace
treaty between Japan and the Republic of China.[15]

Hori's personal position was probably somewhat more sympathetic to Taiwan. He agreed that the PRC was the legitimate
government of China, but he also insisted that Japan's official
relations with Taiwan should be respected and maintained.[16]
As Satō's devoted loyalist, however, he was willing to go a
long way to help build a bridge between Tokyo and Peking so
as to save the Satō government. According to Tagawa's testimony published in the spring of 1972, Hori accepted the view

13. On Matsumura's role in the pro-Peking groups within the LDP, see
Fukui, *Party in Power,* 247–251.
14. *Asahi Shimbun,* April 16, 1971; interview: Noda, February 5, 1972.
15. Interview: Noda, February 5, 1972.
16. Interview: Hori Shigeru (LDP secretary-general), January 24, 1972.

that Taiwan was part of China in his conversations with
Tagawa on August 19 and September 1.[17] A few days before
they met for a third time, on October 13, Hori apparently
wrote the letter along the lines of Noda's June proposal, indicating his wish to visit Peking in person if the PRC agreed to
a dialogue on the basis of the proposal. Before it was given to
Minobe, the letter was apparently cleared with both Satō and
Foreign Minister Fukuda Takeo. The idea was that by sending
it under the name of the LDP secretary-general, its rejection by
the PRC would not directly embarrass and undermine the
credibility of either Satō or Fukuda, whom Satō, Hori, and
other LDP mainstream leaders wanted to succeed Satō as
prime minister. It was therefore important that the heir apparent's prestige and credibility not be further eroded by another
diplomatic blunder.

Despite his reliance on the support of the Socialists and the
Communists for electoral victory, Minobe was essentially an
idealistic academic liberal. He was apparently persuaded that
reconciliation with the PRC was worth achieving even under
the rule and by the hands of his political adversaries in the conservative party. He presented the secret letter to PRC representatives on his way home from North Korea in early November.
A few days later Chou pronounced his government's official
rejection on the grounds that the letter failed to recognize the
PRC as the "sole" legitimate government of China and left
open the possibility of an independent Taiwan by deliberately
referring to it as a territory of the "people" of China.[18] A more
immediate reason was probably Japan's cosponsorship of the
"reversed important question" resolution in the United Nations.[19] In any event, Hori's efforts failed and the Satō govern-

17. *Sankei Shimbun*, March 21, 1972.

18. *Asahi Shimbun*, November 15, 1971; Interview: Tominomori Eiji (re-
porter, Political Affairs Department, *Asahi Shimbun*), April 24, 1972. See also
Nihon Keizai Shimbun, October 24, 1971; *Asahi Shimbun*, November 11, 1971
(evening edition).

19. The "reversed important question" formula defined the expulsion of the
Republic of China, instead of the admission of the PRC, as an "important"
question requiring two-thirds consent. Since the PRC government was known
to be determined not to join the U.N. until the Taipei government left, the
approach was expected to achieve the same result as the straight "important
question" formula which it would replace.

ment's predicament deepened. One significant aspect of this unfortunate episode was that an opposition politician, Minobe, who had been elected Tokyo governor on a joint Socialist-Communist ticket, ran the errand for the LDP government. This set an interesting precedent, as we shall see shortly.

The Japanese government's decision to cosponsor the "reversed important question" resolution was the other event at that time which added to Satō's troubles. The plan to abandon the "important question" formula, which the United States and its allies had so far successfully employed to keep the PRC out, and to replace it with the reversed formula had been discussed in some detail by American and Japanese foreign office officials earlier in the year. The idea had been suggested in January, probably first by the American side, as an option for a joint strategy to defend Taiwan's seat in the General Assembly, if not in the Security Council, in the event the straightforward "important question" formula was rendered inoperative by mounting support for the PRC's admission.[20] While the middle-level officials of the two nations were debating the merits and demerits of various options for action in the U.N., however, a very different kind of discussion on the China issue was under way at the White House, as President Nixon revealed in July. Probably for that reason, in March the American side suspended the joint exploration of the new formula with the Japanese Foreign Ministry officials and remained silent during the next four months, until after the Nixon announcement. In previous years Washington would have firmed up its position and strategy by June and signaled it to its allies, allowing ample time for arduous but indispensable behind-the-scenes work to drum up support for the resolution in the General Assembly in October. The Japanese officials involved were all very concerned, and some were quite frustrated, over the unusual unresponsiveness of their American counterparts.

Japanese reaction was understandably mixed when the Americans took up the plan again after the Nixon announcement and asked the Japanese government to cosponsor the resolution calling for Taiwan's expulsion as an important question

20. My discussion here is based largely on information collected through interviews with several Foreign Ministry officials.

and a twin resolution on dual Chinese representation. In both
the LDP and the bureaucracy there was a sharp division of
opinion as to whether Japan should accede to the American
request. In the Foreign Ministry, intense and often emotional
debates lasted for a full month. It was with a great deal of difficulty that an affirmative decision was finally reached by the
top echelon, represented by the staunchly anti-Communist
Deputy Vice-Minister Hōgen Shinsaku, against the vigorous
opposition of several middle-ranking officials, notably China
Division Head Hashimoto Hiroshi.

In the LDP opposition was so strong and widespread that,
despite the affirmative recommendation the Foreign Ministry
leaders managed to submit after the drawn-out battles among
themselves, the ultimate outcome remained uncertain until the
end of September. When Foreign Minister Fukuda went to
Washington during that month to attend the annual meeting of
the Joint U.S-Japan Committee on Trade and Economic Affairs, the LDP China Committee chairman, Noda, warned him
against committing Japan to the cosponsorship of either resolution.[21] When Fukuda was pressed by Secretary of State William
Rogers to so commit the Japanese government for the sake of
U.S.-Japanese cooperation, LDP Secretary-General Hori re-
minded him by telephone that he was not in a position to endorse such action.[22] Fukuda returned without making a firm
commitment and passed the buck to Satō. Satō held out for a
time against growing American pressure, but finally yielded.
Apart from his concern about the probable impact of Japan's
negative decision on the attitudes of Australia, New Zealand,
and other nations who were still undecided—an effect which
the U.S. apparently emphasized [23]—he was obviously worried
about its possible impact on the U.S. position on the textiles
problem, which was entering the final and critical phase of discussions, and, more importantly, on the actual reversion of
Okinawa, which was scheduled for the following spring. Many
LDP leaders and even some Foreign Ministry officials were

21. Interview: Noda, February 5, 1972.
22. Interview: Hori, January 24, 1972.
23. *Sankei Shimbun,* March 21, 1972; interview: Tanaka Yoshitomo (head,
Disarmament Division, United Nations Bureau), May 11, 1972.

vengeful enough in the wake of the Nixon shocks to turn down Washington's request for Japanese cooperation on this matter. Satō, however, felt that he could not afford to offend President Nixon once again and to suffer further retaliation in connection with such other vital issues as trade and, especially, Okinawa reversion. Another Nixon shock would spell the end of his power in Japanese government at least as surely as an unpopular move on the issue of Chinese representation in the U.N.

The crushing defeat of the "reversed important question" resolution and the smashing victory of the Albanian resolution admitting the PRC at the expense of Taiwan had a sort of Bay of Pigs effect on the Japanese government. As Graham Allison wrote of that incident, the experience "raised the most serious internal doubts about the [Prime Minister's] judgment, the wisdom of his advisers, and the quality of their advice." [24] It certainly hurt the whole cabinet and the LDP, but especially hurt were Satō and his inner circle, such as Fukuda and Hori, and senior officials of the Foreign Ministry. Thereafter an early change of the prime minister and cabinet was a foregone conclusion. The only remaining questions were who would succeed Satō and how soon.

Satō's mainstream coalition in the LDP had among its members two active contenders in the succession struggle, Foreign Minister Fukuda and International Trade and Industry Minister Tanaka Kakuei. Both were closely associated with Satō. Tanaka had in fact been regarded as a loyal member of the prime minister's own faction. Both therefore suffered from the growing unpopularity of the Satō government. But since 1955 every unpopular LDP cabinet has been succeeded by another LDP cabinet, the important thing being a difference of personality and style rather than of policy or ideology. By late 1971 both Fukuda and Tanaka had acquired sizable factional followings of their own and were eminently qualified, in terms of intra-LDP factional politics, to aspire to the position of top party leader. There were three other contenders: Ōhira Masayoshi, Miki Takeo, and Nakasone Yasu-

24. Graham T. Allison, *Essence of Decision: Explaining the Cuban Missile Crisis* (Boston: Little, Brown, 1971), 187.

hiro, all of whom led their own factions. After the spring of
1972, as the contest became progressively intense and as psychological and financial pressures built, the three joined forces
with Tanaka to form an anti-Fukuda coalition.[25] The motivations behind their move were largely tactical and Machiavellian.
There were, however, differences of style, and even of policy,
between Fukuda and his opponents. In foreign policy, particularly with regard to the China issue, Fukuda was considered a
hard-liner, while the other four candidates were believed to be
more flexible and "forward-looking." [26]

Satō resigned in early July, by which time Nakasone had
dropped out of the race. The contest was finally between Fukuda and the Tanaka-Ōhira-Miki coalition. As usual, the voting
delegates assembled at the special LDP conference of July 5
were the 297 members of the House of Representatives and
134 members of the House of Councillors, plus the 47 representatives from each of the party's prefectural federations.[27]
There were, however, two rather unusual and important features about this particular LDP presidential election. One was
that foreign policy in general and China policy in particular
was clearly a dominant issue and the other was that the anti-
Fukuda groups had reached an explicit "policy" agreement in
advance. This agreement, made public on July 2, said in part:
"Normalization of Japan-China relations is now the demand of
the entire nation. We will enter into negotiations [with the PRC
government] with a view to concluding a peace treaty with the
People's Republic of China through [official] contacts between
the two governments." [28]

According to the rules of the LDP, in order to win the party's
presidential election a candidate either had to win a clear-cut
majority on the first ballot, or, failing that, had to place first or
second on the first ballot and then win a majority in the second,

25. "Seiken Kōtaigeki to Nitchū no Hōkō" [The drama of a cabinet
change and the direction of Japanese-Chinese relations], *Sekai,* July 1972, 151.
26. *Mainichi Shimbun,* May 9, 12, 18, and 31, 1972; *Nihon Keizai Shimbun,*
May 24, 1972; *Yomiuri Shimbun,* May 30, 1972. See also Mainichi Shimbunsha
(ed.), *Nihon to Chūgoku: Seijōka e no Michi* [Japan and China: the road to
normalization] (Tokyo: Mainichi Shimbunsha, 1971), 265–72.
27. *Nihon Keizai Shimbun,* July 5, 1972.
28. Text in *Asahi Shimbun,* July 3, 1972.

two-man contest.[29] The three allied candidates promised each
other that if one of them won either first or second place on
the first ballot (the other winner being Fukuda), the two losers
would support him on the second ballot, but if two of them
should win the first and the second places, they would compete
against each other in the second balloting. Tanaka won 156
votes to Fukuda's 150 (Ōhira 101, Miki 69) on the first ballot
and defeated Fukuda 282 to 190 on the second, obviously
thanks to the delivery of the promised faction-bound votes by
the Ōhira and the Miki groups.[30] Tanaka was thus nominated
LDP president and then duly elected prime minister with an
explicit commitment to accomplish normalization of relations
with the PRC.

Actors and Factors of Policymaking
Politicians as Policymakers

As the background suggests, Tanaka, Ōhira, and Miki clearly
took on themselves, in the heat of the LDP presidential election
campaign, an explicit responsibility for and a command position in moving Japan toward reconciliation with the PRC after
forty years of hot and cold war. For one thing, the July 2
agreement did not involve the three factions, except for purposes of winning the election. It was an agreement among the
three politicians as individuals. On specific issues of policy the
factions tend to be uninvolved, and individual leaders are
therefore free to act much as they please without the formal
support or approval of their factional followers. But the agreement was taken very seriously by the three leaders. Miki and
Ōhira joined the new cabinet as deputy prime minister and
foreign minister, respectively, and, following the formation of
the cabinet, both Tanaka and Miki publicly reaffirmed the letter and spirit of the pre-election commitment.[31]

Beyond this, there were serious differences of political style

29. On the procedure, see Fukui, *Party in Power,* 96.
30. *Asahi Shimbun,* July 5, 1972 (evening edition).
31. See "Tanaka Seiken to Nitchū Kankei" [The Tanaka government and
Japan-China relations], *Sekai,* September 1972, 156; "Tenkaiki no Hoshu
Gaikō: Sono Kokusai Ninshiki wa Kawari uru ka" [The conservatives' foreign
policy at the crossroads: can their perspective of international problems
change?], *Sekai,* November 1972, 98–99.

and strategy between Tanaka and Miki which plagued their relationship from the beginning and subsequently led to widening rifts between them. It was largely at Miki's insistence that the commitment on the China issue had been part of the July 2 agreement, and, in fact, Tanaka had mildly protested its inclusion. Miki's personal commitment and his plans concerning the issue were straightforward and well publicized.[32] He was anxious to move in a few bold and dramatic steps. In order to keep alive his image as a serious candidate for the premiership despite being in his mid-sixties, Miki needed some spectacular personal achievement in either domestic or foreign policy. The China issue seemed to promise him an opportunity to impress his colleagues in the LDP and the nation. Tanaka, on the other hand, was shrewd and cautious. Concerned with building his own political empire, he was reluctant to commit himself to a definite course of action before he made certain that it was the safest and most profitable. Despite his media-created image as an outspoken, action-oriented politician, he had not spoken much on the sensitive China issue before July 2, 1972. Ōhira had a more philosophical bent and much greater substantive interest in foreign-policy questions.[33] He was, however, also an extremely cautious and discreet man with prime ministerial ambitions of his own. Tanaka found him congenial and trusted him. There was probably an understanding between the two men that Tanaka would turn over the prime ministry to Ōhira in due course, an understanding which added to the latter's desire to cooperate with the prime minister in their joint undertaking on the China issue.[34]

The command core of the policymaking group which emerged in July was thus not a trio but the duo of Tanaka and Ōhira. This arrangement put a considerable premium on discretion, circumspection, and pragmatism. As the experiences of Tanaka's predecessors had demonstrated—Kishi in a negative sense and Ikeda and Satō in a positive sense—these were in fact the essential ingredients of successful leadership in the Japa-

32. For relevant information, see sources given in n.26 above.

33. Interview: Ōhira, February 7, 1972.

34. This is my own speculation based on conversations with several newspaper reporters personally close to Ōhira.

nese government. Tanaka and Ōhira displayed these familiar
characteristics of LDP leadership nowhere more consistently
than in their dealings with the pro-Taiwan elements within the
LDP itself.

The policy positions and strengths of the anti-Communist,
pro-Taiwan groups in the LDP, represented by the Asian
Group (the Soshinkai) and the Asian Parliamentary Union,
have been discussed elsewhere.[35] These groups remained very
much alive and militant after the Nixon shocks of 1971 and
were ready to challenge the pro-Peking moves of the new Tanaka cabinet. A few weeks before the LDP presidential election
those in control of the party's Discipline Committee officially
impeached the flamboyant pro-Peking leader Fujiyama Aiichirō, as the result of a joint communiqué which he had signed
with the China-Japan Friendship Association (of the PRC) in
Peking on behalf of a delegation of Japanese Diet members.[36]
After the Tanaka cabinet was formed the "hawks" continued to
speak forcefully against normalization through the newly
formed Foreign Policy Roundtable (Gaikō Mondai Kondankai) and elsewhere. Specifically, they opposed the acceptance of the "Three Principles" and the Japanese offer of apol-
ogies for wartime actions.[37] In the middle of August they were
still publicly advocating the two-China policy.[38]

The Tanaka-Ōhira duo tried to cope with the continuing
revolts of the right-wing groups in the party by, on the one
hand, containing them in a party committee controlled by the
mainstream groups and, on the other, appeasing them through
personal tactfulness and concessions. The first line of attack
was attempted by the creation of the Council for the Normalization of Japan-China Relations a week after the July LDP
presidential election. At Tanaka's request Kosaka Zentarō, an
Ōhira faction foreign-policy specialist, a pragmatic liberal, and
a former foreign minister, was appointed its chairman. The

35. Fukui, *Party in Power,* 251–62; Langdon, "Japanese Liberal Democratic
Factional Discord."
36. For details, see *Yomiuri Shimbun* (Osaka edition), May 27, 1972; *Mainichi
Shimbun,* June 2, 1972.
37. *Mainichi Shimbun,* July 15, 1972; "Tanaka Seiken to Nitchū Kankei,"
157.
38. *Sankei Shimbun,* August 17, 1972.

committee, however, quickly proved to be unwieldy and ineffective. It was crowded with both militants and opportunists from both camps and the right-wingers skillfully used it as their principal propaganda forum. When the committee met officially for the first time on July 24 with both Tanaka and Ōhira present, nearly two hundred fifty LDP Diet members joined.[39] The real trouble developed when they began to discuss the substantive issues.

In the meantime, by early August the Tanaka-Ōhira action plan began to crystallize around Tanaka's prospective trip to Peking. The Kosaka council decided at the meeting of its chairman and vice-chairmen on August 2 to approve such a trip, and a week later, on August 9, the council as a whole formally approved the plan.[40] This became the formal recommendation of the party committee, just as Tanaka and Ōhira had hoped, and it was accepted by the party's Executive Council and became an official party policy on August 22.[41] These successive steps carefully orchestrated by the duo, however, aggravated and further provoked the pro-Taiwan groups. During the debates in the Kosaka council on August 15 and 17 they presented their views forcefully.[42]

When the council adopted "Five Principles of Normalization" at Kosaka's suggestion on August 24, the reaction within the LDP was so violent that the statement of innocuous generalities had to be subsequently revised twice.[43] The objections to the five "principles" were that they merely reiterated the 1954 Chou-Nehru Principles of Peace and that they did not include references to the strong feelings in the LDP about the Taiwan issue. During the last week of August the revolts threatened to get completely out of hand and even Kosaka, now confronted by a vote of no-confidence by members of his own council, for once lost some of his poise and expressed misgivings about the ultimate outcome of the entire undertaking.[44]

39. *Asahi Shimbun,* July 24, 1972; *Yomiuri Shimbun,* July 14, 1972.
40. *Asahi Shimbun,* August 2 and 9, 1972.
41. *Ibid.,* August 22, 1972 (evening edition).
42. *Ibid.,* August 16, 1972; *Nihon Keizai Shimbun,* August 18, 1972.
43. *Asahi Shimbun,* August 25 and 30 and September 6, 1972; *Nihon Keizai Shimbun,* September 1, 1972; *Sankei Shimbun,* September 1, 1972.
44. Interview: Kosaka, March 8, 1972.

Apart from the strategy of containment pursued by way of the Kosaka council, Tanaka and Ōhira were discreet in their response to the criticisms of the right-wing groups. Ōhira explained the basic spirit at a press conference on July 7, when he insisted that a party consensus was essential to any diplomatic initiative that he might take on the China question.[45] On July 24, Tanaka and Ōhira attended the first general meeting of the Kosaka council; on that same day Tanaka met with members of the Soshinkai and the Asian Parliamentary Union and allegedly promised to attend the forthcoming meeting of the APU.[46] Throughout this period Tanaka met, frequently and solicitously, with LDP "hawks," such as Kishi Nobusuke, Kaya Okinori, Ishii Mitsujirō, and Funada Naka, right up to and after his China trip.[47]

The last-ditch position of the pro-Taiwan rebels in the LDP was that if normalization of relations with the PRC was to be accomplished, the existing political and economic relationship with the Republic of China should not be sacrified.[48] Their arguments were based on pragmatic calculations about the economic importance of Taiwan to Japan as well as some lofty moral principles and ideological beliefs. After all, about $73 million of Japanese money was invested and some 3,800 Japanese citizens were residing in Taiwan in the spring of 1971, while Japanese exports to and imports from Taiwan in that same year amounted to $760 million and $260 million, respectively.[49] Moreover, as some of their critics speculated, several of the pro-Taiwan LDP members may well have been profiting directly or indirectly from illicit import-license manipulation.[50] On the other hand, actions directly motivated by or related to factional interests were almost totally absent, supporting our view that the LDP factions are largely indifferent to specific policy issues.

45. *Asahi Shimbun,* July 8, 1972.
46. "Tanaka Seiken to Nitchū Kankei," 157.
47. Interviews: Kishi, March 6, 1973; Kiuchi Akitane (secretary to Prime Minister Tanaka), February 24, 1972. On Ōhira's personal call to Kishi's office on August 4, see *Mainichi Shimbun,* August 4, 1972 (evening edition).
48. Interview: Kishi, March 6, 1973; *Asahi Shimbun,* September 6, 1972.
49. *Nikkan Kōgyō Shimbun,* August 14, 1972.
50. This is my own speculation based on conversations with several LDP politicians and newspaper reporters knowledgeable on the subject.

In any event, both Tanaka and Ōhira obviously shared the hawks' desire to keep the lucrative Taiwan connection as intact as possible, partly to deflect the latter's criticisms. As the discussion below will show, while the Chou-Tanaka Joint Communiqué and accompanying statement by Ōhira put an end to formal diplomatic relations between Taipei and Tokyo, informal economic relations survived.[51] Recognition was naturally condemned by the pro-Taiwan groups in the party, but their reaction was restrained, no doubt at least partly because their final demand was partially met. More generally, the deliberately accommodating tactics employed by the duo helped minimize the impact of the intraparty opposition.

In the meantime, preparations for Tanaka's trip and the firming up of the basic terms of reconciliation to be consummated by the trip were progressing elsewhere—in the Foreign Ministry bureaucracy, as one would naturally expect, but also among individuals whom one would not have expected to play a role of major significance. The latter included, centrally, a maverick LDP politician, Furui Yoshimi, and the CGP chairman, Takeiri Yoshikatsu. The bureaucrats neither initiated nor directed the politicians' activities but used them effectively ex post facto. Furthermore, Furui and Takeiri worked closely with each other and with the Tanaka-Ōhira duo.

Furui was an independent-minded and dedicated advocate of pro-Peking policy in the LDP. Since 1959 he had visited China a dozen times, each time deepening his commitment to reconciliation between the two nations.[52] Most recently, he had been to China in December 1971 and again in May 1972. Before the latter trip he had met and discussed the prospects of normalization with both Ōhira and Tanaka, as well as with Fukuda, (then still foreign minister in the Satō cabinet) Miki, and Nakasone. He returned with the distinct impression that

51. *Nihon Keizai Shimbun*, September 14, 1972; *Nikkan Kōgyō Shimbun*, October 1, 1972.

52. The following account is based on an interview with Furui, February 26, 1973. Verification and additional details may be found in Furui, "Nitchū Kokkō Seijōka no Hiwa," and Matsushita Muneyuki, "Nitchū Kyōdō Seimei no Seikaku to Haikei: Nokosareta Kadai wa Nani ka" [The character and background of the Japan-China statement: what tasks remain to be undertaken?], *Sekai*, December 1972, 133–40.

the PRC was now eager to negotiate normalization as soon as a
new Japanese cabinet was formed and that, while remaining
firm on matters of principle, the PRC was extremely open to
suggestion on details. Even on such basic issues as Taiwan and
the U.S.-Japan Security Treaty, Peking seemed far more flexible than on previous occasions. Chou and other PRC officials
were also anxious to know who Furui thought would succeed
Satō as prime minister. Furui predicted Tanaka's victory and
Ōhira's appointment as foreign minister. The Chinese made
clear their wish that the next prime minister would visit Peking
at an early date to discuss normalization, and while Furui did
not bring back any formal proposal from Chou, he passed on
the general but clear Chinese signal to Ōhira.

By coincidence a CGP delegation led by Ninomiya had visited Peking only a few days before Furui. The CGP had been
engaged in an extensive campaign in Japan for "correct understanding" of China ever since the summer of 1971, when party
chairman Takeiri visited the PRC for the first time.[53] The Ninomiya mission was a natural offshoot of that campaign. During
his visit the previous summer Takeiri had told Chou and others
in the PRC government that he expected Tanaka and Ōhira to
replace Satō and Fukuda in the next change of cabinet in
Tokyo. Ninomiya was asked for his opinion about the prospect
and replied that he thought Takeiri had made a correct forecast. When the delegation was met by Chou on May 15, Ninomiya was apparently entrusted with a confidential message to
Takeiri, a message which triggered an important chain of
events when it arrived in Tokyo.[54] It contained an invitation to
the would-be Tanaka cabinet to take up the normalization issue
without delay and for Tanaka himself to visit Peking for that
purpose. Chou promised in the message not to insist on Tanaka's adherence to the "Three Principles" as a precondition to
negotiation, not to shun discussions on specific details, and not
to drive Tanaka to a politically difficult position. Takeiri imme-

53. The following account of the CGP and Takeiri's role is based mainly on
an interview with Takeiri, February 22, 1973.
54. On the delegation's audience with Chou, see *Yomiuri Shimbun*, May 16,
1972; *Mainichi Shimbun*, May 17, 1972.

diately relayed his message to Tanaka and Ōhira, feeling that he must go to Peking soon with Tanaka's reply.

Like Tokyo Governor Minobe, Takeiri believed that the normalization of Japan-PRC relations was important enough to transcend partisanship and he was no doubt personally anxious to see the two nations become friends. But he was also anxious to involve himself in Tanaka's undertaking for other reasons. The CGP was a new party with no distinctive personality of its own. Its leaders, including Takeiri himself, were still small-time politicians whose records of performance were generally undistinguished in both domestic and foreign policy. Nor had they yet recovered completely from the crippling effects of the "freedom of speech" controversy of 1969 during which the party had been crucified by the Communists and the Socialists, as well as broad segments of the public.[55] The China issue offered the battered party and its leaders an opportunity to regain respectability and put an end to its downward slip in popularity among voters.

As we have seen, Tanaka formed a new cabinet on July 6, but both he and Ōhira were still extremely cautious and reluctant to make hasty moves. Takeiri met them frequently but separately while preparing for his next trip to China. On July 13 he publicly offered to "help" Tanaka, if the new prime minister

55. The controversy arose from allegation of the CGP's attempt to prevent publication of books critical of the party. The principal protagonists were CGP leaders on the one hand, and on the other Fujiwara Hirotatsu, the author, and Nisshin Hōdō, the publisher, of *Sōkagakkai wo Kiru* [I accuse Sōka Gakkai] and Naitō Kunio, the author, and Yale Shuppan, the publisher, of *Kōmeitō no Sugao* [The real face of the CGP]. It became a much larger controversy, however, when the other opposition parties, especially the JCP, took stands against the CGP and launched a media campaign on the constitutional issue of freedom of speech. It is interesting to note that Tanaka, who was then LDP secretary-general, was accused of having put pressure on the authors on behalf of the CGP leaders and that the LDP alone maintained an attitude of noninvolvement throughout the controversy. Takeiri was apparently impressed with and appreciative of the LDP's attitude, especially Tanaka's. See Genron Shuppan no Jiyū ni kansuru Kondankai (ed.), *Kōmeitō Sōka Gakkai no Genron Yokuatsu Mondai* [The suppression of freedom of speech by the CGP and Sōka Gakkai] (Tokyo: Iizuka Shoten, 1970); "Kizu tsuita Kōmeitō no Shoseijutsu" [The damaged survival techniques of the CGP], *Asahi Jānaru*, February 8, 1970, 96–104; "Jimin Kōmei Ryōtō no Taishaku Kanjō" [The balance sheet between the LDP and the CGP], *Asahi Jānaru*, March 15, 1970, 4–8.

was ready to make a decision and move toward normalization.[56] This apparently failed to force Tanaka to come up with
his own reply to Chou's message. As a result, Takeiri drafted a
twenty-point proposal of his own and took it to Peking in late
August. It proposed, among other things, that Japan not abro-
gate either the U.S.-Japan Security Treaty or the Japan–
Republic of China Peace Treaty and that the problem of references to Taiwan and Korea in the 1969 Nixon-Satō Joint Communiqué would have to be "shelved." When shown the text of the
proposal prior to Takeiri's departure, Tanaka and Ōhira neither explicitly approved nor objected to it.

When he arrived in China Takeiri was received, as an *Asahi*
correspondent remarked, like a state guest; he was provided
with a special car, a special train, and a special airplane.[57] In
Peking he met and talked with Chou for a total of nine hours
on August 27, 28, and 29.[58] During the first two days of the
closed confidential discussions Takeiri did most of the talking,
explaining and defending his twenty-point proposal. But on
the third day, without prior warning, he was presented with a
Chinese counterproposal of ten points. Takeiri described that
scene to me: "It was translated by an interpreter, word by
word. After each point was translated, I read it aloud for con-
firmation and corrections. While taking verbatim notes of every
word spoken by the interpreter, I was amazed by China's flexibility and was saying to myself, 'This will do, this will do.'"
Takeiri wanted, however, to make reservations on three points
in the Chinese proposal. These related to Chinese demands for
an explicit reference in the forthcoming joint statement on
normalization to the termination of the war, the abrogation of
the Japan–Republic of China Peace Treaty, and the suspension
of Japanese economic relations with Taiwan after normalization. Chou quickly accepted these reservations. Takeiri told
Chou that he would see that Tanaka and Ōhira accepted the
Chinese proposal as the basis of official negotiation between the
two governments. He also assured the premier that Tanaka

56. *Yomiuri Shimbun,* July 14, 1972.   57. *Asahi Shimbun,* July 26, 1972.
58. *Ibid.,* July 28 and 31, 1972; *Yomiuri Shimbun,* July 29, 1972; *Nihon Keizai
Shimbun,* July 31, 1972.

would visit Peking in person and inquired whether the Chinese government would like Tanaka to wait until after the October 1 anniversary celebration of the People's Republic; Chou said that the PRC government was not planning a big celebration that year and that he would prefer Tanaka's visit before that date. The two agreed also on the logistic details of Tanaka's trip, such as the direct, nonstop Tokyo-Peking flight (instead of via Shanghai), the use of the telecommunications satellite, Intelsat, for television coverage of the event, the number of Japanese reporters to accompany the prime minister's party, and so forth.

Detailed minutes of the conversations were kept by the two CGP Diet members who accompanied Takeiri on this trip, Masaki Yoshiaki and Ōkubo Naohiko. On their return to Tokyo these minutes were shown immediately to Tanaka, Ōhira, and Furui and were subsequently turned over to the Foreign Ministry.[59] A couple of copies were given to newspapers with the understanding that they would not be published.

It is thus beyond doubt that a leader of an opposition party, Takeiri, played a leading role in the advance preparation for Tanaka's trip. Moreover, an LDP maverick, Furui, normally far removed from the power center of the party, also played an important part, both through his trip to Peking in May and through his close collaboration with Takeiri in putting pressure on the Tanaka-Ōhira duo. He was to continue to play a crucial role in the final phase of the preparation. But these were not the only volunteers during this period to help Tanaka get to China and accomplish normalization. Except for the Japan Communist Party (JCP), which had been fighting a running verbal battle with the Chinese Communists since 1966, broad nonpartisan support for Tanaka's enterprise emerged by late July.[60]

The Democratic Socialists were divided, and an anti-Peking

59. Interview: Furui, February 26, 1973; Takeiri's reply to my inquiry by telephone, February 28, 1973. See also *Asahi Shimbun,* August 4, 1972 (evening edition).

60. The JCP kept silent on the issue until early September, when it belatedly announced its support for Tanaka's efforts for normalization. See *Asahi Shimbun,* September 7, 1972; *Nihon Keizai Shimbun,* September 10, 1972.

group led by the party's senior leader, Sone Eki, resisted the growing pressure for them to join the bandwagon.[61] By late July, however, Chairman Kasuga was publicly standing with CGP Vice-Chairman Ninomiya and JSP Chairman Narita Tomomi in a non-partisan call for national support for Tanaka's "positive" China policy.[62] More direct and substantial in its effect on the actual decision process was the role of the former JSP chairman, Sasaki Kōzō, who visited Peking in July, ten days before Takeiri. Before his departure Sasaki too met and conferred with both Tanaka and Ōhira. In Peking, he doubtless reassured Chou and other Chinese leaders that the duo was completely serious in their commitment on the normalization issue and that Tanaka was likely to accept Chou's invitation for an early visit.[63] He returned to Tokyo on July 21, four days before Takeiri's departure, with Chou's informal oral invitation to Tanaka and unambiguous signs that the PRC would be flexible on the terms of reconciliation, even on the interpretation of the "Three Principles." With these messages he met with Tanaka on July 22 and Ōhira on July 24 and urged them to go to Peking together before October 1.[64] This pressure must have moved the duo a step closer to their decision to undertake such a trip sometime in the fall.

In considering the roles played by these opposition politicians it is important to note the singularly personal nature of their involvement. It is true that all three opposition parties (again excepting the JCP) were officially behind the activities of their leaders. It is nevertheless striking how much the latter's activities and contributions were perceived in personal terms and how little formal party organizations and general memberships were involved. As I pointed out above, an important division of opinion in the DSP obviously made a partywide consensus difficult. In April 1972 a DSP delegation led by Kasuga

61. *Nihon Keizai Shimbun,* May 21, 1972.
62. *Tokyo Shimbun,* July 26, 1972; Interview: Ōuchi, March 2, 1973.
63. Matsushita, "Nitchū Kyōdō Seimei," 134; Tada Minoru, "Pekin Kaidan wa kaku Okonawareta" [This is how the talks in Peking proceeded] *Jiyū,* December 1972, 136; Furui, "Nitchū Kokkō Seijōka no Hiwa," 145; *Asahi Shimbun,* July 15, 17, and 20, 1972.
64. *Nihon Keizai Shimbun,* July 22 and 25, 1972. Sasaki met Tanaka again on July 27; see *Asahi Shimbun,* July 28, 1972.

had visited Peking and issued a joint communiqué with the China-Japan Friendship Association. This had drawn sharp criticism from Sone and his followers in the party, and the delegation had been forced to distribute a "clarifying explanation" among party members to defend itself.[65] Nor had Kasuga reported formally to the party on the delegation's activities in China.[66] Divisions in the JSP were less visible, but at least one source detected dissatisfaction among the rank and file about the top leaders' actions and such dissension threatened the party's electoral prospects.[67] The most extreme and interesting case, however, was that of Takeiri. As I mentioned above, the notes of his highly sensitive conversations with Chou in July were shown to the three LDP men, Tanaka, Ōhira, and Furui, and then turned over to the Foreign Ministry. They were not given or even shown to the CGP headquarters. Moreover, Takeiri did not make a formal report to the party on his trip and its significant implications,[68] although Deputy Secretary-General Ōkubo, who accompanied Takeiri, did make a partial report to the CGP Central Committee nearly a month after the trip, on August 28.[69] Secretary-General Yano himself was apparently not fully briefed either on the confidential mission of the delegation or the contents of the Chou-Takeiri negotiations.[70]

What does all this mean? It means, to my mind, first, that Takeiri, and to a lesser extent Sasaki and Kasuga, temporarily became part of the incipient policymaking group forming around Tanaka and Ōhira and, second, that it was the individuals and not the opposition parties that became so involved. This points up quite clearly the ad hoc character of the policymaking group and the highly flexible and open nature of its structure. Formal agreements and cooperation between the

65. The text of the joint statement is in *"Kyōdō Seimei no Zenbun"* [The complete text of the joint statement] mimeo., n.d.; see also "Kyōdō-Seimei-chū no Mondaiten ni taisuru Jakkan no Kaimei" [Some explanations on problems in the text of the joint statement] mimeo., n.d. Both were issued by the DSP delegation. See also *Shūkan Minsha,* April 28, 1972.
66. Interview: Ouchi, March 2, 1973.
67. See "Tanaka Seiken no Nitchū Kankei," 156.
68. Interview: Takeiri, February 22, 1973.
69. *Asahi Shimbun,* August 28, 1972 (evening edition).
70. Interview: Yano Junya (secretary-general, CGP), February 21, 1973.

parties as such would not have been possible, given the traditional hostility among them and conflicts of opinion within each. The bureaucratized party organizations, with their entrenched ideological and factional interests constraining their actions from both within and without, clearly were not capable of adapting to and exploiting the rapidly changing environment of domestic and international politics. Only a small ad hoc group of determined, ambitious, and adroit individuals could act effectively in this type of policymaking situation.

Bureaucrats in Action

Officials in the Foreign Ministry's Asian Affairs and Treaties bureaus had been studying the normalization issue more or less seriously and systematically since early 1972. From the beginning the central question was how to respond to the "Three Principles" of normalization on which the PRC was believed to be quite adamant. Specifically, should or could the new Japanese cabinet recognize the PRC as the "sole" legitimate government of China, accept Taiwan as an "integral" part of the territory of China, and renounce the Japan–Republic of China Peace Treaty? Closely related to these three points were the issues of the U.S.-Japan Security Treaty and the "termination of the war" issue.

By late June—that is, sometime before the formation of the Tanaka cabinet—Treaties Bureau officials had reached preliminary conclusions in their investigation of these complex issues.[71] On the first of the three principles, Japan should recognize the "sole legitimate" authority of the PRC. Theoretically, the "U.S. formula" of normalizing relations with the PRC without severing diplomatic relations with Taiwan might have been considered. In practice, however, this would not have been acceptable to Peking and therefore was not a viable option. On the second principle, they concluded that Japan should neither fully accept nor totally reject the Chinese position that Taiwan was part of the China which the PRC represented. The argument was that, while Japan had renounced its claim to the island by accepting the Potsdam Declaration in 1945, the "final

71. *Sankei Shimbun,* June 28, 1972.

disposition" of Taiwan had not been settled either at the 1951 San Francisco Peace Conference or subsequently. In short, the ultimate status of Taiwan remained yet to be decided. However, Japan, having renounced its own claim to the territory, was not in a position to speak on the problem one way or another. The new cabinet's attitude should therefore be, at most, that it fully understood the PRC's position. Regarding the third principle, Japan should not accept the Chinese argument that the 1952 peace treaty was "null and void." If it was null and void, technically it would be impossible even to "renounce" it, as the PRC was insisting. In terms of the general practice of international law, Japan had had the right in 1952 to recognize the government in Taiwan, aside from the question of whether it was wise or prudent to do so. Besides, for a government to declare a treaty null and void retroactively was an act that would inevitably damage its diplomatic credibility in the eyes of the world. On the other hand, conclusion of a formal treaty with the PRC would automatically result in the invalidation of the Taiwan treaty and would therefore resolve the difficulty.

The "termination of the war" problem was also delicate and the bureaucrats' position remained unsettled until July 5. They felt generally that Japan should adhere to the view that the Japan–Republic of China Peace Treaty had terminated the state of war between China and Japan and, therefore, the prospective treaty with the PRC could not terminate it once again, as if the war had continued. Their position on the U.S.-Japan Security Treaty, on the other hand, was quite straightforward and rigid: The treaty could not be tampered with in any way and Japan should not enter into negotiations if the abrogation or revision of that treaty was made a precondition.

These, then, were what may be regarded as the Foreign Ministry's positions on the basic issues as they took shape in the continuous intramural discussions on the subject, including an intensive round of debates among the ministry's China specialists held in Hong Kong in the middle of June.[72] The deliberations continued after Tanaka formed his cabinet in early July

72. *Nihon Keizai Shimbun,* July 3, 1972.

and by the middle of that month produced an intraministry
consensus on "understanding the spirit" of the three principles.[73] It was, however, not until after Ōhira met the visiting
deputy secretary of the China-Japan Friendship Association,
Sun P'ing-hua and the chief of the Chinese Memorandum
Trade Office in Tokyo, Hsiao Hsiang-ch'ien, on July 22 and
agreed to establish an official channel of communications between the Foreign Ministry and Hsiao's office, that the bureaucrats established direct contact with the Chinese government.[74]
Even then the channel was narrow and indirect. All the work
the officials had undertaken so far was therefore largely a theoretical exercise, the effect and utility of which were quite uncertain in the absence of direct feedback from Peking through a
reliable channel. In short, they were mostly speculating in a situation full of uncertainties.

The first tangible feedback that reached the Foreign Ministry
officials was Chou's ten-point proposal brought back by Takeiri
and the notes of the Chou-Takeiri talks turned over to them
after they were examined by Tanaka and Ōhira. In the last
week of July, while Takeiri was still negotiating in Peking, a
small "working group" of officials was being formed in the
ministry to take full charge of the subsequent activities related
to the normalization issue.[75] Officially dubbed the China Policy
Council, it consisted of four individuals: Treaties Bureau
Director Takashima Masuo, Treaties Division Head Kuriyama
Shōichi, Asian Affairs Bureau Director Yoshida Kenzō,
and China Division Head Hashimoto Hiroshi. Vice-Minister
Hōgen maintained a general supervisory role, but the actual
policymaking work was left to the four, especially Kuriyama
and Hashimoto.[76] This pattern of policymaking undertaken by
a small and tightly knit team in cases involving highly controversial or sensitive issues is quite common and well established. But the extent to which the four kept all important
secrets to themselves, aside from Hōgen and Ōhira, was rather

73. *Mainichi Shimbun,* July 11, 1972; *Yomiuri Shimbun,* July 16, 1972.
74. *Asahi Shimbun,* July 23, 1972.
75. *Mainichi Shimbun,* July 28, 1972; *Tokyo Shimbun,* July 29, 1972; *Nihon Keizai Shimbun,* August 3, 1972.
76. Interviews with bureaucrats who have requested anonymity, March 5, 1973; May 1, 1972; March 6, 1973.

extraordinary. There was a feeling among the four officials and their collaborators in the aftermath of the devastating "Nixon shocks" and the U.N. fiasco that they were fighting not only for their own political survival but also for that of the entire career foreign service. At the same time, Tanaka made it unmistakably clear that he would not tolerate breach of confidence or any other blunder on the part of the officials.[77]

Before the Foreign Ministry team took over the bulk of the work, Tanaka and Ōhira made up their minds to go to Peking by the end of September. Their final decision was made most probably during or immediately following their joint meeting on August 4 with Takeiri, who had returned from Peking the previous day.[78]

From this point onward the work shifted largely to the bureaucrats' hands. So far there had been some misgivings among the officials that the PRC might insist on concluding a full-fledged "treaty," rather than a joint communiqué, on the occasion of Tanaka's visit. Takeiri had now returned, however, with the Chinese consent to a communiqué formula, to the great relief of the officials. The remaining and doubtless the hardest part of the work was then to compose the text of a joint communiqué which would be acceptable to both the Japanese and the PRC governments. The text was drafted by Kuriyama

77. Interview: Anonymous, February 24, 1972.
78. This is again my own speculation, based on the following reasoning: Since the spring, there had been a plan among several Japanese groups, including the opposition parties, to invite a large nongovernmental delegation from the PRC to visit Japan within a year. An official invitation was carried to Peking by the JSP's Sasaki in July. By late July, preparations were completed among the twenty-two Japanese cosponsors, and Prime Minister Tanaka had personally approved the plan. During his conversations with Chou a few days later, however, Takeiri suggested and Chou agreed that the plan should be dropped if Tanaka would visit Peking during the fall and also that, if Tanaka planned to do so before October 1, Takeiri would personally announce the cancellation of the plan as a secret signal to Chou that Tanaka and Ōhira had decided to come to Peking sometime in September. On August 5, the day after Tanaka and Ōhira met Takeiri, the cancellation of the visit by the PRC delegation was reported in the Japanese press and attributed to an anonymous source. On August 7, a "government source" reported that Tanaka's trip would be made in September. The "anonymous source" was no doubt Takeiri. See *Asahi Shimbun,* March 25, July 20 and 21, August 4 (evening edition), 6 and 7 (evening edition); *Sankei Shimbun,* March 24, 1972; *Mainichi Shimbun,* July 12, 1972; *Nihon Keizai Shimbun,* August 7, 1972.

in consultation with the other three members of the team, partially on the basis of the earlier Foreign Ministry plan but far
more substantially on that of Chou's ten-point proposal received through Takeiri.[79] There were some intense debates
among the officials, particularly between Kuriyama on the one
hand and the duo on the other, but it appears that Kuriyama
and Hashimoto worked in harmony with each other and that
both won the politicians' confidence and respect. In the later
phases of the operation Hashimoto worked extremely closely
with Ōhira, while Yoshida was frequently left out of the sensitive negotiations between the officials and the politicians and
between them and the PRC government.[80]

By late August the Tanaka-Ōhira duo and the Foreign Ministry team had apparently agreed to make their position
regarding the second of the three principles somewhat less ambiguous and evasive by recognizing China's sovereignty over
Taiwan "in principle" and "as a long-term view."[81] Considering the implications for the Far East clause of the U.S.-Japan
Security Treaty, they could not say much more on this sensitive
issue.[82] By early September a revised Japanese draft of the
joint communiqué was ready, except for the preamble, to be
taken to Peking by Furui. It contained eight points, substantively identical with the ten-point Chou proposal. Omitted from
this Japanese draft were an explicit reference to the renuncia-
tion of the Taiwan peace treaty and mention of the PRC's intention to respect Japanese lives and property in Taiwan when
liberating the island.[83] Furui left Tokyo on September 9, two
weeks before Tanaka's trip. The following day he presented
the Japanese draft to Liao Ch'eng-chih and a group of middle-
level Japan specialists in the PRC government.[84] On September
12, Chou gave him Chinese reactions to the draft and made

79. Interviews with Foreign Ministry officials involved.
80. This is my personal impression based on interviews with several politicians and officials involved.
81. *Asahi Shimbun*, August 24, 1972.
82. The Security Treaty includes multiple provisions on mutual cooperation
between Japan and the U.S. on matters of security in the Far East, while the
Nixon-Satō Communiqué explicitly refers to Taiwan as a "most important factor for the security of Japan" and notes the treaty obligations of the U.S. to
Taiwan.
83. Furui, "Nitchū Kokkō Seijōka no Hiwa," 135.   84. *Ibid.*, 136–40.

several suggestions for further discussion. During the early hours of September 20 (from midnight until 2:00 A.M.) Furui met Chou and other Chinese officials one more time. Later that morning he wrote a detailed report to Ōhira, which was carried back to Tokyo by the Foreign Ministry's China Division head, Hashimoto, who was visiting Peking at the time with an LDP delegation. Ōhira acknowledged receipt of the report by coded telegram on September 21. After he returned to Tokyo, Furui met once more with Ōhira on September 24, the day before the foreign minister left for Peking with Tanaka.

As the foregoing account shows, Furui again played a crucial role during the last phase of the Tokyo-Peking negotiation preceding Tanaka's trip. Several other pro-Peking LDP Diet members also played roles of some significance in the process. Fujiyama was instrumental in the first direct contact that Ōhira had with visiting Sun P'ing-hua. The two met at a reception given in the latter's honor by Fujiyama on July 20 with the obvious intention of bringing them together,[85] and this led to the official meeting between them on July 22. Furui was accompanied during his last trip to Peking in September by Tagawa and Matsumoto Shunichi. The roles of Fujiyama, Tagawa, and Matsumoto were, however, not comparable to Furui's in terms of involvement in and impact on the operations of the policy-making group commanded by Tanaka and Ōhira. It should nonetheless be noted that these LDP politicians acted their own parts in the drama not as representatives of an organized group but strictly as individuals. It seems obvious that Furui's utility to the duo derived from his personal qualities, particularly his close and extensive relationships with PRC leaders. His maverick position in the LDP enabled him, ironically, to act freely and flexibly without being constrained by ties with a formal government, a party office, or an intraparty faction. In other words, his position on the periphery of the factionally dominated politics of the LDP afforded him the vital freedom of action demanded by the dynamic policymaking situation and made him useful to the command core of the policymaking group.

The Foreign Ministry bureaucrats played an extremely im-

85. *Asahi Shimbun,* July 21, 1972.

portant, perhaps indispensable, but clearly subordinate role vis-
à-vis the Tanaka-Ōhira duo. The two highest-ranking officials
each from the Asian Affairs and Treaties bureaus and, to a
lesser extent, Vice-Minister Hōgen were an integral part of
the policymaking group after Takeiri's July trip, positioned just
below the two-man core. Yet theirs was essentially a supportive,
rather than initiatory, role. They were the "mount," trained
and loyal, to carry the Tanaka-Ōhira "jockey." Moreover, the
involvement of the officials was highly personal during the
most intense phases of the operation, much like that of the few
opposition and LDP politicians mentioned above. Hashimoto
worked so closely with Ōhira that he was inaccessible even to
his superiors and to Yoshida. He could and did frequently refuse with impunity to answer questions asked by his superiors
at the meetings of the Senior Officials' Conference.[86]

Despite, or perhaps because of, the inflexibility of a bureaucracy bound by rigid operating procedures, a small and select
group of officials could be temporarily separated to work in an
environment permitting and demanding personal initiative and
innovation. So long as they were working on the project as part
of the special policymaking team they were largely free from
the standard operating procedures and were thus able to interact dynamically with each other and with those outside the
bureaucracy. Although politicians like Furui were mildly un-
happy about the rigidity and unimaginativeness of the bureaucrats' performance,[87] it appears that they were vastly more flexible and imaginative than one would expect a group of
high-ranking bureaucrats to be in a routine operating situation.

Big-Business Groups

What should we make of the behavior of the *zaikai* in the
decision process? Did it control and dominate the major decisions and actions taken by the policymaking group, particularly
the Tanaka-Ōhira duo? There is at least one straightforward

86. This statement is based on conversations with several officials involved. I
discuss the role and composition of the Senior Officials' Conference in "Policy
Making in Japan's Foreign Ministry," in Robert A. Scalapino (ed.), *The Foreign
Policy of Modern Japan* (Berkeley and Los Angeles: University of California
Press, forthcoming).
87. Interview: Furui, February 26, 1973.

advocacy of such a view. Jon Halliday and Gavan McCormack have stated: "The moves preceding Japanese recognition of China show that big business was the main agent of the change in government policy. Tanaka and much of his cabinet belong to the far right of the LDP and would not have undertaken such a switch without the backing and pressure of big business, which still controls the LDP purse-strings." [88] Needless to say, this is a simple application of the power-elite model. There are, however, two major difficulties in this interpretation. One is that, as I will argue shortly and as a quick review of the contemporary newspapers and magazines would convince anyone, the "backing and pressure" came not only from big business but even more powerfully from the mass media, the general public, and the opposition parties. Even on purely analytical grounds it is difficult to say that the pressure of big business was the major factor, for it is impossible to separate that pressure from the equally obvious pressures of the other groups. More relevant to my main argument is the empirical fallacy of the view that "big business" as such moved Tanaka to make the trip to Peking at the time and under the circumstances I have described.

There was a dramatic shift in the climate of opinion among big businessmen in 1971 and 1972 regarding the normalization issue.[89] The pace and magnitude of the change were, however, quite uneven in different sectors of the business community. To generalize, those currently and substantially involved in China trade (e.g., manufacturers of fertilizer, steel, and trucks), those based in the Kansai (western) districts, and those associated with the Committee for Economic Development (Dōyūkai) changed first and with the greatest ease.[90] Firms of the Sumitomo group switched early from Taiwan to the PRC

88. *Japanese Imperialism Today* (New York: Monthly Review Press, 1973), 250. For a detailed description of the process leading up to their conclusions see chapter 4.

89. For a more comprehensive analysis see Sadako Ogata, "The Business Community and Foreign Policy: The Process Leading to Japan's Recognition of the People's Republic of China," in Scalapino's *Foreign Policy of Modern Japan.*

90. Fujita Isao, "Bei-Chū Shinjidai-ka no Nihon Zaikai" [Japan's financial world in the new era of U.S.-Chinese relations] *Kikan Chūō Kōron: Keiei Mondai,* Winter 1972, 240–49.

by accepting "Chou's Four Principles" of Japan-China trade,[91] while those of the Mitsubishi group were very late in doing so. In their previous competition for control of the Taiwan markets, Mitsubishi had beaten Sumitomo, a fact which largely accounts for the difference between the two in their approach to the issue. The delegation of Kansai businessmen which visited the PRC in September 1971 was a much more representative group, supported by the regional business community as a whole, than was the Tokyo group which made a similar trip in November.[92] The latter group was formed with the managing director of the Dōyūkai, Kikawada Kazutaka, as its principal promoter. Earlier in the spring of 1971, Kikawada had called publicly for a "forward-looking" posture on the China issue among businessmen and for a "cumulative increase" of exchanges between the two countries.[93] Long after the China trips of the two business delegations the Tokyo-Osaka differences of approach remained; they could not even form a joint "discussion forum" on China trade without difficulty.[94] It was not until May 1972 that the Federation of Economic Organizations took a position on the issue.[95] In his address to the general meeting of the federation on May 23, FEO President Uemura Kōgorō referred to the increasing number of businessmen visiting the PRC as a "natural trend in the flow of history." In a press conference following the meeting, however, he denied the possibility of sending an FEO delegation to China before the two governments reached official agreement.[96] He also assured the reporters that his view of the issue had not changed, implying that personally he was still opposed to the immediate recognition of the PRC.

91. As spelled out in the communiqué of the March 1971 China-Japan Memorandum Trade meeting, the four principles would exclude from China trade the following categories of firms: (1) those that assisted in Chiang Kai-shek's attempt to retake the mainland or the aggressive acts of the Park regime of South Korea against North Korea; (2) those with substantial investments in Taiwan or South Korea; (3) those that supplied weapons or ammunition to U.S. imperialists committing aggression against Vietnam, Laos, and Cambodia; (4) U.S.-Japanese joint enterprises and subsidiaries of U.S. firms operating in Japan. See Suga *et al.*, *Nitchū Mondai*, 284.

92. Mainichi Shimbunsha (ed.), *Nihon to Chūgoku*, 150–52.

93. Fujita, "Bei-Chū Shinjidai-ka no Nihon Zaikai," 244–49.

94. *Nihon Keizai Shimbun*, March 26, 1972.

95. *Yomiuri Shimbun*, May 19, 1972.   96. *Ibid.*, May 24, 1972.

On the other hand, once the prospect of an early normalization under the new cabinet became definitive even the most pro-Taiwan and cautious among big businessmen made a drastic about-face. To the amazement of their friends and critics, the staunchly pro-Taiwan Mitsubishi firms nonchalantly swallowed Chou's four principles, and even Uemura began to talk about an early normalization.[97] The businessmen's enthusiasm reached a frantic pitch after Tanaka became prime minister, announced his intention to proceed with the plan for prompt normalization, and made public, in early August, his decision to go to Peking in September. Top *zaikai* leaders, including FEO's Uemura and President Nagano Shigeo of the Japanese Chamber of Commerce and Industry, held a series of talks with Sun and Hsiao (of the Chinese Memorandum Trade Office) in early August, and a thirteen-man businessmen's mission visited Peking later in the same month to discuss a long-term trade arrangement.[98] A Mitsubishi-group mission went to China almost simultaneously with the general *zaikai* delegation. Both were personally met by Chou and other top-ranking Chinese officials.[99]

The "Peking fever" thus gripped Japan's big business in the period following the Nixon shocks of the summer of 1971. It should be clearly noted, however, that both real interests and policy postures differed greatly among firms, industries, employer organizations, and geographic regions. In each of these units a degree of consensus did prevail, but big business as a group was by no means united. Second and more important, the leaders of the largest *zaibatsu* in contemporary Japan, the Mitsubishi group, and those of the most influential big-business

97. *Nikkan Kōgyō Shimbun*, June 26, 1972; *Yomiuri Shimbun*, June 29, 1972; *Asahi Shimbun*, July 11, 1972.

98. *Asahi Shimbun*, August 11 and 13, 1972; *Mainichi Shimbun*, August 22, 1972 (evening edition); *Nihon Keizai Shimbun*, August 24 and 31, 1972; *Sankei Shimbun*, August 30, 1972.

99. For relevant comments see Fujita, "Bei-Chū Shinjidai-ka no Nihon Zaikai"; Yamamura Yoshiharu and Yamamoto Tsuyoshi, "Mitsubishi Gurūpu no Karei naru Tenshin" [The Mitsubishi group's spectacular turnaround], *Chūō Kōron*, October 1972, 222–31; "Tanaka Seiken to Nitchū Kankei." A comprehensive list of Japanese businessmen who visited the PRC between October 1971 and September 1972, with their affiliations and other information, is available in *Shūkan Daiyamondo*, September 28, 1972, 18–24.

federation, the FEO, were clearly the last to support immediate normalization. They did not lead the politicians and bureaucrats; rather they followed them, apparently very much against their initial desires to preserve the status quo. On September 11, 1972, FEO's president and vice-presidents met and decided to work toward normalization "if and when diplomatic relations are restored between the two nations through Prime Minister Tanaka's visit to China" and "in conformity with the nation's policy." [100] When he led the Tokyo businessmen's group to Peking in November 1971, even Dōyūkai's Kikawada was anxious above all to avoid giving the impression that he was committed to supporting the "Three Principles" when the Satō government had not accepted them; he did not want to appear opposed to the incumbent prime minister.[101] What impresses one most about the behavior of big business throughout this period is the degree of their opportunism and their apparent desire to conform to the official government line, rather than their bold leadership and initiative.

All this does not mean in the least that big business did not influence the decisions and actions of the policymaking group, including Tanaka and Ōhira. On the contrary, it exerted a substantial amount of political influence on the entire decision process, but this influence was general and contextual rather than specific and binding on particular decisions. Like the influence of the mass media and general public opinion, it was essentially a factor contributing to the generation of a psychological setting favorable to and supportive of the decisions made by the politicians and bureaucrats. In light of the powerful public pressure which had built by early 1972 for a change of cabinet and prompt steps by the new cabinet to establish formal diplomatic relations with Peking, it was really not necessary for *zaikai* to put pressure of its own on Tanaka and Ōhira, even if it did want them to take such steps. In fact, if big business had opposed Tanaka's China trip at the time it was made or the normalization of Japan-PRC relations on the terms that were agreed on, it is highly unlikely that the duo and the policymak-

100. *Nikkan Kōgyō Shimbun,* September 12, 1972.
101. Fujita, "Bei-Chū Shinjidai-ka no Nihon Zaikai," 247.

ing group would have acted very differently. After all, Hatoyama and Kōno had gone to Moscow in 1956 and the Japan-Soviet Joint Declaration had been signed despite open and sustained *zaikai* opposition in a general political setting much less favorable to the cabinet.

The Diet and Public Opinion

As I have already suggested, organizing collective actions at a formal level among the political parties was much more difficult than bringing together a small group of politicians from different parties on a personal and ad hoc basis. For this reason the Diet as a whole did not prove any more effective in promoting a particular line of policy on the China issue than it has done on other occasions. The nonpartisan Diet Members' League for the Restoration of Japan-China Relations attracted a majority of Diet members (379 of 743) when it was first formed in December 1970.[102] All JSP, CGP, and JCP Diet members joined, and so did ninety-five LDP and thirty-six DSP members. In July 1971, barely a week after President Nixon's July 15 announcement, the group tried to have a nonpartisan resolution adopted by both houses of the Diet calling for prompt restoration of diplomatic relations between Japan and the PRC and the latter's "rightful place" in the United Nations.[103] The attempt failed, however, because one after another of the LDP members withdrew their original support under the intensified pressure of the hostile party leadership. A similar attempt was repeated in late fall, but again in vain. As the president of the group, himself an LDP member, ruefully told me later, there was never real rapport between the group and the Satō government, despite the involvement of a substantial number of LDP Diet members.[104] The failure of the group demonstrated the strength of the partisan barrier between the mainstream groups in the ruling LDP and the opposition parties when they confronted each other as organizations. This barrier made it impossible for the Diet to be more than one ad-

102. *Nihon Keizai Shimbun*, December 10, 1972.

103. *Asahi Shimbun*, July 21, 23, 24 (morning and evening editions) and 25, 1972.

104. Interview: Fujiyama, February 17, 1973.

ditional factor in the generation of a psychological context for the decisions and actions of the policymaking group.

Two other groups were formed along more familiar partisan lines, the CGP-sponsored People's Council for the Normalization of Japan-China Relations and the JSP-sponsored People's Congress for the Restoration of Japan-China Relations. Neither suffered from the kind of internal dissension which plagued the Diet Members' League. They indirectly helped Takeiri and Sasaki, respectively, and, more generally, allowed the leaders of the two parties to collaborate with Tanaka without fear of open revolts or criticisms of the rank and file.[105] Neither was, however, directly involved in the highly personal operations undertaken by Takeiri and Sasaki, much less in the decisions of Tanaka and Ōhira.

Behind the actions of all the groups discussed above, there must surely have been the pressure of "public opinion." It is, however, even more difficult to measure the impact of this factor in quantitative terms than to talk about that of a more or less identifiable group, such as an opposition party or *zaikai*. Generally speaking, various opinion polls taken during the period showed that the general public was moderately in favor of an early normalization and that pro-normalization sentiment grew dramatically as the date of Tanaka's trip approached, reaching a state of national euphoria during and immediately following the trip.[106] The only element of incongruity, but one which had been previously observed,[107] was the continuing insistence of about half of the respondents in the various polls on retaining the existing relations with Taiwan after normalizing relations with the PRC.[108] There is again no room for doubt that this state of public opinion contributed to the psychological environment which prompted Tanaka, Ōhira, and

105. Suga *et al.*, *Nitchū Mondai*, 43–44.
106. See *Gekkan Yoron Chōsa*, November 1971, 75; January 1972, 75; October 1972, 75; December 1972, 82. See also Naikaku Kambō Naikaku Chōsashitsu (ed.), "Nitchū Mondai wo meguru Saikin no Ronchō" [Recent trends of media opinion on the Japan-China problem], mimeo. (Tokyo: Naikaku Kambō Naikaku Chōsashitsu, March 1971, July 1971, October 1971, January 1972).
107. See Fukui, *Party in Power*, 240–41.
108. See, for example, *Tokyo Shimbun*, May 1, 1972.

the policymaking group to make the decisions the way they did. The impact of such mass opinion, however, could not have been but extremely diffuse and generalized. Intuitively one would argue that public opinion did not define the precise parameters of specific policy decisions.[109] There was no room for general public opinion—or, for that matter, for the opinions of the several organized groups mentioned above—to enter directly into the tightly insulated and controlled process of decisionmaking in the small action group of politicians and bureaucrats.

A point of critical importance to be noted in an evaluation of the roles played by the opposition parties, big business, the partisan promotional groups, and public opinion is that they were all supportive of the basic direction in which Tanaka and Ōhira were publicly committed to move when they came to power in early July 1972. Before the LDP presidential election of July 5, Tanaka and Ōhira had no doubt been impressed with the rapid change in the climate of opinion on the China issue. They may well have been influenced by the trend of opinion among bureaucrats and businessmen even more than by that among opposition politicians or the general public. After they took over as the new government, however, the swelling pressure for early normalization was really not a serious problem for them. They would probably have been happy to act as expeditiously and boldly as the conservative businessmen and bureaucrats, who were at least as cautious and wary as themselves, wanted them to. Their real problem was rather the continuing opposition of the cross-factional coalition of right-wingers in the LDP. All the agonizing and soul-searching they went through between July 5 and September 29 was caused predominantly by this factor. The opposition elements included many senior LDP men, such as Kishi Nobusuke, Kaya Okinori, and Fukuda Takeo, who were in a position to seriously embarrass, if not overthrow, Tanaka and his cabinet. This was what really worried the prime minister and the foreign minister. And that is why they went directly from the airport to the general meeting

109. Akio Watanabe's contribution to Scalapino's forthcoming *Foreign Policy of Modern Japan* will contain a more comprehensive and systematic discussion of the role of public opinion in Japanese policymaking.

of the LDP Diet members when they returned from China and subjected themselves willingly to questioning, some quite vicious, from the unreconciled hawks. Tanaka had carefully calculated, while still in Peking, the best way to let off the steam of their dissatisfaction quickly and permanently.[110] He knew his basic vulnerability and guarded against its exploitation by his intraparty opponents. This was, then, the essence of the policymaking process of the Tanaka trip.

Conclusions

This case study of Prime Minister Tanaka's 1972 trip to Peking points up several important and interesting facts about "critical" decisionmaking in Japanese government.

For many years successive conservative cabinets had refused to come to grips with the difficult and controversial issue of Japan's political relationship with the Communist government in China. When, finally, further procrastination became impossible under growing domestic and international pressures, a new LDP prime minister was elected and his cabinet formed to deal with the crisis of conservative rule. The change of power was characteristically from one LDP factional coalition to another, but it magically freed the LDP leadership from its bondage to prior party commitments and precedents. Both in the minds of the politicians and in the eyes of the general public the new prime minister was installed with a mandate to depart from—in fact, to reverse—the traditional line of LDP policy on the issue. One may regard this either as proof of essentially healthy political pragmatism or as a sign of unprincipled opportunism and inconsistency. Regardless, the new prime minister responded and adapted to the changing political context of the issue with remarkable facility and effectiveness.

Prime Minister Tanaka and Foreign Minister Ōhira took the initiative in mobilizing and exploiting the support for immediate rapprochement with the PRC which had been building not only in the LDP and the bureaucracy but also among the ranks of opposition politicians, and, at the same time, they took steps to isolate and neutralize opposition in these same groups. There was substantial opposition, both actual and potential, in

110. Interview: anonymous, February 24, 1972.

the LDP, the bureaucracy, and segments of big business, but all eventually fell in line and accepted the inevitability of the reconciliation with varying degrees of willingness or reluctance. Significantly, it was a cross-factional coalition of pro-Taiwan LDP members who fought Tanaka's action with firmest determination and consistency. The disgruntled ministry officials and big businessmen, on the other hand, were almost totally ineffectual in translating their opposition into organized political action.

The process of official policymaking was dominated and controlled almost exclusively by a very small ad hoc group of Diet members and ministry officials. Participating in significant ways were the prime minister and the foreign minister in a commanding position and a few individual LDP and opposition-party politicians and half a dozen Foreign Ministry officials in supporting roles. Altogether the number of actors directly involved in the crucial decisions was not much larger than one dozen. This extremely small but flexible and dynamic action group skillfully manipulated and exploited the changing political environment, both domestic and international, to bring about the Japanese prime minister's historic trip. In the meantime, the three component groups of the celebrated "power elite"—the LDP, the bureaucracy, and big business—were all internally divided and became objects, rather than subjects, of the decisionmaking by the action group.

When compared to the conclusions of previous studies in foreign policymaking in postwar Japan, the findings of this case study seem generally supportive and confirming. There are a few important disagreements, but the area of agreements is much wider. As Donald C. Hellmann had suggested in his study of a similar case, the Soviet peace treaty negotiations of 1956,[111] the role of big business was not conspicuous, much less dominant. As Hellmann and others have argued, the role of the Diet was quite negligible.[112] The analysis of the impact of

111. Donald C. Hellmann, *Japanese Foreign Policy and Domestic Politics: The Peace Agreement with the Soviet Union* (Berkeley and Los Angeles: University of California Press, 1969), especially 98, 129.
112. *Ibid.*, 142–48; Miyasaka Masayuki, *Seifu, Jimintō, Zaikai* [The government, the LDP, and the financial world] (Tokyo: San'ichi Shobō, 1970), 49,

public opinion in this study was incomplete, but my tentative
conclusion generally agrees with those of Hellmann and
George R. Packard [113] that public opinion was not a major de-
terminant in the crucial decisions. Regarding the role of a cabinet, too, my discussion implicitly and indirectly points up its in-
effectuality as a collective actor in a policymaking situation of
the kind. The prime minister and the foreign minister alone
actively participated, while all other cabinet members were shut
out of the decision process almost completely. The central role
of the prime minister was abundantly clear in this case, fully
corroborating the views advanced by Hellmann, and others.[114]
Packard's point about the limitation of a prime minister's leadership, too, was supported by the extraordinary concern shown
by Tanaka over the reactions of his opponents within the
LDP.[115]

Where the findings of my study differ from those of the earlier works, the difference is probably more of degree than of
kind. The role of the Foreign Ministry officials was judged to
be subordinate to that of the politicians in the policymaking
group, as Hellmann also concluded in his case study. In the
present case, however, the bureaucrats nevertheless fully participated in the decisionmaking process. In fact, they played a
central role after August 4, if not before. In the case of the Soviet treaty negotiations Hellmann found ministry officials shut
out far more completely. The reason for the difference seems
to be quite simple. In the China case the bureaucrats worked
with the political leaders; in the Soviet case they had worked
against the political leaders. This difference caused, quite logically, a difference in the extent to which the policymaking process was "self-contained" within the LDP. In the China case it
was evidently far less "self-contained" than it had been in the

85, 152; Masumi Junnosuke, *Gendai Nihon no Seiji Taisei* [The political structure
of contemporary Japan] (Tokyo: Iwanami Shoten, 1969), 306–11.

113. Hellmann, *Japanese Foreign Policy and Domestic Politics,* especially 78,
149; George R. Packard III, *Protest in Tokyo: The Security Treaty Crisis of 1960*
(Princeton: Princeton University Press, 1966), especially 147–52.

114. Hellmann, *Japanese Foreign Policy and Domestic Politics,* 24; Miyasaka,
Seifu, Jimintō, Zaikai, 107; Yomiuri Shimbun Seijibu (ed.), *Sōridaijin* [The
prime minister] (Tokyo: Yomiuri Shimbunsha, 1971), 15.

115. Packard, *Protest in Tokyo,* 347–49.

Soviet case described by Hellmann. More important, however, than the difference between Hellmann's and my findings about the role of the bureaucracy is the difference between his and my findings on the one hand and, on the other, the more "orthodox" view of bureaucratic dominance and control of policymaking processes.[116] This difference is probably more than one of degree and calls for further examination.

Another disagreement of some seriousness between this study and several previous works concerns the role of the LDP factions in policymaking. Hellmann and Packard, among others, assign a role of central importance to the LDP factions and factionalism in the policymaking situations they examine.[117] In the present study the influence of the factions appears to have been far less direct and conspicuous. The major divisions were more explicitly ideological and related to policy, between the pro-Taipei "hawks" and the pro-Peking "doves." As I pointed out in my previous work, such "ideological" divisions in the LDP tend to have factional overtones and implications.[118] It is nevertheless difficult to interpret the views and actions of such individuals as Furui on the one hand and Kaya on the other primarily in terms of factional interests. Neither belonged to a particular LDP faction in 1972. Ehud Harari's view is probably most applicable to the situation observed in this case. He has written: "Factional considerations became overriding at only one crucial point—a point crucial to intraparty, interfactional competition: the election of the party president."[119]

The last and perhaps the most interesting finding which will set this case apart from the previous studies concerns the role of opposition party politicians. Some cooperation between the LDP and the opposition parties was noted by Hellmann in the Soviet case. My finding in the China case is interesting, however, not only because of the degree of such cooperation, which

116. See my discussion in Chapter 2.
117. Hellmann, *Japanese Foreign Policy and Domestic Politics*, 16–17; Packard, *Protest in Tokyo*, 347.
118. Fukui, *Party in Power*, 256–57.
119. Ehud Harari, *The Politics of Labor Legislation in Japan: National-International Interaction* (Berkeley and Los Angeles: University of California Press, 1973), 180.

was quite unusual, but more because of the saliency of the role played by a few individual opposition leaders and the personal nature of their involvement. The prominent contributions made by Minobe, Kasuga, Sasaki, and, especially, Takeiri to the policymaking process of this particular case no doubt reflected the absence in the LDP and the bureaucracy of individuals with the special experiences and qualifications to act as intermediaries between Japan's conservative government and the PRC's Communist government. The situation was obviously unique and is unlikely to be replicated in the future. Even in the future situation involving Japan's recognition of a Communist government, such as North Korea, Laos, or Vietnam, principal participants in the policymaking processes will probably be recruited from the more familiar sources of the party in power and the bureaucracy. The experience is nonetheless important in suggesting the degree of nonpartisan participation that can develop in Japanese government under certain types of international pressures and in response to certain types of foreign-policy issues. This finding will bear further investigation in a broader context of the political culture and elite behavior in postwar Japan.

4. Compensation for Repatriates: A Case Study of Interest-Group Politics and Party-Government Negotiations in Japan

John Creighton Campbell

At the end of the war in the Pacific, 850,000 Japanese families were still living in Asian territories controlled by Japan, having emigrated at various times throughout the twentieth century. Under orders from the victorious powers, they were returned to Japan during the early years of the Occupation. Many were nearly penniless; some had lost touch with any relatives at home; and a few, of the second generation abroad, could not even speak Japanese. Even in war-devastated Japan, the position of these repatriates was particularly difficult.

The repatriates (*hikiagesha*) were quick to organize and seek help from the government. Their first requests were for food, clothing, and aid in establishing a livelihood. However, they soon began to demand monetary compensation for the property they had owned overseas, all of which had been confiscated at the end of the war. After considerable political pressure, a payment of ¥50 billion (about $140 million) was finally granted in 1957.[1] Though the government hoped this grant would settle the matter, the repatriates were dissatisfied and renewed their pressure in the early 1960's. A long campaign—the subject of this chapter—was rewarded by an additional grant of ¥192.5 billion ($535 million) in 1967. My purpose is to ask two questions about this case: first, why was

1. Dollar equivalents are approximate and are based on the contemporary rate of $1 = ¥360. This paper is based on research partially supported by the Foreign Area Fellowship Program, which is not responsible for the conclusions and other opinions. I am grateful for comments on earlier versions by Gerald L. Curtis, Haruhiro Fukui, George Greenberg, and T. J. Pempel.

the 1967 grant made? and second, why for that particular amount? [2]

Background

Citizens banding together to ask something from their government is a fundamental element of politics, in Japan as elsewhere. It is sensible to begin by placing the repatriates within the context of Japanese interest-group politics, leaving for later some ruminations on how they might have fared in other political systems. We may observe first that the National Federation of Repatriate Groups (Hikiagesha Dantai Zenkoku Rengōkai, usually called Zenren in Japan and referred to here as "the Federation") was, as its name indicates, organized for political action in the national arena, since the benefit it sought could be obtained only from the central government and its membership was geographically widespread. Second, its primary channel of influence was the majority Liberal Democratic Party (LDP), rather than an opposition party or a governmental ministry (a main target of many "functional" groups, such as those in the education, agriculture, or labor fields). Third, unlike big businessmen, who influence the LDP through large contributions, the repatriates' apparent source of power was votes. Fourth, the Federation worked on behalf of a relatively narrow and tightly defined slice of the population—essentially its own membership—rather than some broad aggregation, such as parents who send their children to day-care centers, or all small businessmen. Fifth, the benefit sought was simply cash, not a complicated set of regulations or a major alteration in governmental policy. Finally, unlike rice farmers working to keep prices up or groups attempting to raise the amount of war-related pensions every year, the Federation's campaign, though it lasted for several years, was aimed at a single, one-time-only payment.

2. In concentrating on these two questions, I have omitted many details of the repatriates and their organizations, the long legal controversy over compensation, and other aspects of the dispute. To my knowledge, there are no secondary accounts of the repatriates; this analysis is based on unpublished documents, newspaper articles, and several interviews, including three long talks with an official of the National Federation of Repatriate Groups, who asked to remain unnamed, in the spring of 1969.

Several interesting aspects of the overseas-property case may be inferred directly from these characteristics. For example, though it relied on voting power, the Federation's conservative orientation and clear attachment to the LDP meant that a threat to support a rival party would not be credible; therefore its leverage (in Japan's peculiar electoral system) rested on an ability to switch votes *among* LDP candidates in each district. Hence, it was taken more seriously by individual rank-and-file dietmen than by the LDP's leadership. The relatively small size of the group meant that its influence over most dietmen would not be overwhelming, but it also meant that the total amount required to compensate all the repatriates would not be over-whelmingly large; clearly this was a "distributive" issue over which other actors in the political system would see the Federation's demand as competitive with their own interests.[3] How-ever, since the demand was for cash, the Ministry of Finance would almost automatically be opposed. Since the Federation had no strong relationship with a governmental ministry, and since its demand was not of a recurring nature, it was less likely that the problem could be handled by any already routine gov-ernmental mechanism, such as the budgetary process; a special scenario had to be devised.[4]

We will return to these points but we require first an account of what actually happened to the repatriates. Their success in 1967 was the culmination of an effort stretching over more than twenty years. As early as 1946, a number of self-help groups in the Tokyo area banded together to form the Federa-tion, initially so that a variety of goals could be pursued; before long, however, the national organization and even the local

3. Theodore J. Lowi, "American Business, Public Policy, Case Studies, and Political Theory," *World Politics* 16 (July 1964), 677–715. A related point, with reference to veterans, is made by V. O. Key, *Politics, Parties and Pressure Groups,* 4th ed. (New York: Crowell, 1958), 122–23.

4. It is fortunate that despite the sparseness of research on interest-group campaigns in Japan, an exceptionally good study of a quite similar case is avail-able: Haruhiro Fukui, "Compensating Former Landowners," chapter 7 in his *Party in Power* (Berkeley and Los Angeles: University of California Press, 1970), 173–97. Contrasts of both substance and interpretation will be highlighted where appropriate. I might note here that an attempt to show factional influ-ence among repatriate supporters in the LDP had the same results as Fukui's similar analysis (191–92); virtually no relationships could be found.

components were focusing almost exclusively on the issue of financial compensation for lost property. Since American Occupation authorities refused to take special notice of repatriates, it was not until 1953 that the government undertook its first official investigation of the problem. The first advisory council (*shingikai*) appointed for this purpose was entirely "neutral" in composition.[5] However, before it could make its report—and significantly, immediately before the House of Councillors election in July 1956—intense pressure from the Federation convinced the government to dissolve the first council and establish in its place a new twenty-member group (called the "second council," *daini shingikai*) which also included "non-neutral" dietmen and representatives of the repatriates.

For several months this council engaged in legal and principled debate. Representatives of the Federation—in the 1950's and again in the 1960's—had two basic arguments: First, the 1952 San Francisco Peace Treaty (Article 14) had ceded Japanese rights over property overseas to the Allies; since this was an act of state by the Japanese Government, the Federation maintained that under Article 29 of the Constitution ("The right to own or to hold property in inviolable. . . . Private property may be taken for public use upon just compensation therefore") the government had a *legal* obligation to compensate those whose property had been signed away. Second, the Federation claimed that Japan, as a capitalist state, had a *moral* obligation to defend the right of private property. The government consistently opposed these propositions—maintaining, for example, that the Peace Treaty was not an act of state because it had followed unconditional surrender, and that the repatriates should apply to the Allied Powers for compensa-

5. That is, it had several government officials plus "men of learning and experience" (*gakushikikeikensha*), university professors, and a journalist, who are supposed to serve such bodies as disinterested representatives of the public interest. For accounts of the role of such councils in the Japanese political process see Nihon Gyōsei Gakkai (ed.), *Nenpō: Gyōsei Kenkyū*, 7, "Special Number on Advisory Bodies" (Tokyo: Keisō Shobō, 1966); T. J. Pempel, "The Bureaucratization of Policymaking in Postwar Japan," *American Journal of Political Science* 18 (November 1974), 647–64; and Ehud Harari, "Japanese Politics of Advice in Comparative Perspective: A Framework for Analysis and a Case Study," *Public Policy* 22 (Fall 1974), 537–77.

tion.[6] These arguments could not be resolved, and the council's report was accordingly more a political than judicial solution: it recommended that a "benefit" (*kyūfukin*) be paid, rather than either "compensation" (*hoshō*), as the repatriates demanded, or simply a "solatium" (*mimaikin*), as urged by the government.

This report, however, effectively decided the question of whether any money would be paid. In the crucial decision to enlarge the council, as well as in the turbulent negotiations over the size of the grant which followed, it appeared that the personal influence of Ōno Bamboku (a powerful LDP faction leader and at the same time chairman of the Federation) had been decisive.[7] The result, in any case, was a payment of long-term bonds totaling about ¥50 billion to more than three million repatriates. The individual amounts varied from ¥7,000 to ¥28,000, depending on the age of the person at the time of repatriation. An income ceiling was imposed, and the Ministry of Health and Welfare insisted that the grant was *not* compensation for lost property; it was justified only by the great hardships undergone by the repatriates, and was of comparable size to aid given other groups injured by the war.[8]

The repatriates agreed that the 1957 payment was not compensation for their lost property, and they were certainly dissatisfied with the amount. In the early 1960's, when political conditions once more seemed favorable, they decided to try again.

6. The Federation assembled a variety of scholars to testify or write on its behalf; for examples from the 1960's see mimeographed pamphlets released by the Federation written by Ōishi Yoshio (June 21, 1965) and Ōhira Zengo (November 3, 1966). For the government viewpoint and Federation counterarguments, see the similar pamphlet "Zaigai Zaisan ni taishi Kuni ni Hōritsujō no Hoshō Gimu ga aru to Katei shita baai no Mondaiten (An) ni taisuru Hanron" [Rebuttal to draft: problems with the hypothesis that the nation is legally responsible for compensation of overseas property] (December 30, 1965).

7. For example, journalists thought it was significant that the Ministry of Health and Welfare (which handled the affair for the government) was then headed by Kanda Hiroshi, an important member of Ōno's faction. See *Asahi Shimbun*, March 5 and 23, 1957.

8. The maximum grant approximates average monthly expenditures for an urban worker's household in 1957. For details of the grant and analysis see *Asahi Shimbun*, March 15 and 23, 1957.

Deciding the Principle
The Campaign

The government's concern about the symbolic "compensation" issue stemmed from its worry that a precedent would thus be set for others who might have similar claims—notably the landowners whose property was expropriated during the Occupation land reform. By 1962, however, it began to appear that these landowners would, after all, have to be compensated. Observing this development, the Federation sponsored four large national conventions in Tokyo that year, demanding immediate compensation "in full" of ¥1,200 billion (over $3.3 billion). Prior to the July 1962 Upper House election, Ōno Bamboku (no longer formally connected with the Federation but now the LDP vice-president) promised that the question would be reopened.[9]

But the former-landowners problem soon became embroiled in considerable controversy, and the Federation cautiously backed off to a less ambitious strategy: it would ask only for another official government council to make another investigation. In February 1963 the Federation sent its LDP supporters to present this request to party leaders, and it called another of its big national conventions. The LDP leadership was less than enthusiastic—having problems enough at the moment with the former landowners—but the party was facing local elections in April, and pressure was brought to bear through both the National Organization Committee (representing LDP members in local government) and the Cabinet Division of the Policy Affairs Research Council (PARC). A Dietmen's Bill (a measure introduced by members on the floor, which lacks cabinet approval) to establish the proposed council was threatened. Giving in, the party leadership (the "big four") endorsed the proposal on March 30 and passed it along to the government.[10]

9. *Mainichi Shimbun,* February 22, 1963.
10. *Nihon Keizai Shimbun,* February 26 (evening); *Asahi Shimbun,* March 28 and 30 (evening), 1963. "Big Four" is the journalistic term for the LDP's secretary-general, Executive Council chairman, PARC chairman, and vice-president (when there is one, otherwise "big three"). The group functions as the party's executive in important matters. For LDP institutions and processes, see Naththaniel B. Thayer, *How the Conservatives Rule Japan* (Princeton: Princeton University Press, 1969) and Fukui, *Party in Power.*

The government resisted: Prime Minister Ikeda, Finance Minister Tanaka, and Foreign Minister Ōhira were all opposed, and Chief Cabinet Secretary Kurogane had already stated official policy at his regular press conference on March 28. "The problem has already been solved in the form of a solatium," he said, "and the government does not intend to reopen the question and give compensation." [11] Their opposition was strong enough to prevent the appointment of another advisory council for a time, but in early April the government compromised by establishing a small research section (*chōsashitsu*) within the Prime Minister's Office (PMO). Unlike an advisory council, established to deliberate and make recommendations on how a particular problem should be solved, a *chōsashitsu* is simply a bureaucratic organ staffed by officials, instructed to investigate the details of a problem but not offer any proposed solutions. Still, it did represent a "foothold" (*ashigakari*) in the government for the Federation; the question had again been placed on the political agenda and could no longer be ignored. Also, and not unimportantly, a secondary Federation interest was satisfied: the overseas property problem would now clearly be handled not by the Ministry of Health and Welfare, which was unsympathetic to the plight of the repatriates, but by the PMO, a more "neutral" agency (and one which already had ties with the powerful war-related pension groups, whose problems were somewhat similar to those of the repatriates).

Undoubtedly both governmental and party leaders would have preferred to let the matter rest at this stage for some time, but the LDP soon had to face another election.[12] Exactly one month before the polling date, on October 21, 1963, the Federation sponsored another giant convention in Tokyo, attended by 15,000 local representatives. A group of leading delegates was sent to Prime Minister Ikeda's press conference that day. Under considerable pressure, Ikeda promised them that a new advisory council would be established, and after further Federation pressure, the (third) Overseas Property Problem Council

11. *Asahi Shimbun,* March 28, 1963 (evening).
12. Japanese reporters who cover government-party affairs are prone to emphasize that an upcoming election distorts the decisionmaking system. This insight obscures the point that there is *always* an upcoming election, or very nearly so.

was finally announced nine months later in July 1964. Still, even after all their foot-dragging had failed, the authorities apparently hoped they might obtain a report unfavorable to the repatriates' demands, as had recently occurred in the former landowners case.[13] All the members were to be "neutral"—fifteen "men of learning and experience" and five administrative vice-ministers of interested ministries. Exactly as had happened in 1956, the Federation objected to this composition, and by exerting pressure through the party it succeeded in having five dietmen added to the group. Thus the council did not begin deliberating until December 1964. Two questions were put to it by the Prime Minister, Satō Eisaku: is there a necessity for further steps in the overseas-property matter? and if so, how should the matter be settled?

Over the next two years the Federation had two foci of attention. It bombarded the council with data and authoritative-sounding academic opinions, as well as resolutions from periodic national conventions to keep up the pressure. At the same time, steps were taken to strengthen its influence within the majority party. Already in early 1964 an organization of sympathetic LDP dietmen had been formed, called the Dietmen's League for Handling the Overseas Property Problem (Zaigai Zaisan Mondai Taisaku Giin Renmei, hereafter called "the League"). The League began with 90 members, and by November 1965, 168 LDP dietmen had been induced to sign a resolution which endorsed Federation demands and asked the party to establish its own special committee (tokubetsu iinkai) on the overseas-property problem. Appointment of such a body represented the next step in the federation's strategy: as an official party organ, the committee's report and recommendations would become the basis for an official LDP position. The leadership again delayed and in the end did not establish a "special committee," but in April 1966 LDP Secretary-General Tanaka announced the formation of a "Dietmen's Discussion Group on the Overseas Private Property Problem" (Zaigai Shisan Mondai Giin Kondankai, hereafter the "Discussion Group")

13. See Fukui, *Party in Power*, 178.

as an official organ of the Policy Affairs Research Council.[14] Its fifteen members were formally appointed by the PARC chairman, and all were supposed to be selected for their knowledge of both the repatriates' problems and the financial situation of the nation. In fact, the Discussion Group contained no one who opposed the Federation—all but two or three were actually members of the Dietmen's League. The Discussion Group had two chairmen in its brief history, Aichi Kiichi and Ueki Kōshirō. Both were members of the League, senior and influential LDP politicians, and former Ministry of Finance officials (in fact, both later served as finance minister). The Discussion Group later played a key role in the negotiations leading to the final grant to the repatriates.

The Outcome

The government's Overseas Property Problem Council finally issued its report on November 29, 1966. As expected, it was favorable to the repatriates. At the start, the council had apparently been divided into three groupings: several sympathizers, including the dietmen, led by Ōishi Yoshio (a professor of constitutional law at Kyoto University), who argued that the government had a legal obligation to compensate for the lost property; a larger segment made up of "men of learning and experience" and government officials, who opposed any grant whatever; and a middle-ground faction, led by Chairman Yamada Giken (former head of the Board of Audit), who took the position that while no legal obligation was involved, the government should make some payment anyway.[15] By the fall of 1966, when a subcommittee was appointed to draft the report, nearly all council members had come around to the compromise position: "The government is under no obligation to pay compensation for overseas property," the report read, but "as policy [*seisakuteki ni*] it is necessary to make a special grant."

14. According to informants, a "special committee" would have implied that the party had already endorsed the Federation's demands, while "discussion group," particularly with "Dietmen's" added, has a more tentative and investigatory sound. However, it is somewhat unusual to give bodies with such titles the status of official party organs.
15. *Asahi Shimbun,* December 16, 1965.

Recommendations were included on the many technical problems of how the grant should be administered.

The only change made by the full council in the subcommittee's draft was to drop the requirement of an income ceiling for recipients (as had been stipulated in the 1957 award), to reflect the legalistic "property" arguments of the repatriates' sympathizers and downplay the "welfare" orientation of some other members. Still, in hopes of forestalling new demands from others, perhaps even corporations, who had lost property during the war, the report stressed that the repatriates had been deprived not only of material property but also of intangible possessions like pride, human relations, and other basic elements of life. One member commented afterward that although the basic conclusions of the council had long since been settled, working out the pretexts had been hard work.[16]

Although the council was an advisory body, and its report not officially binding on the government, the question of whether or not a grant would be given had now been settled as a matter of practical politics. The government could not easily repudiate such lengthy deliberations. Oddly, it might seem, the report gave no indication whatsoever of how large the grant should be. Chairman Yamada had feared that negotiating an actual amount would tie up the council's deliberations well beyond its already extended deadline. The Federation was pleased, although its reasoning was different: "Since [a specific amount] can be worked out by flexible political negotiations after the report is issued, it is better not to include one." [17] That is, within the political arena, the Federation's substantial influence could be arrayed to best advantage.

Deciding the Amount

If the complicated seven-month process which followed the council's report had been defined as an open conflict between the Federation and its opponent, the MOF, it is doubtful whether a solution could ever have been reached. Their posi-

---

16. *Asahi Shimbun*, February 22, 1967. See also *ibid.*, April 19 and September 17, 1966, and *Nihon Keizai Shimbun*, August 19, 1966. For the fear of setting precedents, see Fukui, *Party in Power,* 180.
    17. *Asahi Shimbun*, October 8, 1966.

tions were too far apart and their attitudes too adamant. However, as would happen in any decisionmaking system, mechanisms came into play which mitigated the degree of conflict. First, the protagonists did not participate directly but were represented by surrogates: Ueki, the chairman of the Discussion Group, for the repatriates, and Finance Minister Mizuta Mikio, who of course was a senior LDP politician, for the MOF bureaucrats. Second, a large and active group of mediators carried messages and generally smoothed relations between these two surrogates. Most important were the prime minister, the LDP leadership, and the director-general of the PMO—all more interested in bringing the dispute to a close than in any particular decision.

Procedure and Criteria

How would all these participants relate to each other? Who would negotiate with whom, and when, and about what? For many kinds of policy problems in Japan, as elsewhere, various institutionalized processes are already "available" in the sense that all participants understand and accept them; they are established by written or unwritten "rules of the game." Solutions to such problems are produced almost automatically in the normal flow of governmental business, though often enough after considerable delay. Because different participants have different interests, conflict does occur in such cases, but interests are channeled and disputes regularized through established structures. The chief example is the budget process. Most proposals which require governmental spending—and this category includes the greatest number, if not necessarily the most significant, of domestic political issues—are evaluated and then approved, rejected, or compromised through the complicated but quite regular budgetary relationships established among the MOF, the spending agencies, and the majority party.[18] Examples of other institutionalized processes include the periodic negotiations over rice prices, railroad fares, and health insur-

18. These relationships are described in detail in my *Contemporary Japanese Budget Politics* (Berkeley and Los Angeles: University of California Press, 1977), or more compactly in my "Japanese Budget *Baransu*" in Ezra Vogel (ed.), *Modern Japanese Organization and Decision-making* (Berkeley and Los Angeles: University of California Press, 1975), 71–100.

ance charges and payments; drawing up long-term plans in various policy areas, and even—in a somewhat different sense—the ritualized "confrontations" between the LDP and opposition parties in the Diet over the most intensely partisan issues.

Since the overseas property problem was a matter of governmental expenditure, it was thought at first that it could be handled by budgetary mechanisms. The budget process for fiscal year 1967 (April 1967 through March 1968) had been delayed by a general election called for January 29, and the final "government draft" was not scheduled to be passed by the cabinet until February 28 (instead of the more usual late December or early January date). The Federation did not succeed in having its demands mentioned in the vague policy statements on the budget released before the election break, or in the budget requests of the PMO (first submitted in September, but always subject to amendment). During the January election campaign, however, many candidates proclaimed support for the repatriates. Even Prime Minister Satō said in a campaign speech, "Since I have been prime minister, problems like compensation for farm land, the normalization of Japan-Korea relations, and so forth have been solved in turn. The only one left over now is the overseas-property problem. This too will be solved during the Special Diet Session, and the 'postwar settlement' will be completed." [19] The Federation cited this statement frequently, interpreting it not only as a general support but as a promise to work for the figure of ¥600 billion (which had just been informally endorsed by the PARC Discussion Group) during the budgetary negotiations to follow.[20] As soon as the election was over, the Federation's giant tent was again erected and more large conventions were held. The MOF, for its part, prepared for the budgetary struggle by establishing an official position of allowing only ¥35 billion, while informally letting it be known that ¥50 billion would be the absolute maximum permitted.[21]

As it happened, the issue was not handled in the budgetary arena, for two important reasons. First, the demand had come

19. Quoted in *Asahi Shimbun*, February 22, 1967.
20. *Asahi Shimbun*, February 7, 1967.
21. *Yomiuri Shimbun*, February 5, 1967.

late in the process and was not submitted by a governmental agency. This meant that the MOF had not had a chance to evaluate a concrete proposal, and had no one with whom to discuss the problem in regular channels. On the other hand, there had been not a few examples in other years of demands submitted directly by the LDP late in the game, and such demands had often been negotiated and settled immediately, so this difficulty might not have been overriding by itself. More crucial was that in February the "gap" (*hiraki*) between demands and offers on the table—formally between ¥1,200 billion and ¥35 billion, or more informally ¥600 billion and ¥50 billion—was much too wide to be resolved through the essentially incremental budgetary mechanism, particularly in the brief period before the budget bill had to be submitted to the Diet. So although LDP leaders did press for a grant during the "resurrection negotiations" stage of the budgetary process, and it was a major topic in the final all-night negotiations of February 27–28, in the end the LDP accepted the MOF's insistence that the problem needed more discussion, and only a small sum for administrative expenses was inserted into the government draft.[22]

Whether or not this apparent setback actually lost any money for the repatriates—at this stage the MOF probably would not have approved as high a sum as that which it finally granted—it did have important procedural consequences. First, a deadline had been lost: now, no one knew when a decision would have to be made. Illustrating the significance of this loss, nearly all public statements by Prime Minister Satō from that time on were mainly concerned with setting various new deadlines, none of which held up until the last possible moment was reached before postponement for another year would become necessary. Second, a new ad hoc process had to be devised. Participants were no longer certain about who would play what roles and precisely how these roles should be defined in terms of appropriate behavior at appropriate times. For example, for quite a while nothing was accomplished while the government and party debated over who had the responsibility to make the

22. Budget bills are almost never amended in the Diet, so the government draft is the final budget.

next concrete proposal.[23] And with no agreed-upon procedures, questions once decided tended to become undecided
and again subject to debate.

Also worth mentioning here is a factor which would have
complicated negotiations however they were structured. No
one was sure what sorts of criteria or standards of judgment
should be applied in reaching a decision. Many repatriates had
kept documents purporting to show how much their property
had been worth, but these materials could not simply be
stacked up to reach a total amount because they were incomplete—many repatriates had none—and yet far too volumi-
nous and difficult to evaluate. More helpful was an estimate of
the total value of private holdings owned by overseas Japanese
made by the MOF at American request just after the war. This
estimate had been $3 billion, and the Federation justified its
original demand of ¥1,200 billion by simply converting this
dollar estimate into yen at 1967 rates ($1 = ¥360).[24] For its part,
the MOF used the very same estimate (although it also cast
doubts on its validity) to defend its insistence that nothing over
¥50 billion could be allowed, justified by converting dollars to
yen at immediate postwar rates, before the great inflation.
When the Federation cut its demand in half for tactical reasons, it switched formulas: accepting the MOF logic of using the
old exchange rate, it multiplied the resulting yen figure by 13
to compensate for inflation. This multiplier of 13 was derived
from the recent settlement of the former landlords' claim, a
precedent also cited by various participants at various times in
two other ways: as an appropriate level for the *total* grant to the
repatriates, or as an appropriate level for the amount *per recipi-
ent* (about 1.7 million landowners as compared to about 3.5
million repatriated individuals). Payments made to other war-
injured groups might seem to be as applicable, but these
turned out to be too low to provide many useful precedents.[25]
So much detail is offered on this point to show that there were
no unambiguously "objective" criteria available which might
have solved the overseas-property problem "rationally,"

23. *Mainichi Shimbun*, March 20, 1967.
24. *Yomiuri Shimbun*, March 5, 1967.
25. *Mainichi Shimbun*, March 13, 1967.

through essentially administrative procedures. The repatriates'
case cannot be regarded as a "corruption" of administration by
the "improper" intervention of political calculations, as some
might claim. The calculations could be nothing but political,
based on reaching a compromise that would be acceptable to all
the major participants.[26] Justifications which appeared to be
"rational" and "objective" were, in the main, simply added on
after a workable compromise had been reached.

The Negotiations

Despite the fact that not solving the problem during the
budget period necessitated the creation of an ad hoc procedure, it should not be thought that subsequent decisions had to
be made in a cognitive vacuum. Amid the uncertainty, much
was understood and tacitly accepted by nearly all participants.
The main assumptions as the process began were: first, some
grant would be given; second, the amount would be decided in
final negotiations between the LDP and the government, specifically the chairman of the Discussion Group and the MOF;
the LDP leadership and the PMO would also play some role;
third, all participants would assume a "bargaining" posture,
willing to take others' positions into account and compromise;
fourth, the final amount decided would be at least as much as
the total grant to the former landlords, though the upper limit
was less clear.

None of these assumptions answered the immediate problem: who would go first? Actually, the Dietmen's League had
already made the initial move just before the end of the budgetary process, compromising its original demand in the hope of
stimulating quick action. In an interview two years later, Ueki
Kōshirō, the chairman of the Discussion Group, remembered how this had come about:

We [the Discussion Group] were sympathetic to the repatriates, but
as dietmen we had to take the position of the government into account. I, in particular, had to say to those who were asking for money
that Japan, at the present moment, simply couldn't afford the entire

26. For an argument that such processes are really "rational" in a deeper
sense, see the writings of Charles E. Lindblom, e.g. *The Policy-Making Process*
(Englewood Cliffs, N.J.: Prentice-Hall, 1968).

amount requested. So I told them that ¥1,200 billion was out of the question. It would be a better method of getting part of the demand to lower their request: "We couldn't even talk about ¥1,200 billion." Then they asked me how much the demand should be, and I suggested cutting it in half. They agreed to this—what else could they do? [27]

However, the League's tactical concession had not been effective; the ¥600 billion figure was still considered much too high to be taken seriously. For a month and a half, all waited for a new proposal. Both Ueki and Tsukahara Toshio, the director-general of the PMO, cited the lack of clear-cut criteria for decision as the reason why the other should go first.[28] Finally, it was Ueki who began drawing up a series of "private plans" and discussing them alternately with his Discussion Group members, who pushed him to go higher, and LDP leaders, who urged moderation.[29] On April 21, the Discussion Group was induced to go along informally with a request in the neighborhood of ¥250 billion. This was the first "ballpark" request, low enough to become the basis for real negotiations rather than rhetorical exchanges.

Ueki vividly recalled how hard it had been to wring a consensus from the Discussion Group:

As chairman, I talked with all the members and asked them how much they thought should be granted. Some said more, some less. Some said ¥200 billion would be fine; some insisted it would have to be the full ¥600 billion. Since they were under a good deal of pressure from the Federation, mostly they were on the high side. So I took a secret ballot. This would allow those who were thinking only ¥100 or ¥200 billion to say so. . . . After talking it over, we basically came to an average of the various opinions, which turned out to be around ¥250 billion. Now, I knew that even this could not be actually paid out, but it did become a standard [mokuhyō] that we could start from, that the government-

27. Interview, June 12, 1969. In 1962, Tanaka Kakuei, then PARC chairman, had played precisely the same role with leaders of the National Farmland League, convincing them to scale down their demand from ¥1 trillion to ¥2–300 billion. Fukui, *Party in Power*, 187.

28. *Mainichi Shimbun*, March 20, and *Yomiuri Shimbun*, March 31, 1967.

29. *Asahi Shimbun*, April 3, 19, and 20 (morning and evening), 1967. The pronunciation of "private plan" is *shian*, which was also used with another first character to mean "test plan."

party negotiations could proceed from. This became the party's position.[30]

Immediately after obtaining this tentative approval for his "private plan," Ueki met with League and Federation officials in an unsuccessful attempt to win their endorsements.

At about the same time, there was movement on the government side as well. The MOF let it be known that although ¥35 billion would be a perfectly reasonable amount, a "political decision" to award a *maximum* of ¥100,000 per household—most would get less—might be possible. Oddly enough, although the statement was quite clear, this offer was immediately misinterpreted by the LDP and the press to mean that the *average* payment per household would be ¥100,000, so that (with an estimated 954,000 households) the new total offer was ¥95 billion.[31] The MOF, making no public complaints about this misrepresentation, began staff-level talks with the PMO over details of the offer.

As "Golden Week" holidays at the end of April brought a pause in the process, four bids were on the table. The Federation was still calling for ¥1,200 billion; the League, ¥600 billion; Ueki's "private plan," backed informally by his Discussion Group, was for ¥250 billion; and the MOF was apparently offering ¥95 billion. The PMO still had not come up with an offer. All of these figures were simply total amounts, not accompanied by detailed plans on how the funds should be distributed among repatriates of different ages, lengths of time overseas, amount of property lost, and so forth. The time for the second round of bidding had come.

The Dietmen's League again moved first. On May 9, its membership passed a resolution authorizing the leadership to be "flexible," and that afternoon League President Nagayama met with the LDP leadership and pressed a new, detailed proposal that totaled ¥314.2 billion. At a Federation mass convention two days later, the group's leadership was severely criticized from the floor for such a "betrayal," but the offer stood.[32]

30. Interview, June 12, 1969.
31. *Asahi Shimbun* and *Mainichi Shimbun,* April 21, 1967 (morning and evening).
32. *Asahi Shimbun,* May 11, 1967 (evening).

This softening gave Ueki the opportunity to come up with another "private plan" on May 15, calling for ¥240 billion; his proposal was criticized at the Discussion Group meeting on May 17, but the members finally did formally agree on a concrete plan that totaled ¥257.9 billion.

Although not an official position of the LDP as a whole, the Discussion Group's proposal was a detailed plan duly passed by an official party organ. The action was therefore back on the government side—LDP Secretary-General Fukuda Takeo noted that the demand would probably have to be softened somewhat, but called on Director-General Tsukahara of the PMO to make a counterproposal, perhaps by using the Discussion Group's draft as the basis for intragovernmental talks with the MOF.[33]

On May 18, the first formal party-government negotiation session was held. The participants were those who would continue until the end: Ueki Kōshirō, the Discussion Group chairman and the participant most sympathetic to the repatriates (although as seen above his sympathy was not untempered by a sense of political realities); the LDP "big three" of Fukuda Takeo (secretary-general), Nishimura Naomi (PARC chairman), and Shiina Etsusaburō (Executive Council chairman); PMO Director-General Tsukahara Toshio; and Finance Minister Mizuta Mikio (also attending this and some later sessions was Chief Cabinet Secretary Fukunaga Kenji, who represented the prime minister). The first meeting deadlocked after Mizuta said that the Discussion Group's draft was not even worth answering.[34] However, the MOF soon leaked news that it might move up from ¥95 to ¥120 billion, and after Prime Minister Satō asked for speedier deliberations at his press conference on May 30, further formal concessions on details of terms of payment were offered by the MOF. As meetings continued, the effective party-government "gap" was between ¥257.9 billion and ¥120 billion.

The time now seemed ripe for an initiative by the PMO.

33. *Asahi Shimbun* (morning) and *Nihon Keizai Shimbun* (evening), May 18, 1967.
34. *Asahi Shimbun*, May 18, 1967 (evening).

Back in March, many observers had expected the PMO to offer something under ¥100 billion, quickly come to agreement with the MOF, and then do battle with the LDP. Later, in May, it had been expected that the PMO would propose a figure over ¥200 billion, allying with the LDP in negotiations with the MOF.[35] It did neither, but instead decided on a third, middle-ground strategic alternative: On June 7, Tsukahara called at the ministry and formally requested a total of ¥165.9 billion. The request was rejected—Finance Minister Mizuta said that ¥120 billion would be adequate—but this detailed draft did serve as a government response to the Discussion Group's proposal, and perhaps also as the catalyst to move the negotiations into their third, and final, round.

With a plausible, middle-ground draft now on the table, the question became which of the two major protagonists—the LDP or the MOF—would move next. The party made the first attempt through its regular decisionmaking channels. Three long meetings of the PARC Deliberation Council on June 13–15 considered the Discussion Group and PMO drafts in detail. The leadership hoped that this body would produce a reasonable recommendation which could be approved by the Executive Council to become the official LDP position, and then be adjusted in quick negotiations with the MOF. However, Federation pressure exerted through the LDP rank and file again prevailed. The League had been active in early June, appointing a thirty-member executive committee to strengthen its voice in intraparty discussions and sending President Nagayama to testify at the Deliberation Council meetings. LDP members from the House of Councillors were the particular targets, since they faced an election a year later, and a meeting of these politicians on June 14 threatened amendments on the floor of the Diet if the Discussion Group draft was modified too much by the leadership. In the end, the Deliberation Council did no more than recommend a few technical adjustments in terms of payment, and delegated all further moves to its chairman.[36]

35. *Yomiuri Shimbun*, March 31, 1967, and *Mainichi Shimbun*, May 22, 1967.
36. *Mainichi Shimbun*, June 15, and *Nihon Keizai Shimbun*, June 16, 1967.

The Executive Council too, in two attempts several days later, failed to overcome its members' reluctance to annoy the Federation and adjourned inconclusively.[37]

It was thus the MOF which came forward. On June 15, word was leaked to the press that three new alternative drafts were being prepared within the ministry. Their totals were ¥130.1, ¥148.8, and ¥157.3 billion; the largest draft differed only in detail from the PMO's offer of ¥165.9 billion. The lower two drafts were of course quickly forgotten—perhaps they had only been prepared to relieve bureaucratic pressures inside the ministry—so the "gap" at this point might be seen as between a government offer of about ¥160 billion and an LDP request somewhere above ¥200 billion (¥257.9 billion was the only party figure on the table, but the leadership had long since indicated its intention to soften this demand). A "gap" of only ¥60–80 billion (about $200 million) could be worked out in face-to-face bargaining sessions. The meetings billed as the "final negotiating sessions" thus began on June 23. Neither side was unified—disagreements continued between Ueki and the "big three" on the party side, and Mizuta and Tsukahara on the government side—and only a few minor terms-of-payment questions could be settled. But a meaningful deadline was at last at hand: the current Diet session had to end on July 17, and allowing time to draw up the necessary legislation and get it passed, a decision was required almost immediately. The participants therefore applied themselves diligently. After a session that began on June 26 and lasted until 5 A.M. on June 27, compromise was reached at ¥192.5 billion.

Even during this final stage of negotiations, the problem which plagued all the participants was the lack of helpful criteria for reaching decisions. How Japanese politicians function in such ambiguous circumstances is nicely revealed in Ueki's own recollections of the last meetings:

> Well, first I was thinking that we [the Discussion Group] had recommended about ¥255 billion, and the repatriates had gotten about ¥45 billion before [in 1957], and subtracting one from the other we come up with about ¥210 billion. From one way of thinking, I thought this

37. *Asahi Shimbun*, June 20 and 24, and *Nihon Keizai Shimbun*, June 23, 1967.

might be a logical result. This amount has nothing to do with the actual overseas property; it is just the difficulties the repatriates had and so forth. But then we might also look at the grant to the former landowners as an example of postwar compensation. . . . They got ¥145–150 billion or so. It was logical that this would become a criterion [*meyasu*] for other problems, like the repatriates. Some said, "Couldn't they put up with something like that?" I myself was thinking along the lines of ¥210 billion, but some others were very concerned about the country's financial problems and thought a grant about the same size as the landowners' would be adequate.

But there were about 1.8 million people covered by the landowner grant, and there were between 2.6 and 3 million repatriates, including children. However, figured as households the numbers are about the same, so many said the same amount of money would be okay. But I said this was too low, they won't stand for it [*tottemo gaman dekinai*] . . . it is cutting too far from ¥600 billion [the League's February demand]. So the other side said, "Well, you asked for ¥250 billion, and this will have to be cut, so why not start discussions from ¥150 billion?" I replied that some of the repatriates had really had terrible problems after the war; why not add about 20 per cent on to the ¥150 billion for that? That would make it about ¥180 billion.

The situation then became a confrontation between ¥210 billion and ¥180 billion. As the next standard [*sono tsugi no mokuhyō*], I thought our side should come down to ¥200 billion, strive for that, and then compromise somewhere over ¥190 billion. This is what happened in the very last stage. We then worked out all the details of payment—the ten year bonds, age limits, division among age groups, and so forth.[38]

In this fashion some $535 million was dispensed by the Japanese government. Immediately after the party-government meeting, the outline of the agreement was ratified by the cabinet and the LDP Executive Council, making it official. It was also approved—not without some grumbling for the record—by the assemblies of the LDP members of both Houses.[39] The formal bill, called the "Draft Law Concerning Payment of a Special Grant-in-Aid to Repatriates" ("Hikiagesha nado ni tai suru Tokubetsu Kyūfukin Shikyū ni kan suru Hōan")

38. Interview, June 12, 1969.
39. Although Executive Council decisions are binding on the party, an assembly is called when "you have to add a little more weight to make the decision stick" (LDP dietman Hara Kenzaburō, quoted by Thayer, *Conservatives*, 249).

was passed by the cabinet on June 29 and enacted into law on July 22 without difficulty.[40] Special windows were established in local government offices throughout Japan to accept applications. Under the formula finally devised, the maximum payment to individuals, which applied to those 50 years old or older at the end of the war, was ¥160,000 (about $445); the lowest payment, to those 1 to 19 years old, was ¥20,000 (about $56). Heirs would receive 70 per cent of the amount due repatriates who had died, and an additional bonus of ¥10,000 was paid to those who had been overseas prior to 1937. All payments were in ten-year bonds bearing 6 per cent interest. The average payment per person was to be about ¥56,000 ($155), which meant an average cash benefit of some $15 per year plus interest for ten years.

Given the small size of this grant relative to the original demands, it is evident that the repatriates were somewhat less successful in the negotiations over amount than they had been in establishing the principle that some compensation would be offered. To account for the difference, we must examine the properties of these two decisional processes. Why were Federation tactics effective in one and less so in the other? Before discussing tactics, however, it is necessary to analyze the fundamental strategy of the repatriates and the resources upon which it rested.

Sources of Repatriate Influence

The Federation itself, in public statements and in interviews granted to the author in 1969, has provided one version of its basic strategy, one which resembles that developed earlier by the National Farmland League and is related as well to strategies said to be followed, successfully, by other Japanese interest groups (rice farmers, pensioners, small businessmen). It is worth exploring in some detail.

Federation Leverage

To begin with, the Federation claimed it controlled a great many votes. Its own estimates of actual membership ranged

40. Note that "payment of a special grant-in-aid" is another neutral term, neither implying nor denying that "compensation" is being offered.

from 720,000 to 850,000 households, or 3 to 3.5 million individuals—probably wildly inflated figures in terms of those who actually paid the annual ¥200 dues but roughly equivalent to the total number of repatriates in Japan.[41] Further, the Federation said that each member would influence the votes of others, relatives and friends, so that it really could command some 10 million votes. Journalists discounted this claim, but most accepted a figure of about 5 million voters influenced by the Federation—a sizable group representing some 8 per cent of the electorate or 12 per cent of the actual number of voters in the 1967 general election.[42]

A group controlling such a large proportion of votes would command the attention of politicians in any country. In Japan, the repatriates' leverage was said to be substantially heightened by the country's extraordinary electoral system. In the competition for three to five seats in the House of Representatives from each district, margins between candidates are often very narrow, and candidates from the same party (particularly in the LDP) spend most of their energy running against each other.[43] Even a small group of voters in a district, therefore, might exert considerable influence on an individual candidate by threatening to shift their support to another within the same party. If an interest group wished to exploit this leverage, it would never support all the candidates of one party; if, say, four LDP candidates are running, one, two, or three would be given support. In fact, the record indicates that most LDP-oriented interest groups opt not to apply this leverage and instead endorse all (or none) of the conservative candidates in a given district, preferring to make no enemies.[44] However, the

41. Estimates of the number of repatriates have included 2.5 million by the Ministry of Health and Welfare in 1957, 3.2 million by the Economic Stabilization Board during the Occupation, and 3.6 million by the Overseas Property Problem Research Section in the mid-1960's; see *Tokyo Shimbun,* February 12, 1957; *Asahi Shimbun,* November 30 and December 14, 1966; and *Nihon Keizai Shimbun,* March 16, 1974. Recipients of the 1957 grant totaled 3.17 million; *Yomiuri Shimbun,* March 5, 1957.

42. E.g., Horiwaka Kiichi in *Yomiuri Shimbun,* March 5, 1967.

43. Such peculiarities are well treated in Gerald L. Curtis, *Election Campaigning Japanese Style* (New York: Columbia University Press, 1971); their effects are analyzed in a dissertation in preparation by Jun-suk Youn, University of Michigan.

44. Curtis, *Election Campaigning,* pp. 180–81.

Federation maintained that it used the electoral system to best possible advantage, by tailoring its endorsements carefully. The example offered by a Federation official was a three-member district with three LDP and two Japan Socialist Party candidates running. The national office of the Federation would select the two LDP candidates and one JSP candidate who seemed most likely to support repatriate demands, based on past records and verbal commitments. Among Federation members who normally support the LDP, those living in one portion of the district would be instructed to vote for one candidate and those in the remaining portion for the other. JSP voters would all be told to vote for the single endorsed Socialist candidate. In a five-member district, three or four LDP candidates could be endorsed, with a similar geographical division.

Lists of Federation endorsees are not available—the official said they are always destroyed immediately after elections, in case local representatives should come to be accused of violations of the electoral law—so it is not possible to determine precisely the degree to which this strategy was actually followed. It is known, however, that the Federation endorsed 286 candidates in the 1967 general election, about 200 of whom were from the LDP (the remainder were JSP or Democratic Socialist Party candidates). This means that almost 60 per cent of the 342 officially authorized LDP candidates were endorsed by the Federation, a figure which fits in plausibly with the strategy outlined above. If in 1967 the Federation consistently endorsed three LDP candidates when five were running, two when either three or four were running, and one when two or only one were running, the endorsement total would be 208, very close to the cited figure of 200.

In maintaining that its votes were influential in securing victory for the candidates it endorsed, the Federation further claimed that 240 of its 286 endorsees were elected. This is a success ratio of 83.9 per cent, which seems impressively high, since the success ratio for all candidates in that election was 54.9 per cent. Many LDP politicians seemed to be suitably impressed: one second-term dietman told the *Asahi Shimbun* that "they are organized all the way down to the city-town-village level. If you promise firmly to back up their demands, they can quickly be turned into a supporters' association [kōenkai]." [45] A former cabinet minister said: "I know their request is thinly justified. But they have a lot of active power, if only because they worked together overseas. If you are their friend, you're safe, but I would be afraid of making enemies of people with such high-handed characters. If I opposed them, they would be bound to tear up my district." [46]

Although Federation spokesmen at times asserted that it was the LDP as a party that was being threatened—one told a party group in 1965, "let us be sure that this problem doesn't bring the opposition parties into power" [47]—it is clear that its strategy was primarily aimed at individual conservative dietmen. Support for repatriate goals from the party leadership or the party as an institution was seen as crucial, but it was to be obtained indirectly by motivating (or coercing) sufficient numbers of the rank and file to apply their own pressure on the upper levels of the party. The key was the Dietmen's League for Handling the Overseas Property Problem (only LDP dietmen were included; this group is the exact functional equivalent to the "advisers" to the National Farmland League). At its height in 1967, the League had enlisted between 213 and 267 members, or 55 to 70 per cent of lower house LDP dietmen and 40 to 50 per cent of those in the upper house.[48] With a majority of the majority party as its enthusiastic supporters, the Federation could hardly fail to move a reluctant government to grant some portion of its demands.

The fact that the Federation did not limit its efforts to the LDP makes this case somewhat different from that of the

45. A feature story in *Asahi Shimbun*, February 22, 1967.   46. *Ibid.*

47. Mike Makoto, Chairman of the Dietmen's League, quoted in *Asahi Shimbun*, December 16, 1965. A resolution circulated at a Federation national convention in May 1967 read, "If the promise to pay compensation of ¥600 billion or more is not kept, we will put all our energy into a movement to bring down the LDP" (*Asahi Shimbun*, May 11, 1967).

48. These and figures below calculated from "Zaigai Zaisan Giin Renmei Meibō" [Register of the Dietmen's League for handling the overseas property problem], mimeo., no publication information but probably originally produced by the Federation prior to the 1965 House of Councillors election. By 1969, some names had been crossed out and many others added in ink. Newpaper estimates of League size were as high as 280 members; e.g., *Yomiuri Shimbun*, March 5, 1967.

former landlords. Its strategy was applied also to the opposition Socialist and Democratic Socialist parties, and both actively supported the more extreme repatriate demands throughout the process; even the Clean Government Party, which earlier had taken a righteous stance critical of LDP handouts to special interests, in the end was won over by pressure from repatriates within the Sōkagakkai, its parent religious association, and became a supporter. Only the Communists remained steadfast in opposition. While probably not a crucial factor in the actual decisionmaking process, this broader support obviated worries about opposition to compensation in the Diet, which had been intense in the former-landowners case, and even allowed the Federation to mention darkly the possibility of a nonpartisan Dietmen's Bill which could be passed over LDP leadership objections.[49]

Leverage Re-examined

By following this carefully devised strategy, said the Federation, irresistible pressure was applied to the government, which eventually had to give in. But if the strategy worked so well, if the repatriates were so powerful, how is it they received only one-sixth the amount they demanded? This nagging question provides sufficient incentive to take a more searching look at the sources of repatriate influence.

First, how many votes did the Federation actually control? Leaving aside the problem of determining the number of dues-paying members, it is clear that there were more than three million actual repatriates who would be eligible for compensation if granted, and it does not seem unreasonable that friends and neighbors might swell the total to five million. Statistics for lower house elections offer no way to substantiate these figures, but, as is true of many interest groups, the Federation also sought influence in upper house elections by sponsoring candidates in the national constituency.[50] In earlier years it had

49. This strategy probably was not available to the National Farmland League because the group it represented was regarded by the left parties as a traditional enemy, socially and politically conservative. See Fukui, *Party in Power*, 181–82.

50. In national-constituency balloting, each voter receives a separate ballot containing a long list of nominees, from which he selects one; the top fifty vote-getters are elected.

run only one, who had always succeeded, but in 1965 two were
endorsed: Furumi Tadayuki, a new candidate who received an
official LDP nomination; and Tsukumi Yasuhiro, another new
candidate, who failed to secure official LDP nomination. As
with the lower house election strategy, the Federation divided
the country in two to maximize its influence: all members in
Kyūshū (where there are large numbers of repatriates)
were instructed to vote for Tsukumi, and those living elsewhere in Japan were to vote for Furumi. About 440,000 votes
would be required to place a candidate among the fifty win-
ners.

The distribution of votes was consistent with the Federation's
strategy in that Tsukumi received 71 per cent and Furumi just
8 per cent of their total votes in Kyūshū. However, much
more significant is that both received surprisingly few votes and
lost: Furumi, with 351,632 votes, finished sixty-third, and Tsukumi, with 221,796, finished sixty-eighth. The Federation must
have calculated that about 900,000 votes were available, or only
one candidate would have been run. But even this minimum
anticipated figure—let alone the 573,428 votes actually tallied—
is well below the estimate of five million votes under Federation
control. Of course, the strategy outlined above pertained to
elections for the House of Councillors, but there is no reason to
believe that voters unwilling to follow Federation recommendations for national-constituency House of Councillors elections (in a year when the repatriate campaign was well publicized) could be counted on for local lower house races. All in all,
there seems to be little direct evidence for crediting the Federation with control of more than five or six hundred thousand
votes—a long way from the claimed five million.

Second, how credible is the argument that the Federation actually decided its endorsements on such a "rational" basis,
choosing one or two less than the number running? Lacking a
list of endorsees or direct evidence about repatriate-group activity in local constituencies, we cannot draw definite conclusions, but it is interesting to observe that at the time of the 1967
general election 202 incumbent members of the Dietmen's
League stood for re-election; an inspection of the list reveals
that in many districts all the LDP candidates were included in
this group, while in others there had been only one or none. In

making its list of about 200 official LDP endorsees, the Federation—to follow its avowed strategy—would have had to *deny* endorsement to dietmen who had already formally attached themselves to the repatriates' cause by joining the League. According to several Japanese political observers I spoke with, such behavior would be unlikely, if only because it could create real enemies. It seems likeliest that even though in a very few cases the Federation might have withheld endorsement from members of its own League, the overwhelming majority of the 202 incumbent League members running would have been supported.

In any case, nearly all those endorsed must have been incumbents: the selections were made by the national headquarters, whose relations were with dietmen in Tokyo. This observation throws light on the third question: How much difference did the Federation endorsement actually make to candidates? As noted, of 286 endorsees (from three parties), 240, or 84 per cent, were elected, a figure well above the success ratio of 55 per cent for all candidates or 70 per cent for LDP, JSP, and DSP candidates in 1967.[51] But about 70 per cent of the endorsees were Liberal Democrats, and the success ratio for all LDP candidates was 81 per cent; moreover, the ratio for LDP incumbents in that election was 88 per cent. Of the 202 League members who ran (all, of course, LDP incumbents), 180, or 89 per cent, won. In other words, membership in the League (and thus possibly Federation endorsement) seems not to have had any effect on chances of LDP incumbents' re-election.[52] In fact, if one assumes that only incumbents were endorsed, the hypothesis—albeit speculative—that Federation endorsement made no difference whatsoever is admirably sustained by the figures available:

51. Success ratios (number elected over number running) are calculated by counting from election lists in *Kokkai Binran* [Diet handbook], 37th ed. (Tokyo: Nihon Seikei Shimbunsha, August 1968), 300–14.

52. Fukui (193) concludes: "there is little doubt that the [National Farmland] League's endorsement made an appreciable difference to the performance of the candidates concerned" in the prefectural constituencies of the 1962 upper house election, because the success ratio of endorsees was 85.5 per cent compared with 78.6 per cent for all LDP candidates. This difference does not seem so enormous to me, particularly since in that case also it is likely that the endorsees were disproportionately drawn from incumbents, with their higher success ratio.

	Federation-endorsed candidates		Partywide incumbent success ratio		Estimated endorsees elected
LDP	200	×	.89	=	178
JSP + DSP	86	×	.71	=	61
	Total endorsed candidates elected			=	239

As noted, the Federation itself claimed that 240 of its endorsees were actually elected.

Fourth, if the Federation's voting power actually made little or no difference to candidates, why should LDP dietmen have been as worried about its purported power, as the quotes above indicate they were? One answer is that not all were. When I asked several LDP dietmen about the repatriates during 1969 and 1970, none could remember whether they had received Federation endorsement in the previous election or not. In a published book-length case study of a single lower house election campaign in Kyūshū in 1967, the repatriates are mentioned only in passing, as one in a list of endorsing groups cited by one candidate.[53] While this evidence is fragmentary, so is that backing up reporters' accounts of dietmen quailing under Federation pressure. My guess is that not many dietmen were very concerned.

Why, then—our fifth question—did so many join the Dietmen's League? There is no reason to doubt that in 1967 somewhat more than half of all sitting LDP dietmen had joined and thus formally endorsed the rather extreme demands of the Federation. However, many such leagues (or "study groups," or "advisers" to an interest group) are organized each year within the LDP, and many attain memberships of half the LDP dietmen or better. For the politician, membership requires only inscribing one's name on a roster and offers a chance to appear at national conventions and wave to potential voters. As Curtis points out, candidates like to have affiliations with as many organizations as possible; furthermore, since it makes little sense for a politician to offend any group unnecessarily, he is unlikely to decline an invitation from a body which makes so few

---

53. Curtis, *Election Campaigning*, 226. This candidate, Ayabe, lost.

demands.[54] Therefore, formal support of Federation demands implied no automatic commitment to work very hard for them.

If my analysis is correct—if the Federation really controlled only a few votes, did not really follow a strategy of maximum leverage, and failed to frighten dietmen into more than *pro forma* support—then the repatriates were no more than a paper tiger, unworthy of serious attention from politician or political scientist. Why then did the LDP leadership and the government, both initially opposed to reopening the question at all, finally consent to make a grant to the repatriates? What were the *real* sources of repatriate influence?

Other Sources

Unfortunately, I am unable to offer a hypothesis as ingenious and neat as the propositions attacked above. Only a few rather subtle factors, which cannot be measured but may constitute a substantial portion of the true explanation, will be suggested.

First, information might have been poor. For example, Japanese newspaper reporters apparently were unanimous in their acceptance of Federation claims of voting strength, or at least they printed them without reference to the dubious evidence of the 1965 House of Councillors election. There is no reason to believe that many dietmen were not similarly credulous.

Second, many conservative politicians, even the relatively young, exhibited a sympathy that is apparently quite genuine for those who served Japan loyally before and during the war, and ran into hard times afterward. Such regard, beyond that dictated by simple vote-counting, would seem to be extended to veterans, war widows, and other groups as well as the repatriates, and might insure at least a friendly predisposition with regard to requests for help.[55]

54. LDP dietmen regard dealings with such interest groups as "a subsidiary strategy of limited usefulness" (*ibid.*, 180). Note also an American congressman's remark about the American Legion's putative electoral power: "I honestly do not believe that the Commander of any post . . . controls any vote but his own. Sometimes, I think he has difficulty telling his wife what to do" (W. H. Ayres, quoted by Key, *Pressure Groups*, 122–23, n. 11).

55. It might be added that the LDP's sympathy for certain other unfortunates, such as the victims of American atomic bombing, has been less marked,

Third, throughout the long process leading up to decision, the Federation sponsored many mass meetings, public demonstrations, and direct petitioning campaigns. Tactics at times became fairly extreme: in 1956, several repatriates had held a hunger strike on top of the Ministry of Finance smokestack in an effort to gain an interview with the minister, and in 1967 a large group had to be removed from the corridor in front of his office by riot police. To "encourage" a favorable report by the Overseas Property Problem Council in late 1966, demonstrations with as many as 10,000 participants were held in Tokyo, and an enormous tent was erected near the Diet Building to serve as headquarters for sixty-five days.[56] While disavowing violence, the Federation evidently laid great emphasis on direct lobbying tactics; in fact, a staff member noted with some pride in an interview that the Federation had originated several demonstration techniques common today, such as outfitting petitioners with slogan-bearing sashes. Whether taken as indications of sincerity or simple nagging, LDP dietmen and leaders (as well as Overseas Property Problem Council members awakened at early hours to receive telegrams) may have been influenced by these efforts.

Fourth, even if most rank and file Dietmen's League members were apathetic, several LDP dietmen, from whatever motives, were extremely active on the repatriates' behalf. Some were repatriates themselves, and others had long ties with the organization. They were constantly pressuring the party leadership and exhorting other dietmen.[57]

Perhaps it would be fair to conclude that the Federation's real plan was rather more subtle than its avowed strategy of mobilizing rank and file LDP support through disciplined voting power. This strategy had only to give the *appearance* of being effective, sustaining a vague impression of repatriate strength and thereby providing the tacticians of the Federation

perhaps because these groups have been associated with left-wing political movements and opposition parties.

56. Respectively, *Asahi Shimbun*, March 23, 1957; Ozawa Teruo, "Bimyō na Yosan no Fukkatsu Sesshō" [The resurrected negotiation of a delicate budget], *Kōmei*, April 1967, 76–79; *Asahi Shimbun*, February 22, 1967.

57. A similar group was extremely important in the former-landowners case; Fukui, *Party in Power*, 181 ff.

and League leadership with room to maneuver within the LDP. Seen in this light, the single most important resource of the repatriates was the political know-how and skill of the managers of their campaign.

Why These Decisions?

We may turn now from the particularities of a Japanese interest group to an examination of the Japanese decisionmaking system. How is it that these strengths proved so effective in the decision to make a grant, but relatively ineffective when it came to settling the actual amount?

Deciding the Principle

The conflict over whether or not the repatriates would receive any compensation was fought in three arenas: inside the Liberal Democratic Party; between the party and the leaders of the government; and inside the Overseas Property Problem Council. It was obvious to the Federation from the beginning that LDP support would be crucial to its cause, and furthermore that the attitude of most party leaders—who like to take a "national interest" stance and had other problems to worry about as well—would at best be cool. The repatriates had no strategy available to threaten the LDP as an organization. On the other hand, it is generally believed in Japanese political circles that the LDP is extremely susceptible to pressure from its backbenchers, and that individual dietmen could be subjected to electoral pressure. The leadership, therefore, could be confronted with a combination of broad-based, if passive, support, as symbolized by the League, and quite active pressure from a few highly motivated friends of the repatriates. Diffident as the leadership might have been, its vital interests were hardly at stake in this issue, so the costs of giving in and endorsing the Federation's demands were low.

The battle in the next arena—getting the council established by the government—was only slightly more difficult. The majority party's favorable judgment was already on record, and activists continually appeared in public forums, particularly in sensitive pre-election periods, to press Prime Minister Ikeda for action. Worried about setting a dangerous precedent, Ikeda (and presumably others in top government posts) delayed as long as possible and then tried to stack the membership of the council against the repatriates, but he too was unprepared to take a determined stand on an issue which was, in personal terms, less than crucial. Similar pressures were brought to bear to forge what probably was the single most significant link in this decisional chain: the agreement in 1964 that dietmen would be added to the "neutral" members of the council, insuring that committed supporters of the repatriates would participate directly in formulating recommendations.

In both these arenas the Federation was aided by two important factors: first, that all these demands had clear precedents in the former landowners case, which everyone perceived as being comparable; and second, that each demand was in itself extremely modest and hard to resist—only further "research" was called for at each stage. The fundamental strategy, pursued quite skillfully, was that of the "camel's nose" (or "foothold"), taking one small step at a time.

Within the third arena, the council itself, it is difficult to ascertain exactly how the majority was converted from opposition to approval over two years, but the fact that some members were strongly positive, while the negative views of most others were based more on abstract principles than on real interests, was undoubtedly important. Then too, few special advisory bodies in any nation ever seem to recommend that no action be taken; several members of the Overseas Property Problem Council were quoted as observing that "it seems only natural that after establishing a council and talking about the problem, the nation should take some step with regard to the repatriates." [58] Additionally, the Federation's mass demonstrations, letter-writing campaigns, and frequently offered expert advice may have played some role in this arena, as in the others.

Repatriate demands were not effectively opposed throughout this process because the only major participant for whom significant interests were threatened—the Ministry of Finance —could not play a large role in any of the three arenas. It had no way to intervene in an intraparty dispute, and its repre-

58. *Asahi Shimbun,* May 1, 1966.

sentation on the council was but one man in twenty. The ministry, it is true, did have good relations with Ikeda, and indeed it is normally expected that a prime minister will back up the MOF on questions of governmental expenditure—perhaps this influence explains the degree of resistance the government did offer over the question of appointing the council and its composition. Still, the norm of prime-ministerial fiscal conservatism is one often violated, and again, the repatriates' demand was a modest one.

Deciding the Amount

When the question at issue became yen, rather than a yes or no, the action shifted to a new arena, with different participants and different rules of the game. The important points are that the final decision was reached in a small group of a particular sort and that the problem was defined as monetary. Direct participation was restricted to a few senior LDP politicians, who knew each other well, shared a certain style of doing business, and had dealt with similar problems in the past; the majority of the group—the "big three" of the LDP, Tsukahara from the PMO, and Chief Cabinet Secretary Fukunaga (when he was participating)—played mediating roles. Even the protagonists were hardly zealous advocates of their causes: both Ueki, representing the repatriates, and Mizuta, as finance minister, were quite ready to compromise, within limits, to speed a solution. Variations in these elements would have changed the process significantly. If the participants had been of two political parties, one side or the other would probably have found partisan advantage in taking the case to the public at some point. Without all the mediators to move things along and suggest alternatives, the two sides could have bogged down on small points. If the rules had been more formal, complete plans might have been required for each change in position, rather than the free-and-easy bargaining style actually adopted. If the meetings had been public, Ueki and the LDP leadership would have come under intense fire from the repatriates after any hint of compromise. Perhaps most significant was the restricted participation: consider the effect if, instead of Ueki, an actual paid representative of the Repatriates' Federation (or even the

Dietmen's League president) had taken part in these sessions, or if a career MOF bureaucrat had participated in place of Mizuta. The negotiations might be going on still, each side seeing lower costs to its own interests in delay, at any given point, than in accepting any possible solution.[59]

The second critical factor was the definition of the problem itself. It was taken as a monetary question, not a matter of principle or of a yes-or-no decision, and money is almost infinitely divisible. The other matters which had to be decided, such as the terms of payment, were considered secondary to and dependent upon agreement over the total size of the grant. Then too, while the amount of money concerned was not inconsiderable, neither was it an enormous proportion of the entire national budget, of such a size as to engage the vital interest of either the LDP or the MOF. Finally—a point emphasized at several junctures—for several reasons there were no unambiguously applicable decisionmaking criteria available, so the participants were relatively free to reach for any pretexts that came to hand (even a 20 per cent bonus or "plus alpha" for "unusual hardships").

It should be understood that neither of these factors was a given. The issue could have been handled in other sorts of arenas, and it could have been defined differently: on a more "rational" or administrative model, for example, each of the complicated terms-of-payment questions, including appropriate relative levels of payment among age groups, might have been decided first, with the total amount of the grant then being settled by adding all these up. That the dispute proceeded in the fashion described was the result of a series of choices less conscious than unconscious—the product of precedents, habits, and unspoken assumptions shared by the participants who, in the last analysis, felt that their long-run interests lay more in maintaining dependable decisionmaking procedures than in any short-run concern for the overseas-property problem.

59. For a related Soviet example, see Zbigniew Brzezinski and Samuel P. Huntington, *Political Power: USA/USSR* (New York: Viking Press, 1963), 199 ff.; see also Sidney Verba, *Small Groups and Political Behavior* (Princeton: Princeton University Press, 1961), 27–29.

Given this process, why was the result ¥192.5 billion? Why not ¥190.1 or ¥200.1 billion? Or why not ¥50 or ¥600 billion? The latter two questions are easy to answer. On the one hand, certainly the amount could have varied by a few billion yen either way without anyone much minding.[60] On the other hand, the MOF would not have tolerated a grant of ¥600 or even ¥300 billion (and would have been strongly supported by the prime minister and probably the LDP leadership), while if the amount had been set below that of the grant to the former landowners, the repatriates might well have been successful in forcing a Dietmen's Bill. In other words, in any such process the expectations of participants define both a floor and a ceiling with a "realistic" or "practical" range of alternatives— "everyone knows" the solution will not fall outside this range. In this case the floor could be identified precisely as ¥145.6 billion, the grant to the former landowners; the effective ceiling was less definite.

We lack sufficient information to generalize—beyond the very specific account provided by Ueki in the extended quotation above—about how some specific figure between the floor and ceiling is chosen. I suspect, however, that a mechanism something like the following operates: that the amount finally decided will be above, but not much above, the mid-point of the "first serious offers" of the two sides. By "not much above" I have in mind a margin of something like 10 per cent; it will be above and not below because the MOF will ordinarily find it in its interest to make a small sacrifice to hasten the decision (and it will reach that point before the requesting side will). Obviously, the problem is determining the "first serious offers"— which might be defined as the first offer by each side which is fairly near the minimum acceptable terms of the other (i.e., the floor and ceiling mentioned above). Operationally, it may be possible to identify the "first serious offers" by when and how they are put forth, the length of time they are maintained, or some other characteristic. In the matter at hand, the first

60. Perhaps a little resistance from the MOF would have been encountered at the ¥200 billion level, since it would worry about future claimants referring to the repatriate grant as "in the ¥200 billion range"; ¥192.5 billion sounds rather like pricing a dress at $39.95.

serious offer by the requesting side was clearly the Discussion Group's demand of ¥257.9 billion, decided on May 17; for the MOF, less clearly, it was probably the informal offer of about ¥120 billion first mentioned in mid-May and then emerging in June as a specific proposal of ¥112.6 billion. The mid-point of the two offers lies between ¥185 and ¥190 billion, just some 5 per cent below the actual grant of ¥195.2 billion.

This hypothesis does seem to represent the bare bones of the overseas-property negotiations accurately; whether or not it describes other similar cases in Japan and how it might compare with equivalent formulations for other political systems are matters which might be attractive subjects for future inquiry.

Conclusions

It would be exaggerating the importance and representativeness of the overseas-property case to draw sweeping conclusions about the nature of the Japanese decisionmaking system. Still, in its relative simplicity, this affair (and that of the former landowners) does stand as something of an "ideal type" of Japanese interest-group politics, allowing us to view certain relationships more clearly than in cases which involve a greater number of participants, weightier issues, or more ambiguous motives. I am therefore encouraged to explore some implications of the analysis above in a comparative context, even though the relative lack of similar studies for other countries means relying on generalizations.

First, it is probably safe to assume that groups more or less like the repatriates in size, degree of organization, and nature of demands exist in many nations.[61] Are such groups likely to be particularly influential in the Japanese political system? Plainly enough, Japan's medium-sized, multi-member, single-ballot electoral system does put the individual dietman (particu-

---

61. This statement is made without much evidence; a brief search has revealed no comparable case studies. There have been politically active repatriate groups in Europe, but they are often more sociologically distinct from the population and, more concentrated geographically and tend to have a wider range of demands. Veterans' groups—especially those seeking a one-time-only bonus payment—could be comparable; see Key, *Pressure Groups,* 118–24. Medium-sized national trade groups of small businessmen are another possibility.

larly a Liberal Democrat) in a position of vulnerability to demands from relatively small groups of voters. Margins of victory can be so small, and switching from one conservative candidate to another so easy, that any dietman must go to some lengths to avoid making enemies. In countries with plurality or proportional electoral formulas, small but unified groups of voters may be influential in a few unusually tight districts, but they could not, as in Japan, apply such pressure effectively in nearly all districts. Hence groups of this sort elsewhere might try instead to influence a few high-level politicians or the leadership of a particular party. Whether or not one believes that the Federation actually followed its avowed strategy of maximizing electoral leverage, the rules of the Japanese electoral game meant that LDP dietmen would be predisposed to see its threats and claims as plausible, convincing enough to warrant signing up in the League. Obtaining broad, if not necessarily intense support from the rank and file of the majority party probably is easier in Japan than elsewhere.

   Second, we might suggest rather hesitantly that the LDP may be more susceptible to backbencher influence than parties in other countries. Certainly the leadership continually compromised with the repatriates' supporters in the party, even though its opposition to a grant had been made clear from the start. This pattern is consistent with the conventional picture of Japanese political leadership as passive, dominated by a need to placate various factions, and reflecting a consensual style of decisionmaking. While not disagreeing with this line of analysis, I do note that it often takes as its reference point the traditional view of "normal" political parties as centralized and oligarchic, while some recent research has emphasized instead the importance of backbencher revolts and the considerable—possibly expanding—autonomy and influence of individual members.[62] However, I suspect that an empirical comparison would nevertheless reveal that the LDP is more likely than most parties to be swayed by rank and file members representing some special interest.

   These two considerations apply to the first process we de-

   62. Samuel H. Beer, *The British Political System* (New York: Random House, 1974), 121–27.

scribed, that of inserting an issue into the political agenda and obtaining a favorable response in principle. It is likely that, for an interest group like the repatriates, these rungs of the policy ladder are easier to climb in Japan than in many other political systems. The process of deciding the amount, on the other hand, seems less distinctive: the sequence of offers and counteroffers that progressively narrow the "gap," the flexible use of any "objective" criterion which might simplify the decision, the overriding commitment to getting problems out of the way—all have been observed in political arguments over money around the world.[63] There are, of course, national variations: Japanese tend to be rather self-conscious about matters of process and are probably more aware than their counterparts elsewhere of precisely where they stand at each point; in this case for example, participants knew how much the "gap" would have to be narrowed before the issue could be settled by a face-to-face bargaining session. Another Japanese characteristic is the proclivity to wind things up in a formal but relaxed small-group meeting, one in which the members know each other well and share an understanding of the situation despite differing roles. In England, such a dispute might be solved by a "chat" between two civil servants in a club; in France, through arbitration by a higher authority.[64] It seems quite possible, however, that the result of such negotiations, once started, might be about the same anywhere—another speculation which might be approached through empirical comparative analysis.

The universe of which our example represents one case is that of relatively small, vote-based interest groups seeking benefits for themselves against governmental resistance. Such groups appear to have a head start in Japan, because of the electoral system and a possibly distinctive organizational fea-

63. Many examples will be found in the budget process literature: Aaron Wildavsky, *The Politics of the Budgetary Process* (Boston: Little Brown. 1964); Hugh Heclo and Aaron Wildavsky, *The Private Government of Public Money* (Berkeley and Los Angeles: University of California Press, 1974); Guy Lord, *The French Budgetary Process* (Berkeley and Los Angeles: University of California Press, 1973); Thomas J. Anton, *The Politics of State Expenditure in Illinois* (Urbana: University of Illinois Press, 1966).

64. Oversimplifications, of course, but see Heclo and Wildavsky, *Private Government,* 76–128; and Michel Crozier, *The Bureaucratic Phenomenon* (Chicago: University of Chicago Press, 1964), 253–55.

ture of the majority party. However, once a problem becomes defined in familiar monetary terms, and participation is restricted, the Japanese government apparently copes with its difficulties as ably as most others.

5. Setting the Price of Rice: A Study in Political Decisionmaking *

Michael W. Donnelly

Early every summer, after the Japanese rice farmer has plucked his rice seedlings from the protected shelter provided by carefully tended nursery beds and replanted them into the soft, muddy soil of the paddy field, the agriculture cycle is briefly interrupted by politics. Since the early days of the Pacific War over three decades ago, the rice farmer has sold most, if not all, of his commercially marketed crop to the government. Until recently he had little choice. During the war and the subsequent Occupation, officially determined prices were well below what the open, free market would bring. But to sell on the black market was to risk fine, crop confiscation, and perhaps even imprisonment. The situation changed in the early 1950's with political independence and the firm establishment of political party government. The farmer could no longer be simply coerced into selling his crop to the government; sufficient economic incentives had to be provided. The extent, nature, and types of incentives came to depend, to a great extent, on decisions made during the annual rice-pricing season.

Like the rice production cycle, the political calendar of events is firm but not excessively rigid. Sudden and unforeseen changes in the political rhythm and climate of the densely complicated political life in Tokyo can force decisions to be made sooner or later than usual. But farmers must be told as early as

* The research for this paper was supported by a grant from the Foreign Area Fellowship Program of the Social Science Research Council. I would like to thank James Morley and T. J. Pempel for reading and commenting on an earlier version.

possible how much they will receive for their crop. Contracts for sales must be made and bargains sealed with collection agents. And so in early June, just as the rainy season settles over much of the countryside, the politics of rice-pricing begins to occupy the time of the political and bureaucratic leaders of Japan's economic superstate who must decide at what level farm incomes should be supported and how the costs will be distributed.

Despite recent changes in the food-control system, the government is still the biggest buyer of domestic rice and so the rice-pricing season is a political wage negotiation which involves not only the farmer but a whole host of participants and interests which are part of the country's political economy of rice. Participants include the cabinet and the prime minister, official and unofficial committees and groups within political parties, organizations of farmers, consumers, and labor, government ministries and administrative bodies, different parts of the financial world, agriculture experts, and the mass media. The process of decision is relatively permeable and so permits maximum participation and the open flow of information. The conflict and bargaining take place not only between the Liberal Democratic Party (LDP) and the cabinet, but also within formal and informal policy networks which cut across organizations and the boundaries of party and government. The season is filled with political rallies, waves of demonstrators visiting the offices of dietmen and the headquarters of the LDP, and protracted, sometimes rancorous negotiations of various kinds.

When the price is finally determined the fiction is sometimes contrived that the price established is just and demonstrably fair since it has been determined by the objective and neutral standards of an elaborate and complicated economic formula. But abstract economic formulas do not make for automatic computations or eliminate the need for political compromise. And while the decision process sometimes appears to be a little bit of political theater, it is nonetheless a matter of prime importance to the political leaders of the Japanese economic superstate.

Rice as an Income Problem

One of the most difficult economic problems in advanced industrial societies is what to do about farm incomes. The process of industrial development and a rising gross national product ultimately lead to the decline of the agriculture population and the labor force.[1] Moreover, despite advances in technology and mechanization, labor productivity almost always rises more slowly in agriculture than in other sectors of the economy. Thus while urban wages increase and most consumers become well fed, many farmers find themselves on an economic treadmill, encountering increased difficulties in keeping up with the rising standards of living enjoyed by those living and working in urban areas. The income problem is especially acute in Japan; the Lilliputian farms averaging only 1.1 hectare in size do not create the conditions for a viable economic unit for most farmers in an economy which has achieved unprecedented rates of economic growth.

Expansion of the scale of production, adoption of new technology, and the intensification or diversification of production offer, in principle, ways for farmers to increase business, cut their costs, and raise net income. However, many small farmers in Japan do not have the opportunity or necessary funds to expand their scale of management, diversify production, or invest in new equipment. Many younger people simply elect to leave agriculture, and those who decide to continue seek supplementary income by part-time employment in other industries.

But there is another means that is often used to help mitigate, although rarely solve, the rural income problem: the use of political power. A decline in the relative numbers, status, and economic position of farmers in industrial societies has not necessarily led to a concomitant decline in political influence. Indeed, threatened by the apparently ineluctable flow of history, farmers and the various organizations which claim to structure their interests are frequently stimulated to greater unity as they seek to use the power of the state to increase

1. For a summary of the research by economists on the topic of economic growth and agricultural transformation see Bruce Johnston, "Agriculture and Structural Transformation in Developing Countries: A Survey of Research," *Journal of Economic Literature* 8 (June 1970), 369–404.

public benefits and protection from some of the undesirable results of industrial growth. They are particularly successful in their efforts if the political party in power is dependent upon rural votes for continuation in office. In such a context of rapid but uneven economic growth, rural political power creates enormous pressure on the politician to do something about rural incomes.[2] In Japan this problem has been strikingly manifested in the struggle over rice prices.

A major issue concerning Japanese economic policy in the 1960's involved the extraordinary rise in prices paid by the government to rice producers. Beginning in 1960 producer prices doubled in eight years from ¥10,405 to ¥20,640 per 150 kilograms of unpolished rice. This rise was far greater than that in prices paid by consumers, which were also officially determined. Producer prices also exceeded almost all other commodity prices and were above general price levels. Rice prices in Japan were at least twice the international price. By 1968 slightly more than 40 per cent of government expenditures for agriculture and forestry were going to rice-related policies. This sudden rise in prices for the benefit of the cultivator was unprecedented in Japanese history and must be understood in terms of very rapid economic growth and the political organization of Japan's rice economy.[3]

One of the results of economic growth in Japan was a growing disparity in productivity and income between agriculture and other sectors of the economy beginning around 1955. The long-term causes and historical implications of uneven economic growth in Japan are complex and beyond the immediate scope of this paper.[4] Politically, however, the growing weakness of the agriculture sector in the late 1950's created political pressure for the government and the ruling LDP to do something

2. See, for example, D. Gale Johnson, *World Agriculture in Disarray* (London: Fontana Paperback, 1973); for an overview of agriculture policies in industrial nations see *Agriculture Policies in 1966: Europe, North America and Japan* (Paris: Organization for Economic Cooperation and Development, 1967).

3. For an explanation which stresses rice as a wage good see Yujiro Hayami, "Rice Policy in Japan's Economic Development," *American Journal of Agricultural Economics* 54 (1972), 19–31.

4. The best work in English on Japan's long-term economic growth is Kazushi Ohkawa and Henry Rosovsky, *Japanese Economic Growth: Trend Acceleration in the Twentieth Century* (Stanford: Stanford University Press, 1973).

for the farmer. It was natural that farmers sought a fair return for their labor in light of Prime Minister Ikeda's Income-Doubling Plan which promised to double the income of every employed citizen in ten years.

The Basic Agriculture Law of 1961 was designed to cope with the growing "farm problem" and income gap. Its general aim was unambiguous: "Agriculture production should increase in such a way as to reduce the disparity in productivity between agriculture and other industries and . . . those engaged in agriculture should earn higher incomes enabling them to make a living comparable to those engaged in other industries." [5] To achieve the goals of the "new constitution" for agriculture, future government programs were to encourage and facilitate a growth in the scale of farm management and thus a system of viable farm holdings which could meet the rising domestic demand for vegetables, fruits, and various livestock products. Rice production was not regarded as an item of special consideration.

Nonetheless, even before the new "constitution" for agriculture had become law a significant change was also made in the criteria used to establish the price of rice. The food-control system was established in 1942, during a period of severe wartime food shortages.[6] A complicated administrative framework was created to completely control the flow of rice and other basic foodstuffs. However, by the end of the Allied Occupation and the recovery of agriculture production only rice continued under direct government control, although wheat and barley received indirect price support.

The Food-Control Law left the price at which agriculture products would be bought and sold entirely to the discretion of the government, operating within the broadest of policy directives. It was simply noted that producer prices would be established "by taking into account costs of production, general prices, and other economic conditions." [7] The consumer price,

5. *Agricultural Policy in Japan* (Paris: Organization for Economic Cooperation and Development, 1974), 42.

6. The official history of the food-control system is *Shokuryō Kanrishi* [History of food control] (Tokyo: Ministry of Agriculture and Forestry, Food Agency, 1972), I–IX.

7. Food-Control Law, Article 3.

on the other hand, was to be set in order to help stabilize the consumer's household budget "by taking into account household expenditures, general prices, and other economic conditions."[8] The criteria for setting the two prices were not the same, nor were the prices necessarily to be set at the same time. For budgeting purposes a special account was established and any deficit in buying and selling operations would have to be covered by funds from the general account.

Over the years a number of price formulas have been devised to translate these general goals into a concrete method of determination. During the 1950's various versions of a parity formula were used, but there was no commitment to keep farm incomes at "parity levels" with nonagricultural incomes. Indeed, no matter how much the parity formula was manipulated, by the late 1950's parity price indices were equal while the urban-rural income gap was increasing. In 1960, after almost a decade of extensive private and public debate, improvement in data gathering and analysis, and tinkering with various statistical methods, a new "income compensation–cost of production" formula was adopted.[9]

The unique feature of the formula was that the level of remuneration for family labor had to be substantially equivalent to average wage rates in manufacturing in order to guarantee "fair returns" to labor. Thus, if rice producers did not increase efficiency of production by labor-saving devices, the government purchase price would rise in order to compensate for the rise in wages received in manufacturing. Under the formula about 60 per cent of costs would be for labor and 40 per cent would be for remaining inputs.

The formula was used to compute the "standard price" only; the price offered the farmer varied according to quality as well as quantity of rice delivered. Additional subsidies were also offered: a bonus for early delivery was provided as an incentive to farmers to deliver their rice in September and October. Since the primary beneficiaries were farmers in the northeast regions of the country, a bonus was offered to farmers in western Japan whose rice strains generally had a higher yield than

8. Food-Control Law, Article 4.
9. See discussion in *Shokuryō Kanrishi*, III, 1–76.

varieties grown in Tōhoku, Hokuriku, and Hokkaidō. Another subsidy was given to farmers who contracted in the early summer to deliver a fixed amount of rice at harvest time.

The new formula marked the beginning of an explicit commitment on income compensation to rice farmers. Nonetheless, it did not follow that a high level of support would automatically be provided. The new formula structured the debate, but its specific application was open to interpretation and disagreement.

The Food Agency and farm groups did not agree on which households should be part of production surveys, how the surveys might be carried out, what costs should be included, and how the findings should be summarized. Thus there was no agreement on the actual cost of producing rice. Differences also continued concerning which urban incomes should be used as a basis for remuneration, how capital interest should be determined, what criteria were to be used to establish land rent, and which years should serve as the base years in the formula. Farm groups urged abolition of the urban-rural price differentials used in the formula to reduce producer prices and insisted that fringe benefits such as health insurance and unemployment benefits received by workers be part of the farmer's remuneration. Labor costs, interest on owned capital, and land rent represented, for most farmers, costs not paid out and therefore direct income. These elements were especially controversial and subject to yearly adjustment.

The Food Agency also asserted that the new formula would obviate the need for various subsidies to rice farmers. Farm groups insisted that the formula established only the standard price and that extra bonuses were required to guarantee the continued production of rice. Competent, technically proficient staff members of farm groups were able to compete with government technicians in analyzing rice prices, meaning that the "facts" of the Food Agency were subject to independent verification and disproof and enabling the farm groups to provide independent, informed advice to politicians who made final decisions. In short, within the technical boundaries of the new price criteria there was room to adjust, tinker, twist, and modify.

The principal government goal for agriculture after 1961 was formally expressed in the Basic Agriculture Law. But basic structural change is no easy matter and requires a period of transition and adjustment, except under extraordinary circumstances which permit a strong dose of authoritarian politics. Moreover, the opposition parties in Japan were militantly opposed to any amendments to the Agriculture Land Law of 1952, which severely restricted the amount of land any individual could own. Corporate ownership was also prohibited by the same law in order to protect the "democratic" results of the land reform.

In the face of constant political pressure from farm groups, politicians turned to rice prices. The country's food-control system was a handy, institutionalized mechanism which could be used to channel immediately subsidies to more than 60 per cent of the nation's farmers. Moreover, four broad features of rice-price politics combined to permit politics to take command for almost a decade: the rural basis of the LDP's electoral support, the nature of agrarian interest-group politics, the character of the decision process, and the issue itself. In brief terms, these features were manifested in the following way:

1. Rural areas were overrepresented in the LDP. This had two implications. In 1960 almost 90 cer cent of Japanese farmers produced rice and studies have shown that farmers in Japan are extremely sensitive to government price policies. Second, rural dietmen were party committee chairmen, leaders of the LDP, and cabinet ministers.

2. A powerful association of agriculture cooperatives could claim the membership of almost all Japanese farmers. Farmers were organized during the rice-pricing season by the cooperatives, whose administrative role was crucial not only to the workings of the food-control system but also for many other agriculture policies. The cooperatives also helped organize the local basis of LDP electoral support. Cooperative leaders as well as other farm-group representatives participated directly in the decisionmaking process. Moreover, there was little intracrop competition in agriculture and all the major farm organizations supported rice farmers.

3. Backbench, rural politicians meanwhile successfully pen-

etrated the decision process by going outside the formal institutions of party and government. Their participation was considered a reality, if not legitimate, not only by party leaders and cabinet ministers but also by high-ranking civil servants.

4. Since the final price for rice was decided outside the process of national budget-making, it was not subject to the constraints of incremental politics which affect other allocation decisions. A revenue surplus permitted a supplementary budget to cover losses in the food control special account.

5. The separation of consumer and producer prices institutionalized the absence of "countervailing power" which might have held prices down. The opposition parties pressed for higher producer prices than even most rural LDP dietmen were willing to support, and labor unions also supported high producer prices despite their demands for low consumer prices. The government's Rice Price Deliberation Council was dominated by high-price advocates.

6. The price issue itself was extremely malleable and the economic constraints on policy could be redefined somewhat each year. Moreover, the new price formula included an almost "automatic" guarantee of annual increases.

But if politics took command in the early 1960's there were also limitations and constraints on political behavior that began to narrow the option of choice. The process of decision is not a closed, autonomous system isolated from the economic changes which give rise to many political issues in the first place and under certain circumstances determine political outcomes.

In virtually all advanced industrial societies, the primary objective of agriculture policies is to improve the income status of a selected part of the population which chooses to remain in agriculture. But using prices as a means to maintain incomes often creates serious economic strains and ultimately places restrictions both on possible political decisions and on the ability of politicians to assist their voting supporters. In brief, using prices as a means of supporting farm incomes often results in (1) serious distortions in domestic prices and international trade; (2) large costs to consumers; (3) a drain on the public treasury and distortion of other agriculture policies; and (4) an unwanted expansion of output of a particular farm crop to the detriment of other crops for which demand is increasing. Most discouraging of all, there is little evidence that farm incomes are much improved by high-price policies in spite of the large costs to taxpayers and consumers.[10] When economic constraints become too severe for politicians to ignore, a change in practice and policy has to be considered.

During periods of policy adjustment and disequilibrium, groups and interests both inside and outside the formal institutions of government hitherto only indirectly involved in policy and decision become manifestly more concerned about goals and policy direction. The policy area received more time and sustained attention by policymakers, and public discussion and partisan debate becomes more lively. Attention was drawn to rice prices after 1966 because of the various institutional and economic interests adversely affected by prices and because of the obvious policy stalemate. The inaction of the government's Rice Price Deliberation Council (hereafter called "the Rice Council") and a prime minister determined to institute changes permitted other parts of the government to take initiatives. Advisory committees of the Ministry of Finance and the Economic Planning Agency as well as committees under the Prime Minister's Office could, with less political difficulties than the Rice Council, examine the various elements of rice programs and, more importantly, could draw up specific recommendations. Advisory councils with no pretense of "representing" all the various interests in the food-control system could deal with questions well beyond the issue of farm income, including the most basic question of all: Why was the government still in the rice business?

The purpose of this paper is to describe and analyze the political process through which rice prices have been determined during the past decade or so.

The Political Economy of Rice

The complexity and diversity of price decisions are reflected in the types of social groups, interests, and organizations which have a stake in their outcome. During the 1960's the following participants or interests were directly or indirectly concerned

10. Johnson, *World Agriculture,* chapter 1.

with the political decisions made during the annual rice-pricing season.

Rice Producers

In 1961, 55 per cent of all arable land was in rice cultivation, and the rice crop accounted for some 48 per cent of the total value of all agriculture production.[11] Of Japan's 5,718,000 farm households almost 5,221,000, or close to 91 per cent, cultivated rice. Among these 68 per cent, or some 60 per cent of all farm households, sold at least some rice to the government. While about 50 per cent of total production was concentrated in the "rice bowl" regions of Tōhoku, Hokuriku, and the northern parts of Kantō, all rural areas had a high percentage of rice farms.

The Japanese farm averages about one hectare in size, and most rice farms are even smaller. In 1962 about 77 per cent of the farms selling to the government were smaller than one hectare. The 3.6 per cent of farms larger than two hectares accounted for 18 per cent of the total amount of rice sold through official channels. The 35.6 per cent of farms smaller than one-half hectare could claim only 10 per cent of total government purchases, while farms between one-half and one hectare supplied 33 per cent. The income derived from rice farming thus had a differential impact. In 1961, 32.4 per cent of all farm households received no "official" income from rice. But 13.3 per cent reportedly relied completely on their rice sale for their agriculture income. Rice accounted for 50 per cent or more of total agriculture income for another 33.6 per cent of all rice farms.

Farm Groups

The National Association of Agriculture Cooperatives, popularly known as Nōkyō, is Japan's mammoth agriculture *zaibatsu*.[12] It is an incredibly complex, loosely knit, and unwieldy organization composed on the national level of three

11. The data on rice farming were taken from *Shokuryō Kanrishi*, III, 383–485, and from *Shokuryō Kanri Tōkei Nenpō* [Annual report of food-control statistics], various issues, published by the Ministry of Agriculture and Forestry.

12. The most comprehensive history of the Association of Agriculture Cooperatives is *Nōgyō Kyōdō Kumiai Seidoshi* [History of the system of Agriculture

economic federations, a central cooperative bank for agriculture and forestry, and, sitting uneasily on top of the whole system, a Central Union of Agriculture Cooperatives. The latter body is responsible for unifying cooperative interests by providing policy coordination and national leadership. These national organizations are linked to prefectural unions and then to some 7,000 local cooperatives, which altogether can claim the membership of practically every farm family in the country.

The network of cooperative facilities which laces the country has been used by the government since 1947 to collect almost all of the rice crop, bringing the cooperatives large service fees for collecting, packing, and storing rice. Moreover, the payment system for government-purchased rice through the central Nōkyō bank has provided sizable funds for other economic operations and has thus helped the local cooperative become the most important economic organization for all farmers.

Politically the cooperatives have always been closely affiliated with the LDP. A number of surveys have indicated that the great majority of cooperative leaders support the party. In addition, the cooperatives run their own LDP candidates. Robert A. Scalapino and Junnosuke Masumi report that in 1958, when changes in the price formula were being debated, 6 per cent of LDP members in the House of Representatives were cooperative officials.[13] A more recent study confirms the continuing importance of Nōkyō to the LDP.[14] Political endorsements and support are always difficult issues for such a diffuse organization, involving a delicate balance between national leadership and local autonomy. On both the national and the local level cooperatives endorse sympathetic candidates, including some Socialists, help organize the vote, and raise political funds. Scalapino and Masumi assert that, at least in the early

Cooperative Associations] (Tokyo: Nōgyō Kumiai Keiei Kenkyūjo, 1967), I–VII.

13. *Parties and Politics in Contemporary Japan* (Berkeley: University of California Press, 1962), 68.

14. *Jimintō* [The Liberal Democratic Party] (Tokyo: Asahi Shimbun, 1970), 47–73.

1960's, the cooperatives were "undoubtedly the most vital affiliation for the conservatives at the mass level." [15]

The annual Nōkyō rice-price struggle, which mobilizes farmers and cooperative officials from all over the country, is organized and coordinated by the Central Union. National cooperative leaders also sit on the Rice Council. The extensive network of communication and policy coordination between agencies of government and private organizations is part of the routine of public policy in industrial societies. The Japanese government has probably never made any major changes in agriculture policy without first consulting with national cooperative leaders.

The National Agriculture Committee System (Zenkoku Nōgyō Kaigisho) is an officially sanctioned, pyramidal structure of the National Chamber of Agriculture, prefectural chambers of agriculture, and local agriculture committees in cities, towns, and villages.[16] The system is an outgrowth of three administrative organizations, including the Agriculture Land Committees, set up during the Occupation to help "democratize" various agriculture policies being carried out during the period. Considerable subsidization by central and prefectural governments, limited elections by farm members, and close liaison with the government in helping to carry out various official policies give the committee system a strong public character. National Chamber leaders also sit on the Rice Council. The national and prefectural chambers claim to be an independent interest organization concerned with the welfare of all the nation's farmers. The chambers work with the Central Union of Agriculture Cooperatives in drawing up rice-price demands but are careful to maintain an independent stance. Members of the agriculture cooperatives sit on the board of directors of the National Chamber of Agriculture. In brief, the system is best perceived as a semi-independent subcontractor of the Ministry of Agriculture and Forestry.

15. Scalapino and Masumi, *Parties*, 90.
16. The best descriptive study of postwar farm groups is Mitsukawa Motochika, *Nōgyō Dantai Hattenshi* [History of the development of agriculture groups] (Tokyo: Meibun Shobō, 1972).

The All-Japan Federation of Farmers' Unions (Zennihon Nō-min Kumiai Rengōkai) is the country's only important farm union group and in the 1960's was closely aligned with the Japan Socialist Party and to some extent with the Communist Party as well. Whereas the cooperatives and the agriculture chambers view rice farmers an entrepreneurs or small business-men entitled to rent and other profits, the farm unions view the rice producer as a worker. Never able to compete with the cooperatives on the local level, the unions in the 1960's were nonetheless particularly successful in the prefectures of Ya-magata, Akita, Niigata, and Nagano, all of which are in the rice bowl. During the 1960's the annual rice struggle was ap-parently the only issue which really mobilized the unions into a national movement. The unions conduct their own local and national rallies and formulate specific price demands. Union members are more willing than a Nōkyō man to "capture" a cabinet minister or conduct a sit-in. Union leaders also sit on the Rice Council.

Three other small farm organizations should be mentioned, although they have not played a significant role in price deci-sions. The National Farmers' Alliance (Zenkoku Nōmin Dōmei) broke off from the Federation of Farmers' Unions when the JSP and the Democratic Socialist Party (DSP) split in 1960. It is, in effect, the rural farm organization for the moder-ate DSP. The National Farmers' General Federation (Zenkoku Nōmin Sōrenmei) is the political election organization for the Central Union of Agriculture Cooperatives. However, it claims independence from the cooperatives and does have local offices in about twenty prefectures. Finally, the All-Japan Rec-lamation Federation (Zennihon Kaitakusha Renmei) is a na-tional organization for farmers who have settled on land re-claimed for agriculture purposes. The importance of all three organizations is that they join together almost every year to jointly sponsor rice-price rallies in support of Nōkyō de-mands.

Market-Related Organizations

Official rice deliveries have been made through an elaborate system of designated wholesale and retail merchants. Until

1968, when the delivery system was greatly modified, there were fewer than 400 wholesale dealers and some 58,000 retailers, the local rice dealers from whom the Japanese consumer makes his purchase. Wholesalers and retailers are organized into national federations. These market-related organizations play no organized role in the politics of rice prices but have been mobilized whenever any changes in the system itself have been considered. They have representatives on the government's Rice Council.

Government Bureaucracy

Since it was established in 1949 the Food Agency has been the governmental hub of the food-control system. Over 20,000 employees are part of the agency, which has its headquarters in the Ministry of Agriculture and Forestry (MAF) and local offices throughout the country to help coordinate and monitor the national flow of rice. The size of the agency is one measurement of the government's involvement in the rice economy. The government price proposal originates in the Food Agency, is recommended to the minister of agriculture for modification and approval, and is then negotiated with the Ministry of Finance (MOF). The Rice Council is attached to the Food Agency, whose staff is responsible for supplying price data, cost surveys, and other economic information to serve as the frame of reference for council debate. The head of the agency invariably rises to the position of administrative vice-minister, the top civil service position in the ministry's bureaucracy.

Compared to other MAF agencies, the Food Agency has a reasonable amount of autonomy and leverage over agriculture policies within its jurisdiction; nonetheless, it is still a part of the MAF and government funds spent on rice come out of the ministry's overall budget. Moreover, the bureaucratic practice of frequent intraministry transfer of elite administrators has helped prevent excessive autonomy. Most of the Food Agency's "foreign policy" (external negotiations with other ministries and the LDP) is coordinated by the MAF under the administrative vice-minister and, of course, the cabinet minister.

The minister of agriculture must consult the Rice Council before a final price is determined. The council's mandate and role has changed since it was established in 1949, but its most general tasks are to point out problems concerning the food-control system, develop proposals to deal with new problems, and discuss alternative solutions. The history of its proceedings is a history of both rice policies and general agriculture policies.

The council's twenty-five members are appointed by the minister, and until 1968, dietmen, including opposition-party members, were selected. The council is expected to bring together the major interests concerned with the food system and nonpartisan experts in hopes that they can arrive at a collective judgment and a unanimous set of recommendations for the minister. Membership has been drawn from producer and consumer groups, former bureaucrats, especially from the MOF and the MAF, leaders of collection and delivery federations, and a variety of neutral sources, such as newspaper editorial writers, commentators, heads of research institutes, and academics, all of whom are collectively known as "men of learning and experience." Occasionally a prefectural governor is also appointed.

Membership turnover each year is minimal, although on occasion some of the so-called neutral members have resigned in protest over the council's operation. The council is certainly an assembly point for diverse views and suggestions not only concerning prices but also concerning the workings of the whole system. Meetings are frequently long and tense since collective agreement on any issue is difficult to achieve. The council cannot reflect the predominant views of the government because of its composition and because agencies of the government are themselves frequently divided. More often the council has served as a platform for partisan members to articulate their views before an attentive press. If the council has sometimes not been able to play a decisive role it is not so much because it lacks legal authority as because it lacks the political ability to bring all the conflicting interests together, balance them, and arrive at a compromise.

The Ministry of Finance is guardian of the public treasury and maker of the national budget. As such it is especially concerned with balanced accounts and the impact of increased prices on general price levels. It is also eager to make the setting of producer and consumer prices a part of the general budgetary process. Supplementary budgets were required every year during the 1960's because unanticipated costs resulted from producer price increases during the summer months. The ministry's concurrence is necessary before any final price decision is made and the finance minister participates in all major negotiations concerning the level of support to be given to producers.

The Economic Planning Agency (EPA) has not been as influential or as actively involved as the MAF and the MOF in price decisions. It is broadly concerned about price levels, wages, and general economic "rationality" in public policies. One of the EPA's advisory committees produced in 1967 the first major criticism of the food-control system; this criticism led to major modifications after 1968.

Political Parties

In 1960, when rice prices started their unprecedented rise, farmers represented the largest socioeconomic category of voters. Approximately 40 per cent of the Japanese electorate could be classified occupationally in agriculture or agriculture-related categories. This rural vote belonged overwhelmingly to the LDP. Moreover, voter turnout is much higher in rural than in metropolitan areas, and the basis of representation in the lower house greatly favors rural voters. The need for reapportionment has long been an issue in Japan; even before the massive migrations to the cities in the late 1950's, it was possible to elect a rural politician with only half the votes needed to elect a representative in certain metropolitan electoral districts.

It was thus axiomatic that the LDP needed the continued support of the farmers and that "feudal loyalties" or appeals to arcane notions of submissiveness to authorities would not suffice to keep their votes. One of the concrete benefits which could be offered was rice prices at a high enough level to help guarantee some kind of income parity with the urban blue-collar worker. The final rice price was always determined by LDP politicians in their role as cabinet ministers or members of a ruling party firmly anchored in rural areas. But it was never an easy decision and the pattern of disharmonies and political fissions which preceded each decision are a central focus of this paper.

The Japan Socialist Party (JSP) was not always directly involved in rice-price decisions. A relatively permanent minority with no widespread electoral support in rural areas, they nonetheless sought a variety of means for impressing the farmer that they were the generous champions of rural economic interests. Through the farm unions and also by participation on the Rice Council they persistently advocated higher prices than the LDP was ever willing to advocate or grant. Simultaneously the JSP advocated low consumer prices.

Involved Spectators

Although they are not at all monolithic, the large-scale economic federations such as the Japan Committee for Economic Development or the Federation of Economic Organizations have all taken their turn at lambasting high rice prices and the workings of the food-control system. The pervasive political influence of the business community is a widely accepted premise in the study of Japanese politics, although with some recent qualifications.[17] Clearly, "the voice of business" is heard in a variety of contexts, including the Rice Council, and had a measurable impact on rice policies in the later 1960's.

A great deal of news ink has been used to examine, denounce, and blast the "political price of rice" over the years. A select group of newsmen and agricultural economists have served on the Rice Council, which might account for the wide publicity given to rice policies and their frequent public analysis in the press.

Consumers and Taxpayers

The price of rice affected the average citizen in two ways. Rice is the most important staple food in Japan. In 1960 the household of the average urban worker still allocated some 10 per cent of its total expenditures for rice, and the percentage

17. See, for example, Gerald L. Curtis, "Big Business and Political Influence," in Ezra Vogel (ed.), *Modern Japanese Organization and Decision-making* (Berkeley and Los Angeles: University of California Press, 1975), 33–70.

was higher among the lowest income groups. While total demand was peaking, rice nonetheless remained an important household expenditure for all Japanese families. Deficits in the special account for food control had to be covered by appropriations from the national budget. The citizen also had an interest in rice policies as a taxpayer. Yet neither consumers nor taxpayers had anywhere near the organizational clout possessed by rice farmers. Moreover, the nation's large labor unions, such as the General Council of Japanese Trade Unions (Sōhyō), while favoring low consumer prices, also aligned with the JSP in support of high producer prices. Only consumer groups, like the Federation of Housewives (Shufu Rengōkai), really spoke out against high support prices.

In 1960 the food-control system was an amalgam of many formal and informal agencies and organizations created in different periods for different purposes and loosely related to each other through administrative allocations, hierarchical authority, collegial responsibility, division of bureaucratic labor, shared political interests, and mutual political support. Different parts of the policy and bureaucratic network could react to political and economic changes and demands with differing degrees of subordination and autonomy. In brief, it was a policy area as wide as economic society itself and one in which the distinctions between state and society were difficult if not impossible to draw.

Stages of Decision

Annual allocation decisions require continuity of practice. In Japan there is a reasonably systematic way of arriving at a choice. Certainly during the period under consideration no two decisions were made precisely in the same way. Nor were influences and pressures exerted uniformly. As in any political system, political power and influence in Japan is sometimes indirect and circuitous and manifested in complicated interpersonal and factional relationships. Nonetheless, there have been distinct patterns in the policy process which have been repeated over time. Although there is some danger in imposing too much clarity and finality on political behavior, the

162   Michael W. Donnelly

following stages of decision can be said to have repeated themselves rather regularly since the later 1950's.[18]

Definition of the Issue and Collection of Information
  The annual price decision begins in late March or so when
economic data are gathered and analyzed by the Food Agency
and the major farm groups. Price and cost indicators are carefully weighted. Economic "facts" deemed useful to win a political debate are incorporated into a neat body of "objective" indicators. The choice of data is extremely important since this
preliminary information describes the current state of the rice
economy and helps delimit the possibilities of later political
choice.
  The farm groups try to keep the issue narrowed to costs of
production and urban wage levels. The Food Agency is concerned with the formula and also with the effect of prices on
other economic variables: the state of supply and demand,
black-market and government prices, rice stocks, consumer
prices, the quality of rice, and other agriculture policies. The
Ministry of Finance is primarily concerned with deficits, budget
constraints, general price levels, international rice prices, and
other economic policies. The crucial differences over prices
and policies usually arise from differing economic interests and
political and organizational responsibilities. Farm groups want
to increase the price by narrowing the issue; the MOF places
the issue into the broadest macrolevel of national economic policy in the hope of preventing excessive increases.
  Of course, information collection involves more than gathering and analyzing raw economic data. The participants in the
decision process are well known to each other and so the "political mood" is evaluated as a prelude to tactical maneuvers. If an
election or cabinet change is forthcoming politicians seem more
ready than usual to seek higher increases. Factional in-fighting
around election time sometimes becomes a subtle part of the
decision process.

  18. A number of political scientists have attempted to conceptualize the political process in terms of stages of decision. The most seminal is Harold Lasswell, *The Decision Process: Seven Categories of Functional Analysis* (College Park:
University of Maryland Press, 1956).

Development of Alternatives

The Ministry of Finance is generally the first participant to suggest a price informally, which then is made known through deliberate press leaks. It is always the lowest possibility. The MOF is concerned less with a specific price formula than with overall budget constraints. Calculations are apt to be made backwards from available resources to specific prices. In the 1960's the supplementary budgets required to cover losses in the food-control special account were regarded as an unmitigated fiscal disaster by the guardians of the national treasury and so the Budget Bureau invariably took the initial position of advocating the "budget price" included in the current general account budget.

The National Association of Agriculture Cooperatives usually announces its demand sometime in April or May at a joint meeting of the central and prefectural unions of the cooperatives. The announcement indicates that the demand price drawn up at the central headquarters has received the formal blessing of prefectural and local cooperative officials although not necessarily all rice farmers. The National Chamber of Agriculture during the 1960's supported the cooperative position but was always careful to emphasize that its price was calculated from independent investigations. During the same period the farm unions announce their demands, which are always well above those of the other farm groups. A major reason for this difference in the early 1960's was that the unions first calculated labor remuneration on the basis of wages received in factories employing thirty or more workers. Later they shifted it to factories of one hundred or more.

By late May or early June two or three possible prices have been calculated and the process of decision reaches the vice-ministerial and cabinet level. The MOF and the MAF are rarely in automatic agreement, and consultation and negotiation at the highest bureaucratic level are necessary before agreement is reached. Agreement is required since a government draft proposal must be submitted to the Rice Council.

Information Dissemination and the Organization of Political Advocacy

The cooperatives' announcement of their demands is followed by mobilization of political support and preparation for demonstrations in Tokyo a few days before the Rice Council begins its deliberations. The rice-price struggle has always been a delicate internal problem for the cooperatives. Each year the local Nōkyō sets up centers where farmers who sell their rice to the government can meet to discuss economic and political issues and decide the level of support which should be demanded. Cooperative ideology insists that these local headquarters constitute the "mother body" of the struggle. In practice, technical skills, organizational and informational leverage, and the sheer advantages flowing from sustained interest and involvement in policymaking mean that while "form" is honored, key decisions are made at the central level. However, in the 1960's there were incidents of "pressure from below" which forced unplanned tactical and strategic changes. Once demands are announced, prefectural and local groups are used to organize letter-writing campaigns, demonstrations, petitions, and fund raising to help finance the travel costs of demonstrators. Tactics vary each year but the fundamental goal is to inundate the government and political parties with postcards and people. Demonstrations of this kind display national unity and political solidarity. This stage of decisionmaking ends with demonstrations in Tokyo by farm groups and meetings of the Rice Council.

Narrowing the Choice

Since the amalgamation of the conservative parties in 1955, no cabinet or agriculture minister has ever been able to make the administrative rice-price decision without extensive consultation with, and the approval of, the LDP. The party has never hesitated to revise or reject cabinet decisions. The party's role has been to give farmers more than what the government is ready to offer but less than what farm groups demand. But it is never an easy decision. The first issue is deciding how to decide.

About two months or so before the final decision, a choice is made by the party leadership either to set up a special investigation committee under the Policy Affairs Research Council (PARC) or to use a joint committee drawn from the permanent divisions of the party. A special committee permits party leadership more flexibility in appointments and thus a chance to broaden the spectrum of party interests in the committee's work. A joint committee which includes nonagricultural divisions would accomplish the same goal.

Whichever route is chosen the committee usually does not begin serious work until after the Rice Council has made its formal recommendations to the minister of agriculture. Since the committee is usually composed of fifty or more members, a subcommittee does the actual work. Government bureaucrats, farm group leaders, and other LDP members are invited to present data and recommendations. The process is not unlike the investigations of an American congressional committee prior to drawing up a piece of legislation.

In the 1960's, parallel to formal party action an ad hoc group of politicians, which came to be known as the "Viet Cong," organized informally to harass and pressure party leaders by enthusiastically supporting the demands of the cooperatives. During this period their number reached 150 dietmen. There was constant communication and coordination among these party stalwarts, members of the formal party machinery, and cooperative leaders in the exchange of information and the working out of compromises. Party negotiations are tense and frequently LDP headquarters are surrounded by farmers conducting sit-ins. The party is tolerant of the sometimes rough and disorderly tactics of its more unrestrained members. The ritualized display of rural political power is a prerequisite for politicians who need the relatively quiescent acceptance by producers and consumers of a price which usually does not satisfy anyone's expectations.

Usually the party's target price emerges from the special committee and the issue moves next either to the PARC deliberation commission or to a joint PARC–Executive Council meeting. On occasion the special committee reports only to the three party leaders, and after consultations the party-government meetings begin. If the target price requires formal party approval the negotiations often become acrimonious and tense. Newspaper photographs have shown low-ranking dietmen who had joined the "Viet Cong" crowded alongside news reporters, an ear tightly pressed to the doors of the closed PARC–Executive Council meeting. It is reported that rural politicians inside the room did not hesitate on these occasions to speak in voices loud enough to be heard by those listening in the hallways. Frequently, cooperative leaders roam the hallways keeping a careful eye on the actions of the dietmen from rice-producing electoral districts.

Finally, after a long debate, including an occasional convocation of all LDP Diet members in a General Meeting of Both Houses (Ryō Giin Sōkai), a party target price is established. In the 1960's it sometimes took more than ten days of maneuvering, bargaining, and cajoling before a final decision could be made.

The Final Politics of Choice

Government and party negotiations bring to a close the rice-pricing season. The government side is represented by the minister of agriculture and forestry, the finance minister, the chief cabinet secretary, and usually the head of the EPA. Their immediate relevant constituents include the prime minister, other members of the cabinet, and the ministries or agencies which they head. Advocates of high prices perceive the cabinet as either weak or helpless victims of political party obstinance. The LDP team is represented by the party's secretary-general, the chairmen of the PARC and the Executive Council, the chairman of the party's special rice-price committee, and the head of the subcommittee which drew up the initial party target price. Their immediate constituents are the PARC and the Executive Council. Lurking not so quietly in the background are rank-and-file dietmen from rural areas.

All participants are members of the same political party. But differences of as much as ¥1,500 per koku (150 kilograms) of rice have separated them. Round figures and specific elements of the price formula are discussed. Although a good deal of informal interaction and discussion precedes formal meetings, it is rare that one meeting will result in agreement. Tentative agreements usually have to be ratified by the party and the prime minister. Such agreements are sometimes overruled by the party even though they had the strong endorsement of the prime minister. Finally an agreement is reached. The price is reported in banner headlines and accompanied by unanimous editorial chagrin that once again prices have been determined in an opportunistic and excessively political manner.

From High Prices to Superabundance: Rice Prices 1960–1968

Of course, to describe politics in terms of "stages of decision" tends to make political behavior and policy debate appear orderly and mechanical. An examination of price decisions in the 1960's shows how unmechanical and messy the political process could sometimes become. The following section traces the changing debate and political process concerning rice prices as it evolved from domination by advocates of high prices to political polarization and deadlock.[19] The deadlock was broken after 1968 as a consequence of a rice surplus and an enormous drain on the public treasury. The solution to the "rice problem" did not remove the rice-pricing season from political life in Japan, however, and rice prices are still determined in much the same way as described above. But a number of key decisions after 1968 did sharply change the nature of the government role in the political economy of rice.

The First Big Push: 1961

The big political push to increase the producer price began in 1961 in the context of a reasonably favorable economic environment. The agriculture parity index had increased by more than 6 per cent from the previous year, and average wages in

19. This section is based on the following sources: newspapers and various periodicals especially *Ekonomisuto* [The economist]; interviews with participants, including journalists; *Nihon Nōgyō Nenkan* [Japanese agriculture yearbook] (Tokyo: Ie no Hikari, annual), various issues; *Nōgyō Kyōdō Kumiai Nenkan* [Yearbook of the Argiculture Cooperative Associations] (Tokyo: Ie no Hikari, annual), various issues; *Shokuryō Kanrishi*, especially vol. III (Prices) which covers the period 1955–1964; Nōrinshō, *Shokuryō Kanri Geppō* [Monthly report on food control] (Tokyo: Ōkurashō Insatsukyoku, monthly), various issues.

manufacturing were up by almost 10 per cent. The Ministry of Finance, with an eye on mounting deficits and a reluctance to permit an increase in consumer prices, advocated keeping the increase to no more than ¥100 per koku. But as early as April, the Food Agency began to calculate a tentative price with the new formula and was soon reconciled to a ¥400 to ¥500 increase. It was also the first rice decision following the enactment of the Basic Agriculture Law and so the "mood" in the LDP was to show the farmer that the party was eager to keep its income support commitment.

Nonetheless, Prime Minister Ikeda along with Finance Minister Mizuta Mikio and Agriculture Minister Sudō Hideo appeared hopeful that they could keep the increase around the ¥500 range. A special Consultative Committee on the Problem of Rice Prices composed of "cabinet-level" policy experts was established by party leaders to determine the LDP target price. Akagi Munenori, a former agriculture minister, was selected as chairman. The usual delicate balance of factional affiliation, seniority, and official party position was honored. While most were agriculture policy experts of some kind, a few politicians known to advocate "more rationality" in rice policies, including Aichi Kiichi and Takami Saburō, were also appointed, so that considerations beyond rice prices might be a direct part of the discussions and debate.

A ten-man subcommittee headed by Shigemasa Seishi, a former administrative vice-minister of agriculture, was responsible for the major part of the committee's work. During the final days of the rice-pricing season the subcommittee met almost daily. Most of its members were regarded as agriculture experts. None was elected from a major urban electoral district and most were from areas which produced a good deal of rice. Four members also served on the MAF's Rice Council: Uchida Tsuneo (Yamanashi), Kuranari Tadashi (Nagasaki), Ōnō Ichirō (Niigata), and Shirai Isamu (Yamagata). Yamanashi and Nagasaki have not been major rice areas; Niigata and Yamagata are in the heart of the nation's rice bowl. These four men played a major role in determining the government draft to the Rice Council on which they would later sit in judgment.

Two days after the LDP organized to deal with the rice decision, the agriculture cooperatives announced their demands for a 14 per cent, or ¥1,509 per koku, increase. The Democratic Socialist Party (DSP) quickly endorsed the demand in a formal pronouncement delivered to Ikeda, Mizuta, and Sudō. In the same week, the farm unions demanded a 28 per cent increase. The JSP supported a more moderate demand and made it clear that they would oppose any government attempt to link considerations of supply and demand with prices. The avoidance of sharp political disagreements with the socialists was a major political tactic of Prime Minister Ikeda and so the positions taken by the two opposition parties became part of the LDP's calculus of decision.

This was the last year that the government and the LDP reached agreement prior to convening the Rice Council. Given the schedule of decision, the cooperatives held their Tokyo demonstration in late June, just as party-government negotiations were about to begin. It was a small but rather clamorous affair which brought together some 3,000 official delegates from all over the country. During the meetings a good deal of grass-roots hostility was especially directed at the Central Union of Agriculture Cooperatives. At one point during the proceedings a band of some twenty farmer-delegates raced onto the stage, wrenched the microphone from a speaker, and denounced the weak-kneed and "ambiguous" leadership. When demands for a more militant movement struck a responsive chord in the audience, the central and prefectural leaders who made up the steering committee were startled and clearly embarrassed. The meeting was followed by demonstrations in the streets of Tokyo and a decision to convene an "Emergency National Convention to Achieve Rice-Price Demands" two weeks later.

The second cooperative convention again brought more than 3,000 delegates to Tokyo. They were joined by some 120 politicians who waved and smiled benignly from the speakers' platform and declared their support of the farmer's "rightful" demands. Upon adjournment the demonstrators hoisted placards and banners which marked their demands and once again marched through the busy streets of the capital. When the march broke up near the National Diet Building, the Nōkyō men dispersed into teams to make their pleas directly to the politicians elected from their districts. The halls of the Diet officebuildings swarmed with petitioners.

The LDP subcommittee met almost daily from June 30. Public hearings were held so that cooperative leaders could make their pleas. After the full committee went into executive session the agriculture minister made the first government offer of ¥10,707.50. This was quickly rejected. Although never stated officially, it appears that the committee target price was ¥11,000. The rejection included a demand for greater capital-depreciation allowances, higher allowances for packing costs, and restoration of advance-offer subsidies, which the government had decreased from ¥100 to ¥50 and was trying to eliminate entirely. A second government offer increasing the price by ¥219 was also rejected.

In the meantime a group of LDP dietmen from the rice areas of Tōhoku and Hokuriku demanded that before any final government decision, the secretary-general convene a General Meeting of Both Houses. Clearly the group believed that in a showdown the high-price advocates in the party would be shown to be in the majority.

A third government offer raised the price to ¥11,002.50. After a half-day of informal consultations this offer was accepted at a formal party-government meeting held at a downtown hotel, a location perhaps reflecting the slightly irregular nature of the policy process. The LDP was represented by the three party leaders plus Akagi and Shigemasa. The government side was represented, as usual, by the ministers of finance and agriculture and the chief cabinet secretary. However, this agreement was rejected when it was brought back to a joint meeting of the PARC and the Executive council for approval. After long debate the same negotiators were instructed to insist once again that the ¥100 subsidies for "advance offers" be restored.

At the next party-government meeting, Mizuta and Sudō were annoyed at this recalcitrance and quickly rejected the demand. Negotiations were broken off, and after the government team consulted with Ikeda it was decided to convene the whole cabinet. Meanwhile, a General Meeting of Both Houses was held at LDP headquarters to explain the state of negotiations. The formal party position received unanimous endorsement. Late in the afternoon at an emergency cabinet meeting the government finally capitulated. The initial government price had been increased by ¥345 and the government draft was readied for the Rice Council.

Protracted political negotiations had delayed the council's opening meeting by two days. The "neutral" members were particularly outraged at the way in which the government draft had been drawn up and bitter that the price had in effect already been decided. The hearings were tense. The only general agreement was that the government draft was not satisfactory: the producer representatives and their supporters thought the price too low; some consumer and neutral representatives decided the price was too high.

A unanimous report was impossible. Instead, the report contained parallel but conflicting reasons for finding the government draft deficient. All members, however, did agree that the consumer price should not be increased during the current calendar year. After the council submitted its report, Ōkawa Kazushi, chairman of the council and one of Japan's most eminent economists, announced his resignation. Five other "neutral" members also resigned in protest over the functioning and role of the council. On the same day the government draft became the official decision.

There are difficult technical problems involved in any attempt to determine what the market price of rice would have been if the free market had been at work. But according to Food Agency calculations, the increase in producer prices in 1961 to ¥11,052.50 per koku placed the producer price above the market price for the first time since 1942. The income provisions which were built into the formula and the widespread political support for high prices meant that only extraordinary circumstances would permit any cabinet or prime minister to bring the price back into line.[20]

20. *Shokuryō Kanrishi*, III, 431.

The Ascendancy of High-Price Advocates: 1962–1964

The nature of the debate and the process of decision remained more or less the same during the next three years. Farm groups continued to demand a price well above anything the government was willing to provide. The cooperatives and other farm groups made it quite clear how and why they differed with the Food Agency in their interpretation of the price formula and continued to bombard politicians, bureaucrats, large economic organizations, consumers, and the mass media with economic evidence in support of their cause. The severely critical treatment accorded the farm groups' demands in the press was an especially vexing problem which alternately angered and depressed cooperative leaders.

In 1962 political tactics of mobilization were refined, in part, because of a threat to the system itself. Shortly after the producer price was established in 1961, Kōno Ichirō, the new minister of agriculture and a powerful faction leader in the LDP, embarked on a personal, somewhat quixotic attempt to move the rice system to indirect control. An MAF committee organized to examine Kōno's proposal and other issues relating to decontrol had not yet made its formal report by the spring of 1962. Although there was little support for Kōno, the cooperative leadership was nonetheless deeply concerned. Demonstrations in Tokyo in the early summer of 1962 were preceded by a massive letter-writing and signature-gathering campaign aimed at demonstrating the political weight of the rice-price constituency. Over 10,000 delegates were then mobilized to attend the national rally prior to the convening of the Rice Council. Following patterns established in the past, formal and informal meetings were held with various members of the LDP and the rally was concluded by a street march. Many delegates remained in Tokyo until the final decision.

Plans for decontrol were shelved in late 1962, but the cooperatives did not rest quietly. In the next two years four million postcards and petitions were delivered to politicians and cabinet ministers. In 1963 some 260 dietmen or their political secretaries were recorded as attending the Nōkyō rally. During the street demonstrations many politicians marched alongside their rural constituents as they made their way through the streets to the Diet buildings. More senior leaders quietly introduced petitioners from their district to other senior members of the party. Each year the number of LDP politicians willing publicly to support the ad hoc intraparty group of "Viet Cong" dietmen grew steadily.

If the function of the Rice Council was to create ultimate agreement from initial disagreement, then it did not do its job very well. Despite changes in the council's format and operations, little unanimity was achieved between 1962 and 1964. Following the resignation of the six neutral members in 1961 it was necessary to change the order of events in the annual decision. No longer was it possible to query the council following party-government negotiations. Negotiations had to take place after the council made its report. To do otherwise was to court unneeded political flak. This change placed the schedule of decision in an established public sequence and provided a handy target date for the farm groups to muster their forces in Tokyo.

Two other changes were made. In principle the proceedings of the council were to be private. But over the years this regulation was gradually relaxed, at first to accommodate the personal secretaries of council members, then to give open access to the press, and finally, in 1957, to admit representatives of producer and other groups. In effect, the debate became public. Since opposition politicians as well as LDP members served on the council, serious political differences appeared exacerbated by the presence of an audience and the possibility of capturing headlines in the news. This audience-playing infuriated the academic and other neutral members of the council, who preferred a more judicious, sober, and detached examination of the problem. Beginning in 1962 the proceedings were once again made private.

It was also decided to broaden the debate in the council by making the questions much less specific. Too much specificity about price levels and other matters encouraged specific answers which then limited the range of political bargaining. Henceforth, when specific calculations were drawn up, they were for "reference" only and not meant to solicit specific approval or disapproval. It was recognized that the council was able to perform a representative rather than an advisory function and that the wrong advice would probably only cause additional embarrassment concerning the "politics of rice."

Debate in the council continued to be rent by very fundamental differences concerning which economic considerations were most central in the calculation of prices. Producer representatives and politicians approached the issue in terms of adequate farm income. Representatives of consumer groups stressed the market system, consumer prices, and the quality of rice. The neutral members attempted to place prices into a broader context of supply and demand, mounting deficits, and the goals of the Basic Agriculture Law, which, in theory, remained the constitution of agriculture policy. Under such circumstances the council could barely eke out a brief report of vague, usually contradictory admonitions let alone anything remotely resembling policy advice or general guidelines. Because of serious disagreements over prices and policy, and widespread political concern over the types of decisions which were to be made, the LDP politicians had the greatest stake in the final decision and it was they, therefore, who made it.

Each year the LDP established a special intraparty committee to handle the rice decision after the Rice Council had made its recommendations. The size and composition varied but it always had an overwhelming "agricultural bias." A new chairman, always a senior member of the party identified with agricultural interests, was appointed each year. A subcommittee of ten to fifteen members handled most of the work. While the membership changed annually, there was never a total turnover. Party members with close ties to the major farm groups were selected, as well as former high-ranking MAF bureaucrats. Party members such as Ōno Ichirō and Shirai Isamu of the government's Rice Council also served on the subcommittee.

The special committee was given authority by the LDP leadership to establish the party's target price. The subcommittee would usually begin its work the day after the Rice Council submitted its report to the minister of agriculture. By this stage in the process the competing figures and accompanying economic evidence were well known. After a few days of hearings with farm group leaders and bureaucrats and a good deal of informal discussion, the subcommittee went into closed session to draw up recommendations which were accepted, although not without occasional controversy, by the full committee. The handling of extra subsidies was especially sensitive and revealed the delicate regional differences in rice farming. When the full committee decided its position the three party leaders were notified, and while a formal meeting of the PARC and the Executive Council was not always necessary before negotiations with the government began, official party approval was, of course, necessary before any final decision was made.

The producer price increased by jumps of 10, 8, and almost 14 per cent during this three-year period, 1962–1964, paralleling to some extent the rise in wage levels in other sectors of the economy as well as price increases for fertilizer, costs of machinery, and the like. As long as income compensation at urban wage levels remained a central part of the price calculation sharp increases were inevitable in a period of rapid industrial growth and growing labor shortages. In this sense, the political pressure exerted by farm groups or the encroachment of the LDP into the administrative decisionmaking process cannot be isolated as the most significant explanation of high prices. Still, there is no question that politics did matter.

One somewhat artifical way to measure the influence of the LDP on the final decision is to compare three prices: the first government offer, the party's target price, and the final price. Table 5–1 does this for the years 1962–1964.

Table 5–1. Rice-price offers compared to final decisions (in yen per koku)

Year	First government offer (A)	LDP target price	Final rice price (B)	Increase of B over A
1962	12,004	12,500	12,177	173
1963	12,785	13,500	13,204	419
1964	13,888	15,616	15,001	1,113

Source: Computed by the author.

The first offer was already a compromise between the MOF and the MAF, with the EPA also being consulted. The final decision was less than the party's target price but more than what the government initially calculated as an appropriate level of support. The problem of anticipated reactions makes it hard to assess the real intentions of the government, but empirical evidence suggests that the cabinet gave in grudgingly and only after it felt certain that a sizable majority in the party supported increases. This was especially so in 1964 when the party insisted on an extra ¥550 subsidy to compensate for loss in rice income due to a shortfall in production.

Annual situations reveal more tangibly the party's strength. In 1962, after two days of protracted discussions the two sides had narrowed their differences to ¥25. When the government side refused to make a final compromise, negotiations were broken off. The party leaders returned to LDP headquarters and convened a joint meeting of the PARC, the Executive Council, and the special rice-price committee to reconfirm the party's stand. A General Meeting of Both Houses was also held to demonstrate unanimous support of the party's position. The cabinet negotiators were obviously surprised by this unanticipated maneuver and decided that only Prime Minister Ikeda could make the final decision. In the face of overwhelming party approval Ikeda had no choice but to grant the final ¥25-per-koku increase.

In 1963, the government side remained intransigent after initial negotiations had begun. The three party leaders convened the rice committee and then a joint meeting of the PARC and the Executive Council to reaffirm the LDP position. No matter what his previous stand on rice prices might have been, once an LDP politician became a cabinet minister he generally would oppose any large increases in prices. In 1963, Finance Minister Tanaka Kakuei, elected from a rice-bowl area in Niigata Prefecture, was extremely stubborn in the face of party demands. A final compromise was possible only after Prime Minister Ikeda and the rest of the cabinet expressed willingness to go along with an increase of ¥419 per koku.

As indicated earlier, the 1964 decision was made in the context of a slight shortfall in domestic production and on the eve of a party presidential election. It was widely reported in the press that high-price advocates threatened to cast blank ballots unless the producer price was substantially increased. Certainly there was less political conflict than during previous years. The government quickly raised its initial offer of ¥14,252, and after one day of bargaining the final compromise of ¥15,001 was reached. It included a special subsidy of ¥550 per koku. The participants also agreed that the formula for setting the price should be examined once again.

Controversy over Subsidies and the Price Formula: 1965

One of the most controversial aspects of rice policies involved the political subsidies (*seiji kasan*) added more or less regularly to the formula price each year as a result of LDP political pressure. Journalists and editorial writers, as well as almost every other critic of the party, invariably seized upon these additions as the embodiment of excessive politicization of the policy process and excoriated the party for what was perceived as a blatant robbery of the public treasury for narrow political benefit.

In 1964, when the ¥550 emergency subsidy was granted, party leaders and the cabinet agreed that a subcommittee of the Rice Council should be convened to re-examine the technical criteria used to establish prices and recommend a clearer, less ambiguous standard with which decisions could be made. The income-support commitment was not to be abandoned; what was wanted was a firmer standard of judgment which would eliminate some of the more malleable aspects of current methods of calculation. A brief summary of the debate reveals contrasting views concerning rice farming and the role the government was expected to play.

The ten-man subcommittee included consumer and producer representatives, neutral members, and one dietman each from the LDP and the JSP. The subcommittee met during the winter of 1964–65 to deal with a wide variety of issues related to consumer and producer prices. However, no conclusive agreement was reached on most items. In the final report three possible revisions of the formula for income compensation and cost of production were offered for consideration.[21]

The first suggestion was simply to continue with the "cumu-

21. For a detailed analysis of this controversy see Sakurai Makoto, "Beika Santei Hoshiki" [Formula for the Computation of Rice Prices], *Nōgyō Kyōdō Kumiai*, July 1967, 42–57; see also *Shokuryō Kanrishi Geppō*, August 1955, 30–36.

lative method," revising only the calculations for land rent. A second "composite income method" with producer group backing was less a concrete proposal than a vague idea aimed at fixing a price so that the composite income of rice farmers was in balance with the income of urban blue-collar workers. Since no concrete suggestions were forthcoming concerning how this was to be accomplished technically, it was not treated as a real alternative by the Food Agency.

The third recommendation was an "index method." The aim was to calculate the price in terms of changes in a set of clearly defined economic indicators using 1964 as the base year. The indicators would include elements already part of the "cumulative method," but the criteria for setting the producer price would be less susceptible to tinkering since the indicators would not be subject to redefinition each year. Farm groups adamantly opposed such a formula, alleging that it was an attempt to permanently freeze low prices. The Food Agency, however, favored such an automatic means of calculation, although they agreed that it should be applied for only three years, after which it would be re-examined.

The cooperatives were also considering the fundamental goals of rice prices, and in early spring revealed a new "balanced family budget" formula which had only been indirectly suggested during the hearings of the rice subcommittee. In a word, they proclaimed that the goal of rice prices should be an overall annual income balance between farm workers and urban blue-collar workers rather than simply a balance in hourly or daily remuneration. Their arguments concerned the nature of agricultural labor and the rightful beneficiaries of increased agricultural productivity.

The cooperatives noted that agricultural production is more than simple physical labor in the paddy field. It is also a managerial process involving planning, study, learning of new skills, and proper administrative organization. To perceive rice farming as similar to hourly factory work was to distort the entrepreneurial elements of farming and to misunderstand the organic nature of production, which requires persistent attention and care. The cooperatives insisted that it was arbitrary and unfair that the current rice price did not take into direct account these necessary elements of the farmer's labor.

The inevitable problem of underemployment was also acknowledged. Farm labor does not observe a regular eight-hour day but fluctuates according to the production cycle, weather, and other natural phemonena. Slack periods should be recognized as a necessary social and economic part of the production process.

A third issue concerned the appropriate beneficiaries of productivity increases. A formula which provided for a balance in hourly compensation meant that as productivity increased and the number of labor hours required to produce rice declined, income derived from rice farming would also automatically decline. This might be fair if the farmer could easily expand his unit of production or find supplementary employment outside of agriculture. But this was difficult for many rice farmers, especially in the areas of Tōhoku and Hokuriku. The cooperatives thus insisted that a new method for determining prices had to be contrived which would return to the farmer appropriate rewards for increased productivity. Otherwise, even if hourly remuneration was in balance, the overall rural-urban income gap would widen further. Government reaction to this new concept of rice prices was, to say the least, negative.

In order to achieve this goal, the cooperatives contrived a rather complicated method of computing a price which would balance the annual household expenditures of rice farmers with household expenditures of urban blue-collar workers. The demand price was calculated at ¥18,986, or 20 per cent higher than the previous year and 26 per cent higher than the previous official price. The National Chamber of Agriculture went along with this new concept of rice prices, although with misgivings and doubt.

The farm unions, on the other hand, continued with their basic formula. The inclusion of profits, interests, and high land rents smacked too much of capitalism and was contrary to the socialist view of the farmer as rural worker. But to provide a basis for higher prices the unions now demanded that labor costs be adjusted to the wage scales in factories employing more than one hundred workers. Thus their demand of ¥22,500 was well above the price advocated by the two more conservative farm groups. These conflicting conceptions of agricultural labor further exaggerated the differences between the groups and made political cooperation in demonstrations and other activities on the national level even more difficult. In 1965 a number of meetings were held between the Central Union of Agriculture Cooperatives and union leaders to explore possibilities of joint efforts. But ideological and political differences and the close ties between the unions and the JSP made efforts for a united struggle impossible.

When the Rice Council was convened in 1965 six different versions of the index and cumulative formula were provided for consideration. The discussions ranged from what the appropriate reimbursement for packing costs should be to whether or not the food-control system should be modified. But when it came time to draw up a unified opinion it was clear that fundamental differences still existed over the purpose of rice policies. Producer representatives and politicians advocated higher prices and supported the cooperatives' demands and their new price formula. The neutral members and the consumer representatives preferred the index method of calculation and a consequent lower level of support. The result was another divided report reflecting the two views.

The process of decision within the party and the final negotiations with the government were reasonably orderly. The special committee appointed to determine the party's target price was composed mostly of reappointments from the previous year. Ueki Kōshirō (Fukui), a former MOF bureaucrat, was made chairman of the committee. Koeda Kazuo (Okayama), who had close ties with the National Chamber of Agriculture, was made head of the subcommittee.

The initial government offer was ¥15,526 based on the index method. The party responded with a demand for ¥16,884 based on the cumulative method of calculation. The final compromise took less than one day. The price was set at ¥16,375, a 9.2 per cent increase over the previous year. The official version of the price made it an index-method calculation and included a contract subsidy for ¥255 per koku. It was clear that no matter what the formula, subsidies would continue to be part of the final decision.

The Scope of Conflict Widens: 1966–1967

The scope of conflict in the annual setting of rice prices has always been rather wide, as measured by the number of participants and the multiplicity of organizations and institutional interests which have been part of the decisionmaking process. Nonetheless, during the first half of the 1960's the organizational and political bias in the process permitted high-price advocates to influence the outcome heavily. While roll calls were never taken to determine unambiguously who was for and who opposed higher prices, there is little question that a majority of the LDP supported the political modifications made each year in the formula price. It was not the work of a small coterie of rural zealots.

However, as government deficits mounted and consumer prices increased, the political controversy surrounding the annual decisions became more intense. From 1957 through 1964 the consumer price had been increased only once. But with steady producer increases the government was forced to increase consumer prices in 1965 and again one year later. Each increase was accompanied by growing criticism of LDP interference in the policy process. The Rice Council became completely polarized and unable to make any recommendations concerning producer prices. The political debate grew more intense as the scope of conflict widened to include segments of the government whose participation heretofore had only been intermittent and peripheral. The policy process during the next two years can be perceived as a further "socialization" of the political conflict as external economic constraints on higher prices became more difficult to ignore. The first challenge came from the Economic Planning Agency. In 1966, an EPA advisory committee directly and unequivocally admonished the government to hold down if not freeze rice prices. This report received wide publicity, no doubt in part because it coincided with a common theme found on the editorial pages of the nation's press.

Shortly after the EPA committee made its recommendations, Prime Minister Satō announced that the government had no intention of raising consumer prices that year. He also proclaimed his belief that producer and consumer prices should be established at the same time. The press made it clear that Satō was determined that the "index method" would be used to set producer prices and that no political additions would be tolerated.

As a further means of holding down the price, the LDP under Secretary-General Tanaka organized a joint committee from the permanent PARC divisions to determine the party's target price. Members of the price and economic policy committees were included on the joint committee to tone down the agricultural bias in its deliberations and recommendations. Akagi Munenori, chairman of the PARC, was appointed head of the joint committee. Akagi served on a number of occasions as minister of agriculture during the 1960's and was known as a reasonably sympathetic ally of rice farmers. Tanaka also indicated that because the Diet was in session party members should not return to their electoral districts to attend rice-price rallies sponsored by farm groups.

The cooperatives and other farm groups responded by organizing their most militant campaign to date. Indeed, the threat of a government attempt to hold down prices persuaded cooperative and farm union officials to try once again to unify their movement by conducting joint demonstrations in Tokyo. It proved impossible on the national level. However, in a number of prefectures in Tōhoku and Hokuriku, local cooperatives participated in demonstrations with the local farm unions. Farm unions also organized with local labor unions in a few prefectures to forge a worker-farmer alliance in support of high producer prices. The labor unions favored low consumer prices and demanded that the government cover the inevitable deficit by spending less on military programs.

During the week before the Rice Council met, farm groups held four separate demonstrations in Tokyo. The Nōkyō rally was attended by more than 16,000 delegates from all over the country. In spite of Tanaka's admonition, some 200 dietmen, including LDP members, appeared at the rally. Another 100 politicians, including five cabinet ministers, sent their representatives. The farm union rally attracted over 12,000 and followed by one day the first large rally ever conducted by the union in western Japan.

Demonstrators clogged the streets and entranceways to the building where the Rice Council began its deliberations. It was clear after five days of debate that the council would have a difficult time producing any kind of report. While many neutral members supported the index method, the press reported that producer members and most of the politicians adamantly opposed any mention of the index method in the final report. After five days of debate it was recognized that no report was possible. The agriculture minister was called at 5:00 A.M. on the sixth day and notified that for the first time in its history the council had no recommendations. The JSP quickly called for the cabinet's resignation.

The negotiations moved immediately to the LDP subcommittee. At the same time a small army of 2,000 or so farm group spectators pitched their tents outside LDP headquarters and began a vigilant sit-in to await the final decision. A target price of ¥18,105 was offered to the whole rice committee and was revised upward to ¥18,559, including a ¥225 subsidy. Without any formal party approval this became the LDP position, and Tanaka and Akagi, along with two members of the committee, were authorized to enter negotiations with the government.

The first meeting was held at LDP headquarters. Outside the building the voices of shouting farmers and politicians could be clearly heard. The "Viet Cong" dietmen were especially vocal during the final days of this season. They claimed to include over 200 LDP members, basing the claim partially on signatures of support collected at LDP headquarters by the demonstrating farmers. At one point during party-government negotiations some 60 of the farmers' more enthusiastic LDP supporters barged into the room where the bargaining was taking place to make their pleas or threats directly. Afterward they announced to the demonstrators outside that "we have just stormed the fourth floor . . . soon the final barrier will be destroyed," a display of support which the press attributed to the knowledge that a general election would be held within six months.[22]

Despite party demands, Prime Minister Satō was determined to keep the price below ¥18,000. When initial negotiations did not produce a compromise, discussions were broken

22. *Asahi Shimbun,* July 5, 1966.

off and representatives from both sides visited Satō at his home, where a tentative compromise of ¥17,875 was reached. However, when Tanaka returned to receive formal party blessings, the bargain was denounced; a formal joint meeting of the Executive Council and the PARC refused to approve Satō's decision.

A brief cooling-off period was needed. After two days of informal discussions a final decision was made. The previous compromise price was increased by ¥2 permitting the party to claim an "incremental" victory over Satō. This made the total price increase 9.2 per cent over the previous year. More important, ¥5 billion was allocated separately to be distributed to rice farmers as a means of encouraging increased production. Rice farmers and their political allies had forced Satō to compromise.

In 1967 cooperative leaders agreed with the LDP and Kuraishi Tadao, the new minister of agriculture, that, to the limits permitted by serious political differences, the rice price should be decided in a "mood of consultation." The cooperatives would not discard their mobilization tactics; but they would try to complement political demonstrations and petition democracy with a public relations campaign to win understanding if not support from the financial world, mass media, major consumer groups, and the MAF. Strategy was established earlier than in previous years and close liaison was maintained with prefectural and local organizations from the beginning of the year.

The government had decided in December to increase the consumer price by 15 per cent beginning in October. This was an attempt to place a ceiling on the subsequent producer price decision. But a more ominous challenge concerned the composition of the Rice Council. In 1964 a special investigation committee on government administration had admonished that the presence of politicians on government advisory committees was a violation of the principle of separation of powers. The LDP agreed to remove politicians from most administrative committees. Given the previous inability of the council to draw up a recommendation on rice prices it was clear that the Satō cabinet would try to remove the politicians from the council.

Another disturbing element for the cooperatives was the quiet but growing split with the National Chamber of Agriculture concerning the "income balance" method of calculating rice prices advocated by Nōkyō. The two organizations had always managed to demand the same level of support. But in early spring the head of the National Chamber admitted to the press that he believed rice prices should be placed within the context of other agriculture commodity prices as well as agriculture policy as a whole.

In a mood of compromise the Central Union of Agriculture Cooperatives held a widely publicized meeting with leaders of the Japan Committee for Economic Development, one of the nation's largest business federations. The cooperative leaders also met with the heads of the major national newspapers. The impact of these consultations is difficult to measure. It is doubtful that views were changed as a result of face-to-face discussions. Certainly the news coverage of the talks showed very fundamental differences. The financial leaders made it clear that the country needed cheaper rice and saw no reason why more rice should not be imported. But the voice of the financial world had been heard before. Cooperative officials also met several times during the spring with Food Agency personnel. Some rather candid exchanges took place not only about the level of price supports but also concerning the future of the food-control system itself. In May cooperative officials also visited Prime Minister Satō to discuss prices.

A decision had to be made by early June concerning the Rice Council. The JSP opposed the removal of dietmen, whose presence gave them a useful opportunity to embarrass the conservative government and demonstrate their support for rice farmers. After a good deal of internal LDP consultations, Prime Minister Satō and Minister of Agriculture Kuraishi decided that since the Diet was in session it would be prudent to postpone a decision. They clearly feared that the JSP would disrupt the legislative routine. This vascillation, however, outraged the neutral members of the council who were anxious to bid farewell to all politicians. According to the press, only after Kuraishi promised that politicians would be removed the following year did they agree to serve once again.

In 1967, for the second consecutive year, the Rice Council was paralyzed and unable to make a recommendation. Three possible prices were included in the materials submitted, and debate went well beyond the virtues and shortcomings of each. Differences related to more fundamental issues concerning the outlook for supply and demand, price and structural policies, deficits, productivity, and the future of Japanese agriculture. But when it came time to draw up the final report the division in the council concerning price formulas persisted. When producer group representatives and JSP members insisted that only the "cumulative method" be recommended in the final report, the council adjourned without any recommendations.

Chagrined at this outcome, LDP leaders and the relevant cabinet ministers decided it was best to handle the decision with as much dispatch as possible. A joint committee composed of members from the party's Agriculture and Forestry Division and its Investigation Committee on Basic Problems for a New Agriculture Policy was established to determine the party's target price. Aichi Kiichi was appointed chairman of the committee and also head of the subcommittee. The committee had already decided to use the cumulative method advocated as a compromise by the farm groups. After one all-night session a target price of ¥19,536 was established.

When the party began its hearings, reports in the press indicated that the MOF was adamantly opposed to increases which would put the price above ¥19,200. However, at the recommendation of Aichi, who was one of the most respected policy experts in the party, the higher subcommittee price was quickly endorsed. Negotiations with the cabinet took less than one day. The final price of ¥19,521 was only ¥15 less than the initial LDP target price.

Considering the usual disarray in the policy process prior to the final politics of choice, it was one of the most automatic decisions the party and government had been able to achieve. No doubt, the swiftness of the final decision was prompted by a desire to avoid deadlock and further political antagonism between party and cabinet. The price was 9.1 per cent higher than the previous year. The same percentage increase for three consecutive years provided evidence that perhaps the best indicator of what will happen in any year is what happened the previous year—assuming, of course, that all variables are constant. In 1968 they were not.

The Rice Problem of 1968

Rice production in 1967 was the highest in the recorded history of the country, totaling almost 14.5 million metric tons. Total demand and average consumption of rice had begun to decline in Japan after 1962. However, except for bumper crops in 1955, 1959, and 1960, domestic supply did not provide all the rice consumed. Indeed, cold weather and heavy rains contributed to shortfalls in production in 1963–1965, creating a minor mood of scarcity. But production recovered in 1966 and the record crop of 1967 began an accumulation of unsold rice which reached 7 million metric tons by 1970. More than any other factor, the ability of the Japanese rice farmer to produce rice on such a scale redefined the rice-price problem. But there were other factors as well.[23]

In 1959 the transfer payments from the general account budget to the special account for food control were only 8.8 per cent of the MAF budget; by 1968 these were 40.6 per cent of the MAF budget and almost 5 per cent of the national budget, taking funds away from other agriculture policies, putting a strain on other economic policies, and representing a dubious allocation of national resources. In part, the deficit existed because the government did not pass on to the consumer all production and administrative costs, but it grew as well because the total amount of rice handled through the control system had increased markedly during the 1960's, creating additional storage and handling costs.

Another problem related to who was actually benefiting from high rice prices. The income compensation–cost of production

23. A number of articles and books have been written about the rice problem in the late 1960's. Most useful for this study were: Ogura Takekazu, *Shokkan Seido wo Kangaeru* [Views on the food system] (Tokyo: Ie no Hikari, 1973); *Shinkyokumen ni tatsu Shokkan Seido to Jishu Ryūtsūmai* [New aspects of the food-control system and the autonomous rice market] (Tokyo: Kokkai Toshokan, 1970); *Nihon Nōgyō Nenkan*, 1969; Kondō Yasuo (ed.), *Nihon Nōgyō Nenpō* [Annual Report on Japanese agriculture] (Tokyo: Ochanomizu Shobō, 1968) Vol. 17; *Chijō*, June 1968.

formula certainly helped support the income levels of some
rice farmers; but this support was skewed in favor of the larger
farms. According to government statistics, in 1968 the average
remuneration for family labor time in rice farming was ¥2,794
per hour.[24] During the same year, the average hourly wage
received by a regular worker in the manufacturing sector in an
enterprise employing five or more workers was ¥1,653. Thus
labor remuneration for rice farming on an average hourly basis
was some 60 per cent higher than average urban wages as
defined above. However, few rice farms were full-time enterprises. Indeed, probably close to 80 per cent of Japanese rice
farms provided 150 days or less of full-time employment each
year.

All farms did not benefit equally from the income-support
program. Thirty-nine per cent of all households selling rice
farmed land smaller than 0.5 hectare, but these farms accounted for only 10 per cent of the total government-
purchased rice crop. Farms between 0.5 and 1 hectare sold 29
per cent. The remaining 23 per cent of farms accounted for
the balance of rice purchased by the government (61 per cent).
Especially noteworthy is that the 5 per cent of farms of 2
hectares or larger sold 25 per cent of the marketed rice.
This group of farm households, concentrated especially in
Tōhoku, Hokuriku, Hokkaidō, and Kita Kyūshū, benefited most from high prices. Smaller farms, especially those of 1
hectare or less, were mostly part-time and relied on supplementary nonfarm income in order to keep up with the rising
standard of living taking place steadily, although unevenly, in
the country.

Price policies were also in direct contradiction to pressures
for import liberalization. The price of rice increased after 1955
until it was at least twice and perhaps as much as three times
the price of rice on the international market.

One of the major goals of agriculture policy since 1961 was
to encourage farmers operating very small farms on a part-
time basis to leave agriculture so that those who remained
could expand their scale of management to become "viable

24. Ōshima Kiyoshi, *Kome to Gyūnyū no Keizaigaku* [The economics of rice
and milk] (Tokyo: Iwanami Shinsho, 1970), 120.

farms" capable of providing an adequate income without heavy reliance on government subsidies or nonagricultural income. Many critics of the food-control system argued that high prices discouraged this out-migration.

Furthermore, since the passage of the Basic Agriculture Law the MAF had encouraged the production of vegetables, fruits, livestock products, and other agriculture crops for which demand was increasing. But rice was the most profitable crop for the Japanese farmer to grow, with the exception of mandarin oranges, and "structural" policies did not provide enough incentive for farmers to begin cultivating crops for which demand had increased. Indeed, it could be argued that with the remarkable technical and mechanical advances made in rice cultivation during the last fifteen years, rice required less attention than other crops and was therefore well suited to part-time farming.

The food-control system had been created because of critical shortages in wartime and a consequent need for the government to intervene in the market in an attempt to prevent price gouging, hoarding, and excessive profits, and thus to help insure a reasonably "fair" allocation of basic staple foods. However, by 1967, even though rice was still officially "rationed," a black market at the consumer level was thriving. Especially in the large metropolitan areas, rice dealers repolished standard rice and added higher-quality rice in order to improve the taste. This was then sold to the consumer who was willing to pay the extra price for better-tasting rice. With superabundance, official allotment of rice became an administrative nightmare.

Not all of the above problems were traceable to excessively high prices. But price policies were certainly not irrelevant. Producer prices nearly doubled in seven years. The MOF believed them to be at least 20 per cent too high. Consumer prices increased as a consequence and critics were quick to point out that higher consumer prices put an upward pressure on prices of other agriculture commodities as well as on general price levels, which in turn helped open the way for higher wage demands during the spring labor offensive. There is considerable room for doubt concerning such simple notions of causality, but it was clear that prices were higher than what they should be in a time of abundance.

It is difficult to discern a clear rice-pricing season after 1967; the issue dominated the political agenda for over a year. It was a foregone conclusion in September 1967 that consumer prices would rise because of deficits in the food-control special account. But the price increase would take place in the context of oversupply and growing stock accumulations. The consumer price was never determined in the context of massive political mobilization, an obdurate and demanding LDP, and the general hoopla and disarray that surrounded the setting of producer prices. The LDP was consulted, but discussions were much more informal since most rank and file politicians were willing to let the cabinet bear the responsibility. The Rice Council was consulted but managed always to make a final report even though the very elements that made the decision on producer prices so difficult found their way into the debate when the council met to discuss consumer prices.

After four days of discussion in 1967 a majority of the council voted to approve the 14.4 per cent increase in consumer prices. During the next months every major daily ran a series of articles examining the food-control system and called for revisions, modifications, and fundamental changes not only in price policies but also in the system itself. While immediate and outright abolition was not considered with much seriousness, the press made it clear to the reader how much the program was costing the consumer and the taxpayer. Faulty bookkeeping, bureaucratic waste, a rampant black market, uneconomic monopolies, and other "ills" of the system were detailed. One article wryly warned that the rice farmer would next demand remuneration for his sleeping time if it included a dream about labor in the paddy field.[25]

The nation's big-business federations also called for a price freeze and restoration of elements of the "free market." These were not just *pro forma* or casually issued public declarations. The most widely discussed proposal from the financial world was issued by the Japan Committee for Economic Development in December.[26] A long and expertly researched document

25. *Asahi Shimbun*, October 4, 1967.
26. For the various proposals see *Shinkyokumen*, 15–29.

based on many months of investigation by a specially appointed committee, it analyzed the rice economy and called for the establishment of an indirect system of control within two years, including specific steps on how it could be achieved.

In the same month Minister of Agriculture Kuraishi announced the record crop. A week later the press reported that the MOF was studying a plan for a system of indirect control as a means to solve the rice problem. In such a system, the government would buy rice at an established minimum price but the producer would be free to sell elsewhere if higher prices were offered. A maximum consumer price would also be established, and authorized rice dealers would no longer have a monopoly on selling operations. In effect, this plan would have returned rice policies to the system of floor and ceiling prices used in the 1930's. Finance Minister Mizuta also announced the policy of an "integrated budget" and abolition of supplementary budgets passed each year to help cover deficits in the food account. An integrated budget would make price decisions part of the annual budgetary process. It would also directly link producer and consumer prices so that if producer prices were increased, then consumer prices would also be raised to cover whatever deficit might be incurred if it had not been anticipated in the general budget. It was meant to be a policy of balanced budgets in the food-control special account.

In January 1968 politicians and representatives from consumer and producer groups were removed from the Rice Council. In their place a "neutral Rice Price Council" composed of nine newsmen, seven academics, and six former government officials was established. After the previous two years of stalemate, Prime Minister Satō and his cabinet were determined to create a council that would recommend changes. The JSP and producer groups were outraged although little was heard from consumers. In Diet proceedings during the spring the JSP persistently badgered cabinet ministers concerning the change, but with the backing of his cabinet and party leadership, Prime Minister Satō would accept no compromise. Interest groups were offered the opportunity to consult with the LDP's rice committee but this was nothing new.

In March, Tanaka Kakuei was again appointed chairman of the LDP's rice committee. A membership of fifty-six dietmen from both houses made it the largest special committee to date. Included were many of the party's most determined high-price advocates. Nonetheless, the selection of Tanaka as chairman was widely interpreted as an attempt by the party leadership to create as much party discipline as possible during the rice-pricing season.

Throughout the spring the MOF, the MAF, and the EPA held separate discussions concerning future rice policies. But while press reports indicated that various alternatives were being examined, no responsible leader including Satō was willing to announce what changes were being contemplated. No doubt a bureaucratic and political consensus had not yet taken shape. Then too, with a House of Councillors election scheduled for early July, LDP leaders and the cabinet did not want to create excessive concern in rural rice areas. In the middle of the election campaign, the LDP officially declared that the party would "preserve the nucleus of the food-control system." Satō also insisted that it was much too early to discuss modifications in the system. However, following the election (in which the party maintained its strength), Finance Minister Mizuta, EPA Director Miyazawa Toshio, and the new minister of agriculture, Nishimura Naomi, each revealed their plans for dealing with rice prices and the food-control system.

The finance minister was first. The prestigious Finance System Deliberation Council had recommended that the government restrict rice purchases, freeze the producer price, and make supply and demand considerations a central part of the producer price formula. Finance Minister Mizuta quickly endorsed these recommendations and added that measures should also be adopted to cut back rice production, establish elements of a "free market" in rice, and return to the goals of the Basic Agriculture Law of 1961. EPA Director Miyazawa strongly urged that every effort be made to determine the producer and consumer prices at the same time.

Nishimura made the MAF position clear in a personal policy statement to top-ranking MAF bureaucrats in the middle of July. He called for "integrated agriculture policies." For the first time since Kōno Ichirō, a minister of agriculture and forestry had formally admitted that the time had come to consider major modifications in the system.

Meanwhile, a producer price had to be set. The party's rice committee began sessions in June by inviting producer and consumer groups, academics, economic federations, and bureaucrats from the various concerned ministries to present their views concerning prices and the system. But no matter how large the official committee might be, it could not accommodate the number of dietmen who were willing to show their support for the farm groups' demands. In early June the ad hoc, informal, and, according to Miyazawa, "illegal" Rice Price Countermeasures Conference, or "Viet Cong," was organized under the chairmanship of Matsuura Shūtarō. Before a final price was set some 200 LDP dietmen publicly supported the position taken by the ad hoc group. But it was the last year the group reached such high numbers.

The rice-price struggle in 1968 was the most tumultuous during the period under examination. The cooperatives used the same techniques of mobilization as in the past and held three large demonstrations in Tokyo. But the organization was on the defensive and did not seem able to respond directly to the challenge to the system itself. When the party was pressed by the cooperatives to explain its pre-election promise to maintain the "nucleus" of the system a joint party-government statement declared the government would: (1) insure the future production of rice; and (2) purchase a sufficient amount of rice to permit adjustment of supply and demand.[27] Rank and file dietmen were not directly consulted before this policy statement was made.

The Rice Council met on July 24 amid a sea of protesting farmers, farm union members, and Nōkyō men. It was asked to consider both consumer and producer prices in the context of mounting deficits, unwanted stock accumulations, and disarray in the market. The government documents proposed a 2.9 per cent price increase, a low level of support which would never have been proposed when politicians and producers served on the council. Debate was lengthy and attention was focused on the issues deemed important by the government bureaucracy responsible for the system, rather than simply on pricing methods. The final report, the longest ever

27. *Ibid.*, 36.

produced by the council, showed that Nishimura had selected the right people. In summary the council recommended: (1) Changes in producer and consumer prices should be interrelated and determined together. (2) The rice farm of average productivity should gradually become the standard household used in price computations; the consumer price should move closer to the appropriate cost price; deficits should be dealt with immediately. (3) The producer price for 1968 should be determined by the income compensation–cost of production formula, but recent changes in supply and demand, deficits, and price levels should also be taken into account.[28] The council also admonished the government to examine rice production levels in light of "integrated policies" and urged that necessary amendments be made to the food-control law to permit the infusion of the market mechanism.

The issue quickly moved to the LDP, but it was three weeks before the party and the government were able to make a final decision. The first government offer was about 3 per cent higher than the previous price and based on the cumulative method of calculation but modified by changes in the definition of the "marginal farm," land rent, and capital-interest returns. These modifications were less important than the level of support. After two days of discussions, an initial figure of ¥20,905 was recommended to the whole committee. This figure was denounced by a number of committee members, and rather than make an ultimate decision, the committee deferred to the Executive Council where support for a higher price was overwhelming. The party negotiation team was thus instructed to start with a ¥21,000 target price.

During the ensuing days of negotiation, bitter denunciations were privately and publicly exchanged, a coke bottle was smashed in anger during an Executive Council meeting, the party leadership attempted parliamentary maneuvers to outflank high-price advocates, the more energetic Viet Cong dietmen threatened to take physical action, and the party counterthreatened to impose official censorship if such action occurred. Some LDP dietmen spoke of offering a no-confidence resolution in the Diet against the cabinet and a few

28. See *Shokuryō Kanri Geppō*, September 1968.

even mumbled aloud about leaving the party. But after a number of formal and informal meetings the cabinet team, with Prime Minister Satō looming large in the background, budged only a little. In a sudden joint press conference the three cabinet ministers, without first notifying the party, announced the government's final stand of 5 per cent. One more negotiation produced a 5.5 per cent compromise, which again was declined by the party. On July 30 the final decision was postponed until after the special meeting of the Diet scheduled to end on August 10.

Ten days of informal negotiation during the Diet session helped produce a final decision. Prime Minister Satō repeated in the Diet his intention of moving toward modification of the system. But eager to make a final price decision as soon as possible, the cabinet finally agreed to a compromise figure of ¥20,640, or a 5.9 per cent increase over the previous year. An additional subsidy of ¥6 billion for "staggered deliveries" was added to make the real increase about 6.4 per cent. A month later, when the neutral Rice Council met to consider the consumer price, the government was pressed to move even faster in restructuring the control system in order to make it more "flexible" and better adjusted to the current circumstances of rice production and marketing.

The Aftermath

The rice problem in 1968 generated a new examination of the food system in light of the Basic Agriculture Law of 1961. It was widely recognized that rice problems were not to be solved simply by tinkering with price formulas. More basic changes were required. After producer and consumer prices were set in the summer and early fall of 1968, the government, the LDP, and the major farm groups all set to work to formulate new approaches which might help restore a balance both in the rice economy and in overall agriculture policies.

An autonomous or "semicontrolled" market was officially established in 1969 when the Diet approved an amendment to the Food-Control Law.[29] The farmer was thus able to sell his

29. For a description of the market changes see Mochida Keizō, "Sengo Beikoku Shijō no Tokushitsu" [Special features of the postwar rice market], *Nōgyō Sōgō Kenkyū* 26 (August 1972), 1–44.

rice directly to designated dealers, which were mostly local co-operatives, without any government inspecting, measuring, or price-setting. The flow of rice was still part of an overall system monitored by the government but price formation was freed from control, a change designed to reduce the amount of government purchases and to improve the quality of rice by permitting consumer preferences to be more freely expressed. The volume in this market increased from 860,000 metric tons in 1969–70 to 1,960,000 metric tons in 1971–72.

In 1969 and again in 1970 the producer price was not increased. But there was no total cut-off of government funds. In 1969 a special bonus of ¥22.5 billion was distributed to producers for fertilizer, agricultural chemicals, and other farming aids. The subsidy amounted to a price increase of slightly over 2 per cent. In 1970 another subsidy of ¥23.8 billion was provided as an incentive to grow rice of better grades. This was approximately a 2.7 per cent increase in price. The price differences between the five grades of rice were also narrowed. Despite subsidies, the government claimed that the price had been frozen for two years. Farm groups agreed.

A provisional crop-diversion program was also introduced in 1969 with a 10,000 hectare target and incentive payments of ¥20,000 per 0.1 hectare of diverted paddy fields.[30] However, as a result of the low incentive payments and the late announcement of the program, less than half the target of 10,000 hectares was diverted. A much larger program was implemented in 1970 aimed at reducing rice output by one million metric tons. Incentive payments were also increased. While the program achieved its limited goal of reducing the amount of land in rice, some 78 per cent was left fallow and only 22 per cent was diverted to other crops. Leaving land fallow in a system of agriculture where land is relatively scarce and other crops in short supply meant a substantial loss of national resources. A new long-range program was established in 1971 to make the transition more rational.

The amount of rice purchased by the government was also restricted starting in 1971 as a result of a second amendment to

30. For these changes see *Agriculture Policy in Japan*, 62–64.

the Food-Control Law. The national limit was set at 7.6 million metric tons in 1971–72 and 7.95 million metric tons in 1972–73. The quota is allocated to each rice producer on the basis of past sales, target quantities of rice reduction, and so on.

Until March 1972 wholesale and retail prices of rice were regulated by a control ordinance which fixed ceiling prices. This ordinance was abolished so that price formation would be determined in accordance with the quality and quantity of rice. However, rice at a "standard price" was still available to consumers through official distribution. Other minor modifications were made in marketing policies, including abolition of the registration system between wholesalers and retailers so that rice became available at department stores and other large outlets. Bonuses were also continued to give producers an incentive to market a higher quality of rice, for which demand had increased.

A principal explanation for the above changes was simply the state of the rice economy. Change was also possible because the effective locus of power within the conservative governing establishment was moved outside the annual rice-price decision process. Initiative on prices and policies was returned to the bureaucracy and to the agriculture division of the PARC, which maintained close liaison with the Food Agency and the MAF. Of course, the LDP was involved in the various modifications of the Food-Control Law, but these modifications were a matter of government routine rather than an answer to political mobilization and demonstrations by farm groups. Of course, the cooperatives did not accept the changes passively. Indeed, the transition was possible in part because the LDP, the MAF, and the cooperatives continued to maintain close liaison and cooperation. The autonomous market was structured so that the cooperatives continued to retain their privileged position in the rice market. Producers and consumers were returned to the Rice Council in 1969. Politicians were not.

These modifications and changes in the rice economy, however, did not bring an end to the rice-pricing season. This will remain as long as the government stays in the rice business. Thus the stages of decision outlined in this paper remained, but in 1969 and 1970 under the determined leadership of

Prime Minister Satō, the government was able to limit increases to special subsidies. Indeed, in the face of the specific need to reorient agricultural policies, the pressure for high prices from the party was not as intense as it had been in earlier years. In 1970 all the opposition parties as well as farm groups were adamantly opposed to an additional year of frozen prices. But power of decision was firmly entrenched in the cabinet and party leadership, and party discipline was reasonably maintained.

Certainly the change in policies affected aggregate farm income. The growth in agricultural income per farm household averaged 12.4 per cent per year from 1960–61 until 1967–68.[31] Subsequently, however, this increase slowed to 3.3 per cent in 1968–69 and 0.4 per cent in 1969–70. According to a report on agriculture policy in Japan by the Organization for Economic Cooperation and Development, this stagnation was caused in particular by frozen rice prices and reduced rice output.[32] Also, the index of producer prices for farm products as a whole rose about 7 per cent per year through the 1960's while prices paid by farmers for agriculture requisites rose at a much slower rate of about 3 per cent. After 1968–69 prices of farm products grew at a much slower pace, and by 1970–71 prices paid by farmers were increasing faster than prices received for agriculture products. Again, a major reason for this was the stagnation in rice prices and the program to cut back rice production.

The rice price did not stay frozen. In 1971 and 1972 the average producer price increased by modest increments of 3 per cent and 5 per cent to reach ¥22,384 per 150 kilograms. But in 1973, when the purchasing unit was changed to 60 kilograms, the price increased by 15 per cent and in 1974 by a whopping 37.4 per cent, making 60 kilograms of rice on the average worth ¥13,615. A good deal of this increase was due to the high rate of inflation which hit the Japanese economy after 1971. The rice price was still set according to the income compensation–cost of production formula and there is no question that costs and wages had increased during the early 1970's. But the rice farmer had not yet become the forgotten man of the

31. *Ibid.*, 26.   32. *Ibid.*, 26.

ruling party and rice prices still served as a means to help support farm incomes.

Thus while rice output had been reduced, it still remained the political commodity par excellence of Japanese agriculture. The food-control special account was still running a substantial deficit and consumer prices were well behind producer prices. In 1973 rice-related programs still accounted for 35 per cent of the MAF budget and almost 4 per cent of the general account budget.[33]

Conclusion

The extremely complicated and subtle interplay of political behavior and economic environment is a central issue in the study of politics. Rice-price politics during the 1960's can be seen as a political struggle over the power to define economic constraints on price decisions. The ability of high-price advocates to restrict the economic environment to comparative income standards opened the way for high prices. But had Japan not experienced an unprecedented period of economic growth and government revenues not increased as much as they did, permitting a supplementary budget, prices would almost certainly not have risen as fast as they did. Of course, it is possible to argue that without rapid industrial growth, rice prices would not have had to rise so fast since the economic decline of agriculture would not have been so rapid. Regardless, high rice prices represented an attempt to help ease some of the economic and political strains which are part of the decline in the economic importance of agriculture in advanced capitalist societies.

Certain consistent features in the rice-pricing process provided opportunities for the LDP and the farm groups to increase the price. Although the final decision was made by the cabinet, the process itself was rather pluralistic in character. Among the more salient features, the following are noteworthy: (1) the units participating in the decision process were roughly equal in power and so had to bargain with each

33. Data furnished by the Food Agency, Ministry of Agriculture and Forestry.

other; (2) there was fundamental disagreement concerning the goals of rice prices; (3) while the range of possible choice was not unlimited, there were many possible choices; (4) not only were clientele groups consulted but their members participated in the policy process; (5) consensus was required before a decision could be made because participants were not hierarchically arranged and power was widely dispersed; (6) there was an unusual amount of public information concerning the dynamics of the process, if not about the exact details of the various negotiations prior to decision.

When prices were more or less frozen, the policy process unquestionably was less pluralistic, in terms of the locus of effective power. LDP leaders and the cabinet were able to impose party discipline. But this was possible less because of a sudden shift in the distribution of power than because the economic constraints on decisions had changed drastically. Moreover, once readjustment of sorts had been established, the process of price decisions continued to manifest the same general pluralistic character it had shown in the past.

6. Pollution and Policymaking

Margaret A. McKean

As a densely populated and highly industrialized society, Japan suffers from severe pollution, perhaps the worst in the world. Even though pollution is often seen as a very new problem faced by the most industrialized societies, Japan has had occasional outbreaks of pollution ever since it began its economic take-off in the Meiji period.[1] But it is in the postwar period that Japan has experienced unrelenting and widespread pollution that has had detrimental effects on both production levels (particularly in agriculture and fishing) and human health.[2]

The Development of Pollution as a Political Issue

Both critics and defenders of the role of industry in Japan's pollution problems agree that pollution has been seriously exacerbated by the nature of Japan's rapid postwar economic growth. Japan has experienced one of the highest ratios of investment to consumption ever known, with an average of 35 per cent of GNP reinvested from 1960 to 1969, and most of this investment has gone into the expansion of productive capacity, continually propelling the further growth of GNP.[3]

1. The best-known case of pollution in the prewar period was at Ashio copper mine from about 1890 on. See Fred G. Notehelfer, "Japan's First Pollution Incident," 351–84, and Alan Stone, "The Japanese Muckrakers," 385–408, both in *The Journal of Japanese Studies* 1 (Spring 1975).
2. For statistics on the economic costs of pollution, see Kankyōchō, *Kankyō Hakusho 1972* [White paper on the environment, 1972] (Tokyo: Ōkurashō Insatsukyoku, 1972), 15.
3. James Morley, "Economism and Balanced Defense," in James Morley (ed.), *Forecast for Japan: Security in the 1970's* (Princeton: Princeton University Press, 1972), 24.

Such high rates could not have been maintained if Japanese business had indulged in the luxury of investing in nonproductive items, including, for example, pollution-prevention technology.[4] Small and medium-sized firms, many of which are highly polluting manufacturing concerns, normally could not afford even rudimentary prevention equipment.[5] Similarly, government expenditures have been channeled into public works to promote industrial expansion, rather than into facilities which might have alleviated pollution.[6] The rising standard of living and the emergence of a consumer economy has further compounded pollution problems.[7]

It is not merely the rapidity with which Japan has expanded its productive capacity which has exacerbated the pollution problem. The pattern and distribution of industrial capacity is also significant. During its growth, Japan placed special emphasis on heavy industry, particularly steel and petrochemicals, which release unusually complex pollutants. Moreover, to run this industrial giant, Japan's energy consumption per unit area is very high: in 1970, Japanese GNP per unit of level area was twelve times that of the United States. Most of this energy has been imported, largely in the form of heavy sulfur oil.[8] Finally, to combat the social imbalances created by extremely rapid ur-

4. See Hashimoto Michio, *Kōgai wo Kangaeru: Yori Kagakuteki ni Yori Ningenteki ni* [Thinking about pollution: more scientifically and more humanely] (Tokyo: Nihon Keizai Shimbunsha, 1970), 9; Matsubara Haruo, *Kōgai to Chiiki Shakai: Seikatsu to Jūmin Undō no Shakaigaku* [Pollution and regional society: the sociology of livelihood and residents' movements] (Tokyo: Nihon Keizai Shimbunsha, 1971), 86–113; Miyamoto Ken'ichi, *Kōgai to Jūmin Undō* [Pollution and the residents' movements] (Tokyo: Jichitai Kenkyūsha, 1970), 24–47; and Tsuru Shigeto, *Gendai Shihonshugi to Kōgai* [Modern capitalism and pollution] (Tokyo: Iwanami Shoten, 1968), 1–79.

5. Ui Jun, *Kōgai no Seijigaku: Minamata Byō wo Megutte* [The politics of pollution: on Minamata disease] (Tokyo: Sanseidō, 1968), 194.

6. For the debate over investment priorities, see "Indices of National Welfare," *Japan Quarterly* 18 (July–September 1971), 260–63; and Ken'ichi Miyamoto, "Local Self-Government and Local Finance," *Developing Economies* 6 (December 1968), 587–615.

7. Hashimoto, *Kōgai wo Kangaeru*, 9; Miyamoto, *Kōgai to Jūmin Undō*, 28; and Ken'ichi Miyamoto, "Japan's Postwar Economy and Pollution Problems," a paper presented to the annual meeting of the Association for Asian Studies, San Francisco, March 1975, 15–29.

8. John W. Bennett, Sukehiro Hasegawa, and Solomon B. Levine, "Japan: Are There Limits to Growth?" *Environment* 15 (December 1973), 7.

banizaton, the Japanese government constructed new bases for heavy industry in rural and semirural areas all over Japan, and the unforeseen effect of this policy was the sudden introduction of large-scale pollution damage into formerly unaffected areas.[9]

Clearly, Japan has achieved its status as an economic superpower only with enormous costs, the most tragic of which have been the diseases that afflict human beings. The best known of these is mercury poisoning, which results from eating contaminated fish. Methyl (or organic) mercury attacks the central nervous system and gradually kills the brain cells, turning the affected areas into a black spongy mass. The disease can attack very slowly, or it can kill in a matter of weeks. Methyl mercury can also accumulate in the placenta of an apparently healthy pregnant woman, causing massive brain damage to the fetus. Two companies have been most clearly responsible for methyl mercury poisoning: Shin Nihon Chisso Hiryō (Chisso) in the city of Minamata, Kumamoto Prefecture, and Shōwa Denkō in Niigata Prefecture. *Itai-itai* ("ouch-ouch") disease in Toyama Prefecture appears to be the result of long-term cadmium poisoning, which causes massive neuralgic pain, gradual decalcification of the bones, skeletal deformation, and extreme susceptibility to fracturing. Death usually results from loss of appetite, physical weakness, and the complications of multiple fractures. The cadmium has been traced to untreated wastes from Mitsui Mining and Smelting in Gifu Prefecture. A third major pollution disease identified in Japan has been "Yokkaichi Asthma," associated with the combined air-pollution effects of several industrial firms in the city of Yokkaichi, Mie Prefecture. In addition to these famous diseases, Japan has the standard array of air, water, and noise pollutions that affect many other industrial nations. By May 1976, there were 1,548 recognized victims of methyl mercury poisoning, including 186 dead, with over 3,500 additional victims awaiting final certifi-

9. The government first created a plan to build fifteen New Industrial Cities during the 1960's, followed by the New Comprehensive National Development Plan (*Shin Zenkoku Sōgō Kaihatsu Keikaku*). Prime Minister Tanaka Kakuei's ambitious program to solve the problems of rural poverty, maldistribution of population, and pollution by moving industry into new self-contained cities of 250,000 was shelved, apparently permanently, during the 1974 Diet.

cation; 350 victims of cadmium poisoning, including 120 dead; 191 victims of hexavalent chromium poisoning, including 24 dead (Kyodo News Service reports these figures as 232 victims including 41 dead); and over 30,000 recognized victims of air pollution throughout Japan, with the actual totals rising rapidly.[10] Paul Ehrlich has called Japan "the canary in the coal mine," a nation so polluted that it functions as a test case of human tolerance levels.[11]

Pollution disease has been the single most important factor injecting the environmental issue into the public domain and forcing the government to respond. In fact, the government's plans for industrial development, although blamed for compounding pollution by their critics, also constitute early attempts to alleviate pollution without sacrificing rapid economic growth. The government's effort to strike a balance between these two goals of pollution control and continued growth will form the core of this study of environmental policy.

Participants in the Process of Environmental Policymaking

It is commonplace to analyze Japanese political power as largely the prerogative of the national government, rather than that of local government organs, and to see the decisionmaking process in turn largely as the province of a relatively unified conservative triumvirate made up of the ruling Liberal Democratic Party (LDP), big business, and the central bureaucracy. Further, much of the analysis of Japanese politics suggests that the major source of political conflict is that which separates this conservative "camp" from the opposing progressive "camp." But the pollution issue provides an instance in which political initiative and the lines of political cleavage fall elsewhere. Indeed, it could well be argued that the initiative for action originates far from the organs of the central government and the

10. Recognized victims are those who are eligible for compensation under the 1969 law for medical relief. There are undoubtedly many additional uncertified cases, particularly in view of surveys showing high levels of pollution all over Japan, not merely at the sites where illnesses have appeared so far. For recent casualty figures, see *The Japan Times*, December 14, 1974; June 7, August 21, August 27, September 3, 1975; and April 7, April 18, and May 5, 1976.

11. Paul Ehrlich, "The Population-Resource-Environment Crisis with Special Reference to Japan" (unpublished manuscript, 1973), 9.

LDP, and that the two camps have manifested nearly as much disunity as accord. Certainly, the victims of pollution are not confined to the political opposition, so there is some pressure among conservatives to regard environmental protection as an important issue. Conversely, it is not only profit-seeking industrialists and stability-minded conservatives, but also labor and the left, who are reluctant to take the expensive step of preventing pollution and making ample restitution to the victims.

Nonetheless, we can classify participants in environmental policymaking according to the centrality of their roles in Japanese politics. First, there are the official participants within the government, the bureaucracy, and the ruling party—the LDP members of the Diet, the cabinet, the ministries, and, one must add, the courts. Then there are those nationally organized interest groups, particularly Keidanren (the Federation of Economic Organizations, or FEO), which share goals and values with the LDP, and which regularly lobby through the ruling party and the powerful sectors of the bureaucracy. Further away from the locus of decisionmaking are the opposition parties in the Diet and the nationally organized pressure groups which attempt to work through them in order to influence policy, particularly organized labor. National environmental policy has finally been determined in this central arena, but most individual pollution controversies have begun and been dealt with primarily at the local level.

Officialdom at the Center

The LDP, business, and most organs of the government have been deeply committed to the idea that Japan's ability to solve its problems depends on continued economic growth. At the same time, as the pollution problem mounted, the LDP lost quite a few seats in municipal levels of government, and particular Diet members from districts where pollution was very serious faced electoral difficulties. The gains of the Japan Socialist Party (JSP) and the Japan Communist Party (JCP) in the 1972 election have frequently been attributed in large part to public dissatisfaction with the LDP's poor record in attending to pollution problems (and to dissatisfaction with the moderate parties as channels of protest). Thus the LDP has been under conflicting constraints in its attempt to create environmental legislation and enforcement which would satisfy its constituents and simultaneously avoid serious disruption of its overall economic programs.

Until the Environment Agency was established in July 1971, the government ministries with chief responsibility for environmental problems were the Ministry of International Trade and Industry (MITI) and the Ministry of Health and Welfare (MHW). Because of the difference in their spheres of competence, their perceptions of the relative importance of different problems, and the inevitable tendency within any bureaucracy for each sector to attempt to expand its influence, conflict between these two ministries has been very severe. MITI and MHW competed for control of investigative commissions appointed to study the origins of the various pollution diseases, and produced widely differing opinions. MITI regards its duty to be the guidance and protection of industry, and it is usually very responsive to the wishes of large-scale business interests.[12] The MHW, with different constituent interests, has viewed pollution more from the standpoint of the victims, arguing that the alleviation of their suffering justified the costs involved, however burdensome the economic hardship might be for industry, government, or society at large.[13]

12. Chitoshi Yanaga, *Big Business in Japanese Politics* (New Haven: Yale University Press, 1968), 95–119.

13. The MHW invariably came up with results that verified theories advanced by the victims, whereas MITI usually found insufficient evidence to draw conclusions or advanced theories which absolved the enterprises from responsibility. In the case of cadmium poisoning, MITI supported Mitsui's theory of hormonal and nutritional deficiencies, whereas the MHW concluded that cadmium was indeed the cause and that the source was Mitsui's smeltery in Kamioka. A similar conflict occurred when the MHW concluded in 1959 that "Minamata disease" was probably due to methyl mercury which probably came from Chisso's effluents. MITI, arguing that the cause was not mercury, successfully pressed for the dissolution of the MHW study group and tried to have the EPA, over which it had more influence, carry on the studies. This conflict persisted when the investigation was resumed in Niigata after 1965, and the MHW concluded in a report of March 1966 that methyl mercury released by Shōwa Denkō was the source of the illness there. MITI intervened and insisted that the study be continued before final conclusions were drawn. As late as January 1968, MITI tried to assert that even if the cause was mercury, the source was too complex to be specified. Nonetheless, when the final report, in the hands of the Science and Technology Agency, did emerge in September 1968, it agreed

Other government agencies have frequently become involved in pollution problems. The Ministry of Construction has a vested interest in pursuing its plans for rapid industrialization and development in rural areas and has objected to the implication that it neglected to supervise development in Japan's crowded urban areas. The Ministry of Home Affairs was responsive to the arguments of environmental activists that different areas needed widely differing programs and more independent authority at the local level, and thus it has favored permitting local areas to deal more aggressively with their own pollution problems than the central government wanted to allow. The Economic Planning Agency (EPA) was occasionally involved in pollution problems; partly because its staff came largely from the Ministry of Finance (MOF) and MITI, its officials normally held views close to the positions of those ministries. Finally, the Prime Minister's Office (PMO) has also been involved, often in an effort to coordinate the competing positions of the various ministries. There has been comparatively little interministerial harmony concerning the pollution issue, a problem that has been of great significance in the development of government policy.

A final official participant in the environmental policymaking process that must be noted is the court system. Obviously, no clear institutional position on the question can be attributed to the courts; however, as will be seen, they have increasingly shown themselves willing to take up environmental questions and in many instances to issue verdicts which are tantamount to policy. The courts' significant role in this issue also seems striking in contrast to the accepted wisdom concerning Japanese courts, which usually suggests that they are the knowing advocates of a conservative government line at worst or somewhat reluctant political actors at best.

---

with the earlier MHW report and asserted further that Chisso was the guilty party in Minamata as well. By the time of the final report, conclusive evidence based on experiments with cats was available which proved the cause and effect relationship between methyl mercury in Chisso's wastes and Minamata disease itself. Chisso discovered this research, suppressed the evidence, and continued to discharge its wastes. After a second outbreak of the disease occurred in Niigata, the researcher involved broke his silence, and his testimony was used in court as proof of Chisso's negligence.

Business Interest Groups

The business community—small and large enterprise alike—
has demonstrated a predictable, consistent attitude toward responsibility and remedies for pollution problems. It is commonly accepted among Japanese environmental activists, and
admitted by many industrialists, that ignoring pollution problems has actually contributed to Japan's spectacular economic
growth in postwar years by permitting tremendous reinvest-
ment in capital expansion. Both small and large enterprises
have argued consistently that they cannot afford to change
their allocation of funds. They point out that they are not efficient operations because of their size, that they cannot afford
to divert earnings into pollution prevention, that they are already being pressed to improve working conditions and offer
higher wages. They have asked instead that the government
provide a variety of different forms of aid to them: grants,
long-term low-interest loans, and aid in financing collective pollution-prevention facilities.

Large enterprises, which offer their employees more pleas-
ant working conditions, relatively high wages, and lush fringe
benefits, cannot claim poverty. But they argue cogently that
they cannot easily alter their investment patterns without
wreaking havoc upon the national economy. First of all, they
are overextended and heavily in debt, often up to 75 per cent
of their assets (whereas American companies never think of
going beyond 15–25 per cent),[14] and in order to pay back these
loans they must continue to expand production and profit. To
divert a large amount of profits to some purpose other than
repayment of current obligations or expansion of capacity to
meet future obligations would drive an efficient, profitable, and
well-managed business into bankruptcy. Large enterprises that
attempt to avert this disaster by raising their prices, they argue,
would destroy their ability to compete abroad and dampen
sales at home, eventually forcing Japanese consumers to lower
their standard of living. Therefore, the larger enterprises conclude that if the government would like to prevent economic

14. John F. Copper and Kenneth R. Stunkel, "The Elusive Goal: Great
Power Status," *Japan Interpreter* 9 (Winter 1975), 295.

chaos and public unrest, it should prevent pollution by providing loans and outright aid even to large industries. Thus, the LDP faces strong pressure from its regular source of funds and support to move slowly on pollution prevention and to avoid asking industry to pay for it.

The Opposition Parties

The LDP and the government receive very different demands from the political opposition. All four of the opposition parties agree that pollution is an important problem which cannot be regarded simply as a necessary cost of further economic expansion, and that government and industry should bear more responsibility, both legal and financial, for solutions. All four have criticized the government's reluctance to develop a unified comprehensive policy on environmental problems, and all have given various aid to antipollution movements in specific cases, normally in the form of moral support, confidential information, skilled political advice, or publicity. Their much greater independence from business makes it much easier for them to advocate policies which would be uncomfortable for industry, and their ideological views incline them in this direction. They are all ready advocates of a popular position on any issue which greatly embarrasses the government in power; they realize that they stand a good chance of increasing their influence at the local level and their membership in the Diet through vigorous antipollution activity.

But the parties differ among themselves in the vehemence with which they express this opposition and in their readiness to compromise with the government on legislation. The Democratic Socialist Party (DSP), as a small and relatively impoverished political party supported by a moderate labor union federation (Dōmei), concentrates its energies on activities within the Diet and is relatively willing to compromise with the LDP, adopting a rather low profile vis-à-vis the pollution issue.

The remaining opposition parties have rather distinctive approaches to the problem. The Clean Government Party (CGP) has remained conspicuous as an advocate of comprehensive environmental controls. While other opposition parties have often been accused of "all talk and no action," the CGP was the first to supplement its pronouncements with scientific surveys in badly polluted areas.[15] In fact, these surveys are responsible for some major discoveries and can be credited with embarrassing the government into conducting official investigations of its own.

The JCP has made tremendous gains in popularity and prestige not only as a result of its vigorous activity on behalf of environmental protest but also because of its conscious attempt to become "loveable" again and to build a more broadly based party organization. Prior to 1972 the JCP concentrated its energies on activities outside of the Diet, largely because it did not have the twenty-seat minimum required to initiate legislation. Relatively independent of labor union support, the JCP has, like the CGP, been comparatively free to assist antipollution movements in various localities.

As the largest of the opposition parties, the JSP is in the best position both to work outside the Diet and to exert pressure on the LDP within the Diet, and it has been active in both areas. Individual JSP dietmen have utilized interpellation sessions in the Diet to publicize the most frightening facts about pollution damage and to expose inconsistencies in the arguments of government spokesmen. However, the JSP has occasionally been hindered by its dependence on Sōhyō, Japan's largest trade union federation.

Organized Labor

The national labor organizations, industrywide associations, and even most regional associations officially oppose industrial policies which will exacerbate pollution, and all demand that industry pay for pollution prevention out of the "excess profits" it allegedly retains by refusing to pay higher wages.[16] However, the level of organization most important to individual labor union members is the union of the individual enterprise. Japa-

15. *Japan Times,* August 18, 1970.
16. See Sōhyō's official stance on pollution in Sōhyō Chōsabu, *Keizai Kōzō no Henka to Rōdō Undō no Shiten, 1971 Nenkan* [Views on changes in the economic structure and the labor movement, 1971 yearbook] (Tokyo: Rōdō Keizaisha, 1971), 196–212; and a special issue of Sōhyō's monthly publication, "Rōdō Kumiai to Kōgai Tōsō" [Labor unions and the pollution struggle] *(Gekkan) Sōhyō,* no. 161 (November 1970), 6–35.

nese labor union members typically see their personal welfare and their short-term material self-interest as tied to the welfare of the company, and they are often hesitant to challenge management decisions, particularly on broad social or economic issues. This paradox in orientation—leftist rhetoric at the national level combined with timidity and even conservatism at lower levels—puts labor in a difficult position with respect to pollution. In areas where industrial development and pollution have become controversial issues, especially where particular companies can be blamed for damage, the labor unions of the offending enterprises have usually taken the side of management. Occasionally these unions have actually participated in underhanded management attempts to obstruct antipollution movements or official scientific inspections.[17]

What is of interest is how this assortment of opposition programs and tactics affects policymaking. First of all, the opposition provides a channel for the voicing of opinions from which the LDP is sometimes insulated. The LDP learns a great deal from the opposition parties that it does not always hear from its own supporters and is sometimes happy to accommodate such suggestions. More often, though, the competition for political advantage gives the opposition the incentive to search for weak points in the government's proposals and to expose them publicly.

Local Levels of Government

Some of the most significant influence wielded on national policymaking has come from the local level. Unlike many other controversies in postwar Japan, pollution became a political issue in specific localities long before it was viewed as a national problem. Naturally, there has been a predictable tendency for

17. The two conflicts over Minamata disease provide conspicuous examples in which the enterprise union of the offending company defended management rather than the antipollution movement, even when some of its own members were afflicted with the disease. See Igarashi Fumio, *Niigata Minamatabyō: Osorubeki Shōwa Denkō no Suigin Kōgai* [Niigata's Minamata disease: the frightening mercury pollution of Shōwa Denkō] (Tokyo Gōdō Shuppan, 1971); Ui, *Kōgai no Seijigaku;* Ui Jun, *Kōgai Genron* I [Principles of pollution, I] (Tokyo: Aki Shobō, 1971); and Honda Junsuke and Kataoka Noboru, *Kōgai to Rōdōsha* [Pollution and labor] (Kyoto: Hōritsu Bunkasha, 1971).

conservative local governments to support the interest of industry, while progressive local governments have generally been more vocal, if not always more active, on the question of combating pollution. Nevertheless, there are cases where the responses of local government bodies have differed markedly from the positions taken by parties at the national level.

For example, in the case of cadmium poisoning, conservative local government bodies took strong measures on behalf of the victims. The Toyama Prefectural Assembly provided medical relief to the victims two years before the central government began to provide such aid, and later charged the polluting company, Mitsui, for a refund of these payments for medical costs, the first time that any governmental body in Japan sued a polluting enterprise for damages. Furthermore, thirty-three of the thirty-six municipalities in the prefecture passed unanimous sympathy resolutions, and in March 1969 the assembly of the town where most of the cadmium victims lived donated one million yen from the municipal treasury toward the victims' court fees. In view of the prejudice demonstrated by the rest of the community up until that time, and the conservative strength in Toyama, these were extraordinary gestures.[18]

But in Kumamoto Prefecture, the city of Minamata, even with its socialist mayor and powerful labor organization, chose to defend Chisso, the major cause of mercury poisoning there, rather than the victims. The fact that Minamata was dominated by "progressive" political forces could not erase the more significant fact that it was also a one-company town, dependent on Chisso for its economic survival. Furthermore, because the vast majority of the victims were fishermen unconnected with Chisso, the population of Minamata divided into two factions. In 1959 there were several skirmishes between fishermen and company workers in which the riot police had to be called.

18. *Itai-itai* victims were not regarded with sympathy for the first decade or so after the cadmium theory was revealed. Nonvictims worried about their ability to sell rice that was suspected of containing cadmium and exerted tremendous pressure on the victims not to go to court. Until the cadmium theory won a hearing in court, other community residents believed the disease to be a hereditary or nutritional problem which reflected poorly on the victims themselves. The doctor who proposed the cadmium theory received anonymous telephone calls, crank letters, and even bomb threats.

Obviously, then, quite a few factors influence the way in which prefectural and municipal governments respond to local pollution problems. In addition to the general ideological propensities of townspeople and elected officials, the occupations and economic roles of the victims are significant, as are the personal relationships among the victims, the suspected polluters, and the local officials. Whether or not there is a diversified local economy is also important. Finally, the strength and sophistication of environmental protest has a decisive effect on the long-term response of local government.

In many cases where conservative local governments have dealt inadequately with pollution, residents' antipollution movements have cooperated with the political opposition, and many have managed to remove their conservative mayors from office (as in Mitaka, Musashino, Kawasaki, Yokohama, Fuji, Usuki, Toyama, Fuchū, and many other cities). In other cases, conservative heads of government have been willing to reverse their views on the pollution issue in order to stay in office, while remaining conservative on other issues.[19] Where leftist mayors have already come into power, pollution problems have sometimes continued. New pollution problems have been particularly troublesome for leftist administrations in Tokyo, Yokohama, Kyoto, and Osaka, although most environmentalists would probably agree that these progressive governments are really a good deal more sympathetic to the cause than the conservative governments they have replaced.[20]

What must be emphasized, however, is that many local governments have been forced by circumstance to be highly constructive and innovative in devising their own local antipollution policies well ahead of national government action. Japan's urban areas in particular had to deal with some of these problems quite early.[21] Much of the local governmental action has

19. Jack G. Lewis, *"Hōkaku Rengō:* The Politics of Conservative-Progressive Cooperation in a Japanese City" (Ph.D. dissertation, Stanford University, 1974).

20. See my "The Potentials for Grass-Roots Democracy in Postwar Japan: The Anti-Pollution Movement as a Case Study in Political Activism" (Ph.D. dissertation, University of California, Berkeley, 1974), chapters 6–11.

21. Tokyo was the first to use its legislative authority as provided in the Local Autonomy Law of 1947, by passing the Factory Hazard Control Ordinance in 1949. Osaka and Kanagawa passed similar ordinances in 1950 and

come in direct response to citizen-initiated movements which must also be recognized as a new and significant aspect of policymaking in environmental issues. Motivated by the desire to protect their own lives and communities, the members of these movements focus their attention on local problems and local leadership. For the most part, they have not yet engaged in lobbying or any other activity designed to have direct impact on national decisionmakers, and they are conspicuously absent when the Diet considers environmental legislation. Only a few national organizations to combat pollution exist, and they function primarily as communications centers for local movements by facilitating the exchange of scientific and legal advice. However, citizens' movements have managed to establish themselves as an important component of the policymaking process at lower levels. Some sympathetic local governments have actually given them a formal place in policymaking by inviting their members to participate on urban planning commissions or in study groups charged with the task of preparing new plans and ordinances for improving the urban environment. As citizens' movements have demonstrated their effectiveness at the local level and in the courts, decisionmakers have grown unwilling to alienate them unnecessarily.

The Evolution of a National Environmental Policy

Environmental policy in Japan began as a series of ad hoc, piecemeal efforts to deal with particular outbreaks of pollution, usually at the local level. As it became clear that such palliatives could neither solve the problem nor quiet growing public alarm about environmental hazards, the government finally assembled a statement of intent to deal with pollution, in the form of the Basic Law for Environmental Pollution Control of 1967. In the absence of enabling legislation and vigorous enforcement, however, the Basic Law proved utterly inadequate, and the pollution issue assumed crisis proportions by 1970. As the configuration of pressures on the ruling party changed, the LDP finally convened an extraordinary session of the Diet in

---

1951, respectively. Tokyo also passed additional ordinances to control noise and smoke in 1954 and 1955.

order to pass additional legislation, to provide its environmental policy with substance as well as flourish, and to enact measures to prevent pollution as well as grant relief to its victims. An unexpected supplement to formal environmental policy was provided by the Japanese judiciary, whose aggressive pollution verdicts became a vital factor in inducing the government to enforce its own policies and industry to comply with them.

Early Legislation [22]

The first national attempt to deal with pollution was in 1953, when the MHW conducted the first national survey of pollution (noise, vibrations, air and water pollution) and its victims. On the basis of the findings, the MHW drafted a law to prevent the contamination of the "living environment." But in the 1950's pollution was not yet considered a major problem, no interest groups were vitally concerned with establishing such a law, and the diseases which subsequently aroused such great concern were not highly visible. Therefore, opposition from other ministries, the government party, and the business community brought an end to these efforts. Nonetheless, as specific problems arose during this period, other laws which included sections on "public nuisances" were passed in connection with the construction of highways and public works. Some localities tried to provide comprehensive environmental control and to deal specifically with air pollution and noise, but such ordinances created within the narrow authority of local government could not solve the problem, nor did local governments

22. The discussion of legislation up to 1970 is based primarily on Hashimoto, *Kōgai wo Kangaeru*, 9–46; Kaji Kōji, *Kōgai Gyōsei no Sōtenken: Kaiketsu no Michi wa* [A general examination of pollution administration: the road to solutions] (Tokyo: Gōdō Shuppan, 1971), 8–77; Kankyōchō, *Kankyō Hakusho 1972* [Environment White Paper], 284–390; *Kōgai Hakusho 1971* [White Paper on pollution] (Tokyo: Ōkurashō Insatsukyoku, 1971), 148–99, 324–47; *Kōgai wo Bōshi, Kokumin no Seikatsu wo Mamoru* [Prevent pollution, protect the lives of the people] (Tokyo: Minshatō Honbu Kyōsenkyoku, 1971), 5–56; Miyamoto, *Kōgai to Jūmin Undō*, 48–77; Nihon Shakaitō Kōgai Tsuihō Undō Hombu (eds.), *Jūmin no Kōgai Hakusho* [A people's White Paper on pollution] (Tokyo: Shakai Shimpō, 1970), 193–276; and Sōrifu Chūō Kōgai Shinsa Iinkai Jimukyoku, *Kōgai Funsō Shori Jōhō* [Report on the treatment of pollution disputes], a periodical which began in September 1971.

propose to control pollution so stringently as to interfere with any other economic priorities.

During the 1950's, several fishing grounds were ruined by pollution, and affected fishermen protested for compensation. Pressed to create some sort of national legislation to take care of these instances, the Diet passed the Water Quality Preservation Law, the Factory Effluents Control Law, and the Sewerage Law in 1958. In 1962, the Diet also passed the Smoke and Soot Regulation Law to control air pollution, causing major jurisdictional disputes because many of the cities designated as problem zones in the new law had already passed their own stricter prevention ordinances. The final resolution of this dispute was that cities and prefectures with tougher standards would be allowed to apply them, but neither government nor industry regarded these laws as limits on their future behavior.

During the 1960's, pollution incidents began to increase, and widely publicized lawsuits involving pollution victims were filed. Cases which affected human health came to the attention of the MHW, but up to this time the various laws which dealt with what we now call pollution allocated funds to MITI and the MOF, and the MHW had none of its own. However, it did have a large miscellaneous fund which it put toward the development of pollution policies. The MHW drafted a bill to establish the Environmental Pollution Control Service Corporation (Kōgai bōshi jigyō dan), whose function was to provide loans and funds for the construction of individual and collective pollution-prevention facilities and for the moving of industrial plants (all voluntary). The MHW also proposed to create an Advisory Commission on Pollution (Kōgai shingikai) under its jurisdiction, to consider the creation of broader environmental legislation. The Diet, in addition to passing both of these MHW drafts into law in 1965, created committees in both the upper and lower houses devoted particularly to pollution policy, reportedly the first such bodies in the world.

Within the bureaucracy, then, it was the MHW which first took independent steps designed to culminate in comprehensive environmental legislation. At the same time, pollution had become a sufficiently public issue by the mid-1960's to attract the interest of the opposition parties, which began to demand that the government devise overall measures to tackle pollution problems. In 1964 and 1965, the DSP actually presented bills to the Diet for a basic antipollution law. This combination of public interest, active work within the MHW, and pressure within the Diet to create environmental legislation eventually produced the Basic Law for Environmental Pollution Control in 1967, similar in design to the earlier bills presented by the DSP.

The Basic Law for Environmental Pollution Control (1967)

The process by which drafts of this Basic Law were batted back and forth between the various ministries and pressure groups to accommodate diverse interests illustrates in a microcosm the various stresses and strains involved in environmental policymaking in Japan. In August 1966, the newly created Advisory Commission on Pollution within the MHW produced its interim report, suggesting that a basic law be written around four principles: (1) human health should have priority over economic growth, (2) pollution should be regulated at its source, (3) polluting industries should be liable for damage even when they are not legally negligent (the principle of no-fault liability, or *mukashitsu sekinin*), and (4) the polluter should bear the cost of prevention. This interim report also suggested that instead of regulating the concentration of effluents for each outlet, which would permit enterprises to release dangerous quantities of pollutants by increasing the number of outlets, standards should limit the total quantities of pollutants any industry may release. The Ministry of Home Affairs supported these principles and added that no-fault liability should apply even to damage caused by effluents within legal standards and that the law should be administered at the local level.

The combined announcements by these two ministries served as "water on the sleepy faces" of MITI and the financial world, both of which had expected that any proposed law would be administered through the central government, where their influence was far greater than at the local level. The FEO released a sharply phrased counteropinion on October 5, 1966: (1) life and health should not have priority over economic growth, which is what permits good health and high living standards; (2) there is no need to fix pollution standards in law; (3)

a polluter who observes the legal standards and is thus not at fault has to be exempt from liability even if damage results; and (4) the government has to bear some burden for pollution; industry should not be solely responsible.

Only two days later, the Advisory Commission on Pollution replied, reassuring the FEO that the principle of no-fault liability would not be applied unconditionally. Rather, the polluter would only be held liable for the amount of damage above and beyond a certain tolerable standard. Legal experts generally agreed, however, that the whole notion of no-fault liability would be useless without a determination of this hypothetical threshold of tolerance.

On November 24, 1966, the MHW finally produced a basic draft of the bill which still retained the principle that human safety would have priority over economic growth. The government sought additional opinions, from the Ministry of Construction, which argued that a special pollution law was entirely unnecessary and that the problem could be taken care of with modest revisions in other laws, and from MITI, which added that the government's lack of social overhead investment was also a cause of pollution and that people's welfare and the well-being of industry should be planned together.

The PMO then formed its own advisory commission to resolve these conflicts in opinion and produced a new draft bill on February 23, 1967. This version included as its basic purpose the so-called harmony clause: "while planning for harmony with healthy economic development, we will protect the living environment and guarantee the public welfare." In contrast to the MHW's insistence that the polluting industry should pay for pollution prevention, the PMO said that government would pay all or part of the costs.

In spite of the gradual drift of the government position in the direction of the preferences of business, the FEO remained unsatisfied and on March 6, 1967, announced its view. The EPA rather than the MHW should be in charge of pollution administration, and the law should place limits on industrial liability. Other business groups, as well as MITI, also spoke out against having the MHW administer the new law and in favor of assigning a considerable portion of pollution-prevention costs to government.

In the Diet deliberations, pressure from the JSP in committee and during interpellation produced some significant modifications in the government's draft. The opposition parties managed to soften the wording of the offensive "harmony clause," forced the government to add that the standards would be periodically revised in the light of new evidence, and added new provisions for a system to resolve pollution disputes and a statement that small and medium-sized firms might need financial assistance but that large companies could pay their own costs for pollution prevention. Another amendment assured greater autonomy to the prefectures in setting up their own advisory commissions on pollution control. Finally, the opposition inserted an amendment requiring the government to report to the Diet on current pollution levels, the effectiveness of measures in use, and plans for improvements in pollution control.

The final bill, incorporating these opposition amendments along with the "harmony clause" and most of the points demanded by business and MITI, was produced on May 16 and passed by the Diet in August 1967. It provided for the establishment at a later date of environmental standards, the system for arbitration and mediation of pollution disputes, and the rules to divide the burden of prevention costs. The law also created two offices within the PMO to administer it and permitted seriously affected areas to establish their own prevention plans in concert with the government. Primary responsibility for enforcing the law would be retained by the PMO, and only a few subsidiary items would be left to the MHW. This Basic Law remained a disappointment to the opposition, whose own drafts had been similar to the original proposals of the MHW. The Basic Law left the most controversial work undone and did not deal at all with relief for the victims of disease. Secondly, all four of the MHW's original points had been removed or eroded by the government's willingness to bow to the wishes of the economic ministries and business pressure groups.

Increasing Conflict and Criticism

From 1967 to 1970, as the government prepared the additional legislation required by the Basic Law, pollution continued to grow worse, various local governments created their own controversial independent policies, the press publicized the testimony about the pollution diseases being considered in the courts, and the opposition parties continued to criticize the government's performance. The process of formulating each subsequent antipollution measure resembled that in the case of the Basic Law: the appropriate organs of the bureaucracy—most notably the MHW and the PMO—would investigate the situation and come up with a proposal which would then be modified in accordance with the objections made by MITI, other ministries, and usually the FEO. The LDP would present this much-modified bill to the Diet, where it would then undergo criticism and occasional amendment by the opposition.

In December 1969 the Diet passed into law a system for providing medical relief to certified victims of pollution diseases in designated geographical areas. The pressure to create such a law had been great because the prefectures and municipalities involved were currently bearing this burden, official cabinet investigations of some of the diseases had concluded that they were indeed caused by pollution, and the plight of the victims was now well publicized. The government bill again was disappointing in its narrow definition of the victims of pollution diseases and in its limited financial aid to them (victims of mercury poisoning in Niigata, for example, would actually receive less from the central government than they had received from the prefecture), but some amendments to satisfy the opposition were made. Most notably, the government agreed to extend coverage to new victims in the future, and to designate new relief zones wherever pollution levels exceeded those in areas already designated as relief zones.

Similarly, the opposition amended the original draft of the law establishing the dispute-resolution system. The amended version of the law required that prefectures create offices to handle pollution complaints in order to give local government additional authority and to make the system more accessible. The opposition also argued that binding arbitration after which disputants might still appeal to the courts was more desirable than the government's procedure, which denied recourse to the courts. Although this suggested modification was not included in the bill passed in June 1970, it was enacted later and came into effect in October 1972.

The opposition parties were able to amend these bills on such matters because MITI and the FEO did not provide much countervailing pressure. The amendments did not require large budgets, nor did they involve money from nongovernmental sources or threaten to disrupt orderly economic growth. When business did feel its interests were threatened, as in the law which apportioned the financial burden for pollution prevention between government and industry and in the setting of environmental standards, the opposition parties were less successful. MITI and business managed to decrease the amount which business would have to provide in each class of expenditure for pollution prevention. A specialized body within the MHW established figures for environmental standards in July 1968, but the FEO demanded a reinvestigation on the grounds that the mining, electric power, oil, and chemicals industries would simply be unable to meet the published standards. As a result, more lenient standards were announced in February 1969.

Initiative at the Local Level

The Basic Law of 1967 was a statement of intent, but until environmental standards were determined and enabling legislation was passed, there was nothing to enforce, and the national government stood vulnerable to the accusation that it was still doing nothing about pollution. Local governments in badly affected areas felt compelled to enact their own ordinances, reviving the controversy about local autonomy versus central control. For example, the city of Kawasaki managed to halve the quantity of soot in the air from 1961 to 1969 by employing its authority over construction and zoning to control air pollution from stationary sources. A smog warning system initiated by the city as early as April 1965 required thirty-eight major factories to change fuels. Furthermore, in 1967 Kawasaki began offering long-term interest-free loans requiring no collateral to help small businesses buy pollution-prevention equipment. Finally, the city initiated its own medical-aid program in January 1970 to supplement the relief available from the central government.[23] That local government bodies, reputedly so weak and impoverished, felt it necessary to take steps of this kind signified to many that much more could be done and that the LDP could not rely on its earlier excuses as a means of delay. The central government had almost unlimited funds and authority by comparison, it was argued, so if local governments could take significant steps, the center should be expected to do even better.

The Tokyo Ordinance (1969)

The conflict between local and central government reached a peak in the controversy over the Tokyo Metropolitan Environmental Pollution Control Ordinance, passed in July 1969 and further strengthened in October 1970.[24] Unlike the Basic Law, which defines environmental pollution strictly as six varieties of damage (increased to seven in 1970), the Tokyo Ordinance defines environmental pollution to mean *any* infringement of the environment, and can thus be applied to yet unforeseen varieties of pollution.

The preamble and general provisions of the Tokyo Ordinance, which describe the obligations of the prefectural governor, of entrepreneurs, and of the citizens, are much more complete than the brief corresponding section in the central government's Basic Law. The Tokyo Ordinance asserts that citizens have the right to a clean and safe environment, as well as

23. *Japan Times,* November 9, 1970.
24. The official English text of the Tokyo Ordinance is available in *The Tokyo Metropolitan Environmental Pollution Control Ordinance and Its Enforcement Regulation* (Tokyo: Tokyo Metropolitan Research Institute for Environmental Protection, 1971), and in *Tokyo Municipal News* 19 (November–December 1969), 13–20. For comments on the ordinance and the controversy it created, see Muroi Tsutomu, "Kōgai taisaku ni okeru Hōritsu to Jōrei [Laws and ordinances on pollution countermeasures]," *Jūrisuto,* no. 492 (November 10, 1971), 166–72; and Noma Hisao, "Tōkyōto no Shin Kōgai Bōshi Jōrei [Tokyo's new pollution prevention ordinance]," *ibid.,* no. 458 (August 10, 1970), 266–269.

the obligation to respect the rights of others to the same environment by not contributing to pollution. In contrast, the national law makes no mention at all of environmental rights and speaks only in terms of citizens' obligations to cooperate with control measures. Similarly, with respect to the responsibilities of government, the national law gives the state the responsibility "to protect the nation's health and conserve the living environment," a modest assignment in comparison to the Tokyo Ordinance, in which "the Metropolis of Tokyo, the autonomous entity of Tokyo citizens, shall bear the maximum responsibility to assure the citizens of the right to a wholesome, safe, and comfortable life, and . . . shall try every possible way to prevent and eliminate environmental pollution." The penal provisions of the national law involve payment of higher fines for each offense, but the Tokyo Ordinance specifically mentions jail and includes additional administrative penalties as well as fines. It also empowers the governor of Tokyo to order factories that violate the ordinance to cease operations and to deny the water supply to offenders who try to continue.

As we have seen, earlier jurisdictional disputes had allowed local units of government with stricter standards than those provided in the national law to apply their own regulations. However, the Tokyo Ordinance of 1969 was sufficiently different from existing national legislation—and sufficiently bolder than previous local legislation—that the government was much offended by its passage. The fact that the ordinance did not refer to "harmony with the economy" was particularly alarming to the government, as were the penal provisions and the comprehensive coverage. The government therefore held that the magnitude of the difference made the ordinance illegal. The government argued that prefectures were required to make their ordinances within the scope of the law, only insofar as they did not violate national laws or regulations. Although the government admitted that within certain specified subject areas prefectural governors did have the authority to provide standards, as in the earlier resolution of this conflict, the government argued that when the national law did not explicitly delegate such authority, duty by duty, local government had no jurisdiction at all.

The Tokyo metropolitan government responded to all of these points in kind. First, local governments were supposed to represent local citizens, not to act as administrative agents of the center. They were empowered by the Local Autonomy Law to take necessary measures to provide for the protection of their citizens' health and safety. Tokyo argued that the central government had already recognized this duty of local government by its willingness to have noise, smoke, and factory hazards regulated at the local level even after the passage of overlapping national laws. Thus for Tokyo to create stiff antipollution ordinances was to comply with the legal obligations of governing, rather than to break any higher law. The dispute was finally resolved when the government abandoned its criticisms and revised its own Basic Law during the so-called Pollution Diet of 1970, an outcome of the growing seriousness of pollution problems.

1970, a Year of Crisis

In 1970, often referred to as *Kōgai Gannen* (The First Year of the Era of Pollution), the Japanese government faced mounting pressure from a variety of sources. Increasing pollution, relentless pursuit of the issue by the mass media, growing public fear of pollution damage, more explicit criticism of national policy from local governments (particularly Tokyo), unfavorable international publicity, and of course that most easily understood threat of all, potential electoral losses, all combined to force the LDP to consider more energetic antipollution measures.[25] The number of pollution incidents increased drastically in 1970, whether one looks at newspaper reports, the number of local complaints filed, the number of cases submitted for mediation, the number of pollution-related cases in court, or the number of antipollution protests.[26] Tokyo experienced several

25. The events of late 1970 mentioned in the text were all cited in the *Japan Times* between August and December 1970.

26. For figures, see Saikō Saibanshō Jimu Sōkyoku, Minjikyoku [Supreme Court of Japan, General Secretariat, Civil Affairs Division], "Tokushu Songai Baishō Seikyū Jiken Sankō Tōkei Hyō [Statistical reference chart on specific damage compensation claims]" (1973). See also Kankyōchō, *Kankyō Hakusho 1972,* 307; *Kōgai Hakusho 1971,* 152–55; and Kōgai Tōchōsei Iinkai Jimukyoku, *Kōgai Funsō Shori Jōhō,* September 30, 1972, 33–34.

periods when photochemical smog was so severe that school-children had to be hospitalized. The city of Fuji saw the first criminal suit brought by a citizens' movement against local industry and government officials.[27] The CGP began revealing the frightening results of its own environmental surveys.[28] Television and the press also played a vital role in publicizing local pollution incidents, in dramatizing the horrors of the twisted fingers, shrunken bodies, and convulsive seizures that accompany pollution disease, and thus in making environmental problems into an explosive national issue. Opinion polls showed that the public was increasingly alarmed about pollution; 71 per cent of the residents in the seven largest cities, 48 per cent of those in other cities, and even 32 per cent of those in towns and villages claimed to be suffering from pollution in a national poll of May 1970.[29]

In late 1970, Tokyo's very popular and progressive Governor, Minobe Ryōkichi, repeatedly criticized the central government for its inadequate measures to cope with pollution, providing as an obvious contrast his own strong proposals and acceptance of responsibility for pollution problems. Even before the LDP had agreed to hold an extra Diet session to deal with pollution, Minobe requested the Metropolitan Assembly to hold an extra session for this purpose. The Tokyo Board of Education also decided to put environmental problems into the public school curriculum one year sooner than the Ministry of

27. See Hoshino Shigeo, Nishioka Akio, and Nakajima Isamu, "Numazu-Mishima-Shimizu (nishi itchō) Sekiyū Kombinaato Tōsō to Fujishi wo Meguru Jūmin Tōsō [The Struggle to oppose the petroleum kombinat (in the cities) of Numazu, Mishima, and Shimizu, and the residents' struggle in Fuji City], in Miyamoto Ken'ichi and Endō Akira (eds.), *Toshi Mondai to Jūmin Undō* [Urban problems and residents' movements], no. 8 in the series Gendai Nihon no Toshi Mondai (Kyoto and Tokyo: Sekibunsha, 1971), 210–83; Kōda Toshihiko, *Waga Sonzai no Teiten kara: Fuji Kōgai to Watakushi* [From the core of my existence: Fuji pollution and me] (Tokyo: Yamato Shobō, 1972); Matsubara, *Kōgai to Chiiki Shakai*, 221–42; Nishiyama Masao, "Fuji Kōgai Jūmin Soshō no Naka kara [Inside the residents' lawsuit on Fuji pollution]," *Shimin* 3 (May 1971), 101–7; and Ui Jun, *Kōgai Genron II* [Principles of Pollution, II] (Tokyo: Aki Shobō, 1971), 166–86.
28. Kōmeitō Kōgai Taisaku Hombu (ed.), *Kōgai Zetsumetsu ni Idomu: Kōgai Chōsa Repooto* [In defiance of extinction by pollution: a report on our nationwide pollution survey] (Tokyo: Kōmeitō, 1971).
29. Yomiuri Shimbunsha, "Kōgai mondai" [Pollution problems], *(Gekkan) Yoron Chōsa* 2 (August 1970), 55.

Education planned to. Minobe announced that Tokyo would buy cadmium-contaminated rice from farmers who would otherwise be unable to sell it and would help them convert their fields to other purposes. The effect of Minobe's criticisms was visible in the response to his rice-buying plan, which the government at first labeled a violation of the Food-Control Law. After a month of appearing callous and indifferent to the plight of these farmers, the government decided to support Minobe, and in addition to donate cadmium-free rice to the affected farmers for their own consumption.

After the summer of 1970, Prime Minister Satō Eisaku's official statements began to display a greater concern for pollution problems as they might affect Japan's foreign trade, whereas earlier statements had emphasized the importance of continued industrial expansion and economic growth. Rather than echoing industry's usual warning that investment in pollution prevention would reduce the volume of Japan's foreign trade, Satō began to warn industry that foreign trade might suffer because Japan was developing a bad international image as a country which exported at low prices by tolerating pollution, just as industry had always admitted. This concern for Japan's image abroad coincided with negotiations between Japan and the United States over environmental standards for the Pacific Ocean, indicating that Satō may also have been reacting to the much-publicized dismay expressed by American visitors, who repeatedly exclaimed that pollution in Japan was unparalleled elsewhere.

Even within the LDP and the government, pressure for more aggressive pursuit of environmental problems arose. The PMO was now in charge of investigating environmental problems and was exposed every day to the enormity of the pollution problem. Yamanaka Sadanori, director-general of the PMO, became increasingly visible during late 1970 as a proponent of firmer measures to cope with pollution. In addition, Prime Minister Satō faced an election in October 1970 when his third term as party president would expire, and the liberal faction leader Miki Takeo decided to challenge Satō's bid for a fourth term partly to make pollution into an issue within the party. Though Satō won, Miki did much better than expected, which most observers attributed to his attempt to reach the general public and the new generation of young LDP Diet members who cared more about policy than about personality-oriented factions.

Whereas the LDP had previously been exposed to persuasion largely from business and the economic ministries, by 1970 the LDP faced pressure from other sources as well. An increasingly concerned public extended well beyond the limits of opposition-party supporters. Some of the most effective antipollution movements in Japan were in areas where the LDP had once known, and now lost, almost unanimous political support. The LDP was losing many prefectural and municipal assembly seats. The exposure of interministerial conflict over the proper handling of pollution contributed to the government's image as incapable of producing and executing coherent policies. The increasing extent of pollution problems and repeated revelations of industrial violations of existing laws and standards made it impossible for the LDP to continue to maintain that all was well. In August, the cabinet announced its intention to revise the Basic Law and to supplement it with other legislation. The opposition parties demanded that an extraordinary session of the Diet be convened to consider these bills, and after much haggling over timing the LDP agreed to call the special session as requested.

The Pollution Diet (1970)

Several themes emerge from an examination of events surrounding the Pollution Diet. First, a wider circle of interests than had spoken out in 1967, including scientists, environmental experts, and labor unions, participated in the 1970's round of legislation. Although these groups could not directly affect Diet outcomes, they clearly felt that an attempt at indirect influence was worthwhile. Second, during the process of interpellation some minor but embarrassing revelations and policy contradictions were exposed—sometimes by LDP interpellators—and some ministers committed themselves to strict interpretation and enforcement of the law. Finally, although business interests elicited some major concessions, the LDP resisted business pressure on other points, and some of the opposition's demands of previous years became law. In December 1970, the Diet passed fourteen laws, five of which had been modified in committee, as well as a resolution praising, but not enacting, the opposition's own bills.[30]

Several major issues divided the participants: the relative priority of human safety and economic expansion (the "harmony clause"), the principle of no-fault liability, the definition of pollution as a criminal offense, the delegation of independent authority to local government, and the unification of the central government's environmental administration into a single independent ministry.

At the outset Prime Minister Satō announced that he was willing to abandon the harmony clause, and MITI actually endorsed pollution prevention even at the risk of economic slowdown. However, even though the purpose of the revised Basic Law was "to protect the health of the nation and to conserve the living environment," environmentalists and the political opposition were disappointed at the absence of any explicit reference to the priority of this purpose over and above the health of the economy.

Another significant change in the new Basic Law was the removal of the notion of no-fault liability under pressure from business groups. Although the 1967 law had contained an almost useless definition of this concept, its inclusion then had been a victory for the environmental movement and the opposition parties, which hoped to expand the usefulness of the definition this time. Instead, in 1970, the Ministry of Justice argued that a workable definition would be too difficult to prepare, requiring designation of all polluting substances and all circumstances where liability would apply, so the principle was dropped entirely.

A very important piece of legislation in 1970 was the "pollution crime" law. The opposition had argued for years that pollution leading to damage to health should be a criminal offense like assault or manslaughter; in 1970 the LDP asked the Min-

30. For additional material on the 1970 Pollution Diet, see Kaji, *Kōgai Gyōsei,* 61–77; Kankyō Hozen Kyōkai (ed.), *Kōgai Nenkan 1972* [Pollution yearbook, 1972] (Tokyo: Kankyō Hozen Kyōkai, 1972), 203–318; *Kōgai Hakusho 1971,* 10–14, 169–78; *Kōgai wo Bōshi,* 57–65; and Nihon Shakaitō, *Jūmin no Kōgai Hakusho,* 194–216.

istry of Justice to prepare a bill providing fines and jail terms for polluters (although this would still be in the civil rather than the criminal code). Such a law would appear to make Japan's environmental legislation the most stringent in the world, but in fact this law applies to a very narrow range of industrial pollution and was not used until 1974. Many members of the LDP were distressed with it and sympathized instead with the FEO's "profound doubts" about the bill, complaining that it was premature to enact penal provisions, or, for that matter, any preventive legislation. The FEO argued that administrative guidelines were enough and that the government's entire slate of proposed legislation was improper because it was unduly "vague" and had been prepared too hastily.

In particular, the FEO and its supporters in the LDP demanded that instead of applying penalties to pollution "which *may be* hazardous to life and health," the law should cover only pollution "which *is* hazardous." The Ministry of Justice at first insisted that it could not make any revisions in view of the fact that its own experts had already screened the law for technical clarity. After what must have been substantial pressure from Satō, who sought party unanimity on the bill, and from the FEO (which was widely accused of threatening to withhold contributions to the LDP campaign for the upcoming House of Councillors election in June 1971 if its demands were not met), the ministry made the requested alteration in wording, feebly explaining that the changes were needed for the sake of legal clarity after all. Thus all preventive applications were effectively removed from the law, so that it could be used only to punish polluters after they had already caused grievous damage to human life.

The 1970 Pollution Diet finally disposed of the controversy over local control by delegating greater powers to local governments. The new Water Pollution Control Law explicitly permitted prefectures to create standards stricter than those of the central government and gave prefectural governors the power to suspend operations of an offending enterprise for up to one year. The revised Basic Law also permitted local governments to enact their own ordinances to meet local needs.

A final problem raised during the 1970 Pollution Diet concerned the proposed creation of an independent Ministry of Environmental Protection to consolidate environmental administration, although the issue was not fully resolved until the next Diet session. Interministerial conflict and the absence of centrally coordinated policies were clearly wasting time and money, diverting officials' attention from other duties, and creating delays advantageous to no one. These conflicts also embarrassed the government and made its own task unpleasant and difficult. In August, the director-general of the Administrative Management Agency declared that no new coordinating agency was needed, but by late 1970 the LDP realized that the pollution problem was serious enough to require more systematic action, and that a part-time advisory commission of twenty experts and a council of officials attached to many different agencies were inadequate. In 1971, the Diet created a new Environment Agency (not a full-fledged ministry) which started functioning in July with broad jurisdiction over environmental problems and responsibility for future policies, coordinating environmental administration, and supervising enforcement of standards.

The Environment Agency faced certain problems at the outset. Of necessity, it was composed of bureaucrats whose initial attachments were to the agencies from which they came, and there were problems of personal loyalties to these other agencies and to pressure groups whose goals conflicted with the stringent regulation of pollution. In contrast to the well-cultivated connections maintained by other parts of the bureaucracy, the Environment Agency had to start anew, building personal contacts and its own power base from scratch.[31]

Nonetheless, there is increasing evidence that a unified administration permitted a more sweeping response to the problem, and that the agency is developing its own esprit de corps as time passes. Dr. Ōishi Buichi, Prime Minister Tanaka Kakuei's first appointee to the post of director-general of the Environment Agency, was an energetic, outspoken environmental crusader. It is quite likely that just as he won the affection of

31. See Donald R. Kelley, Kenneth R. Stunkel, and Richard R. Wescott, "The Politics of the Environment: The USA, the USSR, and Japan," *American Behavioral Scientist* 17 (May–June 1974), 751–70.

the general public for taking strong stands on environmental questions, he transmitted a sense of purpose and enthusiasm to the transferred bureaucrats under him. A later environment minister, Miki Takeo, also fought vigorously on behalf of stringent environmental regulation even after the oil crisis of 1973, and subsequently went on to become prime minister.[32] Evidence of a firm government attitude on environmental issues was provided in 1973 when Japan experienced a nationwide mercury scare after a third outbreak of mercury poisoning and after the discovery of high mercury contamination in all waters surrounding Japan. Both MITI and MHW responded rapidly, setting limits for safe consumption and ordering acetoaldehyde plants to eliminate mercury from the process by 1975.[33] Since 1973, an increasing number of industries have been charged and indicted for violations of the new antipollution laws, have paid large fines, and have made substantial contributions to medical aid or funds for collective pollution-prevention facilities in accordance with the new laws. In 1974, the Environment Agency recommended that all land reclamation in the Inland Sea be stopped until damage to the ecosystem could be kept under control and that environmental impact surveys be conducted prior to construction of any major public works.[34]

The Role of the Judiciary

In addition to all of the action taken by the LDP, the bureaucracy, and the Diet, however, actions taken by Japanese courts must be recognized as having contributed to present policies. Although the four major pollution decisions followed the government's legislative activity, testimony prior to the verdicts in each case began several years earlier and had major political impact, affecting public awareness about the nature and extent of pollution disease and beliefs about the proper role of government and industry in preventing pollution, both inside and out of policymaking circles. The courts' decisions have also set

32. Margaret A. McKean, "Environmental Protection and the Energy Crisis: Japan," in Donald Kelley (ed.), *The Energy Crisis and the Environment: A Comparative Perspective* (New York: Praeger, 1977).
33. "Fisheries and Industrial Pollution," *Japan Quarterly* 20 (October–December 1973), 373–77.
34. *Japan Times,* May 11 and July 1, 1974.

legal precedents which themselves form a substantial portion of environmental policy.[35]

Victims of *itai-itai* disease in Toyama Prefecture filed suit against the Mitsui Mining and Smelting Company, and, after a long court battle, in June 1971 became the first victorious pollution litigants. When Mitsui appealed the case to the Higher Court, the victims more than doubled their demands for restitution, and in August 1972 they were awarded 100 per cent of their enlarged claims. As a result of this momentous legal defeat for a major conglomerate (*zaibatsu*), defendant enterprises in other cases have not attempted to appeal verdicts unfavorable to them. Victims in both Minamata and Niigata have won compensation, in two landmark court decisions, from the respective defendant companies, Chisso and Shōwa Denkō. By January 1975, Chisso had paid ¥20,000 million to certified victims and was searching for ways to obtain liquid funds to pay thousands of victims likely to be certified in the near future. The company was forced to sell several of its subsidiaries, to seek a loan from the government after the oil crisis in order to continue payments to victims, and to tell shareholders that it could not afford to pay dividends.[36]

The fourth major court case was an unusual suit by asthma victims living in Yokkaichi against not one but six defendant enterprises in an industrial *kombinat*. This verdict firmly established the principle of joint and several liability, so that even if each single enterprise releases quantities of pollutants too small to damage human health and within the limits of environmental standards, a cluster of enterprises which together release dangerous levels of pollutants can be held jointly responsible. The court declared that if companies decide to locate together in industrial combines and to engage in activities likely to release contaminating effluents, it is their duty to test their own emissions, to install prevention equipment, and to construct agglomerations of plants only in areas where their total combined emissions will not damage human health. Failure to

---

35. Relatively detailed descriptions of these four cases in English may be found in McKean, "The Potentials for Grass-Roots Democracy," chapter 2.

36. *Japan Times,* April 13 and May 30, 1974, and January 26, 1975.

make these preparations before commencing production and failure to employ the best available prevention technology constitute legal negligence. This verdict is expected to have major impact on cases involving other *kombinats*, to put legal obstacles in the way of massive construction programs currently planned, and to make many existing enterprises vulnerable to lawsuits for failing to use the best available technology.

Each of these decisions has had a cumulative impact on the legal rights of pollution victims and the responsibilities of enterprises. Although the civil code in Japan does not include the principle of no-fault liability for compensation, the courts have widened the definition of "fault" substantially so that it is not difficult for victims to prove negligence. The courts have also declared that epidemiological evidence is sufficient as legal proof of the relationship between pollution as the cause and a disease as the effect. Thus pollution victims have a much greater chance than ever before of winning damages in the courts, and in fact they are turning to the courts with increasing frequency.

Apart from their legal significance, these court decisions have also been the single most influential factor in causing big business to modify its attitudes toward environmental problems. A telling example is the change in behavior of Shōwa Denkō, the defendant company in the suit over Niigata mercury poisoning. In February 1967, before any pollution victims had taken legal action, the president of Shōwa Denkō announced on nationwide television that no matter what the government's medical findings might show, his company would refuse to acknowledge them and would not comply with government recommendations. But four years later, after the first pollution verdict (*itai-itai* disease) was announced and shortly before Shōwa Denkō's own case in Niigata was to be decided, the company said that it would accept whatever verdict was made and would not appeal the case. This dramatic change in attitude was obviously dictated by the new legal circumstances, in that polluting companies would now face court orders rather than government warnings, and legal appeals were likely to be ineffective and costly.

Big business further demonstrated its newly conciliatory position in agreements concluded after these court decisions.[37] Along with the compensation required by the verdicts, the defendant enterprises also agreed to pay commensurate restitution to nonplaintiffs and even to victims who may be certified in the future, which placed at least Chisso in dire financial distress. The enterprises involved also agreed to contribute additional sums to general medical funds for pollution victims, to sign pollution prevention agreements to apply to their activities in the future, and to undertake special measures to help to restore affected soil or water to a cleaner state. Finally, defendant enterprises in the earlier verdicts renegotiated compensation after the largest settlements ever were obtained by Minamata victims in 1973. The renegotiated settlement for victims of cadmium poisoning actually includes a provision for an annual cost-of-living increase. Thus it is clear that the court system in Japan has provided a major channel for pollution victims seeking redress and that it has been an active organ in the setting of legal precedents binding on both industry and government in the area of pollution control.

Summary and Conclusions

All Japanese institutions—government, business, the opposition parties, and labor—were reluctant to respond to environmental problems, finding the necessary adjustments quite painful. After many years of successfully wooing the public with promises of regional development and further industrialization, the government was slow to comprehend the fact that portions of the public no longer find these promises attractive. Only after the various pollution diseases became newsworthy and began to attract the concern of a wider public and of the opposition parties did the government move to create antipollution legislation. Pollution scares persisted, antipollution movements proliferated, and pollution became an issue of sufficient importance to affect the distribution of power in many local governments and in the Diet. Pushed by these and other

37. S. Prakash Sethi, "Business Response to Social Problems and Social Pressures: The Japanese Model," (Institute of Business and Economic Research, University of California, Berkeley, 1974), 51–84.

factors, the government began to tighten up regulatory standards, to seek out and punish violators of the law, to give greater authority to local government, and to promote research and development of cleaner manufacturing processes and improved pollution-prevention technology.

The government also found it increasingly necessary to demonstrate independence from business ties and to enforce laws unfavorable to business. The business community, in turn, was forced to realize that the respect it won for promoting Japan's rapid growth during the 1950's and 1960's was no longer freely given, and that its public image suffered because of pollution. The business community softened its defiant posture of the 1960's when it had argued self-righteously that industry should not be regulated and refused to modify its practices. Instead, it endured a good deal of public humiliation and began to change its rhetoric and policies. Business also modified its attempts to influence legislation. Whereas the FEO insisted on a broad range of demands—and won all of its points—in 1967, in 1970 it exerted pressure only on a few selected points of the most vital importance and did not attempt to block many of the other demands made by the opposition. After the recent verdicts in favor of pollution victims, business resigned itself to abiding by strict new laws and taking positive steps to prevent pollution.

To conclude, this case study in environmental policymaking reveals a great deal about the process of policy formation in Japan and contradicts many of the commonly held assumptions. First, public opinion and the mass media had substantially greater importance in this case than is usual, because they turned pollution into a national issue. What is also unusual is that public opinion became a positive force, advocating certain concrete steps which the government should take, rather than functioning simply as a negative force of disapproval. Local electoral reverses for the LDP and the proliferation of antipollution movements and lawsuits, concrete manifestations of the general public's concern, forced pollution into prominence. This highly charged atmosphere and the LDP's consequent fear of even more upsetting environmental and political crises in the future caused the LDP's own position to move gradually away from total acceptance of business pressure and toward accommodation with the demands of environmental activists and the opposition parties.

Second, whereas many administrative decisions described elsewhere have been made on behalf of some particular self-interested group of potential beneficiaries who lobbied energetically for their cause, the formulation of environmental policy seems to have been a relatively anonymous matter. Neither particular individuals, interest groups, nor LDP factions were conspicuous lobbyists on behalf of antipollution policies. Neither pollution victims nor citizens' movements approached the national government. Thus it would appear that the central government was responding to a general change in social and economic values in society at large, rather than to particularistic appeals.

But most importantly, this case study shows that decision-making in Japan can be a more open process than many have thought, both within the established cluster of power at the center (the bureaucracy, the LDP, and big business) and also in the sense that influence and even policy initiatives can come from beyond the center. Interministerial conflict divided the bureaucracy and provided room for debate and criticism, which affected the legislation that emerged. Furthermore, the issue cut across the conventional conservative-progressive lines of cleavage in Japanese politics and revealed division within the LDP over environmental questions. Some LDP activists became environmentalists to salvage their local political careers, and other LDP Diet members argued for strong legislation and embarrassed their own party colleagues during interpellation. This division deprived the LDP of the confidence and aplomb with which it has often pushed its own programs uncompromisingly through the Diet. Although business leaders agreed upon the goal of minimizing the economic costs of whatever policies finally emerged, they could exert only limited influence. Given the rapidly changing climate of opinion on environmental problems, the LDP and even the economic ministries eventually felt cross-pressures requiring them to resist the industrial lobbies. Furthermore, the political establishment took up environmental problems only reluctantly, being forced to do so by measures taken elsewhere, usually at the local level or in the courts. Thus it would seem that initial pressure, guidelines, and even concrete details of policy can come from outside the political establishment in Japan.

In fact, the environmental issue has demonstrated that those with a reputation for weakness, lack of imagination, and cowardice are actually capable of boldly taking the initiative in designing policies for local needs and in courageously demanding compliance with legal requirements unpalatable to the powers that be. Many local administrative units were forced, by the combination of pressure from local activists and the absence of a uniform national policy, to create their own policies, often including some imaginative programs which the central government later used as models. Despite the commonly held belief that local governments in Japan operate simply as the uninspired and obedient tools of the central administration, and are unable to do otherwise because of their financial dependence on the center and the nature of factional support for local politicians, this is not always the case. Similarly, the courts also demonstrated a new-found courage to issue verdicts which will have an unsettling impact on industrial priorities, business investment patterns, and future government policies.

This case study also reveals the surprising power which the political opposition, accused in the past of unrealistic rantings and futile extremism, can wield. The LDP still manages to control all of the highest executive offices as well as a comfortable number of seats in the Diet, and despite the new and surprising openness of the policy formulation process dealing with pollution, the business world and the economic ministries do often have the last word in policy design. Nonetheless, it is a testimonial to the growing political acumen of the opposition that it has been able to exert so much indirect influence on the legislative process in what are indisputably hostile surroundings. Not only did the opposition parties use their influence in urban areas and their opportunity to debate in the Diet, but by voicing opinions that were more attractive to the public than the increasingly unacceptable arguments of the LDP, they managed to win wide support for their environmental views. Many of their antipollution proposals eventually won endorsement by the LDP itself, thus becoming law. It is also highly significant that the opposition has experienced such success while using methods almost entirely "within the system," an indication perhaps that "the system" in Japan can be responsive, if sluggish, in spite of the overwhelming concentration of political power in a conservative establishment.

7. Policymaking in Japan: An Organizing Perspective *

Bradley M. Richardson

A troubling problem for scholars in public policy analysis is the difficulty of systematizing description and explanation. Political life is sufficiently complex that a priori paradigms are often less than adequate for organizing findings on real-world political processes. As a result many scholars studying public policy prefer the case approach. Still, as Theodore Lowi and others have lamented, case studies typically lead to findings which are hard to integrate into broader paradigms of policymaking.[1] There is seemingly a vicious circle in which general models do not always encompass the varieties of experience found in the real world while case studies often do not adequately serve the purposes of theory building.

The research reported here attempts to alleviate the paradox inherent in efforts to establish a bridge between empirical theory and case studies in research on Japanese policymaking. Like policymaking in other industrialized countries, Japan's is complicated and involves many different actors. As is also the case in other complex societies, specific policy processes are not always easily classified as examples of some general type. Patterns of participation, cleavage, and consensus vary consider-

* Portions of the research reported here were supported by a grant from the Ohio State University Research Foundation. I am indebted to Daniel Moreland and Michael Yosha for research assistance and to Lawrence Baum and Donald Van Meter for helpful suggestions.

1. See Theodore Lowi, "American Business, Public Policy, Case Studies, and Political Theory," *World Politics* 16 (1964), 677–715. For a discussion of this problem as it relates to research on Japan see T. J. Pempel, "Patterns of Japanese Policy Making: Higher Education," prepared for the annual meeting of the Association of Asian Studies, Boston, April 1974, a revised version of which appears here as chapter 8.

ably among policy processes. As a result, scholars have lamented the difficulties of generalizing to universal principles from the seemingly idiosyncratic facets of individual processes.[2]

This chapter suggests a conceptual scheme for organizing and interpreting the policymaking behavior of political actors which is based on the assumption that they come to policymaking processes with different rationales for participation, i.e., different interests, motivations, and role concepts. Particular policy processes in turn involve specific combinations of actors because they engage specific combinations of these rationales. Individual policy processes are hard to classify on the surface because their content or timing have resulted in different combinations of actors, each of which is process-specific. But underlying these seemingly idiosyncratic patterns of participation are more fundamental and general patterns of rationale. Once these are discerned it becomes possible to build classificatory schemes that identify types of processes on the basis of different intersecting patterns of rationales.

The approach suggested here for application to Japan leans heavily on the work of three students of American policymaking: Graham Allison, Theodore Lowi, and Norton Long. Each subscribes to the perspective that *processes* are the appropriate focus of policymaking research. In addition, Allison, Lowi, and Long postulate the presence of multiple actors in most policymaking processes. With certain exceptions cited by Lowi, political issues are seen to engage *multiple* interests, and oversimplified views of the domination of politics by a few elites are rejected. For Lowi, patterns of participation are influenced by the stakes of particular policymaking arenas: elites dominate some kinds of decisionmaking, broad groups are active in others, and narrow interests are accommodated in still a third.[3] Allison, in contrast, views all policymaking specifically as the product of *coalitions* between multiple political actors, without regard to the kinds of actors involved.[4] Finally, Long argues

2. Haruhiro Fukui, "Foreign Policy Making in Japan: Case Studies in Empirical Theory," prepared for the annual meeting of the Association for Asian Studies, Boston, April 1974.
   3. Lowi, "American Business," 688 ff.
   4. Graham Allison, *Essence of Decision: Explaining the Cuban Missile Crisis* (Boston: Little Brown, 1971), especially chapter 5.

that not only are multiple actors present, but in reality political processes are "ecologies of games," a metaphor which emphasizes the fact that the different actors in any policymaking process seek very different kinds of goals.[5] For example, a local road program will involve politicians in their "game" of satisfying different constituencies, the public-works bureaucracy in its "game" of seeking resources at the expense of other agencies, and construction interests in their "game" rewarded by the prize of government contracts. As such, political processes involve not only multiple actors but also multiple frames of reference and rationales for behavior.[6]

The perspective that policymaking should be seen as a process, that most policy processes involve multiple participants, and that all outcomes involve often complex coalitions between multiple actors motivated by different interests guides the following discussion of basic concepts. Once the organizational framework is presented, the utility of examining Japanese policymaking from the perspective presented here is tested by study of several policy processes from 1968. Using an events-analysis approach, this portion of the paper identifies complex patterns of participation in policymaking. Specific roles and motivations, which conform to the categories presented in the conceptual portion of the paper, are inferred from the actions and statements of political actors. Finally, the patterns of actor participation and cleavages between actors discerned in 1968 are employed to suggest more general and pervasive patterns of participation and motivations for participation.

The Rationales for Political Behavior

Some scholars describe political life and policymaking in terms of fairly simple structural paradigms. Particular groups of people are seen as *generally* dominating politics according to their own values or interests. This perspective is shared by both

5. Norton Long, *The Polity* (Chicago: Rand McNally, 1962), chapter 10 ("The Local Community as an Ecology of Games"). Allison also employs the game metaphor; see *Essence of Decision*, 162–63.
6. Long also argues that many games which go on outside politics impinge on political decisions, e.g., the banking game, the construction game, or the labor game. Tangential actors from these who are interested in political outcomes are termed elite onlookers.

elitist and some pluralist political theories.[7] Elitists postulate that a network of persons of high status and influence dominates political life. Some pluralists see political processes as a patterned struggle dominated by a few major groups, such as business, labor, and farmers, the outcome of which contest establishes the rules for all.[8]

These views on the nature of politics and decisionmaking have the advantage of simplicity of statement and generality of focus, and it is certainly possible to say something about political life in most societies by looking at elite strata or the patterns of major group interests. At the same time, these oversimplified versions of political life are of only limited heuristic value to the empirical political scientist. Historical accounts of past authoritarian regimes and contemporary research on the Soviet Union and China inform us that seemingly elitist political systems have extensive internal differentiation and conflict. Creative research on interest-group behavior also indicates that position taking by groups is often designed to accommodate a diversity of specific member interests.[9] In effect, broad analyses of elite or interest structures may be quite misleading in terms of the realities of political decisionmaking. A more satisfactory picture can be gained through analysis of political behavior as manifested in actual political processes.

The analytical perspective employed here examines policy-making behavior by treating individual political actors as the units of analysis. Individual actors, whether specific persons or groups of people, behave in politics in terms of their own motivations and role concepts. Moreover, while there is much that is situational in behavior, the motivations and role sets which lead people and groups to take positions or engage in some kind of action are themselves related to more permanent *frames of reference*. For example, the coalitional politics of the Liberal

7. See the discussion in Lowi, "American Business," especially 678–86, and Nelson Polsby, *Community Power and Political Theory* (New Haven: Yale University Press, 1963).

8. "Structural" discussions of Japanese politics are not uncommon. Among many see Nathaniel B. Thayer, *How the Conservatives Rule Japan* (Princeton: Princeton University Press, 1969), chapter 3.

9. See, for example, Raymond A. Bauer, Ithiel de Sola Pool, and Lewis A. Dexter, *American Business and Public Policy: The Politics of Foreign Trade* (New York: Atherton, 1963), especially 335–38.

Democratic Party is one frame of reference for individual Liberal Democratic politicians' behavior in particular policy processes. Similarly, the interests of different groups and ministries serve as motivations for other actions.

Political actors thus perform policymaking roles or take policymaking positions in reference to some specific rationale for behavior. As we will see, there are multiple rationales in political life. Political actors may simultaneously play roles based on several rationales and may also play different roles at different points in time. Moreover, actors' decisions about what action is appropriate in a particular situation involves not infrequently the choice between behavior appropriate to different rationales.

At least three general rationales are operative in Japanese political life: *advocacy* of interests, *political* advantage, and *institutional* position. The respective rationales and the roles to which they are related (designated in the text by italics) are discussed in ensuing paragraphs.

Most political actors, whether groups or individuals, have interests, that is, specific things they want done through political processes. Interests are the main rationale for the existence and participation in political life of interest groups and many political parties. The situation is less direct for bureaucratic participants. But as Graham Allison has argued, officeholding in functionally differentiated bureaucracies does lead to differences in perspective, and therefore to interests which bureaucrats wish to have politically indulged.[10]

Interests are articulated in the process of *advocacy,* and persons articulating an interest or an alternative proposal for governmental action will be called *advocates.* The goal of advocacy is to have one's needs indulged or one's point of view accepted through the outcome of some political decision or decisions. The frame of reference of advocacy is thus the process of distribution or allocation, regardless of whether the goods distributed are material or whether they are values or points of view.[11] Material distribution includes such diverse outputs as

10. See Allison, *Essence of Decision,* 167.
11. A popular definition of political systems sees the main thrust of political life as the authoritative allocation of values and goods. David Easton, *The Politi-*

highways, tax programs, implementation of a particular kind of
budgetary policy, or choice of a particular foreign-policy alternative; [12] valuational distribution can involve even more varied
items.

The main behavior involved in the process of advocacy is the
act of pressing one's interest or point of view with regard to
some point of controversy or potential choice. Obviously, advocacy involves far more than simply making a statement. Persuasion, exchange of favors, and the search for protectors (or
structured relationships of access to persons who make or influence decisions) are also advocacy tactics.

A second kind of rationale visible in accounts of Japanese
policymaking is that of *political advantage*.[13] For a variety of
reasons, certain political actors are motivated by a concern for
acquiring influence over others. Some want influence in order
to implement their own political views, and for many, seeking
political advantage is the logical extension of advocacy. Others,
however, seek influence to attain a desired position of high status, or simply to carry out official tasks.

Such political influence is often seen as a composite and static
commodity. Some people are believed to have a great deal of
permanent influence, others to have little. In reality, while
some actors undoubtedly are generally more influential than
others, influence in modern political systems is complex.
Rather than being a composite whole, "influence" is really an
aggregation of many small and specific influences. Moreover,
influence is a behavioral phenomenon in that it involves the
manipulation of actors' behavior by other actors. Appreciation

cal System: An Inquiry into the State of Political Science (New York: Knopf, 1953),
130 ff.

12. Unlike Lowi, I prefer to see foreign policymaking as a general alloca-
tional process like domestic policymaking, for the simple reason that foreign
policymaking involves distribution of competing plans, alternatives, and programs. For the actors themselves foreign policymaking is not dissimilar to domestic policy processes. (For Lowi's position on the differences and com-
parabilities between foreign and domestic processes see Theodore Lowi,
"Making Democracy Safe for the World: National Politics and Foreign Policy,"
in James N. Rosenau (ed.), *Domestic Sources of Foreign Policy* (New York: Free
Press, 1967), 295–331.

13. For analogous uses of the concepts of interest and political gain as basic
motivations, see Allison, *Essence of Decision*.

of both the fragmented and behavioral aspects of influence contributes to understanding the "political" motivations of political actors. The compulsion to act in particular ways to enhance one's influence or to minimize the chances of losing influence is ever present, and for this reason political advantage is obviously a frequent motivation for behavior.

Several tactics are used in the process of political advantage. One of the more well-known is the accumulation of support based on debts for past favors or in exchange for promises of future favors. Prime Minister Kishi's promises to multiple potential successors in 1959–60 are a delightful example of the role such favors and obligations play in coalition maintenance within Japan's ruling party.

Such techniques of political manipulation and political influence are well known. Many other ways of seeking influence also exist. The main point is simply that the rationale of political advantage involves position taking different from that governed by the simple logic of advocacy. Appreciation of this difference in rationale facilitates an understanding of the motivations for particular actors' position taking at different times, in different processes, or at different points in particular processes. (Thus initial positions of advocacy may be modified for the sake of gaining influence over others, while some interests may be temporarily sacrificed in order to gain political advantage.)

Where purely political logic prevails particular actors will be termed *politicos*. The adoption of politico roles is particularly common in public policymaking among the central governmental officials of any political system. More leadership is expected from central executives than from other officeholders and the pressures for making specific commitments to particular policy alternatives are great. At the same time, persons in such central offices have achieved and maintained their positions by building coalitions of supporters which in turn restrict their freedom of commitment, at least where differences in opinion among coalition members exist.[14] For this reason, lead-

14. What is said about central executives also holds to a lesser degree for ministers and Japanese party faction leaders in that their behavior is to some extent circumscribed by divisions of opinion within their own "constituencies." My comments on the pressures on central executives and their need for endless

ing Japanese officials inevitably have to consider political costs and advantages which in turn affect their position taking in substantive policy areas. As a result their behavior sometimes seems to consist mainly of ambiguous postures on controversial issues and various techniques of procrastination.[15]

Similar consequences can be seen where positions are predicated on estimates of political costs or advantages in international coalition building or maintenance. In this case, positions are taken on the basis of anticipated effects on relationships with foreign powers. Since central political executives are responsible for foreign-policy leadership to a considerable degree—they are the only political actors who can commit the entire nation to a particular course of action—the roles which they play by necessity reflect the imperatives of international relationships.

A third dimension of motivation is that based on *institutional* roles.[16] It is obvious that officeholders do things by virtue of the particular positions they hold. Yet there is little in the way of a systematic appreciation of the consequences officeholding actually has for policymaking behavior. Governmental position holders participate in policymaking in part because they feel that something is expected from them in the way of performance. Alternatively, overt pressure forces them to take positions or actions, as in parliamentary interpellations or press conferences. The fundamental point here is that the main rationale for some actors' participation in policy processes is their own concept of their role imperatives. Many officeholders would in fact probably prefer not to participate in certain policy processes, given the high costs of participation in terms of time or political advantage. Yet their roles involve frequently inescapable expectations about performance.

The rules and expectations of institutional processes are defined broadly by constitutions and legislation which determine the basic responsibilities and jurisdictions of the main political

consideration of political costs depends heavily on Richard Neustadt's *Presidential Power* (New York: Wiley, 1960).

15. Japanese prime ministers' frequent commitment to "study" particular problems is one example of such procrastination.

16. See Allison, *Essence of Decision*, 164–65, for a similar emphasis on the importance of positions in government to participation in policymaking.

actors. Routinization of policymaking channels supplements these formal legal definitions. Through experience in handling past problems procedures are developed which are applied to new ones. (The methods for determining rice-price supports in Japan are a good example of the development of institutional routines to meet recurring problems.) [17]

To speak of a single institutional process and rationale is of course inaccurate, for there are many institutional processes, role concepts, and motivations. An examination of even fragmentary evidence on policymaking indicates the presence of a variety of activities resulting from the holding of positions or the possession of particular functional assignments. At least six rather distinct types of institutional roles can be isolated. For example, different ministries exhaustively collect statistics, apply laws, develop programs, and engage in an endless variety of activity related to their functional assignment of *implementing* policies and programs.[18] In addition, some institutional actors are asked to provide advice to other actors; this kind of role is called *interpretation.* Political executives and bureaucrats are also pressed for *opinions* in Diet interpellations or in press conferences. In effect, they are asked to explain policies or to rationalize past and present actions. (Such *opinions* should be distinguished from *advocacy,* which involves voluntary expressions of basic interests or policy preferences.) Finally, political actors are not infrequently consulted privately for their views on particular issues. Since neither the content nor the impact of the *consultation* is publicly known in many instances—the actual seeking of opinion may also have been more of a ritual than otherwise—such behavior is different from advocacy or opinion.

It is also clear that some actors play the role of *decider* in pol-

17. Some other examples of the development of routines in Japanese policymaking include the procedures developed to handle intense conflict between ministries or within the Diet. As a result of routinization of this kind prime ministers are not infrequently involved as arbiters in settling interministerial conflicts, whereas a more or less standardized procedure for "normalization" of Diet stalemates exists.

18. For some, policy implementation lies beyond the realm of concerns for *policymaking* paradigms. I do not accept such a view, and believe that policy formulation and policy implementation are intermingled in real-world processes.

icy processes in Japan while others are essentially *ratifiers*. The postwar Constitution anticipated that final decision power would be exercised by the Diet. But the Diet is seldom a decider in a realistic sense, and is more often a ratifier, at least as long as the Liberal Democratic Party's dominant position restricts the opportunities for full play of "normal" parliamentary processes.[19] The cabinet, too, for a variety of reasons often acts as a ratifier rather than a decider.

Though analytically separable it must be noted that there is an intimate connection between holding a particular position in government and the development of interests. As has been observed elsewhere, functional differentiation in modern government leads to differentiation in interests.[20] In Japan for example, MITI has often championed international trade expansion, industrial development, and protectionism, as a result of its traditional concern for implementing economic policies and the Japanese tradition of bureaucratic dominance of some policymaking sectors. Not dissimilarly, the MOF has developed an elaborate array of interests in connection with its role as guardian of the budgetary process.[21]

A more detailed explanation of policymaking behavior would certainly produce a longer inventory of concepts, but the cate-

19. This general point is discussed by T. J. Pempel in "The Bureaucratization of Policymaking in Postwar Japan," *American Journal of Political Science* 18 (1974), 647–64. It should be remembered, however, that the role of the Diet is more complex and varied than my general observations would indicate. For example, amendment by joint agreement between majority and opposition parties has not been uncommon in some periods. See Shigeo Misawa, "An Outline of the Policy-Making Process in Japan," in Hiroshi Itoh (ed.), *Japanese Politics: An Inside View* (Ithaca: Cornell University Press, 1973), especially 33–34. Also it is well known that the opposition parties and their allies have on a few occasions exercised a de facto veto on legislation through intense intra-Diet struggles, supplemented by demonstrations and supported by the press. When these occur the costs of pushing bills through the Diet may become so high that proposals, such as the 1958 Police Duties Bill, are withdrawn for the sake of obtaining passage of other items of legislation. The de facto veto has not worked, however, with regard to some foreign-policy legislation opposed by the Socialists, such as the revisions of the 1960 Security Treaty.

20. Clientele relationships between ministries and organized interests, where they exist, also facilitate ministerial development of advocacy positions on relevant issues.

21. It should be remembered that intraministerial differences certainly exist. An example is the often-noted rift between "internationalists" and "developmentalists" within MITI.

gories considered thus far will suffice for present purposes. The different categories of rationales and policy-process roles are outlined in Table 7-1. At later points in this paper, these concepts will be illustrated further through application to specific events.

Table 7–1. Basic rationales and roles in Japanese policymaking processes

Rationale	Role	Description of Role
Interest	Advocate	Articulates a concrete demand for action or proposes a specific policy alternative
Political advantage	Politico	Makes a statement or takes an action calculated to gain political influence or minimize loss of influence
Institutional position	Decider	Makes a systemically binding choice between different policy alternatives
	Ratifier	Agrees with a prior decision by another actor without interjecting amendments or qualifications
	Implementer	Carries out a program based on prior decisions
	Interpreter	Provides advice on the political or legal implications of policy alternatives
	Opinion provider	Makes a policy statement or explains policy choices after requests by another actor
	Consultant	Gives views on an issue to another actor in private discussions

Some Perspectives on the Japanese Political Process

The application of a behavioral rationale is associated with certain assumptions about the nature of decisionmaking in Japan. These underpinnings should be made clear.

Many studies of policymaking assume that particular major issues are discrete and final events in and of themselves. Thus the Soviet-Japanese Peace Agreement and the U.S.-Japan Mutual Security Treaty revision have become individual subjects for analysis.[22] This differentiation of objects for analysis is a

22. See Donald Hellmann, *Japanese Foreign Policy and Domestic Politics* (Berkeley and Los Angeles: University of California Press, 1969); George R. Packard III, *Protest in Tokyo: The Security Treaty Crisis of 1960* (Princeton: Princeton University Press, 1966); and Robert A. Scalapino and Junnosuke Masumi, *Parties*

methodological necessity in case-study research; however, a different orientation will be adopted here: Policy processes will be viewed as fairly constant streams of functionally differentiated activity. In other words, policymaking involves a myriad of fairly continuous operations and a multitude of "mini-decisions" as well as "'maxi-decisions." Major politicized confrontations are important, but so are routine policymaking activities.

Moreover, routine activities and decisions contribute to the outcomes of major processes and are sometimes as important as more conspicuous and sensational aspects of policymaking. A simple example of this point is found in the three-year process of revising the U.S.-Japan Mutual Security Treaty. Most analysis has focused on the events and confrontations of the spring of 1960. Yet a long period of intrabureaucratic "study," central elite discussion, intra-LDP position taking, and international negotiation took place in the three years before the process reached its peak intensity, and these routine activities prescribed major portions of the positions subsequently taken by political actors in the 1960 confrontations.[23]

The general point is simple: routine processes exist in functionally or substantively different areas and contribute in many ways to the "major" processes which attract public attention and scrutiny. As such, routine political processes need investigation fully as much as "isolated" dramatic decisionmaking. Once the more or less continuous nature of policymaking in different functional or substantive arenas is appreciated, other research perspectives besides the case approach become legitimate. One consequence is that policymaking activities from a specific *time period*—in contrast with a specific issue—can be ex-

---

and Politics in Contemporary Japan (Berkeley: University of California Press, 1962).

23. These comments are based in part on Packard's Protest in Tokyo, in part on an excellent study by Koki Sukegawa of intra-LDP dimensions of the revision process ("Decision Making within the Japanese Liberal Democratic Party," M.A. essay, Ohio State University, 1967), and partly on my own research. Routine processes are discussed as backgrounds to major issues by some scholars, so it is unfair to say that this aspect of policymaking is totally ignored. Moreover, there is no reason to question the legitimacy of looking at major issue confrontations.

amined as valid examples of policy processes. This approach is employed here.

Within the general context of examining routine processes decisionmaking is also seen here as more segmental than is sometimes the case in policy research. Students of policymaking often assume a unity and comprehensiveness not present in reality. Policymaking goes through discrete and independent phases, particular actors are active in some phases and not in others, and particular phases or segments of policy processes may take place simultaneously with little impact on each other. Even in fairly specific substantive areas policymaking thus often resembles a chain of processes or a cluster of processes more than a unitary process.

Obviously, different phases of specific political processes may be interrelated. But for purposes of both empirical accuracy and analytical refinement, it is often useful to see the phases as partially isolated segments of policymaking rather than as a unitary process. In general, appreciation of the segmental nature of processes (when appropriate) facilitates understanding and identification of the motivations which lead particular actors to participate and adopt certain roles. In other words, looking at the behavior of actors in specific contexts makes precise identification of actors' motivations and roles much easier.[24]

It is also important to see that policymaking in Japan is not well coordinated and symmetrical. Some accounts of political life assume that policymaking begins with position taking and proceeds sequentially through deliberation and compromise to decision. Certainly some processes do follow a more or less orderly pattern of this kind. But often some actors take positions as advocates which are never reflected in outcomes, and certain processes seem never to reach a visible conclusion. Moreover, some decisions even precede position taking, as is the case when governmental decisions are followed by ritualized statements of opposition by the JSP or other parties. The asymmetry

24. Both Allison and Long accept the perspective that policymaking is often so weakly coordinated that conceptualization of processes as dominated by a unitary authority structure is highly inadequate. Their observations encourage the view presented here.

and inconclusiveness of some policy processes is reflected in the 1968 scenarios discussed later.[25]

One final qualification is due. There are actually two *kinds* of political processes in Japan, as presumably in most other modern political systems. One, found within the bureaucratic ministries and occasionally in the decisionmaking activities of parties and groups, is semihierarchical in nature. In this case, political actors in subordinate positions typically seek ratification and support of their positions and decisions from persons at "higher" levels in the relevant organizations. In other words, within vertical organizations policymaking by necessity tends to move upward between decision points. This is distinctive from the behavior of persons who speak for organizations or who take individual positions in the more "egalitarian" processes, e.g. where groups, parties, ministries, and central executives are the main actors. The consequences for analysis are interesting. Where processes are semihierarchical, various actors are often brought into the process to legitimate the positions or decisions of lower-level actors. This is often the main rationale for some upper-level actors' policymaking behavior. In contrast, where actors are less constrained by hierarchical role structures, participation patterns are actually simpler; actors speak for themselves or as representatives of groups without the need to seek external legitimation. Realizing that both kinds of processes exist and that they overlap in normal policymaking is fundamental to an understanding of modern political life.

The utility of these organizing concepts was tested in an analysis of Japanese policymaking in 1968 with Japanese press accounts as the main source of information. Through systematic collection of information on all elements of policymaking which came to press attention, fairly complete coverage was ob-

25. Undoubtedly there is more coordination in policy processes than is indicated by press accounts of Japanese politics, which are the basis for the comments here. Still, the extent to which policymaking in Japan resembles a "free-for-all" is remarkable. In at least one of the 1968 policy scenarios examined below, the absence of policy coordination was publicly lamented by a prominent official.

tained.[26] From the many processes identified, seven were chosen for discussion here. The criteria for selection of examples were twofold: avoidance of overlap between similar and tangential processes, such as occurred in the area of trade relations with China, and representation of the overall scope of Japanese policymaking during 1968.[27]

Seven Routine Policymaking "Scenarios"

The organizing concepts discussed earlier were used in the analysis of policymaking in 1968 to delineate patterns of actor participation and role taking. This "test" of the organizing concepts revealed greater variation in participation than is often assumed by scholars of Japan. Cleavage and agreement patterns relating to particular issues could also be readily identified in many cases.

Five categories of political actors have been identified in ear-

26. Using press accounts to develop a systematic data base was inspired in part by the methodology of events analysis used in international-relations research. For discussions of the events approach see Charles F. Hermann, "Comparing the Foreign Policy Actions of Nations," paper presented at the annual meeting of the American Political Science Association, Los Angeles, 1970, and Philip M. Burgess and Raymond W. Lawton, *Indicators of International Behavior: An Assessment of Events Data Research*, International Studies Series no. 02–010 (Beverly Hills: Sage Publications, 1972), especially 45–49. No data source was as suitable for my purposes as newspaper accounts, even given their limitations. Governmental sources, such as the Kampō, provide only formal accounts of output, while Diet committee proceedings and the proceedings of consultative councils lack the scope of press accounts. The main source of newspaper accounts of political life was the U.S. Embassy's *Daily Summary of the Japanese Press.* Use of these translations made possible research using graduate assistants whose competence did not include the Japanese language. The embassy materials in 1968 stressed mainly foreign-policy processes (despite greater attention to domestic affairs in some other years).

27. Proponents of the "tea house" theory of Japanese political processes may find even the above caveats unacceptable. My own research in no way assumes that small-group processes within the LDP and elsewhere are unimportant. What I hope to accomplish by the methodology employed here, is a portrayal of at least some of the general participation patterns in Japanese policymaking.

It should be made clear that the "processes" discussed here were in fact typically portions of processes which began earlier. Also, in many cases critical decisions were taken after 1968. This of course means that all role taking in these issue processes is not captured by the systematic examination of 1968 events and is evidence of the continuous nature of processes, at least in the sense that some lasted beyond an arbitrary one-year period.

lier studies of Japanese policy processes. These include the bureaucratic *ministries*, the prime ministerial–cabinet (executive) *elite*, the *Liberal Democratic Party* and its internal components, *opposition parties*, and *interest groups*.[28] Examination of even a small number of policy processes during 1968 showed complex patterns of participation by the members of these different general categories of actors. The combinations of actors varied between policy processes, reflecting the effects of different combinations of rationales. In addition, the patterns of apparent conflict and agreement were distinctive for specific issues: political actors were on different sides in different situations, and simple overarching patterns of coalitional agreement were not visible.

Policy processes in 1968 were classifiable on the basis of the character of participation and the extent and nature of issue cleavage. The participation and cleavage patterns for each policymaking process are indicated in the titles to the specific issue senarios which follow.

Bureaucratic Dominance and Ministerial Autonomy: Liberalization of Capital Investments and Trade

Ministerial-level deliberations on the liberalization of capital and trade were conducted during most of 1968, with much of the visible activity consisting of announcements by various officials of decisions made autonomously by different ministries. MITI took the lead in terms of the overall volume of announcements. Spokesmen for MITI included Minister Shiina, Vice-Minister Kumagai, Heavy Industry Bureau Directors Honda and Takashima, Economic Affairs Bureau Director Tsurumi, Enterprise Bureau Director Ojimi, and International Trade Bureau Director Miyazawa. The major policy theme manifested in reports of intra-MITI decisions was a form of

28. For example, see Hellmann, *Japanese Foreign Policy;* Packard, *Protest in Tokyo;* Pempel, "Patterns of Japanese Policy Making"; Haruhiro Fukui, *Party in Power* (Berkeley and Los Angeles: University of California Press, 1970), chapters 7–9; Fukui, "Foreign Policy Making in Japan"; Ehud Harari, *The Politics of Labor Legislation in Japan* (Berkeley and Los Angeles: University of California Press, 1973); and Frank C. Langdon, "Big Business Lobbying in Japan: The Case of Central Bank Reform," *American Political Science Review* 55 (1961), 527–38.

progressive protectionism—gradual liberalization of import controls after consideration of domestic effects and development of domestic industrial programs to bolster affected industries. MITI consulted with the MOF, the cabinet, and the Foreign Capital Deliberation Council (a consultative body attached to the MOF) on the pacing of capital liberalization. The Federation of Economic Organizations (FEO) took no visible position on liberalization but reported conducting internal industry-by-industry consultations.[29] The FEO also announced publicly that it would express its positions in meetings of the Foreign Capital Deliberation Council, of which it was a member. During the year timetables for removal of restrictions on various kinds of import commodities were decided, but discussions on capital liberalization were continued into 1969. All decisions taken during 1968 were made at the ministerial level. The cabinet discussed and ratified actions taken by the respective ministries.[30]

Bureaucratic Dominance and Interministerial Cleavage: Selection of Jet Fighters

Implementing its role as the administrator of the Japanese defense establishment, the Defense Agency in 1968 initiated inquiry into the choice of a new jet fighter for the Self-Defense Forces. Staff officers were sent abroad to examine different types of aircraft. The main decision at the ministerial level was left to the Air Staff Office, which recommended procurement of the Phantom F4E. After internal consultation among the administrative deputy director-general, the Defense Bureau director, and the chief of the Air Staff Office, the Defense Agency ratified the Air Staff Office's recommendation. After consultations with Prime Minister Satō this recommendation went to the National Defense Council for consideration. The final decision was delayed, however, by differences within the bureaucracy on the relative advisability of imports versus do-

29. The FEO may have avoided public commitments on liberalization because of differences among its component organizations.
30. This assessment of the nature of cabinet decisions is based on the timing of policy statements and decisions by various actors.

mestic procurement, as well as opposition from the MOF to the scale of the procurement proposal.[31]

Mixed Participation and Low Coordination between Ministries and Political Parties: Reactions to the U.S. Import Surcharge Proposal

Following the United States' proposal in March to impose a surcharge on imports, Japanese leaders considered various responses. Bureau directors from the Foreign Ministry, the MOF, and MITI met in early March to study "countermeasures" to the proposed action. On this and subsequent occasions MITI advocated strong action, consisting of various export promotion and development tactics and restriction of capital investments. The MOF advocated a "wait and see" policy while the Foreign Ministry advocated, among other things, sending a Japanese envoy to Washington to oppose the surcharge plan. The last proposal was accepted by the cabinet on March 12, and EPA Director-General Miyazawa was chosen as envoy. Meanwhile, MITI continued to develop programs to expand exports through the deferred-payments system. It also proposed export cartels and urged reduction of tariffs under the Kennedy Round agreements. Finally, late in March, a resolution was submitted to the Diet urging "blocking" of the United States' surcharge plan. The resolution was supported by all parties in the Diet with the exception of the JCP. Also late in March the Liberal Democrats decided after consultations with the prime minister to send their own representative to Washington to add support. The dominant feature of this stage of Japanese foreign economic policymaking was the lack of coordination between different ministerial and political actors.

Mixed Participation and Interministerial plus Ministerial-LDP Cleavage: Aid to Okinawa.

While temporizing on the subject of the appropriate date for Okinawa's reversion to Japan, the Satō government in 1968 was extending various forms of aid to Okinawa and preparing for extension of domestic administrative programs to the

---

31. I have no evidence on the date of the final decision. One of the problems of press accounts of political life is their greater attention to positions than to decisions.

Ryūkyūs. In this context, uncoordinated efforts were undertaken by various ministries implementing their respective jurisdictional responsibilities: the Ministry of Health and Welfare sought to "unify" the Okinawan social security system with that of the mainland, Labor Minister Ogawa conferred with the U.S. high commissioner about labor programs, and the minister of agriculture and forestry proposed aid for agricultural development. The fragmented nature of these ministerial efforts led to a request from Representative Takase of the U.S.-Japan Ryūkyū Advisory Committee for better coordination of ministerial programs.

At the same time, the LDP's Special Committee on the Okinawa Problem and the Okinawa Problem Deliberation Council, an advisory group to the prime minister, began pressing for big increases in budgetary aid commitments to Okinawa for 1969. The positions of these groups were endorsed by the Prime Minister's Office, which was responsible for Okinawa policy. A 30 per cent increase in aid funds was reportedly urged initially. However, the MOF opposed application of special budgetary criteria for Okinawa, and subsequently Prime Minister Satō committed himself to aid increases only insofar as Okinawa would receive the same amounts of aid as similar mainland prefectures. The dominant features of this process were fragmentation of ministerial efforts and strong differences of opinion between an LPD committee, a consultative group, and the administrative affairs director of the Prime Minister's Office on one side and the MOF on the other.

Mixed Participation, Ministerial–Opposition Party Cleavage, and Intraexecutive Elite Discussions: The B-52's on Okinawa

The Democratic Socialist Party and other groups were opposed to the basing of American B-52 bombers on Okinawa and feared they would be deployed from Okinawa to Vietnam. For this reason, the DSP introduced a resolution in the House of Representatives advocating removal of the aircraft from Okinawan bases. This position was adopted subsequently by Chairman Katsumata of the JSP's Okinawa Survey Mission.

Foreign Minister Miki argued early in the year that Japan could not negotiate on this matter with the United States while the latter retained administrative rights over Okinawa. Prime Minister Satō in March directed the Japanese delegate to the U.S.-Japan Ryūkyū Advisory Committee, Takase, to "study" the problem of the United States' long-range intentions in stationing B-52's on Okinawa. In April, pressed by the Okinawa Problem Deliberation Council's Ohama and others, the prime minister decided to ask the United States to "consider" the Okinawan people's hopes for the removal of the bombers.

The government continued to make cautionary statements on the matter later in the year, particularly after a B-52 exploded at Kadena Air Base in November. Presumably as a result of the multiple pressures and the explosion, Chief Cabinet Secretary Hori in December directed Administrative Foreign Vice-Minister Ushiba to commence negotiations with the United States on "consideration" of the problem.

The Foreign Ministry and opposition parties were the main actors in this issue process early in 1968, but elements within the central executive elite later became involved. The prime minister's initial position, which was to study the problem and its long-range implications, shifted over time in favor of discussing the B-52 question with the United States. This appeared to reflect his adaptation to pressures from within the executive elite and requests for action from other sources. However, his positions on this issue were often clearly politically motivated and consisted of temporizing and letting others in the executive elite take the main initiatives on the issue.

Mixed Participation, Executive Procrastination, and Intra-LDP Conflict: Export-Import Bank Funds and Trade with China

The question was whether or not to use Export-Import Bank of Japan funds in trade between Japan and the People's Republic of China. Supporting the use of these funds were three actors: LPD dietman Furui Yoshimi, a long-time advocate of improved Sino-Japanese relations, the LDP's Foreign Affairs Research Council, which wanted expansion of trade in general, and Minister of Transportation Nakasone Yasuhiro. Opposing the use of the funds was the LDP's Asian Problems Research

Committee, which was pro-Taiwan in orientation.[32] Nakasone's position was especially interesting; he strongly urged general use of the funds even in the face of Prime Minister's Satō's caution that all decisions should be made at the "administrative" level on a case-by-case basis. Satō and his chief cabinet secretary were conscious of the political costs of openly favoring the general use of Export-Import Bank funds as a result of intraparty divisions on China policy and the LDP's general desire to separate trade and political issues, particularly in regard to matters related to China.[33] Nakasone may have been an advocate of the shipbuilding industry's interests on this issue, but it is also likely that he sought to embarrass Prime Minister Satō in view of his own personal ambition to become party leader.[34]

Executive Dominance and Executive-LDP Agreement: Extension of the U.S.-Japan Mutual Security Treaty

Positions were expressed on the issue of extending the U.S.-Japan Mutual Security Treaty throughout 1968, often in response to questions in Diet sessions or press conferences. In this context, Prime Minister Satō was the first to advocate "automatic" extension of the Security Treaty under the 1960 treaty provisions. Other LDP elements, including Vice-President Kawashima, the party's National Movement Headquarters, the Security Problem Research Committee, and the executive officers, subsequently expressed support for automatic extension. The only opposition to the prime minister and the LDP elite during this time came from Transportation Minister Nakasone, who advocated a more "flexible" policy. Ministerial activity during this period consisted of the Foreign Ministry's implementation of the 1960 agreement by preparing

32. The alignments of the "pro-mainland" and "pro-Taiwan" groups are discussed in Fukui, *Party in Power,* chapter 9.

33. Satō may also have been an advocate. He was less "liberal" on China questions than his predecessor, Ikeda Hayato. As in some other instances, it is possible that positions were taken through the complementary motivation of two or three "rationales."

34. Shipbuilding interests were certainly involved, as one of the issues of the Export-Import Bank issue was financing the export of ships. The Ministry of Transportation shares a concern for the shipbuilding industry with MITI.

positions for a meeting of the U.S.-Japan Consultative Committee on Security. The ministry also provided interpretations of
the ongoing treaty, opining that reversion of the Bonin Islands
and the Nuclear Non-Proliferation Treaty would have no effect
on the 1960 security agreement. The Defense Agency also participated in preparations for the joint Consultative Committee
meetings.

Multiple Policymaking Patterns and Rationales

At least three broad patterns of participation can be identified in the seven policymaking situations analyzed. In the first
two cases, activity was concentrated within the bureaucratic
ministries, with nonministerial political actors playing only limited roles in the overtly visible processes. In contrast, in one
issue (the extension of the Security Treaty) bureaucratic actors
played only limited roles, and the main public participants were
components of the executive elite and the political parties.
Finally, four issues (the import-surcharge problem, aid to Okinawa, B-52's in Okinawa, and trade with China) represented
examples of mixed participation, where elements of four of the
major actor constellations—the bureaucracy, the central executive elite, the Liberal Democrats, and the opposition parties—
were active to some degree.[35]

Within these three types of participation there were multiple
patterns of cleavage and different kinds of role taking on the
part of particular political actors. Bureaucratic participation
took at least three forms: interministerial agreement, interministerial cleavage, and interministerial fragmentation or autonomy. Ministerial roles include advocate, decider, opinion
provider, and implementer.

The central executive elite, and especially the prime minister,
took quite different positions in different policymaking situa-

35. Interest groups, notably the FEO and the Japan Automobile Association,
were active on the trade-liberalization issue, but otherwise little group activity
was seen. More of the issue scenarios reviewed here involve foreign-policy issues, and it is likely that interest groups would be more active in domestic issues. Moreover, there may have been groups "present" in these seven issues
whose interests were articulated through clientele relations with ministries. Finally, it is obvious that the use of press materials in general and press translations in particular involves some hazards where adequate coverage of groups'
position taking is concerned.

tions, ranging from consultant and politico to advocate and decider. In one context the central executive elite provided leadership through advocacy of specific substantive positions. Elsewhere the role of the central executive elite was more that of arbiter or decider of last resort. Positions were taken only under pressure from other political actors for resolution of problems or differences of opinion that had emerged at lower levels.

The role of party components was also complex. LDP organs took clear and open advocate roles in both the Okinawa-aid and China-trade issues. In these two instances the timing of statements led to the inference that LDP organs actively contributed to policymaking, probably influencing the final decision in the case of Okinawa aid and contributing to a decisional stalemate in the case of China policy. In the import-surcharge issue, all of the parties played ritualistic roles, advocating that something be done without taking substantively detailed positions. Finally, advocacy in the B-52 case involved the opposition parties in typical protest positions on an issue involving relations between the United States and Japan.

In each of the seven issues, motivations attributable to the different rationales discussed earlier can be seen. The principal positions taken by different actors are summarized in outline form in Table 7-2.

The logic of *advocacy* was most clearly visible and constituted the most easily discernable rationale for participation. In several instances, advocacy reflected highly visible positions articulated by actors in particular issue areas over long periods of time. In a sense, this "characteristic" position taking was akin to the "patterns of interests" advocated as an analytical construct by Samuel Beer and Adam Ulam.[36] Elsewhere, positions reflected adaptation to situations, or at least less highly visible cleavages, as occurred when the LDP Okinawa or Foreign Affairs committees advocated positions on aid to Okinawa and the U.S.-Japan Security Treaty.

Five distinctive advocacy or interest dimensions could be discerned in the seven issues under examination:

1. *Partisan* differences on Japanese security problems and

36. *Patterns in Government* (New York: Houghton-Mifflin, 1960), 51–59.

Table 7–2. Participation and role taking in seven Japanese policy processes, 1968

| | Bureaucratic Participants | | | | | | | | Executive | |
Issue	Labor	Wel-fare	MAF	Trans-port	De-fense	MITI	MOF	Foreign	Prime minister	Cabi-net
Jet fighters					Adv		Adv		Cons	
Trade liberalization						Dec	Dec	Adv	Opin	Rat
Okinawa aid	Impl	Impl	Impl				Adv		Adv	
Import surcharge						Adv	Adv	Adv		Rat
China trade				Pol		Opin			Pol	
Security treaty				Pol	Impl			Impl	Adv	
B-52's								Interp	Dec	

Note: Certain participants have been omitted for the sake of simplicity. Abbreviation of roles are as follows: Adv—Advocated a substantive position; Cons—Consulted i informal discussion of policy proposal; Dec—Made a substantive decision; Im

U.S.-Japan security relationships. These familiar cleavage patterns have been observed at many points since the early postwar period and were present in LDP components' endorsement of "automatic" extension of the Security Treaty and in the opposition parties' pressure for removal of B-52's from Okinawa.[37]

2. *Intra-LDP* differences were most visible in the China trade issue. As had been the case for several years, individuals and groups favoring close relations with Taiwan or with the mainland were active in expressing opinions, in this case on the appropriateness of using Export-Import Bank funds in trade with mainland China.

3. *Intra-LDP* position taking by intraparty policymaking organs was also present. The Special Committee on the Okinawa Problem was an advocate of increased aid to Okinawa, and the Security Problem Research Committee and the Foreign Affairs Research Council (a suborgan of the Policy Affairs Re-

37. Although there are some basic issue cleavages in Japanese politics, this comment should not be taken to imply that all positions and differences have been static. Within the JSP, for example, there has been multiple position taking within the general context of internationalism, neutralism, and opposition to American involvement in East Asia.

articipants			Party Participants						
hief abinet ec'y	Okinawa problem delib. council	PMO admin. affairs director	LDP Vice- Pres.	LDP top officials	LDP foreign affairs research council	LDP Okinawa problem special comm.	LDP Asian problems research comm.	JSP	DSP
	Adv	Adv				Adv			
				Adv				Adv	Adv
					Adv	Adv			
			Adv	Adv					
dv	Adv							Adv	Adv

—Implemented an administrative function; Interp—Interpreted legal implications of policy alternatives; Opin—Expressed an opinion; Pol—Took a position for political motivation; Rat—Ratified position taken by another participant.

search Council) expressed positions on the Security Treaty issue.

4. *Prime ministerial* commitment on the Security Treaty question was clear and unambiguous.

5. *Ministerial* advocacy was visible in four of the seven issues. The MOF's concern for maintaining the integrity of the budget process was expressed in both the jet fighter and Okinawa aid issues; the Defense Agency's jurisdictional interests were present in its positions vis-à-vis the positions taken by the MOF on jet purchases; the PMO Administrative Affairs Director's involvement in Okinawa problems led to his support for aid increases.[38]

The logic of *advocacy* is reflected in these examples; specific interests or points of view led political actors to take different roles in policymaking. The logic of *political advantage* was also a motivating factor for some actors. At times, it explained the particular roles assumed, while other considerations accounted

38. For a discussion of the budgeting principles guiding MOF position taking see John Creighton Campbell, "Japanese Budget *Baransu*," in Ezra Vogel (ed.), *Modern Japanese Organization and Decision-making* (Berkeley and Los Angeles: University of California Press, 1975), 71–100.

for their participation per se. Thus, Prime Minister Satō took *politico* positions as the result of pressures exerted on him as the incumbent of his office. Elsewhere, political considerations determined not only the content of position taking but also the decision to participate.

At least three cases of role taking which reflected political calculations could be discerned in public accounts of the seven processes.

1. U.S.–Japan relations were present as a reference point in Prime Minister Satō's early reluctance to press for removal of B-52's on Okinawa. Exertion of undue pressure on the United States at this point could have adversely affected Satō's main objective of gaining the United States' commitment to the early reversion of Okinawa to Japanese control. U.S.-Japan relations may also have been one of Satō's referents in regard to positions on China trade, and consideration of American positions on China could have been a basis for his leaving trade decisions to administrative components of the government. Certainly there is precedent for drawing this inference about the prime minister's behavior on China policy matters, although causality was obviously complex.[39]

2. The Liberal Democrats' *intraparty* coalitional process was not a frequent rationale in position taking in the seven issues studied here. Faction leaders have taken *politico* positions in the past on such issues as the U.S.-Japan Security Treaty revision or re-establishing relationships with the Soviet Union.[40] However, the positions of Minister of Transportation Nakasone on both China trade and the Security Treaty extension were similar in certain senses to past faction leaders' behavior. Since the Ministry of Transportation was not directly involved in the Security Treaty and only tangentially an interested participant in

39. Much the same "logic" may have contributed to the absence of strong positions on Prime Minister Satō's part with regard to the import surcharge question. As was suggested earlier, Satō's action on China policy had more than one plausible rationale as the basis. The possible "logics" include: (1) a *politico* role associated indirectly with the intra-LDP coalition process; (2) a *politico* role associated with concern for maintenance of the U.S.-Japan coalition; (3) an *advocate* role reflecting his own positions on relations with the mainland.

40. See again Hellmann, *Japanese Foreign Policy,* and Sukegawa, "Decision Making."

China-trade policymaking, Nakasone's position was in each case probably politically motivated. Nakasone's outspokenness in Japanese policy processes is well known and has reflected at some times his "candidacy" for the presidency of the party.

Finally, Prime Minister Satō's decision to leave China-trade policymaking to administrative decisionmakers was in itself plausibly related to the party's coalition process, given the degree of intraparty controversy on China policy. It is true that the Diet members and groups concerned with the China controversy were not the same participants as those typically involved in the intraparty factional coalition process. Still, it is reasonable to believe that Satō, like other LDP executives, was sensitive to nonfactional as well as factional cleavages within the party and to the possibility that nonfactional dissatisfactions could lead to factional disaffection.

3. *Interparty opposition* processes are a plausible referent in the opposition of the JSP and DSP to the B-52's on Okinawa and the import-surcharge issue. Inferring simple motivations for opposition-party behavior in Japan is extremely risky, as specific statements may simultaneously reflect ideological positions, commitment to the "opposition ritual" as a form of self-legitimation, and pragmatic political considerations. For this reason, *politico* roles must be seen as complexly intertwined with other kinds of motivations. JSP and DSP opposition to the U.S. surcharge and the pressure they exerted for removal of B52's from Okinawa stressed the unreliability or arrogance of the LDP's American allies, as well as giving these parties a chance to express their positions on related issues.[41] For this reason, *politico* roles can be inferred as well as position taking motivated by *advocacy*.

Institutional rationales can also be inferred from position taking and participation in the seven issues. Constitutional definitions of the responsibilities of the prime minister and his cabinet place these actors in central positions in many policy processes, even when they do not choose to play the role of advocate. Thus, in the establishment of a tentative policy on the

41. Among them were: opposition to U.S. "imperialism," opposition to the Vietnam War, espousal of neutralism in Japanese foreign policy, and articulation of the positions of labor union clientele groups.

U.S. import-surcharge proposal, the cabinet acted mainly as a *ratifier* of the position of the foreign minister. The cabinet's presence in the policy process was dictated by institutional logic rather than by its assertion of special interests or political considerations. On another occasion, Prime Minister Satō was *consulted* by the Defense Agency director in connection with the purchase of jets for the Self-Defense Forces. He was also an *opinion* giver, and thus a minor participant, in policymaking in the area of trade liberalization.[42] Finally, the prime minister ultimately made a *decision* to press for "consideration" by the United States of the problems associated with stationing B-52's on Okinawa and played a *politico* role on the China-trade issue simply because of the requisites of his position as the leading foreign-policy executive.

In some cases institutional rationales led to interests and to advocacy of particular positions. This could be seen in the prime minister's leadership on extension of the Security Treaty. His position as top executive served as a basis for commitment, as had occurred with other prime ministers' positions on major foreign-policy issues. As is well known, commitments of this kind were made even when intraparty or other political costs were sometimes high.[43]

The logic of *institutional position* can also be applied to the behavior of particular ministries. Ministers are often required to make policy. The establishment of administrative routines and traditional definitions of jurisdictions make it natural for ministries independently to decide or implement policies, as on trade liberalization or the extension of aid programs to Okinawa. Occupancy of positions in these cases led to taking the initiative in policymaking and to participation in policy processes. This is not surprising. But the institutional-game rationale is separate from the rationales of advocacy or political advantage, even

42. Satō's expression of an opinion on the probable course of Japan's trade- and capital-liberalization policy took place in a press conference. Since the wording of his statement was fairly noncommittal, I saw this as different from an instance of personal advocacy of a specific position.

43. A popular line of thinking assigns the commitments on major foreign-policy issues of Prime Ministers Hatoyama, Kishi, Ikeda, and Satō to the desire to make a major contribution to Japanese foreign relations for the sake of historical recognition.

though institutional rationales may lead to ministerial *advocacy* of positions in broader contexts, such as the MOF's defense of the budget in the face of pressures for more Okinawa aid. Similarly, the logic of institutional processes led to the routine *implementation* of characteristic tasks, such as the Foreign Ministry's and the Defense Agency's preparations for international conferences. Finally, the Foreign Ministry's *interpretation* of international events is another example of participation on the basis of the institutional rationale.[44]

Japanese Policymaking: Toward an Integrated Conceptual Scheme

The analysis of seven Japanese policy processes in 1968 has shown many patterns of participation. Different combinations of political actors were found in each of seven issue areas, and the patterns of cleavage differed between processes. The patterns of *participation* were the result of the combination of three separate policy-related rationales: the logic of advocacy, the logic of political maneuver, and the logic of institutional position.[45]

Charting participation in terms of actors' rationales is a step toward adequate conceptualization of policymaking in Japan. The method discussed here has several implications for Japanese public policy research.

Concepts that facilitiate systematic delineation of participation patterns should be an important contribution to future Japanese policy analysis. Most empirical work on Japanese policymaking has taken the form of case studies, and though the findings provide valuable depth and illustrate actors' motivations and patterns of influence in ways that cannot be accomplished by the methodology employed here, case-study results inevitably face the problem of relevance. Moreover, as was

44. The Foreign Ministry's role as interpreter of foreign events and points of international law reflects the "routinization of processes" embodied in internal jurisdictional assignments. Haruhiro Fukui, "Policy Making in Japan's Foreign Ministry," in Robert A. Scalapino (ed.), *The Foreign Policy of Modern Japan* (Berkeley and Los Angeles: University of California Press, forthcoming).
45. Actually only surface evidence of coalitions and cleavages could be observed. The actual personal relationships which underlie coalition building are not usually reported in newspaper accounts of political life.

noted earlier, some bridging conceptual scheme is needed if the findings from case studies are to serve the purposes of theory building, or even simply adequate description.

The main advantage of this approach lies in its emphasis on systematic organization of information through the use of common concepts. It also seeks to go behind the substance of actors' behavior, which is what is reported in most case studies, to consider the reasons for such behavior. The concepts identified are somewhat crude and will certainly be refined through future analysis, but even at this point they permit systematic portrayal and analysis of several issue patterns which displayed a considerable variety of participation and cleavage. Certainly other devices for systematic analysis of policymaking in Japan will be forthcoming. Also, as systematic knowledge of Japanese policymaking increases, important problems of comparative analysis involving Japan and other nations can be broached.

The findings on 1968 processes are also important, even though the main purpose of looking at policymaking in 1968 was to show the utility of a specific conceptual approach. Some general writings on Japanese politics assume that the outcome of most policymaking is the result of intimate interaction between three major actors: the bureaucracy, the LDP, and "big" business. The findings reported here do not completely contradict this interpretation because the data sources used do not generally permit inferences about patterns of informal "behind-the-scenes" communication and influence. Still, identification of multiple participation patterns represents an advance over simpler views of the Japanese political process. Patterns of participation between the parties, the central executive elite, and the ministries varied in terms of the actors visibly present, the roles they played, and the patterns of cleavage among them. The findings thus dispel the impression that there are simple and permanent coalitions between a few major actors who dominate all of policymaking in Japan. Even if the major actors have been identified correctly by generalists the intricacies and complexities of their internal participation and conflict have not in many cases been given due recognition.

8. Patterns of Policymaking: Higher Education

T. J. Pempel

There is no single pattern of policymaking in the area of Japanese higher education. To those exposed, either directly or through the media, to the snake dances, street demonstrations, university takeovers, and urban guerrilla tactics of the various factions of the Japanese student movement and their explosive encounters with the government's extremely well-equipped and highly disciplined mobile police force, the image most forcefully conveyed is one of intense public-private controversy, rooted in diametrically opposed visions of society. Such a perception is bolstered by the knowledge that an antigovernmental, Marxist tradition is solidly entrenched among the faculty members of at least Japan's more prestigious universities and that these individuals are quick to categorize any number of actions by the Japanese government and the Ministry of Education as resurgences of prewar authoritarianism, militarism and illiberalism, only to find these charges countered by government officials as little more than the unrealistic sloganeering of socially dangerous dogmatists.

From the perspective of the education specialist, such an impression may mask a more significant pattern: enrollment expansion and technical reorientation accompanied by little or none of the major controversy that has surrounded such problems in much of North America and Western Europe. Controversy between the government and student or faculty groups is seen therefore as little more than an inevitable, but largely irrelevant, epiphenomenon in the broader pattern of smooth government-directed adjustment to new social and technological realities.

From still a third perspective, this pattern of "successful adjustment" has been at best partial, and at worst nonexistent, given the fact that Japan's private universities, which have taken on the bulk of the expansion, have been in dire economic straits over most of the postwar period but until very recently have been unsuccessful in their efforts to convince the government that they provide a service sufficiently public in nature as to warrant the government's financial assistance. Nor has the government been sympathetic to the economic difficulty of achieving a higher education if one is from a lower socioeconomic bracket. Seen in this light, public policymaking in higher education has been anything but a sanguine process of rational adjustment to new realities; instead it has reflected a pattern of blind resistance to them.

Undoubtedly other images of more or less importance could be identified within the area of higher education alone. A central point to stress is the limited utility of an examination of Japanese public policymaking from a single perspective, based largely on the functional category of the issue involved. Higher education is more than a single entity and there is no reason to assume that the key variable in explaining differences in the ways in which higher educational or any other public policies are formulated is the simple identification of the particular governmental agency which has the ultimate legal responsibility for such formulation.

If in fact public policy has been formulated in vastly different ways even within the rather narrow area of higher education, one must still ask whether each and every formulation is *sui generis,* requiring a great number of in-depth case studies before any "understanding" is possible, or whether in fact certain commonalities or patterns of policymaking cannot be identified even on the basis of a much more limited number of empirical studies. The answer, I think, is the latter. Familiarity with many recent studies suggests at least intuitively certain striking similarities, even as one recognizes certain equally striking differences. The problem is to find the best method of dealing with both real similarities and real differences without unfairly distorting either.

Even though empirical studies on policymaking in Japan

have been appearing more frequently, as Chapter 2 has made clear, they are still relatively sparse when compared, say, to such studies regarding the United States or even Britain. Consequently, any effort to develop an all-inclusive and heuristically relevant typology is likely to result in more wasted effort than insight. At the same time, in view of the fact that most existing typologies of policymaking are specific to the U.S., an attempt to apply any one of them unquestioningly to the Japanese context could well obscure rather than illuminate important variations taking place in the different cultural context.[1]

The development of Weberian ideal types appears more promising as a basis for analyzing many existing studies and as providing suggestiveness and flexibility for future research. Generated through a combination of induction and deduction, such types can be used as intellectual maps against which to highlight particular aspects of known realities, as well as to isolate critical factors which must be investigated further. In each case the map prescribed by the ideal type(s) can be compared to empirical realities, and significant gaps between the map and perceived reality can be targeted for future theorizing and/or empirical investigation. All the while such ideal types remain flexible enough for readjustment in light of new factual discoveries.

Although a number of different ideal types could be conceptualized, this chapter suggests the significance of three in particular: policymaking through camp conflict, pressure-group pluralism, and incremental policymaking. Several dimensions surrounding the policymaking *process* vary sufficiently in each type to warrant separate classification. Further, such variation is largely a function of the interplay between differences in what will be called the *nature of the issue* and differences in *political structures* most relevant to those issues. A word of explanation about each is in order.

1. On the other hand, my thinking has been significantly influenced by the U.S. studies of Theodore Lowi, most notably "American Business, Public Policy, Case Studies, and Political Theory," *World Politics* 16 (July 1964), 677–715, and "Four Systems of Policy, Politics and Choice," *Public Administration Review* 32 (July 1972), 298–310.

It is important to begin by examining the most significant aspects of variation in the policymaking processes. Variation along four dimensions seems to warrant particular attention: the political actors involved, the manner in which they are aligned on a specific question, the intensity of conflict among them, and finally the organizational matrix within which that conflict is resolved and through which the policy is formulated.

The number of relevant political actors on individual questions of public policy is almost infinitely variable, but it is clear that some cases involve a wide range of actors, both public and private, while in others the number is far more narrow. In certain instances, these actors will be relatively flexible in the types of political alliances they will seek to form, reflecting the adage about politics making strange bedfellows; on other questions political arrangements will be almost totally inflexible, with coalitions and alliances obstinately and immutably set. Again, on the level of conflict, it is clear that some political situations will result in a mix of comparatively calm adjustment and horse trading with little more than a few flamboyant speeches to mar the prevailing tranquility, while in others the tactics employed escalate dramatically, in extreme instances even to the verge of civil war. Finally, certain policies will be largely the result of legislative action; other items will be primarily an outgrowth of executive or administrative fiat; still others will involve coordination between public and private bureaucracies. And, of course, many will involve various hybrids of these and other matrices of resolution.

What accounts for such wide variations? Here it will be argued that two major contributing factors are critical: the nature of the issue under dispute and the relevant political structures. It was suggested above that issues are not best approached in terms of the ministries having legal jurisdiction over them. At the same time there is growing recognition of the fact that the issues themselves or aspects of them, may be far more relevant in defining the process of policymaking than was frequently assumed to be the case.[2] There is much less agree-

2. For example, Theodore Lowi, "Four Systems of Policy"; William H. Riker, *The Theory of Political Coalitions* (New Haven: Yale University Press, 1962); Lewis A. Froman, Jr., "An Analysis of Public Policies in Cities," *Journal of Poli-*

ment, however, about exactly which aspects of any issue are the most analytically significant. Nor is it at all clear that understanding the issue per se is sufficient to predicting the process. In particular, the structural features of the political system seem all too frequently to get lost in the focus on issues as the independent variable. Here the interplay between both factors will be analyzed, rather than focusing exclusively on one or the other.

In regard to the nature of any particular issue, at least three components seem particularly significant: divisibility, scope, and affect. Some issues are almost infinitely divisible; they can be broken down into a multitude of small items and small decisions, many of which are subject to various alterations, thus making the entire policy amenable to political compromise. The standard example would be the "pork barrel" where every river drainage created, every municipal auditorium improved, and every new bridge constructed is subject to bargaining and almost infinite compromise is possible, providing "something for everyone" (or at least everyone who counts politically). Of a radically opposite nature are nondisaggregable items demanding either a "yes" or a "no" decision. Either Okinawa is, or it is not, returned to Japanese control; either China is granted recognition or it is not; either the Self-Defense Forces are constitutional or they are not. These issues obviously admit little or no room for compromise, and thus when differences of opinion emerge regarding them, policymaking becomes a high-conflict, zero-sum game.

A second key element is the scope of a particular issue. Some policies are diffuse, affecting, for example, all citizens relatively equally. These are quite different from policies affecting specific subgroups such as farmers, veterans, or businessmen. Other things being equal, the former are likely to generate far

tics 29 (February 1967), 94–108, and "The Categorization of Policy Contents," in Austin Ranney (ed.), _Political Science and Public Policy_ (Chicago: Markham, 1968); Murray Edelman, _The Symbolic Uses of Politics_ (Urbana: University of Illinois Press, 1967); Heinz Eulau and Robert Eyestone, "Policy Maps of City Councils and Policy Outcomes: A Development Analysis," _American Political Science Review_ 62 (March 1968), 124–43; William Zimmerman, "Issue Area and Foreign-Policy Process: A Research Note in Search of a General Theory," _American Political Science Review_ 67 (December 1973), 1204–12; _inter alia_.

more general interest than the latter. At the same time the intensity of the response is likely to be far less for precisely the same reason, while policies affecting a narrower, more specific group can be expected to result in highly intense concern and activity by the sectors or groups affected. In other words, diffuse policy matters will generate diffuse but potentially widespread response; specific policy will generate more narrow but potentially more intense and focused response.

A somewhat related, but isolable, dimension of issue-specific variation is the emotional content, or affect, of the issue. Certain issues, for a wide variety of reasons, almost automatically trigger strong emotional responses and therefore are far less amenable to incremental accommodation and more likely to generate antagonistic and volatile policymaking than issues lacking such affective overtones. This is certainly true in Japan, where issues such as military spending, control over protest activity, nuclear weapons, moral education, university administration, and relations with the U.S., South Korea, Taiwan, and China have long been highly controversial, usually involving clear-cut splits between Japan's progressive and conservative camps. The historical residue of such controversy is embedded in the shibboleths surrounding them: "End U.S. militarism and imperialism"; "The U.S. is Japan's number one ally"; "No two Chinas (or Koreas)"; "University self-governance"; "Socially responsible education"; "Freedom of association"; "No right to disruption"; and the like. Once an issue becomes engulfed in such vitriolic emotionalism, its ideological past becomes a part of the policymaking present. A particular item of U.S.–Japan relations which comes to be categorized by political elites, the media, and the public as militarily related is almost certain to have a line-up of political actors and a pattern of interaction comparable to those that characterized previous militarily related U.S.-Japan issues, as if the dominant factor is the category of issue, rather than the specifics of any particular proposal. Specifics become less significant than symbols. And when an issue becomes publicly identified as part of such larger, recurring symbolic issues, when it is seen as touching on an ideological fault line between the opposing conservatives and progressives, policymaking takes on far more ritualized conflict than when it is not.

Such a perspective suggests why large variations in the processes of policymaking can be attributed to the nature of the issues involved. Nevertheless, it is difficult to argue that the issue per se can explain all of the major variations in policymaking process. For one thing, legal and administrative regulations in most political systems prescribe explicit formal steps that must be taken on different items. For example, certain issues are constitutional in nature and the constitution must be revised before they can be changed. International treaties must be formulated in specific ways. Certain other items are explicitly designated in law, and changes in them must be made through the prescribed legislative process. Still others are the province of some particular agency, insuring that regardless of the divisibility, scope, or affect of the issue, that agency with its own organizational idiosyncrasies is sure to be a participant in the policymaking process. Such features, often seemingly obvious, cannot be ignored in considering policymaking variations.

Finally, one can not ignore political resources. In discussing the scope of issues, it was noted that some issues will leave their impact on a broad, unorganized class or sector of the populace—consumers, women, the middle class, auto users, commuters, or other groups. Others will affect groups represented by far more explicitly political organizations, such as blue-collar workers, farmers, big business, or the residents of particular communities, to name but a few. Clearly the probability of political action by the latter is far greater than for unorganized interests. Of at least equal importance is the fact that success is more likely for certain groups than for others. Thus certain aspects of policymaking in postwar Japan can only be explained if one is conscious of the governmental dominance of the conservative Liberal Democratic Party (LDP) and its predecessors, as well as its close ties to the big-business community and the agricultural sector. The same can be said of the correspondingly far lesser power of organized labor and the political parties of the left. A clear-cut imbalance of power between two competing sides in any dispute, or a relative equality of power between them, is bound to dictate different tactics to each; it also certainly will influence the outcome of their interaction. At least these two political variables of structure and power distribution, then, must be examined in addition to variations in any issue as likely contributors to variations in policymaking processes.

A number of variables have been discussed, both in policymaking per se and as contributors to its variation, most of them with a wide range of possible values. Obviously the number of *possible* interrelationships they could manifest borders on the infinite. Yet to examine all such combinations would be not only cumbersome intellectually but useless for practical purposes since the variables do not interrelate in a totally random manner and most of the logically plausible interactions are unrelated to known realities. In actuality, the variables tend to cluster and combine in such a way that one can construct ideal types of interactions that approximate most significant real-life policymaking situations.

To begin, what was earlier called policymaking by camp conflict is characterized by a process involving many powerful and well-organized actors, arraying themselves along fixed camp lines, and demonstrating a high level of political conflict. Resolution is rather clear-cut, usually after the interaction of the Diet, the cabinet, and the national bureaucracy, often in combination with a great deal of nongovernmental action ranging from media campaigns through street protests.

In sharp contrast, incremental policymaking is marked by a much lower number of usually not very well organized political actors, interacting in a much more fluid, less conflict-ridden manner, and resolvable largely through a series of discrete but eventually related actions of a single bureaucratic agency or subagency. In short, policymaking through camp conflict and incremental policymaking manifest processes which are almost antithetic to one another. Policymaking through pressure-group pluralism, in turn, reflects something of a mid-point on most of the variables identified: comparatively few well-organized participants, more than in incremental policymaking but fewer than in situations of camp conflict; a fluid but not totally mercurial flexibility in alignment; conflict about midway between the other two extremes; and a process of resolution that is relatively clear-cut and largely bureaucratic but usually involves more government agencies than most incremental cases and necessitates greater internal governmental coordination.

These processes, in turn, are associated with different issue types and different structural factors. Issues that are settled through patterns of camp conflict tend to be high in affect, low in divisibility, specific but relatively broad in scope; they also usually involve legal or constitutional, as opposed to administrative, questions and powerfully opposed and well-organized political groups. In contrast, incremental policymaking is associated with issues that are low in affect, high in divisibility, and general in scope; they are far more likely to require administrative decisions and usually involve few if any well-organized and powerful groups from the private sector. Again, policymaking through pressure-group pluralism is identified with mid-points on most of the variables. Table 8-1 summarizes these features.

These skeletal generalizations take on flesh in an examination of several policymaking situations in Japanese higher education. In each case different issues have been resolved through these different policymaking processes. Nevertheless, while the three types of process emerge as distinct from one another, there is within the patterns certain internal variation, mostly in terms of eventual outcome, which is also explored. Thus the general patterns are made concrete, but with greater dynamism and flexibility than is often the case in ideal-type constructions.

Policymaking Through Camp Conflict

Policymaking in the area of university administration has been among the most controversial, politically salient, and publicly visible issues in Japan; it is surely so within the more narrow arena of higher educational policy. Most issues involving university administration have been of limited disaggregability and high ideological affect. Their importance plus their uncompromisable nature has meant that policymaking in this area has generally been characterized by pitched battles between

Table 8-1. Patterns of Japanese policymaking

	Issue			Structure				Process	
	Scope	Divisi-bility	Affect	Institutional requirement	Power resources	Actors involved	Cleavage	Intensity of conflict	Locus of resolution
Camp conflict	Broad and specific	Low	High	Constitutional-legal	Many powerful and well organized participants	Many	By camp	High	Diet, cabinet, bureaucracy
Pressure group pluralism	Narrow and specific	Medium	Medium	Legal-administrative	Few participants but usually well organized	Few	Fluid groups vs. one another and/or government agencies	Medium	Central bureaucracy, often public-private agreements
Incrementalism	Narrow or diffuse	High	Low	administrative	Disorganized if any	Fewest	Disorganized interests vs. usually one government agency	Low	Bureaucratic agency

rather unified political camps—progressives versus conservatives. While such issues have by no means been of high salience to all sectors of Japanese society, their impact has been quite wide and specific among academic groups, political organizations, and much of the informed public. Widespread media coverage, high public interest, and the involvement of a large number of governmental organs, ranging from advisory committees and bureaucratic subsections to the cabinet and the police, have also characterized policymaking in this area.

Some historical background is important in understanding why the issue has taken on such a character. Japan's entire university system was under relatively strict governmental control through most of the prewar period, and recurring struggles took place during the 1920's and 1930's between a government seeking even more control and faculty members seeking greater autonomy.[3] This tradition continued into the postwar period, though the balance of power shifted conspicuously in favor of the faculty during the early years of the U.S. Occupation.[4]

Many faculty members purged before the war returned to their universities; leftist student organizations flourished; faculty members deemed to have been unduly cooperative with the military regime were purged or forced into early retirement and faculty and student power began to thrive on campuses throughout the country. Moreover, political sentiment on campuses ran strongly in favor of the progressive camp and the best universities became progressive strongholds, while the conservatives and the government they controlled became identified by many on campuses as enemy forces.

3. On the history of Japanese universities and problems of university-government relations, in English, see Herbert Passin, *Society and Education in Japan* (New York: Columbia University Teachers' College, 1965), and Michio Nagai, *Higher Education in Japan* (Tokyo: Tokyo University Press, 1971); in Japanese, Nagai Michio, *Kindaika to Kyōiku* [Modernization and education] (Tokyo: Tōkyō Daigaku Shuppankai, 1969); Ikazaki Akio, *Daigaku no Jichi no Rekishi* [History of university self-governance] (Tokyo: Shin Nihon Shinsho, 1965); Ienaga Saburō, *Daigaku no Jiyū no Rekishi* [History of academic freedom] (Tokyo: Kōshobō, 1962); *inter alia*.

4. Kazuo Kawai, *Japan's American Interlude* (Chicago: University of Chicago Press, 1960); Kaigo Tokiomi and Terasaki Masao, *Daigaku Kyōiku* [University education] (Tokyo: Tōkyō Daigaku Shuppankai, 1969), especially chapter 1.

As the Occupation's initial flirtation with such "democratization" gave way to economic pressures and the exigencies of the Cold War, and as the Japanese conservative camp consolidated its control over the offices of government, the heightened antigovernmental protests at many universities turned the unchecked autonomy of the universities into a serious issue. For the Japanese government and its SCAP (Supreme Commander for the Allied Powers) supporters a key concern was to re-establish some semblance of control and to check the rising power of the left.

The earliest major test of strength between the two came in 1948, when the Ministry of Education in conjunction with the Civil Information and Education Section (CI&E) of SCAP generated a legislative proposal which would have drastically reduced faculty power by creating "governing boards" on each campus with broad powers in the selection of the university president and control over budgetary and personnel matters. Board membership would be more than two-to-one nonacademic. The proposal also included provisions for the creation of a national-level "advisory board" which would have broad coordinating powers over universities throughout the country. Its membership also included nonacademics, most of whom would be appointed by the minister of education.

The comprehensive nature of the proposal left little room for compromise, and strong reaction came quickly. Virtually all academic groups, from the new student organization, Zengakuren, through more liberal organizations such as the Japan Science Council and the Council of National University Presidents, took up positions vigorously opposed to the new plan. Debate centered on the question of governmental intervention in the universities' governance, and after a long process of public debate and demonstrations, revision, more debate, more revision, and finally legislative formulation and submission in 1951, the bill died in the Diet without ever coming to a vote, although the government had the votes to push it through. The almost uniform opposition of the entire academic community was bolstered by similarly unified support from the political left, including both the Socialist and Communist Parties and union federations. Moreover, the media and the general public demonstrated significant agreement with the academic-progressive position on the autonomy of the university.[5] Thus the government had few allies or resources with which to push the long conflict to ultimate victory.

This pattern in large measure was repeated in two additional attempts to alter the university administration system by legislation, the first coming during the period 1951–1954, and the second in 1960–1963. In both instances, the government, relying on advisory committees, conservative party organs, and the Ministry of Education, formulated legislative proposals that would have significantly centralized decisionmaking powers within Japanese universities and broadened the potential for government control of both faculty and students. Responsibility for personnel and disciplinary matters would have been transferred from the faculty conference to the university president, who in turn would have become explicitly subject to the authority of the minister of education, both in his appointment and in his general authority on campus. Clearly both these factors would have represented signal power gains for the government and would have allowed very close official supervision and influence over most important campus activities.

In both of these cases, intense political battles occurred along camp lines and the government again failed to gain passage of its proposed legislation. As in 1951, a unified academic community in conjunction with political progressives—primarily the JSP and JCP, and their labor union allies—vigorously opposed the government. Again winning the support of significant segments of the media and the public, the progressive-academic coalition successfully blocked legislative action until the proposals eventually were withdrawn. Alternative policy demands and a growing quietude among student groups undoubtedly weakened the government's commitment to force the issue; at the same time, student protests became less vociferous as legislation became less imminent and as other policy demands came

5. Ikazaki, *Daigaku no Jichi,* 103; Kaigo and Terasaki, *Daigaku Kyōiku,* 596–607; Ohara Seiji, "Daigaku Hōan no Suii" [Developments in the plan for a university law], *Refarensu,* September 1954.

to receive higher legislative priority.[6] In terms of policymaking process the important point to note is the similarity between these unsuccessful attempts at legislation: the wide involvement of a variety of well-organized political actors, their arrangement along camp lines, the vigorous conflict surrounding the process, and the fact that the key efforts at resolution were highly public legislative proposals.

All of these factors were present in the government's final attempt to centralize the university administration, which culminated in 1969; the only key difference was in outcome. This time the government succeeded in passing its legislation, a factor which, as will be seen, resulted largely from a shift in the political powers of the opposing groups.

While Japanese students have long been activists, the protests of the late 1960's went far beyond anything that had occurred earlier in scope, intensity, and duration. Major "incidents" on Japanese university campuses for the period 1950–1964, as tallied by police, averaged fewer than one per year.[7] In 1968, the Ministry of Education calculated that 116 universities experienced significant conflicts, and in 1969 there were major protest activities at more than 75 schools per month.[8] Police figures for this period also indicated heavy activity on university campuses: in 1968, 31 campus actions involved more than 10,000 police and resulted in 425 arrests; for 1969 the figures were up to 938 campus actions involving 243,000 police and resulting in more than 3,500 arrests.[9] Moreover, these figures

6. Of particular concern in 1963, for example, was Japan's treaty with South Korea, and cabinet debate over university measures continually connected the two problems legislatively. *Asahi Shimbun,* January 19, 1963; *Mainichi Shimbun,* January 23, 1963; *Nihon Keizai Shimbun,* January 23, 1963.

7. Nomura Heiji, *Seifu-Jimintō no Daigaku Seisaku* [The university policies of the government and the LDP] (Tokyo: Rōdō Junpōsha, 1969), 43. Of course, much of the focus of student protest in the 1950's had been off-campus, so these figures cannot be taken as measures of total student activity.

8. Ōhashi Hisatoshi, *Shiryō: Daigaku no Jichi* [Source materials: university autonomy] (Tokyo: Sanichi Shobō, 1970), 265 (from data provided by the Ministry of Education).

9. To seasoned American radicals the number of police actions and arrests in 1968 may seem low; however, they reflect primarily a general policy of noninterference by police in university affairs through the first half of 1969 and a policy of making as few arrests as possible on campuses. The police statement of policy at this time is produced in *Asahi Shimbun* (evening edition), Feb-

represent only on-campus disputes and police actions. Off campus, student activists engaged police in numerous additional confrontations.

Most dramatic of all, at Yasuda Hall, Tokyo University, a year-long student strike was broken as over 8,500 riot police armed with duralumin shields, armored vehicles, water canons and a tear-gas-spraying helicopter engaged radical students wielding iron pipes, stones, hatchets, rivet guns, gasoline, poison, explosives, and a flame thrower, in a televised battle that lasted two days.[10] Although not all protests reached such levels of violence, rocks, iron pipes, glass, wooden staves, and Molotov cocktails became standard equipment for demonstrating students, and violence was commonplace.

Since the protests in 1965 and 1966 were fundamentally localized on individual campuses and concentrated on such particularistic issues as tuition, control of dormitories and student unions, and curriculum,[11] government officials encouraged administrators to curtail protests on their own by calling the police,[12] and thus drove a wedge between different sectors of the university community.

As protests escalated, and as university officials seemed increasingly unable to cope with them, the government more frequently threatened to alter administrative controls, thereby creating an even more ambiguous situation for administrators

ruary 13, 1968, and *Mainichi Shimbun* (evening edition), February 13, 1968. Relations between police and the university community, are discussed *inter alia* in Inoue Seiji, "Daigaku Jichi to Keisatsuken" [University autonomy and police authority] *Hōritsu Jihō,* Special Issue, January 1970, 108–17; Okudaira Yasuhiro, "Daigaku to Keisatsu" [Universities and police], *Jurisuto,* no. 426 (June 1969), 63–70.

10. Stuart Dowsey (ed.), *Zengakuren: Japan's Revolutionary Students* (Berkeley: Ishii Press, 1970), 156–57.

11. A causal analysis of the earlier disputes is compiled in *Jurisuto,* no. 347 (June 1966), 46–51. Regarding the later disputes, see the listings in *Shūkan Asahi,* September 13, 1968; *Sandē Mainichi,* February 20, 1969; *Sankei Shimbun,* July 3, 1968. A related analysis which attempts to deal with the specific catalysts to student protest and the issue of university alienation is Nagai Michio, *Daigaku no Kanōsei* [Possibilities for the universities] (Tokyo: Chūō Kōronsha, 1969), 11–118.

12. Mombushō, *Gakusei Mondai ni kansuru Daijin Danwa oyobi Tsūtatsu nado,* [Speeches, communications, and other items of the Minister of Education concerning the student problem] (Tokyo: Mombushō, 1970), 38–45.

and many faculty. Clearly unfavorable for the most part to student demands for increased participation and to student violence, administrators and faculty were at least as hostile to suggestions of direct government intervention in their universities or alterations in university administrative structures.[13] The Ministry of Education finally announced that it would no longer rely on simple cooperation with university administrators but was willing to take steps of its own to curtail protest activities.

In November 1968 the ministry called on its advisory body, the Central Education Council, to consider more explicit governmental measures to meet the growing tide of protest. From then until April 30, 1969, when the council issued its report, the Ministry of Education increasingly favored taking legislative steps aimed at major changes in university-state relations.

When the government proposed specific legislation, the entire political complexion of the problem took on most of the classical dimensions of previous government-university controversies, and numerous academic and progressive-led demonstrations took place against the bill, culminating in a flurry of bipolar conflict in the summer of 1969.[14] Yet while formally the

13. *Ibid.; Asahi Shimbun,* December 2, 1967.
14. The increase in public and media attention that took place at this time was remarkable. Journalist Fukashiro Junrō notes somewhat plaintively how he sought in vain for statements of policy by the major political groups during the summer and fall of 1968; "Daigaku Mondai ni tai suru Seitō no Taishitsu" [The predispositions of the political parties toward the university problem] *Gendai Seiji,* June 1969, 6–7. The issue had somehow remained "nonpolitical" at least to the extent that most normally involved political bodies had not even issued statements on the subject. By late fall, however, the situation had changed remarkably, and political interest and action escalated in the following months. In November 1968 the police began to issue monthly statistics on the number of university conflicts that had occurred or were still in progress. In November and December 1968 all five of the major political parties put forth tentative plans, proposals, or recommendations on the university problem. So too did the Japan Science Council, the Japan Teachers' Union, the Japan Federation of Employers' Associations, and dozens of other groups with more or less political relevance to universities. Most are reproduced in Yamamoto Tokushige, *Daigaku Mondai Shiryō Yōran* [Handbook of source materials on the university problem] (Tokyo: Bunkyū Shorin, 1969), 425–39. Newspaper headlines were dominated by university-related stories, public-opinion polls tapped every conceivable dimension of the problem, and books and articles on the university and the student problem quintupled between 1967 and 1969. Kitamura Kazuyuki's figures show a jump in books on the subject from 25 in

university community was united against government legislation and the LDP and the business community supported it, the apparent unity along conservative-progressive lines concealed more fundamental divisions on questions related to student power and violence where the conservatives were unified and the progressives badly split.

Only the "new left" students and their most far-left allies were in general agreement on tactics and power demands, while the JCP and its student allies (the Minsei) openly denounced violence. Furthermore, organizations of university administrators and many faculty members who had on earlier occasions generally supported progressives rather than conservatives were at this time more in agreement with the latter on questions of student participation and tactics. This split between progressives and the academic community left the advocates of intervention in a comparatively strong position. Seemingly, no other alternative could both end the violence and retain limits on the political power of students.

The report of the Central Education Council's special subcommittee in April 1969 managed to blend these three elements—student power, tactics, and legislation—so effectively that granting the government greater administrative powers including the power to intervene in university disturbances emerged as a logical necessity.[15] To the extent that public opinion is any indicator, the presentation of the case as involving these three highly interrelated elements was successful. Polls show that those who disapproved of the law in the abstract had a clear plurality, but those who saw no alternative when combined with those who approved of the law made an even more impressive and "realistic" majority.[16]

The final version of the bill drawn up by the Ministry of Education in consultation with senior LDP leaders during the summer passed quickly on August 7, 1969. A temporary mea-

---

1967 to 275 in 1969 and an increase in articles from 401 to 1,746. *Daigaku Gakusei Mondai Bunken Mokuroku: 1965–1971* [A Bibliography on higher education and students in Japan 1965–1971] (Tokyo: IDE, 1971).

15. The report is reproduced in Yamamoto, *Daigaku Mondai Shiryō Yōran,* 425–39.

16. *Asahi Shimbun,* May 29–30, 1969.

sure to last only five years, the bill granted substantial powers
to the university president and more especially to the minister
of education, particularly as regards control over protest activities and the administrative and personnel matters related to
them.[17] Most fundamentally, the minister was given the power
to suspend all education and research functions in any university where a dispute lasted more than nine months or where a
dispute of six months' duration recurred within one year after
it had been settled. During any such suspension, government
funding for student scholarships and faculty salaries would be
fully or partially curtailed and the time of suspension would
count toward neither graduation for students nor promotion
for faculty.

This law was the first major legislation affecting the overall
governance of the universities since the earliest reforms of the
Occupation. In one sense, it was the culmination of a long government drive to significantly centralize powers within the university and to sharply alter the balance of power between the
universities and the government—something the government
had been unable to do under the late Occupation, in 1954 and
in 1963. Certainly many of Japan's progressive scholars have
offered such an interpretation.[18]

Although the nature of the issue and the structural political
variables were roughly comparable to those of the earlier cases
where the government had not succeeded, two factors did
change sufficiently to insure the government's legislative success in 1969. The issue of university administration was complicated by the introduction of the subissues of violence and student power, and these in turn divided the previously united
progressive camp and the academic community sufficiently so
that their ability to prevent government action was muted.
They also led to public and media demands for strong action
by the government, whereas in earlier cases both had opposed
such actions. Consequently, the government was willing to risk

17. Text of law is in Tabata Shigejirō *et al.* (eds.), *Sengo no Rekishi to Kihon
Hōki* [History and fundamental regulations of the postwar period] (Tokyo:
Yūshindō, 1970), 239–44.
18. For example, Nomura, *Seifu;* Nagai Ken'ichi, *Kenpō to Kyōiku Kihonken*
[The constitution and bases of authority in education] (Tokyo: Keisō
Shobō, 1970).

greater political capital to end these protests, insuring in the process substantial increases in its own power over university administration.

Despite the differences in eventual outcome, the picture of policymaking that emerges from these cases is quite comparable. Each time, the issue involved primarily nondivisible components of high ideological salience to important and well-organized actors in opposing camps, making compromise exceptionally difficult and camp conflict the dominant mode of resolution. While an objective assessment of long-run political factors surely favored the government's gaining legislative victories in all cases, however, the unity of the progressive camp and academic circles in the earlier situations combined to make the costs of such a victory exceptionally high, and the desired changes in university administration were simply not worth the price to the government. When the scope of student demands and tactics to achieve them radically altered public opinion, though, and simultaneously divided academics and progressives on several important subquestions, the government was quite able to achieve success.

Policymaking through Pressure-Group Pluralism

University administration has been a decisional area involving policymaking through camp conflict: the arena affected is broad; numerous nongovernmental groups are involved in pressing or opposing demands; political parties and their internal organs are highly active; many governmental institutions are involved, including bureaucratic and legislative committees, full and special sessions of the Diet, one or more cabinet ministries, the cabinet itself, and the Prime Minister's Office; the policymaking process has generally been a media event worthy of McLuhan; the total political resources invested have been extremely high; and most fundamentally there has been a high degree of ideologically based camp conflict throughout the policymaking interactions. A rather different pattern of policymaking involves the call by some private nongovernmental group for official action on narrow, rather specific problems which may or may not be opposed by other private groups or by sections of the government. Several specific issues illustrate

this general pattern, again with important intrapattern variations. Key educational demands of two different groups will be
examined: "big business" and private university officials.

The Japanese big-business community, primarily through
its peak organizations—Nikkeiren, the Japan Federation of
Employers' Associations (JFEA); Keidanren, the Federation
of Economic Organizations (FEO); and Nihon Keizai
Dōyūkai, the Japan Committee for Economic Development
(JCED)—as early as October 1952 pressed the government to
increase the specialization of higher educational institutions
and their graduates. At that time a JFEA "Opinion Paper on
the Re-examination of the New Educational System" argued
that although the great majority of university students entered
the business world after graduation, the educational perspective ignored them in their capacity as potential employees. The
report criticized "the lack of integration between [general] education courses and specialized courses" and called for increased
specialization throughout the higher educational system.[19]
Many subsequent proposals from JFEA, FEO, JCED, and the
Kansai Economic Federation between 1954 and 1961 reiterated
and concretized these early demands.[20]

With relative uniformity the reports all called, among other
things, for science and engineering facilities of higher quality,
for an increase in the number and competence of technical
graduates, for postgraduate training of industry personnel,
and for the creation of five-year industrial and technical
schools which would combine the last three years of high school
with two years of college and would emphasize vocational training. The demands were based on data showing the relatively
poor "production" of scientists and engineers in Japan as com-

19. The report appears in Yamamoto, *Daigaku Mondai Shiryō Yōran*,
475–76.
20. For example, "Futatabi Kyōiku Seido no Kaizen ni tsuite" [A second
proposal on the reform of the education system], which is analyzed in Kaigo
and Terasaki, *Daigaku Kyōiku*, 447–49, and reproduced in Yamamoto, *Daigaku
Mondai Shiryō Yōran*, 477–78 under the title "Kyōiku Seido Kaizen ni kansuru Yōbō" [Demands in regard to the reform of the education system].
See also, *inter alia*, "Shinjidai no Yōsei ni taiō suru Gijutsu Kyōiku ni kansuru Iken" [An opinion on scientific education to respond to the demands of a
new age], reproduced in *ibid.*, 479–82.

pared to other industrial nations and the economic significance of greater university responsiveness to business demands.

The economic motivation behind the propositions was obvious. A larger pool of well-trained scientists, technicians, and engineers in the tight Japanese labor market would be of clear benefit to large technical manufacturing firms; businessmen throughout the world have made similar demands. Nonetheless, more overt political motivation was not absent. In their November 1960 statement, for example, JCED stated: "For the development of a healthy democracy we must train a common-sensical middle class which will serve as a stable social force." They also said that "in order to bring students into the camp of democracy and capitalism the financial world must make cooperative moves toward students. For these purposes, it will be most effective to rely on a movement for 'industrial and university cooperation.' " [21] Such explicitly political motives, though, remained very much in the background of discussion, and the demands were pressed as predominantly those of an interest group requesting particular help from the government, albeit that of a group providing the main financial support for the government party.

The earliest element in the demands to be officially considered was the request for the creation of the five-year technical schools. In the fall of 1952 the JFEA began a concentrated two-year campaign aimed at forcing the junior colleges created after the war to focus their attention on industrial and work-oriented education; [22] most of the students in the two-year colleges were enrolled in the fields of literature, homemaking, law, and economics, with well below 10 per cent in the occupationally more relevant fields of science, engineering, agricultural sciences, and nursing.[23] Constant public and private pressure from the business world was exerted on the Ministry of Education, and in the fall of 1955 Education Minister Mat-

21. *Asahi Shimbun,* July 10, 1960; also in Nomura Heiji et al., *Daigaku Seisaku—Daigaku Mondai* (Tokyo: Rōdō Junpōsha, 1969), 666.
22. E.g., *Asahi Shimbun* (evening edition), October 26, 1952; *Mainichi Shimbun,* October 31 and November 15 (evening edition), 1954; *Asahi Shimbun,* November 1 and November 5 (evening edition), 1954.
23. Mombushō, *Kyōiku Tōkei Shiryōshū* [Collected education statistics] (Tokyo: Mombushō, 1970), 45–56 (my calculations).

sumura announced plans to submit the question to its main advisory body, the Central Education Council.[24] The ministry proposed in December 1957 to cease recognition of the junior colleges beginning April 1, 1959, and to establish occupationally oriented Specialist Colleges (Senka Daigaku) beginning in 1960.[25]

The junior colleges collectively opposed any such changes, which would have required not only a reversal of their collective philosophy but also major financial outlays. Through the Junior College Association they brought counterpressure within the LDP, particularly on upper house members of the party, and the plan which had been ratified by the Education Committee of the lower house was revised modestly.[26]

The plan was resubmitted to the lower house Education Committee. Still, however, the positions of the business world, the LDP, the bureaucracy, and the junior colleges were not reconciled. Finally, after much debate, an organizationally irrational but politically sensible compromise emerged in which junior colleges would be allowed to continue, their aim being to provide both general and professional education for secondary-school graduates and also to develop the intellectual and practical abilities required for their future careers and practical life.[27] Meanwhile, a new law providing for the creation of a totally separate system of five-year technical colleges in line with business demands passed quietly through the Diet. Since then these schools have produced large numbers of middle-level technical personnel and have received the acclaim of the business community.

Business made demands in several other areas. In addition to the creation of the higher technical schools, they sought a pol-

24. *Mainichi Shimbun,* September 14, 1955, dealing with *tanka daigaku* and *senka daigaku,* both of which phrases were in use at the time for the newly proposed institutions.
25. *Mainichi Shimbun,* December 9, 1957.
26. *Asahi Shimbun,* November 1, 1958; *Tokyo Shimbun,* March 3, 1959; *Yomiuri Shimbun,* March 9, 1959. This pressure came in conjunction with upper house elections and parallels that exerted by the repatriates, as noted by John Campbell in Chapter 4.
27. School Education Law, Article 69.

icy of institutional specialization and differentiation at the university level. The U.S. Occupation had revised the prewar system, making general education and the four-year university the keystones of higher education, on the premise that these in turn would create and sustain a critical citizenry who would support democracy and be a bulwark against future authoritarianism. From the perspective of Japanese business and industry this new system succeeded simply in producing a generation of "overeducated" youth whose theoretical orientations interfered with their ability to perform well in the business world after graduation.

Such discontent was articulated again through a series of position papers, combined with private lobbying and other pressures, subtle and overt. In contrast to the efforts to have the junior colleges transformed into technical schools, which met opposition from junior colleges and their association, most of the demands for specialization and differentiation ran into less organized opposition. Part of the reason for this is that the demands being made were far less damaging to any group's interests than was the case regarding the junior colleges; part must be attributed to the internal division of organizations representing the four-year colleges and universities; and part must be attributed to the fact that the university system as set up by the Americans was never universally accepted by Japanese academics.

In any event, in response to business pressure, the government made changes in three related areas: general education requirements were lessened; emphasis on scientific and technical training was increased; and major structural differentiations were built into the system between "research-oriented" institutions (*sōgō daigaku*) and "ordinary universities" (*tanka daigaku* or *daigaku*) where the focus was almost exclusively on teaching.

The process by which these changes were made was almost entirely intrabureaucratic. In 1954, for example, the Ministry of Education issued an administrative directive (*shōrei*) which spelled out the initial differentiation between institutions oriented toward teaching and those whose raison d'être was research.[28] In 1956 a second directive formalized the distinction. Huge gaps in budgeting and in the size and quality of graduate facilities and research institutions subsequently deepened it. The 1963 report of the ministry's Central Education Council on reforming the university system was oriented around this basic distinction, and the 1971 report of the council, heralded as Japan's Third Educational Revolution, took them even further.[29]

On the question of general education, too, the shift was accomplished bureaucratically. The University Standards, which were the basis on which the Ministry of Education granted charters to universities, originally required two years of general liberal-arts education in all universities. In the face of criticism from the business community, which was later taken up by a few members of the LDP, the Ministry of Education in June 1954 exempted medical and dental programs from such requirements, by directive, and in 1956 it issued another directive, which affected all courses of study,[30] reducing by 20 per cent the required general-education offerings. The directive also dropped several broad areas from the required course offerings and allowed more specialized subjects to be substituted. Foreign-language study was de-emphasized, and an additional 20 per cent of the total general-education requirement could be fulfilled by introductory or prerequisite courses for subsequent specialization.[31] These new regulations therefore both weakened the requirements for a university's overall offerings in general education and foreign languages and allowed specialized courses to be included in the calculation of the general-education credits needed for a student's graduation.

Despite these changes, pressure in business circles continued

28. "Kokuritsu Daigaku no Kōza ni kansuru Shōrei" [Administrative directive on chairs in the national universities], Administrative Directive No. 23 (1954) of the Ministry of Education.

29. Chūō Kyōiku Shingikai, "Kongo ni okeru Gakkō Kyōiku no Sōgōteki na Kakujū Seibi no Tame no Kihonteki Shisaku ni tsuite" [Concerning basic measures for the overall expansion and consolidation of future school education], report dated June 11, 1971.

30. "Daigaku Setchi Kijun," as in Mombushō, *Mombu Hōrei Yōran 1971* [Handbook of Education Ministry laws and ordinances] (Tokyo: Teikoku Chihō Gyōsei Gakkai, 1971), 177–91.

31. *Ibid.*

against the general-education program, and in 1963 a special Ministry of Education research committee was established to investigate the University Chartering Standards. After two years it submitted a report to the minister of education calling for the elimination of any minimum general-education requirement.[32] Some organized counterpressure from several academic groups developed, and there was a delay in the implementation of the report as quiet accommodations were sought.[33] Finally, however, in August 1970 the Ministry of Education issued a ministerial directive containing a second major set of revisions that further reduced the general-education requirements.[34]

A final dimension of the government's response to business concerns its decision to increase the number of science and engineering graduates. The first systematic effort in this regard came in 1957, when the Ministry of Education decided, in consultation with several of its advisory and study committees, to increase the entry quota for freshmen enrolled in science and engineering departments by 8,000 as part of a five-year economic plan aimed at meeting the alleged shortage of graduates in these fields. By 1960 this target had almost been met; however, in October of that year the Economic Council's "Plan to Double the National Income" declared that a suitable growth rate would require an increase of 170,000 scientists and engineers in Japan between 1960 and 1970. It therefore called for long-range planning in conjunction with the universities to overcome the predicted shortage.[35] The Science and Technology Council in the Prime Minister's Office echoed this demand with its "Comprehensive Plan for the Advancement of Science and Technology during the Next Ten Years."[36]

The Ministry of Education initially proposed to increase the

32. The report is in Mombushō, *Atarashii Daigaku Setchi Kijun: Ippan Kyōiku* [The new university chartering standards: general education] (Tokyo: Mombushō, 1970), 113–36.

33. The reaction of the Japan Educational Society's Committee for the Study of the University System to the draft report is given in *Kyōikugaku Kenkyū*, March 1966, 91–95; the reaction of the Association of National University Presidents in Mombushō, *Atarashii Daigaku*, 137–54; and that of the University Accreditation Association in *ibid.*, 155–62.

34. Directive No. 21, 1970.

35. Report is in Nomura, *Daigaku Seisaku*, 667–70, *inter alia.*

36. *Ibid.*, 672–81.

enrollment in science and engineering departments by 16,000 per year starting in 1961. The business federations countered that such an increase would be insufficient; eventually an increase of 20,000 per year was established as a goal for the years 1961–1964.[37] This was subsequently revised upward each year and the annual number of graduates in these fields nearly tripled between 1960 and 1970.

The shift was again achieved through essentially bureaucratic means, largely under the control of the Ministry of Education: changes in the entry quotas for specific university departments, encouragement to establish or expand existing science and engineering departments, and financial inducements such as special funding for private university expansion in the sciences.[38]

The picture that emerges, then, is of a government policy consciously formulated and implemented to alter the structure and content of the higher educational system in such a way as to make it increasingly specialized, occupation-oriented, and responsive to the needs of big business. That such a policy has been followed should occasion little surprise in light of the early history of Japanese higher education, the close ties between business and government in Japan, and the comparatively unified desire of both these groups for a higher education system responsive to "social needs." In fact, however, "social needs" have been equated with "business demands" by both groups, and there is a striking failure on the part of both to distinguish the concepts of effective or market demand from those of human or social need.[39] The 1971 report of the Central Education Council clearly equates "social need," "social demand," and "business demand."

The process involved in meeting such business demands, though, shows several contrasts with that involved in university-administration issues. Perhaps most noteworthy in a structural

37. "Gijutsu Kyōiku no Kakkiteki Shinkō saku no Kakuritsu Suishin ni kansuru Yōbō" [Demands in regard to the establishment and promotion of a policy for epoch-making advances in technological education], *ibid.*, 682–83.

38. A special subsidy to encourage science education in private universities was begun in 1956. Mombushō, *Wagakuni no Kōtō Kyōiku* [Higher education in Japan] (Tokyo: Ōkurashō Insatsukyoku, 1964), 133 (hereafter WP '64).

39. See, *inter alia*, Robert Paul Wolff, *The Ideal of the University* (Boston: Beacon Press, 1969), 36 ff.

sense is that whereas university administration was an issue which had the Diet as the focal point of key decisions, coping with business demands took place almost exclusively through bureaucratic agencies, bureaucratic directives, and alterations in bureaucratic practices. Party organs, the Diet, and the cabinet were for the most part not significantly involved, except for the relatively noncontroversial legislation regarding junior colleges and technical schools. Moreover, public awareness of the issue and media attention were quite low. Finally, such conflict as was generated over the various subissues came, not from the major power blocs in the antigovernmental camp, but rather from specific groups or interests explicitly affected by the proposed changes. For the most part, the process involved a rather classical replication of the interest-group pressure(s) and governmental response(s) that form the core of the pluralist interpretation of politics.

While this pattern was also generally followed in the case of private-university demands for increased government aid, it would be a mistake to infer, as is the pluralist tendency, that the requests of all organized interests are as quickly and effectively dealt with. Even though the forms of policymaking were comparable, the demands of private-university officials were met far more reluctantly and with far more subsequent governmental controls than were those of the business groups.

Government aid to private universities has been a problem since the end of the war. Private universities were highly concentrated in Tokyo before the war, with the result that most suffered severe bombing damage. This, combined with high inflation immediately after the war, left most institutions with almost no financial resources. Some ad hoc aid was given to private universities immediately after the war, but the new Local Autonomy Law and Article 89 of the 1947 Constitution were interpreted by the government as preventing the distribution of public funds to private institutions, with the result that virtually all assistance was stopped.[40] Eventually some minimal aid was given in the form of long-term loans; health, death, and hospitalization benefits to private-school teachers; and spe-

40. WP '64, 119–28.

cial loans to build new facilities for training science and engineering students. But in all these cases the monies involved were trivial compared to the operating costs of the private institutions; between 1960 and 1965, for example, government aid averaged less than 3 per cent of the expenses of private universities.[41]

Private universities grew dramatically in number and as a proportion of the total higher education system during the 1950's and the 1960's: 51.7 per cent of all universities and 66.5 per cent of all students were in the private sector in 1949; by 1973 the figures were 73.2 per cent and 78.5 per cent, respectively.[42] If junior colleges are included the percentages are even higher. But as their collective importance increased their individual financial conditions deteriorated. Tuitions, entry fees, and additional "donations" from students skyrocketed; [43] bank loans were increasingly relied on for operating capital; and in turn interest payments on borrowed money began to occupy an ever mounting portion of most universities' budgets. In 1967 they constituted 7 per cent of the total private-university budget.[44] The result was that the private universities came to present a curious juxtaposition to the improving economic conditions in the country as a whole.

The private universities—individually, through their several federations, and through the quasi-governmental Japan Science Council, which was made up primarily of university faculty members—issued numerous public statements stressing their importance to the nation and engaged in relentless private lobbying through the Ministry of Education, seeking response to their demands along much the same lines as had the

41. Mombushō, *Wagakuni no Kyōiku no Ayumi to Kongo no Kadai: Chūō Kyōiku Shingikai Chūkan Hōkoku* [The course of Japanese education and future problems: interim report of the Central Education Council] (Tokyo: Ōkurashō Insatsukyoku, 1969), 412–13.

42. Mombushō, *Wagakuni no Shiritsu Gakkō* [Private schools in Japan] (Tokyo: Ōkurashō Insatsukyoku, 1967), 234; Mombushō, *Mombu Tōkei Yōran* [Handbook of education statistics 1974] (Tokyo: Ōkurashō Insatsukyoku, 1974), 54–55.

43. Statistics in *Mombu Tōkei Yōran* and Ōsawa Masaru, *Nihon no Shiritsu Daigaku* [Private universities in Japan] (Tokyo: Aoki Shoten, 1968), *passim.*

44. William K. Cummings, "Japan's Educational Revolution" (paper delivered to Association of Asian Studies annual meeting, Chicago, March 30, 1973), 53–54.

business federations.[45] The "campaign" was more poorly organized and coordinated than that of the business community, however, and the government, especially the Ministries of Finance and Education, continued to maintain the position of "no support, no control." (The absence of government funding preserves the autonomy of the private institutions.) Not infrequently the charge was leveled that in fact the government's position would have been more aptly stated in reverse: until we get control, we will provide no support. Certainly, the antigovernmental positions taken on a number of political issues by prominent private-university faculty members and administrators did not help their cause. This, coupled with the private universities' adamant insistence that aid in no way be allowed to compromise their independence, undoubtedly contributed to the government's reluctance to grant the requested aid. But most fundamentally, the government was giving primary attention to an economic policy of rapid growth in which any "unnecessary" expenditures for social overhead received very low priority.

Finally, in July 1965 the Ministry of Education, in response to these pressures and to the deteriorating financial conditions of the private universities, consented to establish a temporary investigating committee to suggest policies for the promotion of private schools. After two years of investigation the committee issued a series of important recommendations. Accepting the logic that private universities performed an important national function, the report called for increased funding through the government's Association for the Promotion of Private Schools and through politically opportune measures such as increased scholarship assistance to students and tax relief for donors to private universities. The committee was divided, however, over the more important question of aid for personnel expenses; the report recommended further study and stressed the importance of Article 89 of the Constitution as a barrier to such aid.

45. Funding requests issued in November 1957 and November 1959 are in Nihon Gakujutsu Kaigi, *Kankoku-Seimeishū* [Collected advice and declarations], Vol. 2 (January 1957–January 1963). Additional requests made almost annually can be found in subsequent volumes of the same series.

The Ministry of Education responded by extending the period for construction aid, increasing the scholarship program, setting up plans to encourage private donations, and allowing funds previously reserved for aid only to science and engineering students to be used by students in other disciplines. It also submitted a budget request to the Ministry of Finance calling for approximately $28 million in relief over a three-year period.[46] Significant in principle, the actual monies involved remained but a trivial portion of the actual costs of the private universities.[47]

The truly significant breakthrough came only in June 1969, a period, it will be recalled, of intense student protest, much of it widely attributed to the poor conditions of the educational environment. At that time the Central Education Council in recommending measures to improve higher education suggested among other things the need for substantial governmental subsidies to private institutions based on some fixed proportion of their actual needs. However, in the interim report and in the final report a year later, the issue of funding was tied to the need to increase the "public character" of the private universities through central governmental planning for all higher education and rigid investigation and evaluation of the uses to which the funds were put.

The Ministry of Education in its 1970 budget proposals to the Ministry of Finance included a request for significant new funding for private universities. Coming as it did in a climate of intense governmental concern over student protests, the request was favorably received by the previously more tight-fisted Ministry of Finance. After wide consultation the cabinet proposed a system of substantially more government funding, including the partial subsidization of faculty salaries.[48]

46. Ōzaki Jin, "Shiritsu Daigaku" [Private universities] in Shimizu Yoshihiro (ed.), *Nihon no Kōtō Kyōiku* [Japanese higher education] (Tokyo: Daiichi Hōki, 1968), 180–88.
47. Ministry of Education, *Educational Standards in Japan, 1970* (Tokyo: Ministry of Education, 1971), 247.
48. Nihon Kyōiku Shimbunsha, *Nihon Kyōiku Nenkan 1971* [1971 yearbook of Japanese education] (Tokyo: Nihon Kyōiku Shimbunsha, 1971), 209, 219–21.

After the education committees of both houses of the Diet added several "supplementary resolutions of clarification" which detailed the operating procedures and emphasized that the bill was in no way intended to compromise the autonomy of the private universities, the bill passed both houses unanimously in April.[49] The amounts to be made available to private universities promised to be substantial, with up to 50 per cent of faculty salaries eventually to be governmentally subsidized.

Numerous new potentials for control came with the money, however. The foundation dispensing the funds was governmental in nature, with the minister of education appointing the major personnel; grants were not to be automatic but based on individual, reviewable requests; in the meantime, various financial and personnel data had to be regularly reported by the recipients. Clearly, numerous private-university officials, while anxious to receive the added funds, were chary of the potential abuses of the new system, and few saw it as the unqualified boon they had hoped for.[50]

A number of key features in the policymaking processes involved in settling these two different issues are rather similar. First, the demands were made publicly of the Ministry of Education and to a lesser extent the LDP. Second, the demands, although they had clear political components, were largely economic in nature; while they were frequently assessed in terms of national needs and social demand, rather than as the demands of a specific interest group, they lacked the highly ideological nature associated with issues of administration. Third, most of the important decisions were made by bureaucratic agencies and their advisory committees; cabinet and legislative decisionmaking, where it occurred, was largely uncontroversial and ratificatory. Fourth, the entire process lacked the publicity and ideological conflict that dominated the politics of university

49. *Ibid.*, 209.
50. In a confidential interview with a senior official of a major federation of private universities I was told that such concerns were groundless, only to be later called aside by the official's next-in-command and told that in fact such fears were quite strong, and his reading of a number of clauses in the new legal arrangements left him convinced that governmental efforts to control the private schools had been explicitly included.

administration. Policy thus emerged as something approximating the vector sum of the competing forces involved rather than as zero-sum victories and defeats.

Revealing differences between the two processes exist, however, particularly in the levels of success achieved by the two groups and in the concomitant demands made by the government. Certainly one factor to note is that the business organs were more in harmony over their demands than were the private university federations. Both were represented by several peak associations, but the business associations' voices blended as a chorus while the private-university associations' were far more cacophonous. The three peak associations of private universities held drastically different philosophies, reflecting the different sizes of their constituent members. The League of Private Universities of Japan, for example, representing the larger, older universities, tended to be officially less anxious about aid and more concerned about protecting its membership from government interference than, in particular, the Association of Private Colleges of Japan, which represented the more numerous smaller institutions. The two thus rarely acted in harmony. The Japan Science Council, meanwhile, whose members come from public and private institutions, rarely coordinated its actions with private-university groups.

Economics, too, must be noted as a factor differentiating the issues. Increasing the specialization of universities required various inducement funds, and the amounts involved were significant both in terms of absolute monies for new and existing departments in the specialized fields within publicly funded institutions and in the less quantifiable sense of deferred opportunity costs. However, the amount of absolutely new budget items required for specialization in no way approached the level of funding that might have been required to salvage the floundering private universities, and long-term commitment to the latter would have shown a much less tangible payoff. Relatedly, the business demands were explicitly articulated in terms of future contributions to the government's overall policy of high economic growth, while the demands of the university federations had to be seen as contradictory to that policy.

Still, a third very important factor must be added to account for the differences in response to the demands of the two groups. Big business is of far more political import to the governing conservatives than are private university administrators, for financial, political, and ideological reasons, and this difference undoubtedly accounted for a great deal of the government's quicker and more favorable response to business demands.

Despite the differences in response there remain again broad similarities in the policymaking processes of both cases which are notably different from those of the process described above as policymaking through camp conflict. Moreover, the consciousness of decisionmaking in both of these cases (and in total policymaking) as well as the fact that policy implementation was governmental differentiates the pattern in particular from that involving incremental policymaking.

Incremental Policymaking

If some issues of a highly ideological nature, broad and specific scope, and an inherently zero-sum nature almost invariably become decided in a highly publicized, camp conflict-ridden environment at the highest levels of government; and if others, being more interest-group-specific, inherently divisible, and of lower ideological salience, are decided most frequently at lower levels under less controversial circumstances; still a third policymaking syndrome can be identified: that of incremental policymaking.

Robert A. Bauer speaks of policy as involving those decisions and actions "which have the widest ramifications and the longest time perspective, and which generally require the most information and contemplation." [51] It would be a mistake, however, to conclude that policies must by their very nature involve conscious, deliberate, and visibly articulated decisions; to do so is unduly to restrict the meaning of the term. As Peter Bachrach and Morton S. Baratz have suggested, there is a policymaking phenomenon which appears to be decisionless since "policy choices are frequently made in the absence of clear-cut, once-and-for-all decision. They simply 'happen' in the sense

51. Robert A. Bauer and Kenneth J. Gergen, *The Study of Policy Formation* (New York: Free Press, 1968), 2.

that certain steps are taken that are necessary but preliminary to a decision; and the sequence of steps acquires . . . a life of its own." [52] Sometimes institutions do not formally consider certain matters for clear-cut decisions, and yet it is meaningless to deny that they have policies in those areas. This is particularly so when they engage in actions which are systematically and consistently based upon a single line of thinking and have significant and unidirectional consequences. Such consistency in action must surely be recognized as "policymaking." One area in which policymaking of this sort has occurred in Japanese higher education has been in regard to the question of enrollment expansion.

During the prewar period, Japanese higher education was extremely elitist. Only 4 per cent of the relevant age cohort were attending any institution of higher education in 1940; only about one-quarter of these were in universities; and only a minuscule proportion attended the high-prestige "Imperial Universities," graduates from which generally secured the most advantageous positions.[53] The U.S. Occupation sought to induce greater egalitarianism by consolidating the system in accord with an American model. The four-year university was to be the new keystone; tracking was to be eliminated, and the university degree was to become generally more accessible to qualified students. Reorganizing the many kinds of prewar institutions into new four-year universities was a confused process, but by the end of the Occupation 7.5 per cent of the age cohort were attending institutions of higher education.

As has been noted elsewhere, however, the real expansion in university enrollments came after this and was attributable to actions not of the Occupation but of the Japanese government.[54] These actions lacked the character of explicit choice involved in the policies discussed in the previous sections. Instead, enrollment expansion emerged as an outgrowth of incremental actions within the Ministry of Education which allowed for the creation of numerous new private universities

52. *Power and Poverty* (New York: Oxford University Press, 1970), 42.
53. Passin, *Society and Education,* 104.
54. T. J. Pempel, "The Politics of Enrollment Expansion in Japanese Universities," *Journal of Asian Studies* 33 (November 1973), 67–86.

and which removed virtually all regulations on quality, giving the universities an implicit inducement to expand as the popular demand for diplomas increased.

Following the rapid changes of the Occupation, and in the face of a recession that raised serious doubts about the employability of university graduates, the Ministry of Education initially sought formally and informally to *constrain* any increases in the university population and to focus attention on improving existing facilities. Particularly important in this process were restrictions on the issuance of charters for new universities. Provisional charters were eliminated, and the ministry's Council on University Chartering was ordered to examine all qualifications rigidly with the aim of allowing no new universities.[55]

Subsequently strong political pressures were exerted on influential members of the newly formed Liberal Democratic Party by groups and individuals seeking to establish new universities, usually through an upgrading of their own junior colleges or high schools. As a result the LDP threatened budgetary retaliation if more political sensitivity were not shown in granting charters. The Ministry of Education responded by revising its chartering standards and instituting a process of individual, politically motivated exceptions to the "no new charters" policy.[56]

In 1962, in the face of an improved economy and the front edge of the postwar baby boom, additional inducements to expansion took place: increased funds were made available to the Private University Promotion Association and requirements for consultation between university officials and the Ministry of Education concerning revision of entry quotas were dropped.[57] During the same period an even more important factor began to affect the expansion of enrollment: the nonenforcement of a variety of legal minimum standards within universities. These standards, enforceable by the Ministry of Education, are based on a university's annual student entrance quota and deal with

55. *Mainichi Shimbun,* August 13, 1955; *Sangyō Keizai Shimbun,* September 15, 1955; *Asahi Shimbun,* September 9, 1956; *Education in 1955: Annual Report of the Ministry of Education* (Tokyo: Ministry of Education, 1957), 87.
56. *Education in 1955,* 87.   57. WP '64, 37–38.

various minimum facilities such as full-time faculty, classroom space, library facilities, and the like. Moderately enforced during the mid-1950's, these standards became the subject of a twofold deviation: first, the quotas came to bear no relation to the size of a university's actual entering class, many institutions exceeding their quotas by over 100 per cent; and second, the minimum standards, even on the basis of the irrelevant entrance quotas, were never enforced by the government, resulting in ever widening gaps between the written standards and the realities in most universities.[58] As a consequence, universities could be created or expanded with little need to insure quality education.

As a consequence of these various actions and nonactions the number of universities and students jumped drastically between 1962 and 1968. In the last year of the Occupation (1952), twenty-one new universities had been created and student enrollment was nearly 40 per cent higher than the previous year. During the period 1954–1957, when the ministry sought to control expansion, only seven new universities were created and the average annual increase in the number of entering students was about 2,750. From 1958 through 1961, twenty-two new universities were established and the average annual increase in the number of entering students rose to 9,750. From 1962 to 1968, 122 new universities were established and the average annual increase in the number of entering students rose to a phenomenal 20,860.[59]

An overview of the process of enrollment expansion makes clear the gap separating it from the camp-conflict policymaking of university administration or the pressure-group pluralism of specialization and private-university aid. Most noteworthy is the absence of any overt identifiable governmental decision to expand enrollment. Instead, policymaking took the form of a series of seemingly separate but in reality interrelated decisions on matters which had the cumulative effect of encouraging expansion. The unidirectionality of the government's actions and the tangibility of the results make it clear that the government's policy was to allow maximum expansion.

58. Pempel, "The Politics of Enrollment Expansion," 71–73.
59. Based on calculations from Mombushō, *Kyōiku Tōkei Shiryōshu*.

Also noteworthy is the fact that like policymaking in matters that are interest-group-specific, many key policy decisions were made within the bureaucracy with a minimum of publicity and virtually no significant cabinet or legislative participation. However, the bureaucratic actions related to enrollment involved simply insuring the conditions likely to encourage expansion; the actual decisions to expand were made by individual universities, not the government. Thus the government policy was not self-enforcing as in the cases previously examined; rather it required the activities of nongovernmental institutions for its fulfillment.

One of the major reasons why policymaking in this area was different from the others is the nature of the issue. Even though the universities benefited to the extent that they could expand as they saw fit, the expansion policy must really be said to have served the bulk of the Japanese citizenry—or at least that portion of it sufficiently well off financially to allow their offspring to take advantage of the new openings. Furthermore, these broad benefits were granted in a manner not likely to threaten the existing interests of any politically significant sector of society, not even in the sense of the mild pluralist competitions occasionally arising in matters relating to specialization and private aid to universities. Nor did the issue touch on any ideologically salient fault lines. Any ideological overtones the issue may have had were those of almost universally acceptable democratization. Anyone opposing enrollment expansion ran the risk of being dubbed elitist.

The issue also required little expenditure of financial or political resources by the government. Pushing through an unpopular university-administration measure could cost dearly in public image and political resources; aiding private universities and increasing specialization meant budgetary changes. Enrollment expansion, on the other hand, coming as it did primarily through expansion in private universities, cost the government very little economically, yet paid off handsomely in meeting the latent demands of Japan's emerging middle-class families anxious to insure a university diploma for their offspring. The benefits generated thus became a virtually costless component of the broader climate of "peace and prosperity" through which the conservatives sought to strengthen their popular support.

If the nature of the issue differentiates it from those examined earlier, it must be noted that structural political factors were not irrelevant to the outcome of the policymaking process. Japan's capitalist economy and its conservative, somewhat paternalistic political rule no doubt influenced the implicit decision to expand and to do so by relying on the private, rather than the public, sector. The presence of an expanding, more affluent middle class, coupled with the coming of age of the more tangible postwar baby boom during the middle and late 1960's influenced the policy. Further, it is clear that the discretionary powers of the Ministry of Education played a significant role, especially in the changes in the chartering process and in the nonenforcement of minimum legal standards.

Summary and Conclusions

Most fundamentally this chapter has sought to demonstrate that there is no single pattern of policymaking in Japan, even for issues within the same functional category. Rather, there are at least three qualitatively different syndromes of policymaking which diverge widely on such matters as the degree of conflict present, political alliances, publicity and media coverage, organs of ultimate decisionmaking, and degrees of political involvement. One pattern, which is here labeled policymaking through camp conflict, is dominated by high involvement, attention, and conflict; a wide range of political actors are involved, hostilely arrayed along camp lines, and the ultimate policy usually emerges from the Diet and/or the cabinet. A second pattern, associated with interest-group demands for specific governmental benefits, is marked by much lower levels of interest, conflict, and involvement and is normally settled through bureaucratic measures. Conflict resolution tends to involve nonideological pluralist bargaining, and if and when Diet or cabinet decisions are necessary, they are of a far less controversial nature. Finally, a pattern called incremental policymaking has been identified, which is dominated by a series of interrelated decisions that establish policy only through their cumulative impact.

These different syndromes appear to be activated most basically by the nature of the issue about which the policymaking is taking place—its disaggregability, its ideological salience, and its scope—combined with structural political factors such as legal requirements and political resources. Different clusters of such variables elicit very distinctive policymaking responses. At the same time, fluctuations in specific political resources at particular points in time allow for significant variations in outcome within these general patterns. This was certainly the case among the several university-administration policies examined, and in the greater governmental response to the demands of big business than to those of private-university administrators.

These findings are of course subject to all of the standard caveats concerning the preliminary nature of the work, the limited data base, the need for further refinement, and so forth. No model or paradigm is presented; at best the three types provide an initial framework from which to begin defining certain key parameters of Japanese policymaking. Yet examination and understanding of this problem is essential whether one's ultimate aim is to assess the power balance within Japan, or, more normatively, to ask questions concerning the degree of democracy in Japanese political processes, or to take a prescriptive approach aimed at suggesting partial or total alteration in the present policymaking processes. Dealing with any of these problems requires a clear conceptualization of how policy has been formulated in the past. The higher educational material in this chapter should provide some useful facts on this account. In addition, since the types set forth seem to bear a close relationship to known realities from a variety of other areas they should also contribute to the theoretical groundwork for future research.

9. Conclusion
T. J. Pempel

The broadest conclusion emerging from this book is that Japanese policymaking is extremely heterogeneous. The findings of the individual chapters make it difficult to speak meaningfully of any single policymaking process in Japan; no two essays point to precisely similar processes; most, in fact, describe processes that operate in strikingly different ways. The government at times appears to be capable of major innovation, such as, for example, occurred in its moves to arrange for improved relations with China, to reshape university administration, and to extend the Security Treaty with the United States. In other instances, however, such as pollution, compensation for the repatriates, investment liberalization, and university-enrollment expansion, the government remained basically inert until forced to respond to overwhelming pressure from broad subsectors of the domestic society, or from foreign governments.

In some cases policymaking was closed and relatively out of public view, such as Tanaka's visit to Peking, the reaction to the U.S. threat of import surcharges, and decisions to make higher education more specialized. In others, such as the B-52's on Okinawa, the pollution problem, university protest in 1968–69, and the setting of rice prices, it is difficult not to conclude that vast numbers of individuals and groups were critical to the eventual outcome, and dominance of the process by a small elite is impossible to infer.

In a few instances, personal relations and individual leadership seem critical; in others, social forces achieved such a driving momentum that individuals seem to have been swept along, capable at best of incremental influence on the much broader social tide.

Much the same diversity appears concerning political institutions. The Diet was a critical institution in the passage of pollution-control measures in 1970, in all cases involving university administration, and, to a lesser extent, in setting rice prices and in reacting to the U.S. proposal for an import surcharge. Such instances in isolation could easily lead one to conclude that the Diet is actually, as well as constitutionally, "the highest organ of state power." Yet the Diet was irrelevant to Tanaka's visit to Peking and in university-enrollment expansion and was pertinent to the 1970 extension of the Security Treaty only insofar as the government and the ruling LDP sought to prevent the problem from being actively considered there.

Local government and the courts, to cite other institutional examples, are generally accorded minimal significance in Japanese policymaking studies, and indeed they appear to have been totally uninvolved in most of the cases analyzed here, but their significance in problems of industrial pollution make it dangerous to infer that either lies on the periphery of national policymaking. Whether ignored unfairly by past researchers or propelled to new significance as a result of new issues, these institutions have clearly become critical to this important issue, and one can no longer presume them to be insignificant in national policymaking.

Similarly, the opposition parties, which not infrequently seem the embodiment of irrelevance in the face of the "real politics" purportedly taking place within the LDP, the upper levels of the civil service, and the big-business federations, were in fact essential in determining at least the outer limits to policy choice in the case of the B-52's on Okinawa, university-administration efforts, and many pollution measures. Moreover, individual opposition-party members played vital roles in the negotiations with the People's Republic of China preceding Tanaka's visit. From another perspective, any assessment of Sōhyō and the JSP as leftist and "people-oriented" must confront the reality of their reluctance to sacrifice votes, jobs, or the wages of union members when confronted with a choice between industrial polluters and Minamata victims.

Similar variety exists in the policymaking contributions of the bureaucracy, individual ministries, advisory committees, the media, the various peak associations of labor, agriculture, and business, and virtually every other sociopolitical institution. None plays an absolute, clear-cut, and unvarying role. Nor is it easy to generalize for the entire policymaking spectrum about phenomena such as the significance of ideology, the tendency toward compromise or conflict, lines of political cleavage, popular participation, or the importance of technical versus political criteria in decisions.

Many existing generalizations about Japanese policymaking must thus be re-examined. Factionalism, which is allegedly inevitable in Japan, seems to have had little impact on most of the cases examined here. Cultural explanations, based for example on *oyabun-kobun* or *giri-ninjō,* useful as they may be in differentiating aspects of Japanese policymaking behavior from that in other societies, are of little import in capturing significant intrasocietal differences such as those analyzed here. Moreover, since a number of policies have clearly come from the top down, the general predominace of *ringisei* is questionable. Finally, the wide differences in opinion and the ever shifting lines of political cleavage make it impossible to sustain any claim that policymaking in Japan involves the largely harmonious interaction between government and society that is implied in the notion of "Japan, Inc." [1] In short, there is tremendous diversity in Japanese policymaking, defying most existing generalizations.

Despite this diversity it is also clear that some policymaking processes bear striking similarities to one another. The essays by both Richardson and myself attempt to establish bases on which to extract patterns from among the multiplicity of policymaking situations, and most of the material in the other essays

1. The notion of "Japan, Inc." is presented in many studies for and by U.S. businessmen. Typical is Eugene J. Kaplan, *Japan, The Government-Business Relationship: A Guide for American Businessmen* (Washington, D.C.: U.S. Department of Commerce, 1972). See also Herman Kahn, *The Emerging Japanese Superstate: Challenge and Response* (Englewood Cliffs, N.J.: Prentice-Hall, 1970), chapter 4. For a useful antidote, see Gerald L. Curtis, "Big Business and Political Influence," in Ezra F. Vogel (ed.), *Modern Japanese Organization and Decision-making* (Berkeley and Los Angeles: University of California Press, 1975), 33–70.

can be readily incorporated into either approach. Donnelly's analysis of the annual setting of the rice price, for example, Campbell's analysis of government benefits to repatriates, and Richardson's assessment of financial aid to Okinawa all parallel that which I have called pressure-group pluralism. By the same token, the issues of pollution control and B-52's on Okinawa were resolved by a process analagous to policymaking by camp conflict. While what I have called incremental policymaking is a pattern less widely examined, the decision automatically to extend the U.S.-Japan Security Treaty seems to fall into this pattern in many respects.

Other combinations and patterns could be formed along different lines. Tanaka's decision to visit Peking involved largely a once-and-for-all problem, in which a sequence of mini-decisions led up to one major decision which, once made, was largely irreversible. This was similar to the processes which led to the purchase of Phantom F4E's, and the compensation of repatriates and pollution victims. Considered on an annual basis, most of the decisions concerning the price of rice are also parallel. University-enrollment expansion, pollution control, and decisions concerning the use of Export-Import Bank Funds in trade with China, by way of contrast, all necessitated a series of overlapping and reconfirming decisions over much longer periods of time, with numerous opportunities for minor adjustments or significant revision.

The empirical material presented is rich enough to provide many other combinations and distinctions. What is highlighted will depend on one's intellectual and research interests, regarding both policymaking itself and the types of broader implications sought about Japanese politics. But in using the material in such an inductive way it is important to realize that three quite different bases of explanation have been offered as leading to variations in policymaking process. Furthermore, the cases are examined at different levels of analysis.

Beginning with the types of explanations, differences in policymaking are seen to result from variations in the nature of the issue, from variations in political institutions and structures, and from variations in political roles. Each author usually relies on one or two, and though none utilizes all three, they all could usefully be kept in mind in reading any one of the cases. It would be well to examine each briefly, as well as some of the conclusions they suggest.

That variations in policymaking may be the result of variations in the issues around which policymaking occurs is evident first from the simple organization of studies by functional areas (environment, agriculture, education, foreign policy). This method does in fact isolate quite different arenas of power, such as the nongovernmental groups, the bureaucratic agencies, and the internal organs of political parties and the legislature most directly involved. Nevertheless, as was noted in Chapter 8, such a functional approach is but a first approximation in the analysis of policymaking differences within a single country; certainly other factors involving the nature of the issue must be considered as well, and most of the papers assess the relationship between issue and policymaking process as more complicated than functional categorization alone.[2] Several examine a variety of factors which differentiate issues *within* the same functional area; others examine the manner in which an item takes on a different problematic character under varied sociopolitical circumstances. Issues with a high ideological content, for example, are associated with policymaking different from that occuring around issues lacking such ideological moment, regardless of functional specificity. Issues that affect large and powerful interests are handled in quite a different manner from those that do not. Issues requiring disaggregable financial allocations differ in the manner of their resolution from zero-sum, winner-take-all situations. Issues which are extremely technical give far more political leverage to bureaucratic and/or party experts than those which revolve around personalities or which are more glibly reducible to partisan slogans.

A second basis for explanation throughout the book is the contribution made by political institutions and structures to policymaking variation. Japanese law mandates different legal procedures for different circumstances. Some items must

2. The most noteworthy statement of this position is perhaps in Theodore J. Lowi, "American Business, Public Policy, Case Studies, and Political Theory," *World Politics* 16 (July 1964), 677–715.

legally be dealt with through the legislative process; others are reserved for the courts; still others can legitimately be handled through some component of the bureaucracy, such as an advisory committee, a public corporation, or a single cabinet-level agency; some, finally, are legally given over to quasi-public or private organizations.

Additional structural features also emerge as influencing the manner in which policy is formulated. Campbell and Donnelly, for example, in their separate essays, show the importance of advisory committees as integral components in shaping the policymaking processes. Rice-price advisory committees with different memberships altered the nature of conflict around the setting of the rice price at different times. The mere establishment of an advisory committee to examine the claims of the repatriates was itself a victory for them, as well as a major step toward the problem's resolution, according to Campbell. From a somewhat different perspective Fukui stresses the importance of the smallness and ad hoc nature of the group at the core of the decisionmaking process behind Tanaka's decision to go to China.

When decisionmaking power is left to a diversity of autonomous nongovernmental agencies, such as happened in university enrollment, coordination of policymaking efforts is far less likely than when a high degree of governmental aggregation occurs, such as took place in the arrangements for Tanaka's visit to China or the decision to liberalize trade and investment. When private interests are united and politically strong, they are naturally far more likely to be successful in their demands on government agencies than when they are not, as is suggested by a comparison of the situation of the rice farmers, the repatriates, and big business on the one hand with that of private-university administrators, the early pollution victims, and the opposition parties regarding B-52's on Okinawa on the other.

The third type of explanation concentrates on personalities or roles. Fukui in his essay on Tanaka's visit makes clear how important individual motivations and actions can be to the process whereby an issue is resolved. Were it not for the talents of a limited number of Foreign Ministry diplomats, had important members of opposition parties not been willing to play quiet and cooperative roles in laying the groundwork, had Tanaka not been capable of exploiting the "honeymoon effect" of a new prime minister, it is unlikely that the policymaking would have gone forward as it did. This is not to say that Tanaka would never have gone to China or that relations between the two countries would not have been normalized had these personal factors been different, but it is clear that individual decisionmakers took actions critical to the shaping of the policy that eventually emerged. A similar argument can be made for the role played by Ueki Kōshirō and a few others in the settlement of repatriate compensation or for Prime Minister Satō's personal actions in the Okinawa reversion period. Specific actions by many individuals were necessary, if not sufficient, in the development of various distinct policies.

An important component of such individual influence is role perception and motivation, a matter given the most particular attention in Richardson's chapter. As he notes, each political actor in his time plays many different, and occasionally competitive, roles; or as Clinton Rossiter puts it in his discussion of American presidents, the person in office may wear many different hats.[3] Which hat is worn is often critical to the manner in which policy evolves. Different chapters make this point in various ways, but in the aggregate all show that certain organizations or individuals with presumed political significance are not equally interested or effective in influencing the outcome of all issues and that they may take different types of positions under different circumstances. Compare, for example, the strong presence of the Finance Ministry in some issues and its total absence in others; or the role of Nōkyō in rice prices and its irrelevance in matters involving Export-Import Bank funds. Though important in the repatriates' case, Ueki was not particularly relevant in any others. Big business, while interested in and powerful enough to influence large segments of pollution legislation, was essentially uninvolved in the shaping of Tanaka's decision to visit Peking.

Given the diversity of policymaking situations in Japan and the limited amount of hard information on many problems, it

3. *The American Presidency* (New York: Mentor, 1956).

is hazardous at this stage to state categorically that one of these three—issues, structures, or roles—is inherently more significant in determining the policymaking process. Also vague are the circumstances under which one becomes more significant than the others and the ways in which all three interact to shape both patterns and variations within those patterns. Yet it is clear that the three factors are more complementary and mutually influential than contradictory. Their influences run in similar rather than opposite directions in terms of the policymaking they predict.

Issues and political structures, for example, are clearly not independent of one another. Certain structures aid in defining the parameters of an issue and frequently influence the overtones associated with it. Issues in turn can influence structures: certain categories of issues almost automatically attract the interest of specific pressure groups; particular policy questions necessitate certain legal requirements concerning policymaking structures; a change in mass or elite expectations or the emergence of new issues requires new structural arrangements for solution, and so forth. Roles often develop in accordance with the position an individual or a group holds in certain political structures, or in response to changing issues. From a different perspective, an individual can sometimes manipulate a particular role, thereby shaping the historical issues of his time and the structures through which he operates.

Such mutual reinforcement and complementarity among these three types of explanations make it difficult to offer any categorical statements about the particular influence of one versus another, though ironically more data should eventually allow greater parsimony. In the meantime, generalizations about Japanese policymaking made on the basis of any single study or combination of studies must be sensitive to the particular type of explanation offered, and to the possibility that a different type of explanation might suggest an alternative interpretation. Similarly, one must be sensitive to the fact that the studies here, as with most other policymaking studies, operate at two different levels of analysis.

Some studies devote the bulk of their attention to the interactions of state and society, while others are more concerned with intrastate behavior. The former examine efforts by the state to enforce certain forms of social compliance (the purest example, perhaps, being government efforts to revise the university administration system) or they look at efforts by social groups to influence state and governmental behavior (such as arose in the rice-price, repatriates, and pollution problems). Regardless of the direction of influence examined, the principal concern is with the interaction between society and the state, the reactions of one to the stimuli of the other. This is quite different from studies which examine intrastate or intragovernmental behavior in policymaking such as the chapter on Tanaka's visit to Peking and most of the cases in Richardson's paper.

In principle, any instance of policymaking could be examined at either level, and most authors would probably agree that significant activities occurred at both levels in the situations they analyze: focusing on social-state interactions is not to deny that a good deal of personal interaction and intraelite "wheeling and dealing" took place on numerous details; similarly, those who focus on intrastate behavior would surely agree that it did not take place in a social vacuum. But a clear distinction is possible in the importance attached to each level in the specific cases analyzed.

The type of explanation offered and the level of analysis at which it is offered are critical to the conclusions that emerge. In a situation of total information, all data should triangulate toward compatible predictions. Total information, of course, is a rarity in any analytic situation. As a consequence, one must be sensitive to the dangers implied in the adage of the three blind men describing an elephant based only on their individual touching of tusks, legs, and tail. The result is three seemingly incompatible descriptions, despite the elephant's unmistakable unity to a sighted person. Complicating policymaking analysis even more is the fact that with time the "elephant" grows, ages, and moves from place to place. Hence sensitivity to longitudinal variation in both the type of explanation and the level of analysis is essential.

An issue which seems permanently ideological and conflict-laden at one time frequently looses its political bite in another. Child-labor legislation, women's suffrage, the income tax, and the organizing rights of unions were once volatile issues in the United States around which virtually unanimous consensus has now formed, while issues such as abortion, affirmative action, busing for integration, energy policy, and pollution have sprung to prominence after long periods of seemingly total irrelevance, nonexistence, or social consensus.

The same can be said for structures and institutions, which, despite the impermeability the terms imply, are also subject to major temporal fluctuations and take on varied dimensions. The repatriates, for example, were a most important group in a problem of great moment to them, namely, compensation for properties lost as a result of the war, but once this issue was settled, their political significance disappeared along with their raison d'être. The group preparing for Tanaka's visit to Peking, pre-eminent as it was in that single instance, was distinctly ad hoc, and when the visit was completed the group dissolved. From the opposite direction, the citizens' movements so critical to pollution and consumer issues in the late 1960's and early 1970's were nonexistent in the early 1950's; even into the early 1960's they were politically epiphenomenal.

The roles and motivations of individual and group actors are more than fixed and uniform appendages. Outlook and behavior fluctuate with changing circumstances; new problems and new information can force adjustments in perception. Organizations and individuals learn, taking on new roles and changing their behavior accordingly.

Finally, one's level of analysis is highly sensitive to changes in perspective. In general, the longer the time perspective on a problem the more likely one is to include social-state interactions, while a narrower time perspective is almost essential for exclusively intrastate analysis. Consequently, broadening the time span of any intrastate analysis is almost certain, in a complex society, to force inclusion of social influences by, or on, state actors, while narrowing a social-state analysis can lead to a more state-centric perspective.

This impact of time can be seen in almost all of the individual chapters, though it is perhaps most clear in long-term assessments such as those of the problems of rice prices, university administration, and pollution. The point to be made is quite simply that any relationships that seem to emerge inductively among issue, structure, and role, or between these and some particular level of analysis, must be seen in a dynamic context, for all are generally in flux, with the result that seemingly clear relationships are often unstable.

Finally, it is important to realize that these three types of explanations and these two levels of analysis, while they may converge concerning many aspects of the policymaking process per se, begin from strikingly different epistemological assumptions, assume different units of analysis, and often suggest different criteria by which behavior is assessed. As a consequence, choices of one over another are not without normative implications.

Interpretations based on role, for example, begin with the individual and the group as the key units of analysis; structural interpretations assess the interactions of institutions and organizations; and issue-based interpretations examine complex problems arising in an ideological and historical context.

Such differences, in turn, rest on vastly different presumptions about the nature of man. Interpretations based on role, for example, are clearly rooted in the belief that individuals are more than passive respondents to their environment and that autonomous decisions by certain individuals significantly shape the issues and structures of their time. As such the approach is quite compatible with theories of the Great Man in History. In contrast, interpretations based on structure or issue are inclined to treat individuals as little more than the socialized agents of institutional position, historical context, and structural interactions. A purely structural interpretation, moreover, would suggest that structures shape issues far more than the reverse and would be parallel in many ways to systems approaches to politics. As such it would be opposed to issue-dominated explanations, which presume that ideas and ideologies are crucial in shaping the structures and role players of history. There is, consequently, an element of historical determination in issue-dominated approaches, and they are intellectually comfortable with the old adage, "There is nothing so powerful as an idea whose time has come." Analyses of social-state interaction rest much more heavily on the belief that social groups can generate government response or frustrate government efforts than do those which look largely at intrastate relations with minimum attention to extra-governmental inputs.

Sensitivity to such differences in both the types of explanation and the levels of analysis is important as a backdrop to any attempt at utilizing the findings of individual cases of policy-making for full-scale assessments of Japanese politics. Just how important is ideology? The answer will depend on whether one begins with issues, roles, or structures as the basis for investigation and whether one analyzes society-state or intrastate behavior. To what extent is Japanese politics conflictual? The writer using issues as the prime unit of analysis will undoubtedly suggest that the answer depends on the problem under consideration, whereas a structuralist is more likely to conclude that it depends on which organizations and institutions are most predominantly involved, and the writer with a role approach will suggest that the answer lies in the motivations and perceptions of the groups and individuals involved. Examining a case at the intrastate level is almost sure to reveal at least some elements of conflict; efforts by the state to ensure certain forms of social behavior or by social actors to force certain types of action by the state may or may not generate a highly conflictual response. Just how strong are peak associations in Japan in their dealings with the state? Examining an issue in which a comparatively strong organization has confronted a comparatively weak government ministry will lead to one answer, while a different choice of issues and structures would suggest the reverse. Analysis at the intrastate level is almost certain to provide different conclusions than one at the society-state level.

It would be unfair to reduce all discussion of the broader implications about Japanese politics to such questions of philosophical persuasion and methods of analysis, but the point is definitely germane. If one is to draw meaningful conclusions about Japanese politics, one must be clear about the approach being taken and the criteria being used. This is assuredly also the case in any examination of normative questions about the degree of democracy in Japanese politics.

Fukui in Chapter 2 notes the tremendous disagreement among existing studies on whether Japanese policymaking is dominated by elites or is openly pluralistic. A reader committed to one of these perspectives will undoubtedly find ample evidence to support his or her preconceived notions. Those looking for evidence that Japanese policymaking is elite-dominated can point to the small group of top LDP leaders and senior Foreign Ministry officials who were clearly at the hub of all key decisions surrounding Tanaka's visit, unknown to the Japanese public or even to the other politicians and bureaucrats around them. And if the business community, which is usually presumed to be an important component of elite rule, was not important to this decision, government actions were by no means antagonistic to its long-run interests. Certainly the peak business federations were important in changing the higher educational curriculum, in the matter of capital and trade investments, and in Japan's reactions to the U.S. surcharge proposal, where, at a minimum, they set the boundaries within which the government bureaucracy formulated policy.

Further evidence for elite dominance could be found in the large role played by the senior echelons of the bureaucracy and top LDP leaders in aspects of university-enrollment expansion, the extension of the U.S.-Japan Security Treaty, much of the negotiations concerning compensation to repatriates, the purchase of Phantom F4E's, and, with some flexibility in interpretation, even in the setting of the rice price.

The committed pluralist could quickly counter that rice farmers and repatriates, neither usually seen as part of Japan's "elite," were quite successful in influencing certain policy matters. So, ultimately, were the administrators from private universities and pollution victims—at least those represented in court cases. Furthermore, there are cases in which the allegedly ruling elite was clearly unable to effect its will in the face of committed opposition. The earliest two attempts to control university administration provide good examples. Moreover, opposition parties as well as individual opposition members, the court system, local governmental organs, LDP backbenchers, and trade union federations were at times important advocates and actual participants in many of the instances of public policymaking examined here. From such evidence, any alleged elite may be so all-encompassing as to be meaningless, at least to the predisposed pluralist.

The elitist would, of course, be quick to argue that such factors have been basically irrelevant compared to the broader significance of a political system structured to sustain political conservatism and a capitalist economy, while the pluralist could counter that although capitalism and conservatism are undeniable elements of Japanese politics, "the capitalists" and "the conservatives" are frequently divided on important issues; different positions are vigorously advocated; intraelite divisions are readily identifiable; and external political forces have shown themselves most capable of advancing many of their interests against them.

This highly significant elitist-pluralist debate regarding Japan is not any more subject to ready resolution than it is in the more general form in which it has emerged for the United States and other "Western democracies." [4] The cases presented here provide no unambiguous evidence on the question. It is clear that one's approach influences the implications to be drawn. One who begins by choosing a limited number of individuals as the unit of analysis, for example, is more likely to conclude that policymaking is rather closed and elitist than one who begins by looking at broad historical movements over a longer period of time. One who examines policymaking in terms of state influences on society will produce different conclusions than one who begins by looking for societal influences over the state.

The ultimate question of Japanese democracy, of course, is broader than simply determining the degree to which policymaking is elitist or pluralist, and the criteria for an assessment of democracy in Japan would depend, again, on the approach taken.

For the researcher relying on a role-based analysis of policymaking, the key to democracy would have to lie in the interests, motivations, norms, and morality of the individual role players.

4. There have been numerous contributions to this debate, but some of the more relevant are collected in Chaim I. Waxman (ed.), *The End of Ideology Debate* (New York: Simon and Schuster, 1968).

To what extent are these compatible with those of the broader public? To what extent are elites sensitive to mass needs? In contrast, a structural interpretation would be inclined to evaluate the openness of formal channels whereby interests can be meaningfully articulated. What recourse is there for the group with a gripe? An issue-based explanation would have to confront still different questions: To what extent can political issues be generated "from below" in society? Who defines issues within the polity? Do all, or only some, issues receive significant attention? Obviously these suggest very different criteria by which to judge the degree of democracy in Japan, and the position one takes will inevitably rest on many unproven and unprovable assumptions. Clearly, concluding that Japan's formally democratic and participatory political institutions are alone sufficient to insure a democratic polity is an extremely limited perspective.

Clear and comparative criteria are essential to any such broad normative assessments. For example, is the comparison between Japan of the mid-1970's and Japan of the 1930's? If so, contemporary policymaking is surely more open to social influence and less hierarchical in nature. Is one comparing Japan with the countries of North America and Western Europe? In such a situation, differences may be quite significant, but overall similarities are likely to be as striking. Is one asking about the correspondence between practice and ideal? If so, policymaking in Japan, as anywhere, is almost surely going to fall far short. In any case, the answers are not likely to be without ambiguity and thus the words of David Landes on interpreting prewar Japan seem more broadly applicable: "It is important to keep [the] primacy of the political in mind while steering the bark of historical interpretation. On the one hand is the rock of overexpectation; on the other, the whirlpool of underestimation.[5]

The studies in this book reveal some of the many complexities of Japanese policymaking and defy oversimplified judgments about the totality of that country's politics and society.

5. David S. Landes, "Japan and Europe: Contrasts in Industrialization," in William W. Lockwood (ed.), *The State and Economic Enterprise in Japan* (Princeton: Princeton University Press, 1965), 145.

My own concluding observations attempt to set up some guide-posts for their interpretation, but in doing so they may thrust the individual chapters into somewhat different directions than were strictly intended by their authors. I hope this will not dis-tract from their individual foci, but rather will suggest at least one context within which they may take on a collective import beyond the sum of their parts. At the same time the parts should not be lost sight of. The great promise here is that the in-depth analysis of cases plus the broader overview will enable a rich awareness of the complex interactions that make up Jap-anese policymaking, as well as the extensive implications inher-ent in such complexities.

Annotated Bibliography

This bibliography is intended to be a preliminary guide to some of the most representative and useful literature on contemporary Japanese policymaking. As such it should be a helpful starting point for the beginner and a first checklist for the specialist. Several rules of thumb have guided me in the selection of materials. First, only English-language works have been cited. Second, textbooks were excluded, even though many include sections on policymaking. Third, I have tried to include what I admittedly arbitrarily felt to be the most useful items, regardless of their specific contents. Thus a number of items listed cover roughly the same areas. At the same time, I have excluded what I considered to be less substantial items on problems which are adequately covered; when items which of themselves might be of marginal theoretical importance covered areas on which little or nothing else was available, they were included. Finally, works that focus primarily on political structures such as the cabinet, labor unions, or the civil service have by and large been excluded, as have cultural interpretations of the so-called Japanese character, even though both are important to policymaking. A few exceptions which seemed to be particularly oriented toward interaction between structure and process have been included.

Chapters in books have been listed separately where the bulk of the book was not devoted to policymaking; where the reverse is the case, the book alone has been cited.

Anyone interested in pursuing Japanese policymaking in some particular area or in greater depth should also be aware that many English-language publications are available from Japanese government agencies as well as from international organizations such as OECD and UNESCO. These rarely deal explicitly with the process of policymaking but are important as guides to changes in official policy. More detailed work on specific areas will also be aided by the use of English-language editions of Japanese newspapers such as *Asahi Shimbun*, *Mainichi Shimbun*, and *Yomiuri Shimbun*, as well as *The Japan Times*. The U.S. Embassy in Tokyo publishes daily translations of Japanese newspapers and weekly translations and/or summaries of Japanese magazines. And, of course, further direction can be secured from the bibliographies contained in many of the items included here.

"The Antitrust Law Under Fire," *Japan Quarterly* 14 (April–June 1967). Discusses industry's pressure on the government for anti-trust-law revisions.

Arasaki Moriteru. "Okinawa's Reversion and the Security of Japan," *Japan Interpreter* 6 (Autumn 1970). Includes a discussion of how the LDP position on Okinawa was developed.

Baerwald, Hans H. *Japan's Parliament: An Introduction*. London and New York: Cambridge University Press, 1974. A useful examination of the Japanese legislature with details on several major controversies over policy.

———. "Nikkan Kokkai: The Japan-Korea Treaty Diet." Lucian W. Pye (ed.), *Cases in Comparative Politics: Asia*. Boston: Little Brown, 1970. A detailed assessment of how Japan's treaty with South Korea passed the Diet.

———. "Parliament and Parliamentarians in Japan," *Pacific Affairs* 37 (Fall 1964). How a bill gets through the Diet, with the 1963 law covering unemployment relief measures used as a case example.

———. "Tensions in Japanese Politics: Coal and Korea," *Asian Survey* 3 (April 1963). Discusses the government's policies of nationalizing the coal-mining industry and normalization of relations with Korea, as well as the fight with the opposition to effect both policies.

"Basic Trends: Political: Bureaucracy on the Move," *Japan Quarterly* 6 (January–March 1959). Examines the Kishi government's effort to pass the Police Revision Bill and a labor law revision.

Bieda, K. "Economic Planning in Japan," *Economic Record* 45 (Melbourne), (June 1969). A useful overview of key government plans during the late 1950's and 1960's.

Bryant, William R. "Japanese Businessmen and Private Economic Diplomacy," *Japan Interpreter* 6 (Summer 1970). Description of private economic diplomacy in terms of economic missions, roving ambassadorships, international businessmen's conferences, and joint economic committees.

———. *Japanese Private Economic Diplomacy: An Analysis of Business-Government Linkage*. New York: Praeger, 1975. Studies the efforts of Japanese businessmen to promote trade and "good will" abroad with government sanction.

Bullard, Monte R. "Japan's Nuclear Choice," *Asian Survey* 14 (September 1974). Examines international and domestic forces which determine Japan's nuclear policy, focusing on the close relationship to foreign policy, foreign trade, domestic economic development, and domestic politics.

Campbell, John Creighton. *Contemporary Japanese Budget Politics*. Berkeley and Los Angeles: University of California Press, 1976. A longitudinal examination of Japanese budgetmaking which concludes that the process is highly incremental and even less fluid than that in the U.S.

Choi, Sung-il. "Politics-Economics-Public Policy Linkages in Japan, 1965–1969," *Asian Survey* 15 (May 1975). A factor analysis of aggregate data for prefectures is used to try to explain policy output variations.

Clapp, Priscilla A., and Morton H. Halperin (eds.). *United States–Japanese Relations: The 1970's*. Cambridge: Harvard University Press, 1974. Eleven contributors deal with a variety of foreign-policy issues.

"Coal and the Government," *Japan Quarterly* 10 (January–March 1963). Summarizes the findings of the Coal Survey Commission of 1962 which led to subsequent policy revisions.

"Consumerism," *Japan Quarterly* 20 (July–September 1973). Notes the rise in activity of consumer groups acknowledging that consumer consciousness in Japan is not yet very high.

Cummings, William K. "The Conservatives Reform Higher Education," *Japan Interpreter* 8 (Winter 1974). Describes the education reform movement since the Occupation focusing on reforms in the late 1960's and early 1970's.

Dore, R. P. "Textbook Censorship in Japan: The Ienaga Case," *Pacific Affairs* 43 (Winter 1970–71). An examination of the political issues in the major case of postwar textbook censorship.

Duke, Benjamin C. *Japan's Militant Teachers*. Honolulu: University of Hawaii Press, 1973. A pressure-group study of one of Japan's most militant unions with attention to its role in several educational policy changes.

Duncan, William Chandler. *U.S.-Japan Automobile Diplomacy: A Study in Economic Confrontation*. Cambridge, Mass.: Ballinger, 1973. Analysis of Japanese government-business cooperation in a controversial area of economic foreign policy.

"Fisheries and Industrial Pollution," *Japan Quarterly* 20 (October–December 1973). Summary of citizen protest and bureaucratic efforts concerning the third outbreak of Minamata disease.

"The Five-Day Week," *Japan Quarterly* 18 (October–December 1971). Explores MITI's promotion of a five-day workweek in its plan "Trade Strategy for the 70's."

Fukui, Haruhiro. "Economic Planning in Postwar Japan: A Case Study in Policy Making," *Asian Survey* 12 (April 1972). Posits that Japanese economic planning is characterized by "limited pluralism," and that the opposition has little influence. Analyzes the "Occupation," "Korean War," and "LDP dominance" periods to show conservative cooperation in economic planning and opposition impotence.

———. *Party in Power: The Japanese Liberal-Democrats and Policy-making*. Berkeley and Los Angeles: University of California Press, 1970. Includes three case studies of LDP-government interaction in policymaking: relations with China, compensation for former landlords, and constitutional revision.

Goldsborough, William West. "Environments of Economic Development, the Open Economy and Public Policy: The Case of Japan since 1945." Ph.D. dissertation, University of Nebraska, 1974. Examination of the process whereby Japan has liberalized its economic position with emphasis on national-international linkages.

"Government Bonds to the Rescue," *Japan Quarterly* 13 (January–March 1966). Briefly reviews the government's economic policy and actions in face of depression.

Grad, Andrew J. "Land Reform in Japan," *Pacific Affairs* 21 (June 1948). Outlines the U.S. Occupation's land reform law and its acceptance and implementation.

Hadley, Eleanor M. *Antitrust in Japan*. Princeton: Princeton University Press, 1970. A book on an issue of political economy which can be read by noneconomists.

Halliday, Jon, and Gavan McCormack. *Japanese Imperialism Today*. New York: Monthly Review Press, 1973. An analysis of Japan's military policy and relations with Asia and the U.S. that provides a number of critical observations on policymaking as well.

Harari, Ehud. "Japanese Politics of Advice in Comparative Perspective: A Framework for Analysis and a Case Study," *Public Policy* 22 (Fall 1974). An examination of the policymaking role played by advisory committees.

——. *The Politics of Labor Legislation in Japan: National-International Interaction*. Berkeley and Los Angeles: University of California Press, 1973. A study focusing on the attempt to secure bargaining rights guaranteed under ILO Convention 87 within Japan. Many useful observations on labor policymaking and the role of advisory committees.

Heidenheimer, Arnold J., and Frank C. Langdon. *Business Associations and the Financing of Political Parties: A Comparative Study of the Evolution of Practices in Germany, Norway and Japan*. The Hague: Martinus Nijhoff, 1968. Focuses primarily on peak business associations, their political campaign mechanisms, and their consequent influence.

Hellmann, Donald C. *Japanese Foreign Policy and Domestic Politics: The Peace Agreement with the Soviet Union*. Berkeley and Los Angeles: University of California Press, 1969. A case study of domestic and international interactions.

"Help for the Shipping Industry," *Japan Quarterly* 10 (April–June 1963). Summarizes why government help was necessary, and how it came about.

Henderson, Dan Fenno (ed.). *The Constitution of Japan: Its First Twenty Years, 1947–1967*. Seattle: University of Washington Press, 1968. Although primarily legalistic in orientation, the book includes several useful chapters on the policymaking role played by the courts in certain areas.

Henderson, Gregory, S. W. Barton, Johannes A. Binnendijk, and Carolyn E. Setlow (eds.). *Public Diplomacy and Political Change—Four Case Studies: Okinawa, Peru, Czechoslovakia, Guinea.* New York: Praeger, 1973. Concerns the impact of the mass media and other public agencies on foreign policy; half of the book concerns the Okinawan reversion.

Hirosige Tetu [Hiroshige Tetsu]. "The Role of the Government in the Development of Science," *Cahiers d'Histoire Mondiale* 9 (Winter 1965). An historical study which includes a section on the postwar period. The focus there is primarily on new government structures to deal with science and industry.

Hitchcock, David I., Jr. "Joint Development of Siberia: Decision-Making in Japanese-Soviet Relations," *Asian Survey* 11 (March 1971). Examines the various factors and motives which have influenced decisionmaking in these discussions.

Huff, Rodney L. "Political Decisionmaking in the Japanese Civilian Atomic Energy Program." Ph.D. dissertation, George Washington University, 1973. An examination of the impact of technology on the Japanese political system and the political response to technological change, focusing on Japan's peaceful atomic research.

Ide, Yoshinori. "Administrative Reform and Innovation: The Japanese Case," *International Social Science Journal* 21 (1969). A survey of governmentally proposed changes in the administrative structure during the mid-1960's and the response engendered.

——. "Structure and Function of the Decision-Making Process in Japanese Urban Development Planning," *The Second International Symposium on Regional Development.* Tokyo: Japan Center for Area Development Research, 1969. Looks primarily at prewar policymaking legacies as they affect the postwar emphasis on planning. A key concern is local influence versus central direction.

Ishida Takeshi. "Interest Groups under a Semipermanent Government Party: The Case of Japan," *Annals of the American Academy of Political and Social Science* 413 (May 1974). A brief examination of the interrelationship between interest groups and government.

Isomura, Eiichi. "Urbanization and City Planning Policies," *Developing Economies* 10 (December 1972). An examination of Japan's planning and housing policy formation, issues rarely examined elsewhere.

Itō Noboru. "The Reform of Japanese Education," *Japan Quarterly* 3 (October–December 1956). Mainly the author's interpretation of the postwar education reforms; also mentions the government's criticisms of SCAP's actions.

Itoh, Hiroshi (ed.) *Japanese Politics: An Inside View.* Ithaca: Cornell University Press, 1973. A collection of translations of Japanese articles, several of which are important general analyses of policymaking or specific case studies.

Jan, George P. "Japan's Trade With Communist China," *Asian Survey* 9 (December 1969). While reviewing the development of Sino-

Japanese trade from 1949, this article also examines the changing policies and reactions of the Japanese government to the CPR's position on trade.

Japan, Economic Planning Agency, Planning Bureau. *Economic Planning in Japan.* Tokyo: EPA, 1970. An official interpretation of how the Economic Planning Agency arrives at its long-range proposals.

Katō Hidetoshi. "Sanken: A Power above Government," *Japan Interpreter* 7 (Winter 1971). Analysis of the economic influence of a high-ranking business advisory group.

"Keeping ILO Waiting," *Japan Quarterly* 12 (April–June 1965). Summarizes why ILO Convention 87 met opposition in Diet.

Kirkpatrick, Maurine A. "Consumerism and Japan's New Citizen Politics," *Asian Survey* 15 (March 1975). An attempt to document the effectiveness of community-oriented consumer activists.

Kitamura Kazuyuki and William K. Cummings. "The 'Big Bang' Theory and Japanese University Reform," *Comparative Education Review* 16 (June 1972). An examination of government plans to reform higher education in light of previous efforts during Meiji and the Occupation, as well as student protest activities of the late 1960's.

Konno, Genpachiro. "The Problems of the Transportation Policy in Japan—Highway Modernization Policy," *Papers and Proceedings of the International Symposium on Regional Development.* Tokyo: Japan Center for Area Development Research, 1967. Largely an analysis of the substance of highway policy, the paper also makes a few observations on a policymaking area not widely covered.

Kuroda, Yasumasa. "Protest Movement in Japan: A New Politics," *Asian Survey* 12 (November 1972). Examines the nature of citizens' movements and points out their significance to the future politics of Japan.

Langdon, Frank C. "Big Business Lobbying in Japan: The Case of Central Bank Reform," *American Political Science Review* 55 (September 1961). An examination of the unsuccessful effort by the Federation of Economic Organizations and the Federation of Bankers' Associations to make the Bank of Japan more independent of the Ministry of Finance.

——. *Japan's Foreign Policy.* Vancouver: University of British Columbia Press, 1973. A detailed description of the main foreign-policy activities under the Ikeda and Satō cabinets.

——. "Japanese Liberal Democratic Factional Discord on China Policy," *Pacific Affairs* 41 (Fall 1968). An examination of the intra-LDP debates over future relations with the People's Republic of China. The article argues that the LDP is crucial to foreign-policy formation in this area.

——. "Organized Interests in Japan and Their Influence on Political Parties," *Pacific Affairs* 34 (Fall 1961). Discusses the influence of various business groups through money and personal contact on the LDP, briefly mentioning several specific cases.

——. "Strains in Current Japanese-American Defense Cooperation," *Asian Survey* 9 (September 1969). Most of this article discusses the development and change in the LDP position on Okinawa reversion.

Long, T. Dixon. "Policy and Politics in Japanese Science: The Persistence of a Tradition," *Minerva* 7 (Spring 1969). A broad overview of major shifts in science policy including an examination of government efforts in research and development, cooperating with the private sector, and the importance of advising and coordinating functions in the determination of policy.

Maeno, John R. "Postwar Japanese Policy toward Communist China, 1952–1972: Japan's Changing International Relations and New Political Culture. Ph.D. dissertation, University of Washington, 1973. Primarily an analysis of international impacts on domestic policy-making, the study also examines the impact of political opposition and conservative leadership on the formation of policy toward China.

Matsumoto, Tomonori. "Finance Moves in on Politics," *Japan Quarterly* 17 (April–June 1970). Basically a description of businessmen's groups and ideas, but includes some specific instances of government-business cooperation, notably on trade liberalization.

McKean, Margaret A. "The Potentials for Grass-Roots Democracy in Postwar Japan: The Anti-Pollution Movement as a Case Study in Political Activism." Ph.D. dissertation, University of California, Berkeley, 1974. A pressure-group study on a new political issue.

Miyamoto, Ken'ichi. "Local Self-Government and Local Finance," *Developing Economies* 6 (December 1968). A historical examination of the relationship between central and local funding and urban policy.

Miyazaki, Isamu. "Economic Planning in Postwar Japan," *Developing Economies* 8 (December 1970). A brief but useful overview of the government's various economic plans and their evolution.

Morley, James W. (ed.). *Forecast for Japan: Security in the 1970's.* Princeton: Princeton University Press, 1972. A collection of essays which, while not primarily on policymaking, make a number of useful observations on the process as it relates to security problems.

Nakamura, Akira. "The Politics of Air Pollution Control in Los Angeles and Osaka: A Comparative Urban Study." Ph.D. dissertation, University of Southern California, 1973. Examination of interest-group activities and decisionmaking at the local level.

"Nature Conservation," *Japan Quarterly* 19 (January–March 1972). Reviews the case of a citizens' group which received support from the Environment Agency in their fight against a highway near Oze.

Nishimoto Kōichi. "Nōkyō: Pressure from the Co-ops," *Japan Interpreter* 7 (Summer-Autumn 1972). Description of the Agricultural cooperative and its political influence.

Ogino, Yoshio. "The Dairy Industry," *Japan Quarterly* 10 (January–March 1963). Examines the purpose of the Basic Agriculture Law, including its relevance to dairy industry growth.

Okimoto, Daniel I. "Japan's Non-Nuclear Policy: The Problem of the NPT," *Asian Survey* 15 (April 1975). Examines the political reasons for delay in Diet ratification.

Ozaki, Robert S. *The Control of Imports and Foreign Capital in Japan*. New York: Praeger, 1972. A detailed examination of a crucial area of political-economic interaction.

———. "Japanese Views on Industrial Organization," *Asian Survey* 10 (October 1970). Along with the history and ideological basis of the government's notion that "bigness is goodness," Ozaki examines government and business positions on the huge Yawata-Fuji Steel merger.

Packard, George R., III. *Protest in Tokyo: The Security Treaty Crisis of 1960*. Princeton: Princeton University Press, 1966. The most detailed case study of the controversy surrounding the U.S.-Japan Security Treaty.

Park, Yung Ho. "The Electoral Reform Laws of 1962: A Case Study of the Japanese Policy-Making Process." Ph.D. thesis, Champaign-Urbana, University of Illinois, 1968. Seeks to demonstrate that LDP Diet members, in spite of their access to and involvement in all stages of policymaking, are far from an omnipotent political force, and that they are subject to major restraints on their efforts to influence policymaking.

———. "The Governmental Advisory Commission System in Japan," *Journal of Comparative Administration* 3 (February 1972). Examines some of the salient aspects of government advisory commissions: their composition, operations, methods of decisionmaking, functions, and uses in the process of policy formation.

Pempel, T. J. "The Bureaucratization of Policymaking in Postwar Japan," *American Journal of Political Science* 18 (November 1974). Suggests that the role of the bureaucracy in policymaking has been expanding due to a change in its powers to draft legislation, to issue bureaucratic directives, and to control advisory committees. The period covered is 1945–1970.

———. "The Dilemma of Parliamentary Opposition in Japan," *Polity* 8 (Fall 1975). Suggests that compromise and confrontation are the two options for the parliamentary opposition in Japan, with each option carrying serious negative consequences for the advancement of opposition goals.

———. "The Politics of Enrollment Expansion in Japanese Universities," *Journal of Asian Studies* 33 (November 1973). A study of incremental policymaking where the policy outcome has been more than originally expected.

Plath, David W. " 'Ecstasy Years'—Old Age in Japan," *Pacific Affairs* 46 (Fall 1973). Although this article concentrates on nongovernmental interest in the elderly, it does discuss Tanaka's position on retirement age, court action, and opposition parties' criticism of the present National Pension plan.

"Pollution Case Law," *Japan Quarterly* 20 (July–September 1973). Analyzes the precedent establishing relief for victims of Minamata disease.

"Publish and Be Damned," *Japan Quarterly* 17 (July–September 1970). Examines the cooperation between the LDP and CGP concerning efforts by the CGP and Sōka Gakkai to prevent publication of a book critical of the latter.

Quester, George H. "Japan and the Nuclear Non-Proliferation Treaty," *Asian Survey* 10 (September 1970). Analyzes implications of NPT for Japan, describes the reactions of Japanese political parties, and discusses the future of NPT in Japan.

Rix, Alan G. "Tokyo's Governor Minobe and Progressive Local Politics in Japan," *Asian Survey* 15 (June 1975). Analyzes the Tokyo "garbage war" in an effort to show the problems of local administration and citizen participation.

Scalapino, Robert A., and Junnosuke Masumi. *Parties and Politics in Contemporary Japan.* Berkeley: University of California Press, 1962. Includes a detailed look at the 1960 debate surrounding the U.S.-Japan Security Treaty.

Sissons, D. C. S. "The Dispute over Japan's Police Law," *Pacific Affairs* 32 (March 1959). A step-by-step recapitulation of the debate over the bill including arguments by both government and opposition.

"The Soviet-Japanese Negotiations in London," *Japan Quarterly* 2 (October–December 1955). A brief summary of the problems involved and of what Hatoyama was trying to do.

Steiner, Kurt. "The Revision of the Civil Code of Japan: Provisions Affecting the Family," *Far Eastern Quarterly* 9 (February 1950). Includes an outline of the revision process with the position of different politicians.

Steslicke, William E. *Doctors in Politics: The Political Life of the Japan Medical Association.* New York: Praeger Special Studies in International Politics and Government, 1973. A pressure-group study of JMA influence particularly within the Ministry of Health and Welfare.

———. "Doctors, Patients, and Government in Modern Japan," *Asian Survey* 12 (November 1972). Examines the changing role of doctors in Japan as influenced by government control over licensing and health insurance.

———. "The Political Life of the Japan Medical Association," *Journal of Asian Studies* 31 (August 1972). A study of the JMA's pressure-group activities on matters of health insurance and the sale of medicine to patients.

Stockwin, J. A. A. "Continuity and Change in Japanese Foreign Policy," *Pacific Affairs* 46 (Spring 1973). Compares U.S.-Japan 1960 "crisis of communication" with the situation in 1971, perceives Japanese foreign policy as based on broader U.S.-Japan relations, and gives a general discussion of recent foreign policies in light of this premise.

——. *The Japanese Socialist Party and Neutralism: A Study of a Political Party and Its Foreign Policy.* Melbourne: Melbourne University Press, 1968. An examination of the JSP's policymaking process on the issue of neutralism with observations on national foreign policymaking as well.

——. " 'Positive Neutrality': The Foreign Policy of the Japanese Socialist Party," *Asian Survey* 2 (November 1962). Discusses how an internally divided JSP arrived at the foreign policy of "positive neutrality" and how they apply it to certain situations, notably China and Korea.

"Strain on the Constitution," *Japan Quarterly* 21 (January–March 1974). Discusses the Naganuma missile-site trial, noting the tension between the court's policymaking and government desires.

Tachi, Minoru. "The Population Problem," *Japan Quarterly* 5 (January–March 1958). A statistical article detailing growth of the population problem and problems caused thereby. Includes a brief discussion of the evolution of contraception and abortion laws.

Taira, Koji. "Public Assistance in Japan," *Journal of Asian Studies* 27 (November 1967). Public assistance since the Meiji period is reviewed, looking at the greater need for such assistance in the present period.

Takizawa, Makota. "Okinawa: Reversion to Japan and Future Prospects," *Asian Survey* 11 (May 1971). Full review of the Okinawa issue from the perspective of both U.S. and Japanese decisionmakers.

Thayer, Nathaniel B. *How the Conservatives Rule Japan.* Princeton: Princeton University Press, 1969. Not explicitly a policymaking study, this book includes a chapter on policymaking within the LDP which provides general insights beyond the party.

Thurston, Donald R. *Teachers and Politics in Japan.* Princeton: Princeton University Press, 1973. Primarily an interest-group study, the book includes a number of useful observations on the policymaking interface between the Teacher's Union and the Ministry of Education.

Tsuchiya, Kiyoshi. "The Coal Industry," *Japan Quarterly* 9 (October–December 1962). A summary of the main points of the MITI coal industry commission policy as of 1959 and 1962.

United States Department of Commerce. *Japan: The Government-Business Relationship.* Washington: U.S. Government Printing Office, 1972. A critical examination of ties between the Japanese government and big business from the standpoint of the U.S. businessman. Includes three case studies of economic policymaking.

Vinacke, Harold M. "The Growth of an Independent Foreign Policy in Japan," *Pacific Affairs* 38 (Spring 1965). What the Japanese have done since the Occupation to establish autonomous foreign relationships without reference to the U.S., especially with Asia.

Vogel, Ezra F. (ed.). *Modern Japanese Organization and Decision-making.* Berkeley and Los Angeles: University of California Press, 1975. A collection of useful essays on a variety of policymaking and decision-making situations.

Ward, Robert E. "The Commission on the Constitution and Prospects for Constitutional Change in Japan," *Journal of Asian Studies* 24 (May 1965). An assessment of the report, a critique of its value, and the domestic and foreign factors affecting prospects for constitutional revision.

Weinstein, Martin E. "Defense Policy and the Self-Defense Forces," *Japan Interpreter* 6 (Summer 1970). How the LDP sees the role of the SDF, and what policy is therefore pursued.

——. *Japan's Postwar Defense Policy, 1947–1968.* New York: Columbia University Press, 1971. Examines how policymakers in Japan have sought security in the context of ties to the U.S. and domestic opposition to expanded military presence.

Whittemore, Edward P. *The Press in Japan Today: A Case Study.* Columbia: University of South Carolina Press, 1961. Focuses primarily on the 1960 Treaty controversy, with an exploration of the political implications of the media.

Willey, Richard J. "Pressure Group Politics: The Case of Sohyo," *Western Political Quarterly* 17 (December 1964). Using the pressure-group framework of Eckstein, the focus is on the ideological basis of labor's peak federation.

Yamamura, Kozo. *Economic Policy in Postwar Japan: Growth versus Economic Democracy.* Berkeley and Los Angeles: University of California Press, 1967. A study of U.S. Occupation policies directed against prewar financial combines and the basic reversal of this policy and the shift toward monopolies since.

——. "Growth vs. Economic Democracy in Japan, 1945–1965," *Journal of Asian Studies* 25 (August 1966). Tries to show how high economic growth has been accompanied by less "economic democracy" and how the government's antimonopoly and taxation policies influence this situation.

Yanaga, Chitoshi. *Big Business in Japanese Politics.* New Haven: Yale University Press, 1968. A detailed study which sees big business as dominating government decisionmaking.

Yang, Alexander Ching-an. "The Policy-Making Process in Japan's Policy toward the People's Republic of China: The Making of the Liao-Takasaki Trade Agreement of 1962." Ph.D. dissertation, Columbia University, 1969. A case-study examination of the trade agreement that allowed Japan to trade with China while not extending diplomatic recognition.

Yoshino, M. Y. *Japan's Managerial System: Tradition and Innovation.*

Cambridge: MIT Press, 1968. Though primarily a study of problems internal to industry, it includes important observations on government-business interactions.

Yoshitomi, Shigeo. "Regional Development and Administrative Machinery in Japan, Particularly in Relation to the Development of Metropolitan Region," *The Papers and Proceedings of the International Symposium on Regional Development.* Tokyo: Japan Center for Area Development, 1967. Focuses primarily on problems of administrative coordination for regional development.

Index

Administrative Management Agency, 230

Advisory Commission on Pollution, 216, 217-18

Advisory committees, 16-17, 34, 56-57, 106, 109, 152, 181, 206, 218, 255, 279, 281, 310, 313; *see also* Advisory Commission on Pollution; Central Education Council; Overseas Property Problem Council; and Rice Price Deliberation Council

Advocacy, rational of, 243-44, 261-63

Agricultural incomes, 145-152

Agricultural Land Law, 150

Agriculture, 17, 143-200, 201, 257, 275, 310; *see also* Landlords, compensation of

Agriculture land committees, 155

Aichi Kiichi, 111, 168, 186

Akagi Munenori, 168, 170, 182-83

All-Japan Federation of Farmers' Unions, 156

All-Japan Reclamation Federation, 156

Allison, Graham, 70, 240-46, 251n

Ambrecht, Biliana, 58

Anderson, James E., 52, 57

Anton, Thomas J., 141n

Ashibe Nobuyoshi, 26n

Association for the Promotion of Private Schools, 297

Association of Private Colleges of Japan, 300

Asukata Ichio, 46

Ashida Hitoshi, 41

Ayres, W. H., 132n

B-52, 257-58

Bachrach, Peter, 301

Baerwald, Hans, 28n, 33, 36, 42, 63n

Baratz, Morton S., 301

Basic Agriculture Law, 147, 150, 168, 174, 189, 195

Basic Law for Environmental Pollution Control (1967), 214, 217-19, 224; Tokyo Ordinance, compared to, 222-23; revisions, 227-29

Bauer, Raymond A., 242n

Bauer, Robert A., 301

Baum, Lawrence, 239n

Beer, Samuel H., 140n, 261

Beller, Dennis, 35n

Belloni, Frank P., 35n

Bennett, John W., 202n

Bonin Islands, 260

Bronfenbrenner, Martin, 31

Brzezinski, Zbigniew, 137n

Budget-making, 113, 114-15, 148, 150, 248, 257, 263

Bureaucracy, 15, 16, 22-35, 37-38, 44, 51, 77, 84-90, 100-101, 157-59, 204-7, 215, 227, 248, 252, 254, 260, 268, 275-76, 290, 299, 306, 310; *see also* Policymaking, dominance in, 254-56; and entries for individual agencies and ministries

Burgess, Philip M., 253n

Business, 15, 22-25, 39, 44, 90-95, 190, 268, 275, 310; China relations, and, 90-95; higher education, and, 285, 288-94, 300-301; pollution, and, 204-7, 208-9, 215, 217, 227-38; *see also* Business federations; Federa-

Business (*continued*)
tion of Economic Organizations; Japan Committee for Economic Development; Japan Federation of Employers Associations; Kansai Economic Federation
Business federations, 18, 25, 91; *see also* Federation of Economic Organizations; Japan Committee for Economic Development; Japan Federation of Employers' Associations

Cabinet, 254, 265, 276, 279, 295, 306
Cadmium poisoning, 203-4, 212, 212n, 232
Camp conflict, policymaking through, 19, 271-87, 311
Campbell, John Creighton, 16, 40, 59n, 263n, 311, 313
Central Education Council, 284-85, 292, 294, 298
Central Union of Agriculture Cooperatives, 154-56, 169, 180, 185
Chiang Kai-shek, 92n
Chief Cabinet Secretary, 166
China, People's Republic of (PRC), 16, 54, 60-102, 242, 273, 308, 311, 313-14, 317; "Three Principles," and the, 64, 82, 86; "termination of war" between Japan and, 85; trade with, 258-59, 260-61, 262, 264-65, 311
Chisso, 203, 203n, 206n-7n, 232-34
Chou En-lai, 64, 67, 75-83, 86-89, 93
Citizens groups, 18, 46, 213, 236; *see also* Consumers
Civil Information and Education Section (CI & E), 280
Clapp, Priscilla, 63n
Clean Government Party, 64, 78, 79, 83, 95; People's Council for the Normalization of Japan-China Relations, CGP and, 96; pollution, CGP and, 209, 225; repatriates, CGP and, 128
Consumers, 160-61; *see also* Citizens groups
Cooperatives, agricultural, 154-55, 163, 169, 178, 193; *see also* Farm groups; National Association of Agriculture Cooperatives; Unions, farm
Copper, John F., 208n

Council of National University Presidents, 280
Council on University Chartering, 303
Courts, 18, 205, 207, 220-21, 231-34, 237, 309
"Critical" decisionmaking, 61n, 98-102
Crozier, Michel, 141n
Cummings, William K., 296n
Curtis, Gerald L., 39, 47, 59n, 103n, 125n, 131, 160n, 310n

Davis, David H., 51n, 52n
Decisionmaking, stages of, 161-67; *see also* Policymaking
Defense Agency, 255, 260, 266-67
Democratic Socialist Party, 64, 81-82, 95, 156, 169, 257, 265; repatriates, and DSP, 128; pollution, and DSP, 209, 217
Destler, I. M., 63n
Dexter, Lewis A., 242n
Diet, 23, 24-25, 32-33, 42-44, 95-98, 99, 170, 216-17, 219, 227-31, 247-48, 248n, 256, 276, 290, 295, 298-99, 306, 309; committees, Diet, 26, 39-40, 290; House of Councillors, Diet, 71, 121, 192, 290; House of Representatives, Diet, 71, 154, 257, 290
Dietmen's Discussion Group on the Overseas Private Property Problem ("Discussion Group"), 110-11, 113, 114, 117-24, 139
Dietmen's League for Handling the Overseas Property Problem ("The League"), 110, 127, 130-31
Donnelly, Michael, 17, 313
Dowsey, Stuart, 283n
Duke, Benjamin C., 34
Dye, Thomas R., 23n

Easton, David, 243n
Economic growth, 201-2, 208, 297; *see also* Industrialization
Economic Planning Agency, 152, 159, 166, 175, 181-82, 192, 207, 218
Edelman, Murray, 273n
Education, *see* General education; Higher education; Universities
Ehrlich, Paul, 204
Elections/electoral system, 16, 108,

109, 121, 125-32, 139-40, 150, 159-60, 192, 226-27, 229, 235

Emmerson, John K., 31, 45

Endō Akira, 225n

Energy, consumption of, 202-3

Environment Agency, 206, 230-31

Environmental Pollution Control Service Corporation, proposed, 216

Etzioni, Amitai, 52n

Eulau, Heinz, 273n

Export-Import Bank, 258-59, 262, 311, 314

Eyestone, Robert, 273n

Factionalism, 35-37, 51, 70-72, 76, 101, 162, 236, 310

Factory Effluents Control Law, 216

Farm groups, 153-54, 198; see also Cooperatives, agricultural; and names of specific groups

Farms, size and description, 153, 188

Federation of Economic Organizations (Keidanren), 26, 30, 39-40, 92, 94, 160, 205, 217-18, 220-24, 229, 235, 255, 260n, 288

Federation of Farmers' Unions, 156

Food agency, 38, 149, 157, 162, 168, 178, 185, 197

Food control, 144, 147-48, 150, 152, 187, 189, 192; see also Food Control Law; Rice price

Food Control Law, 195, 197, 226

Foreign Capital Deliberation Council, 255

Foreign Ministry, 16, 17, 68-69, 77, 84-90, 100, 256, 258, 259-60, 267, 313; China Policy Council, of, 86; Treaties Bureau, of, 84

Foreign Policy Roundtable, 74

Froman, Lewis A., Jr., 272n

Fujita Isao, 91n-94n

Fujiwara Hirotatsu, 79n

Fujiyama Aiichirō, 41, 54, 65, 74, 89, 95n

Fukashiro Junrō, 284n

Fukuda Takeo, 67, 69-72, 77-78, 97, 120

Fukui, Haruhiro, 15-16, 27n, 33n, 36n, 41n, 44n, 63, 72n, 74n, 96n, 101n, 103n, 105, 108n, 110n, 112n, 118n, 128n, 130n, 133n, 240n, 254n, 259n, 267n, 313, 320

Fukunaga Kenji, 120, 136

Funada Naka, 76

Furui Yoshimi, 42, 64, 77-78, 81-83, 88-90, 258

Furumi Tadayuki, 129

Gabe Masao, 46n

General Council of Japanese Trade Unions (Sōhyō), 34, 40, 161, 210-11, 309; see also Labor

General education, 288-94

Gergen, Kenneth J., 301n

Greenberg, George, 103n

Halliday, Jon, 29, 91

Halperin, Morton H., 55, 55n-57n

Halpern, A. M., 63n

Hara Kenzaburō, 123n

Harari, Ehud, 28, 37n, 43, 56, 57n, 101, 106n, 254n

Hasegawa, Sukehiro, 202n

Hashimoto Hiroshi, 69, 86-90

Hashimoto Michio, 202n, 215n

Hatoyama Ichirō, 95, 266n

Hayami, Yujiro, 146n

Heclo, Hugh, 141n

Heidenheimer, Arnold J., 30n

Hellmann, Donald C., 36, 45, 99-101, 249n, 254n, 264n

Hermann, Charles F., 61, 61n, 253n

Higa Mikio, 45n

Higher education, 269-307; enrollment, expansion in, 269, 301-6; technological orientation in, 269, 288-94; see also Junior colleges

Hikiagesha, see Repatriates

Hiyane Teruo, 45n

Hōgen Shinsaku, 65n, 69, 86, 90

Honda Junsuke, 211n

Hori Shigeru, 65-70, 258

Horikawa Kiichi, 125n

Hoshino Shigeo, 225n

Hsiao Hsiang-Ch'ien, 86, 93

Huntington, Samuel P., 137n

Ienaga Saburō, 279n

Igarashi Fumio, 211n

Ikazaki Akio, 279n, 281n

Ike, Nobutaka, 28n, 44, 47n

Ikeda Hayato, 37, 41, 73, 109, 134, 136, 147, 168-69, 176, 259n, 266n

Ikeda Masaaki, 26, 27, 34, 51

Income-Doubling Plan, 37, 38, 41, 51, 147, 293
Incremental policymaking, 19, 271-77, 301-6
Industry, 17-18
Industrialization, 202-3, 204, 226; see also Economic growth
Inoue Seiji, 283n
Institutional position, rationale of, 246-49, 265-67
Interest groups, 16, 25, 51, 104-5, 205, 242, 254; see also entries for specific groups
International Labor Organization Convention 87, 37, 43, 56
Ishida Takeshi, 24, 25, 27, 33
Ishii Mitsujirō, 76
Issue, nature of, 272-75, 305-7, 311-12, 315-19, 322
Itai-Itai disease, see Cadmium poisoning
Itō Daiichi, 37, 38n
Itoh, Hiroshi, 26n, 248n
Iwai Akira, 26

Japan Automobile Association, 260n
Japan Committee for Economic Development (Keizai Dōyūkai), 91, 92, 94, 160, 185, 190-91, 288-89
Japan Communist Party, 79, 81, 95, 256; agriculture, and JCP, 156, 185; higher education, and JCP, 280-81, 285; pollution, and JCP, 210; repatriates, and JCP, 128
Japan Federation of Employers' Associations (Nikkeiren), 288-89
Japan, Inc., 310
Japan Medical Association, 37, 39, 40, 44
Japan-Republic of China Peace Treaty, 80, 85
Japan Science Council, 280, 296, 300
Japan Socialist Party (JSP), 43, 79, 83, 95, 156, 160, 180, 183, 251, 265, 309; agriculture, and JSP, 156, 191; higher education, and JSP, 280-81; People's Congress for the Restoration of Japan-China Relations, and JSP, 96; pollution, and JSP, 210, 219; repatriates, and JSP, 128
Japan Teachers Union, 34, 43

Japanese Chamber of Commerce and Industry, 93
Japanese Political Science Association, 24, 25, 33
Johnson, D. Gale, 146n, 152n
Johnston, Bruce, 145n
Judiciary, see Courts; Ministry of justice
Junior colleges, 289-91, 296

Kahn, Herman, 310n
Kaigo Tokiomi, 279n, 281n, 288n
Kaji Kōji, 215n, 228n
Kanda Hiroshi, 107n
Kansai Economic Federation, 288
Kaplan, Eugene J., 310n
Kasuga Ikkō, 64, 82, 83, 102
Kataoka Noboru, 211n
Katsumata Seiichi, 257
Kawai, Kazuo, 279n
Kawanaka Nikō, 28, 35n, 38, 46
Kawasaki City, 221-22
Kawasaki Hideji, 64
Kawashima, Shōjirō, 259
Kaya Okinori, 76, 97, 101
Keidanren, see Federation of Economic Organizations
Keizai Dōyūkai, see Committee for Economic Development
Kelley, Donald R., 230n, 231n
Key, V. O., 105n, 132n, 139n
Kikawada Kazutaka, 92, 94
Kishi Nobusuke, 36, 37, 41, 54, 65n, 73, 76, 97, 245, 266n
Kitamura Kazuyuki, 284n
Kiuchi Akitane, 76n
Kobayashi Naoki, 26, 41, 42n, 44
Kōda Toshihiko, 225n
Koeda Kazuo, 180
Kōenkai, see Support associations
Kojima Akira, 40, 59n
Komori Takeshi, 66
Kondō Yasuo, 187n
Kōno Ichirō, 95, 172, 192
Kōno Kenzō, 27
Kosaka Zentarō, 65n, 74-76
Kuhn, Thomas, S., 48
Kumagai Tasaburō, 254
Kumamoto Prefecture, 212
Kuraishi Tadao, 184, 185, 191
Kuranari Tadashi, 168

Kuriyama Shōichi, 86-88
Kurogane Yasumi, 109

Labor, 33, 44, 145, 210-11, 257, 275, 281, 310; *see also* General Council of Japanese Trade Unions; Unions, farm
Landes, David, 322
Landlords, compensation of, 55, 105, 105n, 108, 110, 116, 117, 118n, 135, 138
Langdon, Frank, C., 30, 44n, 63n, 254n
Lasswell, Harold, 162n
Lawton, Raymond W., 253n
League of Private Universities of Japan, 300
Lee, Chae-Jin, 63n
Levine, Solomon B., 202n
Lewis, Jack G., 47, 213n
Liao Ch'eng-chih, 88
Liberal Democratic Party (LDP), 15, 16, 17, 22-35, 42, 43, 51, 55, 79n, 140, 150, 242-43, 254, 256, 260, 268, 275; Asian Group (Soshinkai), 74, 76, 258-59; Asian Parliamentary Union, 74, 76; China Policy, and LDP, 66-67, 95-98; Council for the Normalization of Japan-China Relations, 74; Executive Council, 75, 121-23, 165-66, 170, 175-76, 184, 194; Foreign Affairs Committee, 261; higher education, and LDP, 280-81, 285, 290-92, 299, 303; internal disagreements (*see also* Factionalism), 69, 70-72, 74-77, 250, 250n, 253n, 258-59, 262, 264-65; National Organization Committee, 108; Political Affairs Research Council, 108, 111, 121, 165-66, 170, 175-76, 182, 184, 197, 262-63; pollution, and LDP, 204-7, 211, 215, 220-22, 226-31, 235-38; presidential election, 71-72, 96; rice prices, and LDP, 159-60, 166-67, 181-87, 190, 194-95, 197; repatriates, and LDP, 108, 115, 117-24, 127; Special Committee on the Okinawa Problem, 257, 261, 262
Liberalization (investment and trade), 254-55, 266, 308, 313
Lindblom, Charles E., 117n

Local Autonomy Law, 224, 295
Local government, 18, 211-14, 215-16, 220-21, 223, 229, 237, 309
Lockwood, William W., 31, 39-40, 322n
Long, Norton, 240, 241n, 251n
Lord, Guy, 141n
Lowi, Theodore J., 49, 50, 52, 57, 105n, 239, 240, 242n, 244n, 271n, 272n, 312n

Makoto Mike, 127n
Marshall, A. W., 51n
Masaki Yoshiaki, 81
Mass media, 91, 220, 235-36, 279, 281, 284n, 310
Masumi Junnosuke, 27, 32, 38, 41, 51, 52, 100n, 154, 155n, 249n
Matsubara Haruo, 202n, 225n
Matsumoto Shunichi, 89
Matsumura Kenzō, 66
Matsushita Keiichi, 33
Matsushita Muneyuki, 77n, 82n
Matsuura Shūtarō, 193
McCormack, Gavan, 29, 91
McKean, Margaret A., 18, 47, 231n, 232n
Meter, Donald Van, 239n
Methyl mercury poisoning, 203-4, 206n-7n, 211n, 220, 233-34
Miki Takeo, 65, 70-73, 77, 226, 231, 257
Mills, C. Wright, 23
Minamata City, 212
Minamata disease, *see* Methyl mercury poisoning
Ministry of Agriculture and Forestry, 38, 155, 157-58, 163, 166, 175, 184, 187, 192, 197
Ministry of Construction, 38, 207, 218
Ministry of Education, 34, 225-26, 269, 280-81, 284-87, 289-301, 302-4, 306
Ministry of Finance, 18, 26, 37, 40, 55, 105, 112, 114-24, 135, 137-39, 152, 158-59, 162, 163, 166, 168, 175, 189, 192, 207, 216, 248, 255, 256-57, 263, 267, 297-98, 314; Budget Bureau, and, 163
Ministry of Health and Welfare, 18, 39, 44, 107, 109, 206-7, 215, 216-21, 231, 257
Ministry of Home Affairs, 38, 207, 217

Ministry of International Trade and
Industry, 18, 37, 38, 206-7, 216,
217-21, 228, 231, 248, 248n, 254-55,
256, 259n
Ministry of Justice, 228-29
Ministry of Transportation, 38, 259n,
264
Minobe Ryōkichi, 65-68, 79, 102,
225-26
Minsei, 285
Misawa Shigeo, 25, 27, 28, 39, 42, 43n,
248n
Mitsubishi, 92, 93
Mitsui, 212, 232
Mitsukawa Motochika, 155n
Miyamoto Ken'ichi, 29, 38, 42n, 46,
202n, 215n, 225n
Miyasaka Masayuki, 99n, 100n
Miyazawa Kiichi, 256
Miyazawa Tetsuzō, 254
Miyazawa Toshio, 192-93
Mizuta Mikio, 113, 120-22, 136-37,
168-70, 191-92
Mochida Keizō, 195
Moreland, Daniel, 239n
Morley, James, 143n, 201n
Muroi Tsutomo, 222n

Nagai Ken'ichi, 286n
Nagai Michio, 279n, 283n
Nagai Yōnosuke, 24-26, 33, 56n
Nagano Shigeo, 93
Nagayama Tadanori, 119, 121
Naitō Kunio, 79n
Nakajima Isamu, 225
Nakasone Yasuhiro, 42, 70-71, 77,
258-59, 264-65
Narita Tomomi, 82
National Agriculture Committee Sys-
tem, 155
National Association of Agricultural
Cooperatives (Nōkyō), 150, 153-56,
163, 169-70, 172-73, 178-79, 182-87,
193, 314
National Chamber of Agriculture, 155,
163, 179-80, 185
National Defense Council, 255
National Farmers' Alliance, 156
National Farmers' General Federation,
156
National Federation of Repatriate
Groups (Zenren), 104-7, 108-34, 140

National Tax Administration, 38
Nehru, Jawaharlal, 75
Neustadt, Richard, 246n
New Industrial City Program, 38
Ninomiya Bunzō, 64, 78, 82
Nishimura Naomi, 120, 192, 194
Nishioka Akio, 225n
Nishiyama Masao, 225n
Nixon, Richard, 63-68, 70, 76, 80, 87,
88n, 95
"Nixon shocks," 65, 70, 87, 93
Noda Takeo, 65n, 68-67, 69
Noguchi Yūichirō, 42n
Nōkyō, see National Association of Ag-
ricultural Cooperatives
Noma Hisao, 222n
Nomura Heiji, 282n, 286n, 289n, 293n
Notehelfer, Fred G., 201n
Nuclear Non-Proliferation Treaty, 260
Nuclear weapons, 45

Ōe Shinobu, 29, 32
Ogawa, Heiji 257
Ōgawara Yoshio, 65n
Ogata, Sadako, 91n
Ogura Takekazu, 187n
Ohara Seiji, 281n
Ōhashi Hisatoshi, 282n
Ōhira Masayoshi, 65n, 70-90, 94,
96-98, 109
Ōhira Zengo, 107n
Ohkawa, Kazushi, 31, 31n, 146n, 171
Oil crisis (1973), 231
Ōishi Buichi, 230
Ōishi Yoshio, 107n, 111
Ojimi Yoshihisa, 254
Okinawa, 41, 45, 63, 70, 273, 314; aid
to, 256-57, 260-61, 262-63, 266;
B-52's on, 257-58, 260, 262-66, 308,
311, 313
Okinawa Problem Deliberation Coun-
cil, 257, 258
Ōkubo Naohiko, 81, 83
Okudaira Yasuhiro, 283n
Ōno Bamboku, 107, 108
Ōnō Ichirō, 168, 174
Opposition, 16, 33, 42-44, 67-68,
81-84, 91, 101-2, 198, 205, 209-10,
216-17, 219-21, 227-28, 237-38, 254,
258, 261, 275, 309; see also entries for
each of the opposition parties
Ōsaki Jin, 298n

Ōsawa Masaru, 296n
Ōshima Kiyoshi, 188n
Ōshima Tarō, 46n
Ōuchi Keigo, 64n, 82n, 83n
Overseas Property Problem Council,
    109-10, 111-12, 133, 134-36
Ozawa Teruo, 133n

Packard, George R., 36, 37n, 41n, 43,
    44n, 45, 100, 101, 249n, 250n, 254n
Passin, Herbert, 63n, 279n, 302n
Pempel, T. J., 28, 29n, 32, 33, 34, 103n,
    106n, 143n, 239n, 248n, 254n, 302n,
    304n
Phantom F4E, 255-56, 263, 266, 311,
    320
Photochemical smog, 225
Police, 279, 282-84
Police Duties Bill, 248n
Policymaking; elitist perspective of,
    22-35, 50, 241-42, 320-23; empirical
    studies of, 14-15, 239-40, 267-68,
    270-71; ideal types of, 270-77; and
    implementation, 57-58, 247n; in-
    stitutional processes of, 113-14;
    pluralist perspective of, 35-48, 50,
    241-42, 320-23; studies of, 14, 15-16,
    22-59, 308-23; theoretical studies of,
    14-15, 239-41, 268; typologies of,
    51-53, 240-41
Political advantage, rationale of, 244-
    45, 264-65
Political parties, 159-60; see also entries
    for individual political parties
Pollution, 18, 46, 201-38, 308, 311,
    316, 317; development as a political
    issue, 201-4; see also entries for
    specific pollution problems such as
    Itai-Itai Disease; Methyl Mercury
    Poisoning; Yokkaichi Asthma
"Pollution Diet," 18, 227-31
Pool, Ithiel de Sola, 242n
Pressman, Jeffrey L., 57, 58
Pressure group policymaking, 19,
    103-42, 143-200, 236, 242, 271-77,
    287-301, 311
Pressure groups, see Interest groups,
    Pressure group policymaking
Prime Ministers Office, 109, 117-24,
    152, 207, 218-21, 226, 257, 263
Private University Promotion Associa-
    tion, 303

Public opinion, 45, 79, 91, 95-98,
    99-100, 224-25, 231, 235-36, 284-85,
    287
Pye, Lucian W., 63n

Ranney, Austin, 273n
Rationales for political action, 243-49,
    261-67
Redford, Emmette E., 52
Repatriates, 16-17, 55, 103-42, 308,
    313, 314, 316-17
Rice price, 17, 143-200, 247, 311, 313,
    316, 317
Rice Price Deliberation Council, 151,
    152, 155, 156, 157-58, 160, 163,
    164-65, 168, 171, 172-74, 177,
    181-87, 190-91, 193-95, 313
Rice producers, 153
Richardson, Bradley, 18, 310-11, 314,
    316
Riker, William H., 272n
Robinson, James A., 61n
Rogers, William, 69
Roles, 242-49, 311-12, 313-15, 317-19,
    321-22
Rosenau, James N., 52n, 244n
Rosovsky, Henry, 31, 146n
Rossiter, Clinton, 314

Sakai, Robert K., 31n
Sakurai Makoto, 177
San Francisco Peace Treaty, 60, 106
Sasaki Kōzō, 82, 83, 87n, 96, 102
Satō Eisaku, 41, 63-73, 77-80, 88n,
    94-95, 110, 114-15, 120, 181-85,
    191-92, 195, 198, 226, 228, 255-59,
    264, 266, 314
Sato, Hideo, 63n
Satō-Nixon Joint Communique (1969),
    63–64, 80
Scalapino, Robert A., 27, 90n, 97n,
    154, 155n, 249n, 267n
Science and technology, 31, 288-94
Science and Technology Agency,
    206n-7n
Science and Technology Council, 293
Self-Defense Forces, 255-56, 273
Sethi, S. Prakash, 243n
Sewerage Law, 216
Shibuya Takeshi, 56n
Shigemasa Seishi, 168, 170
Shiina Etsusaburō, 120, 254

Shimizu Yoshihiro, 298n
Shinohara Hajime, 25
Shinojima Hideo, 26
Shirai Isamu, 168, 174
Shōwa Denkō, 203, 232-33
Small and Medium-Sized Enterprises
　Organization Bill, 41-42
Smoke and Soot Regulation Law, 216
Society, Japanese, 15, 315-16
Sōhyō; see General Council of Japanese
　Trade Unions
Sōkagakkai, 128
Soma Masao, 27n, 35n
Sone Eki, 82-83
Soukup, James R., 31, 39
South Korea, 63
Soviet-Japanese Peace Settlement
　(1956), 36, 45, 60, 99, 249, 264
Soviet Union, 54, 242
Specialist colleges, proposal to create,
　290
State, Japanese, 15, 106, 109, 117,
　315-16, 319
Steslicke, William E., 37, 38, 39, 40n,
　41, 42, 44, 47
Stockwin, J. A. A., 35n, 43
Stone, Alan, 201n
Structures, political, 275-77, 306-7,
　311-13, 315-19, 322
Students, 44, 281-85; New Left, 285,
　see also, Universities; Zengakuren
Stunkel, Kenneth R., 208n, 230n
Sudō Hideo, 168-70
Suga, Eiichi, 63n, 96n
Sukegawa, Koki, 250n, 264n
Sumitomo, 91
Sun P'ing-hua, 86, 89, 93
Supporters' Associations (Kōenkai), 23,
　127
Supreme Commander for the Allied
　Powers (SCAP), 279-80
Suzuki Yukio, 26

Tabata Shigejirō, 286n
Tada Minoru, 82n
Tagawa Seiichi, 66-67, 89
Taguchi Fukuji, 26
Taiwan, 62, 66, 68, 76-77, 84-85, 96;
　Japanese economic relations with,
　77, 80; see also 60-102
Takami Saburō, 168
Takashima Masuo, 86

Takashima Setsuo, 254
Takeiri Yoshikatsu, 77-83, 86-88, 90,
　96, 102; visit to Peking, 79-81
Tanaka Kakuei, 16, 42, 62, 70-99, 109,
　118n, 176, 182-84, 191-92, 203, 230,
　308-9, 311, 313-14, 316-17, 320
Tanaka Yoshitomo, 69n
Taniuchi Ken, 28n
Technical colleges, 290
Terasaki Masao, 297n, 281n, 288n
Textiles, dispute with U.S. over, 63, 69
Thayer, Nathaniel, 27, 28, 35n, 108n,
　123n, 242n
Thurston, Donald R., 34, 43
Tokyo Metropolitan Environmental
　Pollution Control Ordinance, 222-
　24
Tominomori Eiji, 67
Toyama Prefecture, 212
Tsou, Tan, 63n
Tsuji Kiyoaki, 26
Tsukahara Toshio, 118, 120-22, 136
Tsukumi Yasuhiro, 129
Tsuru Shigeto, 202n
Tsurumi Kiyohiko, 254

Uchida Tsuneo, 168
Ueki Kōshirō, 111-13, 117-20, 122,
　136, 180, 314
Uemura Kōgorō, 92-93
Ui Jun, 202n, 211n, 225n
Ulam, Adam, 261
Unions, farm, 156, 163, 179, 180, 182,
　193
U.S. Import Surcharge Proposal, 256,
　260, 261, 265-66, 308
U.S.-Japan Committee on Trade and
　Economic Affairs, 69
U.S.-Japan Consultative Committee on
　Security, 260
U.S.-Japan Mutual Security Treaty
　(1960), 29, 41, 54, 60-61, 78, 80, 84,
　85, 248n, 249-50, 264; extension of,
　259-60, 261-62, 266, 308, 311, 320;
　Far East clause, 88
U.S.-Japan Ryūkyū Advisory Commit-
　tee, 257, 258
Universities, 19, 277-307; enrollment
　expansion in, 302-6, 308, 313, 320;
　private, 270, 288, 295-301, 302-3,
　307, 313 (see also Association for the
　Promotion of Private Schools, As-

sociation of Privae Colleges of Japan); protests in, 281-87, 308
University administration, 277-87, 307, 308, 316, 317
University chartering standards, 293
University funding, 295-301
University standards, 292
Ushiba Nobuhiko, 65n, 258

Verba, Sidney, 137n
Veterans, 56, 132
Vogel, Ezra F., 39n, 113n, 160n, 263n, 310n

Wang T'ai-p'ing, 64
Watanabe Akio, 45, 97n
Watanuki Jōji, 26
Water Pollution Control Law, 229
Water Quality Preservation Law, 216
Waxman, Chaim I., 321n
Weinstein, Martin E., 37, 41, 45n
Wescott, Richard R., 230n
Wildavsky, Aaron B., 57, 58, 141n

Willey, Richard J., 33, 34n
Wolff, Robert Paul, 294n

Yamada Giken, 111, 112
Yamamoto Tokushige, 284n, 285n, 288n
Yamamoto Tsuyoshi, 93n
Yamamura, Kozo, 31, 40
Yamamura Yoshiharu, 93n
Yamanaka Sadanori, 226
Yanaga, Chitoshi, 30, 206n
Yano, Junya, 83
Yasuda Hall, 283
Yokkaichi Asthma, 203-4, 232-33
Yosha, Michael, 239n
Yoshida Kenzō, 65n, 86, 88, 90
Yoshida Shigeru, 41
Yoshino Bunroku, 65n
Youn, Jun-suk, 125n

Zaikai, see Business
Ziegler, L. Harmon, 23n
Zengakuren, 280; see also Minsei; Students
Zimmerman, William, 52, 273n

**POLICYMAKING IN
CONTEMPORARY JAPAN**

Designed by R. E. Rosenbaum.
Composed by Vail-Ballou Press, Inc.,
in 10 point VIP Baskerville, 2 points leaded,
with display lines in Optima bold.
Printed offset by Vail-Ballou Press
Warren's No. 66 text, 50 pound basis.
Bound by Vail-Ballou Press
in Joanna book cloth
and stamped in All Purpose foil.

Library of Congress Cataloging in Publication Data
(For library cataloging purposes only)

Main entry under title:

Policymaking in contemporary Japan.

  Bibliography: p.
  Includes index.
  1. Japan—Politics and government—1945–   —Addresses, essays, lectures. 2. Public administration—Decision making—Addresses, essays, lectures. 3. Policy sciences—Addresses, essays, lectures. I. Pempel, T. J., 1942–
JQ1626 1977.P64   354'.52   77-4514
ISBN 0-8014-1048-7